The growing significance of environmental problems such as ozone depletion, global warming and pollution generate increasing scepticism about the modern claim that the technological transformation of nature invariably progresses human welfare. Michael Northcott examines the character and causes of modern environmental problems, and argues that they are linked with fundamental changes in religious belief, and in the human moral and social ecology, as well as with new technological and industrial processes. He finds in the Hebrew and Christian traditions, and especially in natural law ethics, a belief in the intrinsic connection of the moral qualities of human relationships and societies and the stability and harmony of the natural world. He argues that principled ethical responses to environmental problems will therefore depend on principled ethical responses to the civilisational problems of modern societies, including growing divisions between rich and poor, the breakdown of stable families and communities, the loss of virtue and the decline of religion, as well as on the recovery of respect for the laws and harmonies of nature.

THE ENVIRONMENT AND
CHRISTIAN ETHICS

NEW STUDIES IN CHRISTIAN ETHICS

General editor: Robin Gill

Editorial board: Stephen R. L. Clark, Antony O. Dyson,
Stanley Hauerwas and Robin W. Lovin

In recent years the study of Christian ethics has become an integral part of mainstream theological studies. The reasons for this are not hard to detect. It has become a more widely held view that Christian ethics is actually central to Christian theology as a whole. Theologians increasingly have had to ask what contemporary relevance their discipline has in a context where religious belief is on the wane, and whether Christian ethics (that is, an ethics based on the Gospel of Jesus Christ) has anything to say in a multi-faceted and complex secular society. There is now no shortage of books on most substantive moral issues, written from a wide variety of theological positions. However, what is lacking are books within Christian ethics which are taken at all seriously by those engaged in the wider secular debate. Too few are methodologically substantial; too few have an informed knowledge of parallel discussions in philosophy or the social sciences. This series attempts to remedy the situation. The aims of New Studies in Christian Ethics will therefore be twofold. First, to engage centrally with the secular moral debate at the highest possible intellectual level; second, to demonstrate that Christian ethics can make a distinctive contribution to this debate – either in moral substance, or in terms of underlying moral justifications. It is hoped that the series as a whole will make a substantial contribution to the discipline.

A list of titles in the series is provided at the end of the book.

THE ENVIRONMENT AND CHRISTIAN ETHICS

MICHAEL S. NORTHCOTT

Lecturer in Christian Ethics and Practical Theology,
University of Edinburgh

CAMBRIDGE
UNIVERSITY PRESS

Published by the Press Syndicate of the University of Cambridge
The Pitt Building, Trumpington Street, Cambridge CB2 IRP
40 West 20th Street, New York, NY 10011–4211, USA
10 Stamford Road, Oakleigh, Melbourne 3166, Australia

First published 1996

Printed in Great Britain at the University Press, Cambridge

A catalogue record for this book is available from the British Library

Library of Congress cataloguing in publication data
Northcott, Michael S.
The environment and Christian ethics / Michael S. Northcott.
p.   cm. – (New studies in Christian ethics)
Includes bibliographical references and index.
ISBN 0 521 44481 0 (hardback) ISBN 0 521 57631 8 (paperback)
1. Human ecology – Religious aspects – Christianity.
2. Christian ethics.   3. Environmental ethics.
4. Ecology – Moral and ethical aspects.
I. Title.   II. Series.
BT695.5.N68   1996
241'.691–dc20   96–13022   CIP

ISBN 0 521 44481 0 hardback
ISBN 0 521 57631 8 paperback

*To Lydia
with love*

Contents

General editor's preface

This book is the tenth in the series New Studies in Christian
Ethics. Each book has worked closely within the remit of the
series, namely to engage centrally with secular moral debate at
the highest possible intellectual level, and to demonstrate that
Christian ethics can make a distinctive contribution to this
debate – either in moral substance, or in terms of underlying
moral justifications. Some authors have used this remit to
examine a moral theme of current importance – rights, justice,
power, responsibility, plurality and moral action. Others have
examined issues – sex, gender and feminism. Michael Northcott
offers a challenging examination of a major and highly topical
issue on which Christianity often seems very vulnerable, namely
the environment.

Can Christian ethics realistically offer a distinctive justification of environmental ethics when its own history in this area
appears to be so dubious? And, even if it can, how does
Christian ethics hope to shape human action on the environment when only a minority of the world's population is
Christian? The sheer dimensions of environmental ethics
appear to be so huge and the record of Christian responses to
that environment so doubtful. Some argue that it is only secular
voices that might hope to change humanity's lamentable history
of environmental degradation.

Michael Northcott is well aware of the immense difficulties
here. His first book, *The Church and Secularisation* (Lang, 1989),
showed that he had the right combination of theological and
sociological skills to tackle such an area. In this early book he
offered a sharp critique of industrial mission and urban ministry

in the North East of England. Within it he noted that those engaged in mission and ministry often have quite different aims and agendas from those who are the recipients of their work. The analytical skills developed through this research were then supplemented by experience in a non-Western context, lecturing for five years in an ecumenical seminary in Malaysia. This combination of analysis and experience has now borne fruit in his present study of *The environment and Christian ethics*.

This study starts with a necessary account of the factors responsible for the present environmental crisis – such as global warming, pollution, soil erosion, deforestation, species extinction, over-population and over-consumption. The cultural and ideological contributants to this catalogue of human failings are examined next. There are indeed forms of Christianity which have hardly helped to preserve an environment threatened by human behaviour. Only then does Dr Northcott offer a critical examination of the ethical and theological responses that can and should be made on this crucial issue. Like the other authors in the series, he does finally believe that a theistic vision has a powerful contribution to make to ethical discussion. It may even offer a better hope for the future of the world than a purely secular vision.

This is an uncomfortable book largely because the subject it tackles is itself so uncomfortable. As humanity increasingly degrades its own environment, voices of real wisdom are needed. Michael Northcott's book is, I believe, a part of this much needed wisdom.

ROBIN GILL

Preface

In the three years in which I worked on this book the environment moved in and out of the frame of public debate in Britain. In 1992, when I began, it was much in the frame, particularly during and after the Rio Earth Summit. In 1995 as I write this acknowledgement, the idea that Western civilisation faces an environmental crisis is much less in public view. More commonly people are exercised by the crises in employment and in human moral ecology which are manifest in recent developments in Britain and beyond. In this book I argue that the environmental crisis is intricately connected with the human crises of moral ecology and of unemployment, and that the demise of economic justice and moral purposiveness in the global order is directly related to the increasing pace of environmental breakdown. Consequently the reorientation of modern societies towards the biological limits of the planet will not be achieved without a related quest for justice and the common good in human affairs. I also propose that vital resources for both projects may be found in an ecological repristination of central features of the Hebrew–Christian tradition, including the Hebrew vision of created order, the Christian understanding of the Trinitarian creator and incarnate redeemer, and natural law ethics, a tradition of ethics also manifest in classical and Eastern religious thought.

The theological orientation which underlies this book has been formed in a range of contexts; in experiments in alternative living in various Christian communities and churches, not least Saint Margaret's Church in Durham, and in my studies at departments of theology, religion and ethics respectively at the Universities of Durham, Sunderland and Edinburgh, and at the Seminari Theologi Malaysia in Kuala Lumpur. I am especially grateful to the Department of Christian Ethics and Practical Theology at Edinburgh for the time its members have enabled me to find to prepare this book. In my environmental interests I have been much influenced by a five-year sojourn in Malaysia, with its extraordinarily rich, though sadly shrinking, natural inheritance, including steamy rainforests and pristine coral islands. I have also enjoyed an informal association with the Centre for Human Ecology in the University of Edinburgh, whose staff and visiting lecturers have guided a personal interest in environmental issues into what I hope is a more disciplined intellectual engagement.

Much of the research for the book was undertaken in the National Library of Scotland, to whose librarians I owe a great debt. I am also grateful for the help of librarians in the National Science Library of Scotland, New College Library, Edinburgh University Library and the Bodleian Library in Oxford.

A number of people have read parts or drafts of the whole of the manuscript and I am especially grateful to Professors Stephen R. L. Clark, Duncan B. Forrester, Robin Gill and Richard H. Roberts, all of whom responded with vigorous criticisms to what they read. I cannot claim to have overcome all the deficiencies which they observed in earlier drafts, nor that what follows conforms to the approaches they would variously have preferred to the subject matter treated. But I remain immensely grateful for the seriousness of their engagement. The book would have been considerably weaker without it.

I am also grateful for the support of the former Religious Studies Editor at Cambridge University Press, Alex Wright, and to Robin Gill, the series editor, who have borne with missed deadlines and changes in conception very well indeed, and encouraged me to believe that the project was worth pursuing to the end. I am also indebted to my copy editor Audrey Cotterell for her assiduous efforts to enhance the accuracy and reduce the obscurity of my text. As to any errors and obscurities that remain, I hope readers will draw them to my attention.

Writing is hard and at times lonely graft. I would not have been able to complete this book without the support of my wife Jill and my children Lydia, Ben and Rebecca. They have borne the long absences in libraries, and the tapping of the word processor in the study, and they have dragged or welcomed me back from the distraction of too much cogitation. Of all the family Lydia is most exercised about the issues treated of in this book, and at present is mapping out her life plan in terms of a personal and career response to some of them. It is to her that I dedicate this book.

Acknowledgements

Biblical quotations are from *The New English Bible* and *The Revised English Bible* published by the Oxford and Cambridge University Presses in 1975 and 1989 respectively.

CHAPTER ONE

Frogs, floods and famines

In 1991 in the South of England gardeners and naturalists reported a mass death of frogs in garden ponds, small lakes, commons and village greens. Scientists were unable to say what had caused their death on such a large scale, but hundreds of children and parents, many of whom had created a habitat for these creatures to thrive, were disturbed. The suspicions of the scientists, and the people who saw them die, was that pollutants in the environment, in the water and the air, had become too much for these sensitive creatures, which, like all amphibians, absorb substances in the atmosphere and water through their skins as well as their lungs. Perhaps the frogs represented an involuntary early warning. If they cannot survive in our gardens, how long will it be before the earth becomes too toxic for humans as well?

For many people around the world the environmental crisis is already a matter of survival, for themselves and their children: for millions of people in the Sahel region in Africa whose degraded lands will no longer support their livestock and crops; for the residents of Chernobyl in the Ukraine dying of cancer after a nuclear disaster which the industry had always said could never happen, and the sheep farmers in the Lake District who still cannot sell their contaminated sheep in the market eight years after the accident; for the land Dayaks and nomadic Penans of Sarawak in Malaysia whose ancestral home, the million-year-old tropical forest is being systematically and greedily cut down to be burnt as disposable chopsticks or waste construction materials in incinerators in Japan.

Opponents of environmentalism argue that the dangers are

overrated and that calls for a new ethic, or a new religious focus on the place of humanity in the natural world, are the result of the exaggerated picture of doom that ecologists and environmentalists have painted.[1] However, as we survey the range of impacts which human activities in less than a century have made on the planet and its ecosystems, it should become apparent that there is indeed a crisis, and a crisis of momentous proportions. The extent of the crisis seems to require not just new environmental regulations, or new technologies which make less impact on the natural world, though these are surely needed, but a radical change to the predominant direction of human behaviour in modern civilisation. As the global system of the money economy and industrial production and consumption reaches peoples in every corner of the planet, it is the very nature of that system, and of the life-styles which it sponsors, which are called into question.

CLIMATE CHANGE AND GLOBAL WARMING

The single most pervasive and potentially cataclysmic factor in the ecological crisis is that of climate change. Local climate change is already a feature of life in many tropical and sub-tropical regions. Formerly forested areas converted to grass-land, cash-crop agriculture or concrete cities, undergo dramatic climate changes as the cooling effects of tree cover are removed. The tropical canopy acts as part of a micro-climate which recycles and controls both precipitation and sunlight by a combination of warming and cooling mechanisms so as to maintain temperatures and soil fertility at levels suitable for the great diversity of life forms to which the tropical forests are home. Once the forests are removed the natural cooling effects of recycled moisture are disrupted, precipitation decreases or becomes irregular and soil moisture is reduced as the capacity of the tropical ecosystem to absorb and recycle precipitation is diminished. Tropical cities of concrete buildings on a landscape dominated by asphalt become unbearably hot places to live without manufactured air-conditioning with its high energy consumption. Dried-up river-beds and brown denuded landscapes, such as those which surround Manila on the formerly lush tropical island of Luzon in the Philippines, are indicators of the devastation that this kind of local climate change can induce.

Such local climatic changes are in themselves warning enough of the dramatic and potentially catastrophic effects of human activity on local ecosystems and climate systems. However, the earth is now faced with a much greater change in its climatic system, not just in particular continents or regions but globally. The surface temperature of the earth is kept at an average of 15 degrees Celsius, giving a temperature range which is ideal for life, by a combination of gases in the atmosphere which produce a natural greenhouse effect. The warmth of the sun's rays is reflected off the earth's surface and trapped in the atmosphere and the air, and the earth itself is warmed. This natural construction of a climate ideal for life is what scientists identify as the greenhouse effect.

Most scientists and ecologists now believe that the amount of carbon dioxide – the most important of the naturally beneficial greenhouse gases – which human activity is currently generating, together with rises in other greenhouse gases such as methane and nitrous oxide, is leading to an enhancement of the naturally occurring greenhouse effect: this is the prognosis of global warming. The International Panel on Climate Change report that in the last 100 years, roughly the period of industrial activity on the earth, a real warming of the planet has taken place of between 0.3 and 0.6 degrees centigrade.[2] This warming is thought to have occurred as a consequence of the enhancement of the natural greenhouse effect. Two-thirds of this enhancement has come about through the burning of fossil fuels, which have increased the amount of carbon dioxide by 25 per cent since the beginning of the Industrial Revolution, and have increased the concentration of carbon dioxide in the upper atmosphere by 0.05 per cent per year, so that there is now 10 per cent more carbon dioxide in the atmosphere than thirty years ago.[3] 6 billion tonnes of carbon are produced every year by fossil-fuel burning, and a further 2.6 billion tonnes of carbon originate from the burning of forests. The production of methane, the second most important greenhouse gas, has risen as a consequence of increased agricultural activity to feed the growing human population and of the rising demand for farmed meat, cattle and rice paddy being the primary sources of methane. Methane is also associated with natural gas and coal production.[4] Nitrous oxide, another greenhouse gas, is emitted in growing quantities from power stations, factory chimneys and car exhausts, while chlorofluorocarbons (CFCs), a manufactured product which has a warming effect 10,000 times that of carbon dioxide, have also further enhanced the greenhouse effect.

The forecasts of the IPCC of the future effects of global warming are sobering. They predict on the basis of a business-as-usual scenario – that is to say a maintenance of current levels of fossil-fuel burning and greenhouse gas production – that global mean temperature will rise at 0.3 degrees centigrade per decade for the next 100 years, leading to a rise of 1 degree centigrade by 2025 and 3 degrees centigrade by the end of the next century. The rise in temperature will be greater on land areas than over seas. The report highlights the possible effects of large increases in Central North America – the grain basket of the Western world – Southern Europe, the Sahel region of Central Africa and Australia. Central North America will experience a 2–4 degree centigrade warming in winter, and an increase in precipitation, while in summer it will experience a 2–3 degree warming and a 5–10 per cent reduction in precipitation. These predicted temperature shifts are theoretically enough to change the ecology of entire regions, and the IPCC predict a range of startling effects including the occurrence of tropical diseases in formerly temperate climate zones, increases in flooding in coastal zones, exacerbation of drought conditions in arid areas. Vegetation will not be able to adapt fast enough to the rapidity of climate change which is predicted in the next century and areas such as sub-Saharan Africa and Southern and Eastern Asia may see a one-fifth reduction in food production consequent upon increased heat.

Already the signs of the effects of global warming can be observed in a measurable global sea-level rise of 10–20 centimetres, in the retreat of a number of land glaciers around the world and signs of melting of the Antarctic ice shelf. The IPCC also point out that in the 1980s five of the warmest years were recorded since meteorological records began. The future effects of global warming are not easy to predict with precision. According to the IPCC one of the more predictable effects will be a sea-level rise of 6 centimetres per decade, leading to a 65-centimetre rise by the end of the next century. Ice equivalent to 5 metres of global sea level is currently submerged in the ice-floes of the Antarctic. If this ice were to gradually melt, and there are already signs that it is, the results would be even more catastrophic than the predicted steady sea-level rise. Coastal regions, ocean cities and islands such as Mauritius and the Maldives, would be affected by severe flooding and might eventually become uninhabitable. Ten per cent of the population of Bangladesh live on lands which would be regularly flooded with a sea-level rise of around 50 centimetres. Tidal cities like London, Venice and Bangkok, island cities like Hong Kong and Singapore, and river deltas such as the Nile, Niger, Yangtze, Mekong and Mississippi would be severely affected. At the same time the staple food-producing areas on many continents would be affected by temperature rises and precipitation loss in ways which could threaten world food supplies. On the other side of the equation, areas which are presently uninhabitable, or not susceptible to productive agriculture, might become habitable and productive with climate change. Some animal species would probably migrate to higher ground. Large areas of frozen subsoil in Northern Russia might become capable of sustaining new forests or farmlands. But great uncertainties remain in the prediction of the effects of climate change. At its worst climate change may pose a fundamental threat to the delicate balance of temperature, gases, vegetation and moisture which provide the conditions for life on earth.

Global warming is directly related to the industrial consumption of energy and the production of greenhouse gases in affluent industrialised economies. Two-thirds of global carbon emissions arise from fossil fuel utilisation for power generation, transportation, domestic heating, cement-making, gas and coal-mining and industrial manufacturing. Most of these emissions still originate in the rich North, while the burning of forests, resulting principally from rural migration in the Third World as prime lands are enclosed for commercial farming, contributes one-third of the increase in carbon dioxide. By 2025 the projected population increase to 8 billion people will necessitate 60 per cent more fossil fuel consumption than now, and this assumes that most of these additional people will not attain Western levels of wealth and consumption. The World Watch Institute estimates that the world's 400 million cars alone emit 500 million tonnes of carbon dioxide into the atmosphere every year, or 17 per cent of the global output of carbon dioxide.[5] If all the millions of bicycles in China were swapped for cars at some point in the next fifty years, or if two-thirds of families in the South were to acquire refrigerators and electric light, then the prognosis for global warming would be even worse.

A vocal minority of scientists continue to contest the global warming theory. They believe it is a sign of the arrogance of contemporary humans to imagine that human activity is significantly affecting the climate system of the planet. The measured rises in global mean temperatures in this century, and the sea-level rises, can be explained, they argue, as consequences of the gradual warming which has been going on since the last mini-ice age in the sixteenth century, rather than as anthropogenic changes. Sceptics also point to the varying behaviour of the indicators of climate change. Thus even though glaciers are receding in many parts of the world, glaciologists have found that glaciers in South America are advancing again after receding for many decades. But although a minority of scientists continues to dispute it, the weight of scientific opinion is now on the side of the global warming hypothesis, as startling evidence of significant climate change continues to mount. In 1995 Norwegian scientist Ola Johannessen and his colleagues reported that an iceberg the size of Oxfordshire broke off from the Larsen Ice Shelf in the Antarctic, the Wordie Ice Shelf broke up and ice connecting James Ross island to the Antarctic Peninsula disintegrated.[6] Advocates of the hypothesis had predicted that its first substantial effects would be observed in these two ice regions. As this book was about to go to press reports emerged of the latest findings of the IPCC which indicate a new consensus amongst scientists that global warming is already taking place, and new and much more apocalyptic fears that, unless drastic action is taken, global warming could accelerate out of control by the end of the next century.

The hypothesis that the climate is changing as a consequence of the extent and character of industrial and agricultural activity on the surface of the planet is a real possibility which not even the most sceptical scientist can rule out on present evidence. Some action has already been agreed at an international level. The Global Climate Convention, ratified after the United Nations Conference on Environment and Development, the 'Earth Summit' held at Rio de Janeiro in 1992, committed the largest producers of carbon dioxide and other greenhouse gases to stabilisation and reduction targets, despite fierce resistance from some of these producers, most notably the United States of America. But the small reductions agreed by the developed countries will be more than taken up by advancing development in less developed countries and global energy consumption and fossil-fuel burning will continue to increase. More radical change in energy production technologies and in energy use are needed.

POLLUTION

The potential environmental problems arising from the enhancement of the greenhouse effect point to the ambiguous character of that phenomenon popularly known as pollution.[7] Many 'pollutants' are in fact naturally occurring substances, such as carbon dioxide, whose concentrations in the atmosphere, waters or lands of the earth have increased as a consequence of human activity. The issue is whether this anthropogenic increase in the prevalence of certain substances in the world, and the introduction of manufactured substances, represents a real long-term threat to life on earth or to human life. The possible threats to human and non-human life from pollution are many and various. The surface of the biosphere which sustains the only life forms known in the universe is no more than twelve kilometres from bedrock or ocean floor to airless space beyond the upper atmosphere. The damaging effects of pollution are recorded on this fragile 'skin' from receding and polluted water aquifers deep underground to changes in the gases of the upper atmosphere.

The discovery of a hole in the thin protective layer of ozone in the upper atmosphere in 1985 set alarm bells ringing in the scientific community. The precise identification of the ozone hole over Antarctica by a British scientist testing atmospheric gas levels with instruments on a balloon, and its confirmation by satellite evidence, led to an urgent scientific quest to identify the cause. The now widely accepted theory emerged that the depletion of atmospheric ozone which caused the Antarctic hole and a general reduction in atmospheric ozone from 2 to 11 per cent originated from human pollution of the atmosphere in the form of CFCs, which are used as refrigerants, aerosol propellants and plastic expanders. The hole is caused by increases in the amount of suspended chlorine in the upper atmosphere, which neutralises ozone. The existence of the hole locally reduces the greenhouse effect, which in turn results in the formation of ice clouds and ice particles which enhance the ozone depletion.[8] The widening hole over the Antarctic is appearing for longer periods every year and covering larger areas, while there is also now a seasonal thinning of ozone over the Arctic, which again is growing in size and duration year by year.

The depletion of the ozone layer weakens the protection the atmosphere provides to human and non-human life from the damaging effects of too much ultraviolet light. This weakening will result in an increase in human skin cancers and eye cataracts, an increase already measurable in areas nearest to the Antarctic. It will also have effects on human immune systems, and on plant and animal life, including the destruction of plankton on which the ocean food chain depends, and the blinding of fish and mammals exposed to increased ultraviolet radiation. The human populations of Chile, New Zealand, Iceland and even Northern Scotland may soon have to begin taking precautionary measures if they are not to experience a significant increase in skin cancers. Evidence from the nearest city to the Antarctic, Punta Arenas in Chile, indicates that already 3.7 times the normal quantity of ultraviolet B radiation is reaching the earth's surface. Increasing blindness in cattle and sheep, blind fish in the Tierra del Fuego, changes in plant and mammalian life-cycles, and a growing incidence of cataracts in human eyes and of severe sunburn and skin cancers are already being recorded in this region.

The discovery of the Antarctic ozone hole, and the thinning of ozone over the Arctic, sharpened perceptions in the scientific community of the significance of pollution, and amongst the general public and politicians. One of the most hopeful indications of the willingness of humanity collectively to respond to the environmental crisis is the global agreement on ozone depletion known as the Montreal Protocol, which was concluded by thirty-six national governments in 1987. The agreement committed signatories to a reduction in the production of CFCs by 20 per cent of 1986 levels by 1993, and by another 30 per cent by 1998. It rapidly became apparent with further research that there was an urgent need to reduce production more quickly. A new agreement was signed by ninety-two countries in London in 1990, committing them to phasing out all CFC production by the year 2000, and to ceasing production of other ozone-depleting chemicals such as halons and carbon tetrachloride. An agreement was also reached on a subsidy for the cost of transferring CFC-substitute technology to Third World nations.[9]

Ozone in the upper atmosphere may be vital to life but its disappearance is an unseen and relatively recent phenomenon. Air pollution has a much longer and more visible history and is responsible for a much greater range of effects on the health of human and non-human species. Air pollution, like global warming, originates primarily from energy and industrial production processes and from human transportation systems. The most significant contemporary source of air pollution is road transportation. Vehicle exhaust emissions, including carbon monoxide and nitrous oxides, petrol additives such as lead and benzene, and unburned fuel particulates from diesel engines, are linked with various diseases including asthma and bronchitis, with reductions in immunity to infection, with certain cancers and with damage to child development. Some studies have found an increased incidence of infectious disease amongst those living close to busy roads, while increases in childhood leukaemia and in the severity and frequency of asthma attacks are also thought to be linked with increases in road traffic emissions, though the precise causes of recent dramatic rises in the incidence of childhood and adult asthma remain unclear.

Industrial emissions are often removed from cities and their environs by tall chimneys but ultimately return to the lower atmosphere in the form of air pollution at places determined by wind pattern and climatic conditions. Oil and coal-fired power stations are the major source of sulphur dioxide and, along with vehicle emissions, of nitrogen oxides which return to the ground in the form of acidified droplets of water known as acid rain. The pervasive ecological effects of this kind of air-borne pollution are now showing up in the world's forests. The first indications of a problem in the forests were observed in the Plenderwald forests of Germany in the 1970s. Foresters noticed that pine trees were losing their needles, and branches were turning sickly yellow and brown instead of green, and then trees began to die. In 1982 34 per cent of trees in West Germany showed signs of damage and in 1988 52 per cent.[10] Some species such as silver fir were particularly susceptible and by the late 1980s 80 per cent of these had died in affected areas.[11] Ecological damage to forests was also observed in many other countries, including the United States and Britain, although government scientists were reluctant to recognise the problem, or to attribute it to air-borne pollution. There is still controversy about the causes of forest decline, but its effects are now observable on deciduous as well as coniferous trees. Leaf canopies are thinner than they used to be, leaves fall earlier and more quickly, trees grow more slowly, and tree roots are thinning. In many parts of the world trees are slowly dying.

German scientists have proposed a 'multiple stress hypothesis' that explains tree decline and death as a function of a combination of factors which include air-borne pollutants, soil and rain acidification and climate change.[12]

Water pollution is the next most pervasive form of pollution after that of air pollution, affecting water in every form of its presence on earth from subterranean aquifers to rivers, lakes and oceans. The principal causes of ocean pollution are oil spillage, the dumping of chemical and human waste in coastal waters from waste pipes, and in the deep sea by ships and the outfalls of polluted rivers carrying loads of industrial and human effluent or silt from human activities such as logging. The 'out of sight, out of mind' principle is one which has been pursued by humanity living on the edge of the ocean for centuries. When humans were relatively few in number, and most pollutants occurred from natural processes, the oceans were able to cope. However, the quantities of toxic chemicals and of human waste that are now piped or shipped to the sea have begun seriously to impact upon ocean ecosystems.

The deep oceans are showing the effects of billions of tons of toxic contaminants dumped in the seas over many decades. The quantities of heavy metals, petroleum and plastics by-products which are now in the oceans become concentrated through ocean food chains in the fat of higher mammals, especially seals and whales. Those whales which have survived the onslaught of industrial whaling are now threatened with extinction by pollution. Even the polar seas and ice-caps are showing signs of pollution from human industrial farming and manufacturing. In the North polar region ice-floes and the Arctic Sea are polluted with soil from dust storms in degraded agricultural areas in China, Central Asia and North America, and with toxic waste from the polluting industries of the Northern hemisphere.[13]

The shallow North Sea, between Britain and Europe, is one of the most heavily polluted oceans in the world. Hundreds of thousands of tons of heavy and poisonous metals such as mercury, chromium and cadmium were dumped in the sea in just one seven-year period between 1975 and 1982, and similar amounts of plastic and oil-refining residues.[14] These quantities of toxic chemicals represent a serious threat to all forms of sea life. Shellfish absorb significant amounts of waste metals which in turn may harm the health of those who consume them, both human and non-human, while vertebrate fish in the North Sea show signs of genetic damage, disease and reproductive deficiency.

Rivers and estuaries are also subject to a range of pollution hazards. Industrial effluent, sewage and agricultural products – fertiliser, pesticide, silage and slurry run-off from intensive animal-rearing systems – are the principal sources of river pollution. Chemical works and oil refineries are notorious polluters. Chemical companies traditionally locate their plants next to river estuaries, using river water as cheap, often free, dispersal mechanisms for toxic waste. In Britain fines are rarely applied even when legal limits for pollution are exceeded.[15] The River Avon, which flows for hundreds of miles through some of the most beautiful English countryside, is subject to the outfall from nineteen sewage works which regularly used to pump out raw sewage, and also to significant pesticide and fertiliser residues from intensively farmed rape seed and wheat fields. Fish and eels in the river are not safe for human consumption because of high levels of the pesticides DDT and dieldrin.[16]

The third major type of pollution is the pollution of the soil. Rachel Carson's *Silent Spring* was an epoch-making book in the history of environmentalism. She systematically described the environmental consequences and health hazards involved in the introduction into the environment of thousands of toxic substances by industry and agriculture, particularly since the Second World War.[17] Many of these chemicals had originated in the quest for deadly chemical weapons during the Second World War. Agents which were originally designed for killing humans were also highly effective in killing insects. DDT (dichloro-diphenyl-trichloroethane) was widely used after 1945 in agriculture and turned out to be highly persistent in the environment, spreading from fields to rivers and oceans through the food chain to mammals and humans, and is even found in mothers' milk.[18] It was responsible for the symbolic demise of the peregrine falcon in both Britain and America, and is gradually being phased out of use, at least in the developed world, because of its resistance to biological breakdown. However, other synthetic pesticide substitutes for DDT, such as dieldrin, are even more toxic. Dieldrin acts on the nervous system and destroys the liver. Many pesticides and herbicides are carcinogenic and highly dangerous to humans, and yet the use of such toxins is permitted by agricultural regulations throughout the world, which, for example, in Britain allow commercially grown wheat to be sprayed with fungicides only ten days before it is harvested. Even organically grown foods contain tiny traces of these toxins because they are now so pervasive in the natural world. These chemicals have serious effects on the ecology of the soil, degrading its organic life, as well as being absorbed into plant tissues. They also undermine the natural balance of species. As chemicals sprayed on the crops and the ground kill off some species, other species in the absence of their natural predators become more profligate.

Another major source of ground pollution is domestic, industrial and toxic waste. As Chris Rose notes, the United Kingdom, uniquely amongst developed countries, continues to pursue a policy of 'dilute and disperse' towards environmental emissions and waste of all kinds.[19] Environmental consultants estimate that 50,000–100,000 hectares of land are contaminated by toxic waste in the UK. Planning authorities regularly approve the siting of domestic housing on former waste dumps and contaminated land, leading to situations like that on a new housing estate in Greenwich where residents saw blue smoke rising from their back gardens, a result of toxic waste combustion.[20] Britain's principal method of domestic waste disposal is landfill, and until very recently there was no requirement to provide infrastructural facilities to control leachates and gas emissions, and such requirements are still very lenient compared, for example, to those in Germany. However, industrial waste far exceeds domestic waste in bulk and toxicity. The favoured British 'method' of disposal of toxic industrial liquid waste is mixing it with domestic waste in landfill sites. The resultant chemical cocktail produces gases, and leaches into the soil, and is already poisoning ground-water supplies in parts of England as the toxins pass underground into the water table. In one survey of UK waste sites, over 3,000 were found to pose a threat to water supplies.[21] Regulation of these sites is controlled by a handful of inspectors operating with minimal resources. Filling holes in the ground with toxic waste is inexpensive and as a consequence Britain is a major net importer of toxic waste. In the United States past neglect of the problem of toxic waste and land pollution is being radically addressed by retrospective legislation which is requiring past producers of waste, and their insurers, to fund the very expensive process of removing the toxins, purifying the soil and restoring the landscape. The enormous costs of this clean-up programme are among the factors behind the collapse of certain syndicates in the Lloyds Insurance market in London, which carried the insurance risk for many of the companies responsible for the pollution. The near-collapse of this central institution of the world insurance market is an indicator of the destabilising potential of neglected environmental pollution hazards on the economic institutions which fund industrial investment and production.

SOIL EROSION AND DEFORESTATION

Significant features of the environmental crisis can be linked with the intensification of agriculture, and associated animal husbandry practices, which have become characteristic of modern industrialised farming. Topsoil erosion, such as that which gave rise to the agricultural depression of the North American dust bowl in the 1930s, and was associated with the groundnut disaster of the Horn of Africa, is seen by many ecologists as one of the most imminently life-threatening features of the environmental crisis, for without topsoil there will not be enough food for the ever-growing global population. One-third of US farmland is threatened by soil erosion while world-wide 6 million hectares are lost to agriculture every year because of erosion and desertification, and a further 21 million rendered uneconomic.[22] Globally 3.5 billion hectares of land, equivalent to North and South America combined or 40 per cent of the world's arable land, are affected by desertification.[23] Annually 24 billion tons of irreplaceable topsoil are being eroded and eventually washed into the oceans.[24]

Topsoil is more vital to human survival than almost any other natural resource, for without topsoil we cannot feed ourselves. It is also an irreplaceable resource. The intensive chemically sustained commercial production of wheat or corn removes between one and two inches of topsoil for each harvest.[25] It can take anything from 100 to 2,500 years for 2.5 centimetres of soil to be formed, depending on climatic conditions.[26] High inputs of oil-based chemical fertilisers and pesticides, the impacts of excessive tillage and heavy machinery, together with the unsustainable mining of water from deep aquifers which are now becoming depleted, threaten both long-term soil stability and future supplies of drinking water, while the chemical run-off from intensively grown crops poisons ground water and rivers, and chemical residues in food and water threaten human health.[27] Species diversity is also reduced as hedgerows, trees and non-productive vegetation are cleared, and wetlands drained.

Soil erosion, desertification, chemical impacts and deforestation are all closely related to commercialised agricultural production methods. According to E. G. Nisbet, the central factor in the increasingly persistent nature of drought in the Sahel and elsewhere is the loss of natural vegetation and consequent climate change.[28] The famines which have become characteristic of parts of sub-Saharan Africa are a consequence of agricultural abuse of the land by colonial and post-colonial landowners looking for quick returns from cash crops which are unsuitable for the cleared bush and forest land.[29] The picture was very different before colonial times, as Walter Rodney points out in *How Europe Underdeveloped Africa*.[30] The characteristic Western picture of Africans as malnourished, and of African lands as eroded and drought-prone, contrasts markedly with the abundance of vegetation and food, and the well-developed physique of most Africans, before the advent of

European farms and plantations.[31] The product of intensive agricultural practices, surplus food, also creates great problems for indigenous agricultural practices in Africa and elsewhere. Subsidised surpluses, dumped on world food markets, often in the form of food aid, have the effect of depressing the value of indigenous agricultural products in developing countries and reducing the incomes of the poorest farmers.[32]

But poor farmers are also the originators of extensive soil erosion, in Africa, in Asia and in Latin America. Again bad farming methods are partly to blame.[33] However, much of this erosion arises from the farming of marginal lands by peasants excluded from lands formerly used for subsistence farming but expropriated by governments and commercial farmers for export-oriented cash crops. In 1960 a World Census of Agriculture found that approximately one million land holdings of more than 200 acres occupied two-thirds of the agricultural land while 109 million holdings of less than five hectares, or 79 per cent of all world farms, occupied just 7 per cent of the land.[34] According to Paul Harrison, despite urgently needed land reform in some countries, the problems of land inequity and landlessness have got much worse since then, not least because of the high costs of the more intensive farming encouraged by governments and aid agencies in the wake of the 'green revolution', which introduced fast-growing hybrid seeds and increased chemical inputs and mechanical harvesting into much of Third World agriculture.[35] Richard North argues that landlessness is not a problem if the landless family has adequate opportunities of acquiring money for housing and food from non-agricultural employment.[36] However, for many dispossessed farmers in the Third World, and particularly in Africa, no such alternative and adequate employment opportunities exist to traditional subsistence farming on communal lands and family plots.

Deforestation is also a major cause of soil erosion. The effects of deforestation can be seen particularly clearly in the historic clearance of trees which took place in the Mediterranean basin. The original forest in this region stretched from Morocco to Afghanistan as recently as 2000 BC.[37] From the cedar forests of

Lebanon to the hillsides of Greece, from Italy to Libya, and from Central Spain to Morocco, trees were cleared for ship-building, grazing land and agriculture to feed the growing armies and population of the Roman Empire, so that by the time of the fall of Rome in the fourth century large areas of North Africa, the Empire's bread basket, had been reduced to desert, and large parts of Spain, Greece and southern Italy were subject to soil erosion, land degradation and rising temperatures.[38] Environmental degradation, and the difficulty of supplying adequate amounts of food from the impoverished soil for the armies and population of Rome contributed to the eventual fall of the Empire.[39] Similar problems beset other ancient civilisations. The demise of the first great cities of ancient Mesopotamia, Ur, Kish, Uruk and Lagash, as well as biblical cities such as Jericho, also seems to have been related closely to unsustainable agricultural practices, deforestation and soil erosion.[40]

What ancient civilisations managed to achieve in certain circumscribed regions of the earth – the Mediterranean basin, Mesopotamia, the Indus valley – twentieth-century industriali-sation and commercial agriculture is achieving on a global scale. Deforestation in both temperate and tropical areas proceeds at an extraordinary rate. Of the remaining 8 million hectares of virgin tropical forest, roughly 1 per cent a month or 400,000 hectares a week is subject to logging extraction or burnt by peasant cultivators and charcoal burners.[41] In South East Asia and Amazonia vast areas are already completely denuded of trees. In their place is left either a wasteland of leached soils and weedy scrub plants, or grassland capable of supporting cattle or subsistence agriculture for a few years before the soil loses its fertility. Current rates of destruction of tropical forest mean that in twenty years' time only small tracts will survive outside of Zaire and New Guinea, where 'back-ward' governments have not exploited the forest at the same rate as those in South East Asia and Latin America.

One of the principal causes of deforestation is commercial logging for the industrial utilisation of tropical hardwoods as cement moulds in building construction, for chipboard and

plywood, chopsticks and furniture. Selective logging of the
largest trees leaves behind great devastation. Loggers who may
only harvest the largest 2 per cent of the trees destroy at least 25
per cent through logging roads, bulldozing and damage to
other trees, and this is in well-managed logging concessions.[42]
In logging concessions in Sarawak a colleague who observed
the practice at first hand described to me how whole hillsides
are destroyed by the extraction of one or two large trees. As the
large tree is cut it brings down many smaller trees, while the
loggers themselves then cut large numbers of small trees to
provide a slip-way on which to drag the tree down to the river.
This slip-way is then dressed with gallons of diesel oil to make it
slippery and reduce the effort required to get the tree down to
the water or the logging track. The ecological devastation
caused by this kind of activity is far greater than the impacts of
logging described by proponents of sustainable tropical timber
extraction.[43] There are few examples in the tropics of forests
which have been commercially logged over time which have
not been extensively degraded, and their capacity to support
indigenous peoples, and non-human species, dramatically
reduced.[44]

The logging roads may in the end be the cause of even more
damage than tree extraction activity, for these roads open up
the previously inaccessible forest so that after logging is completed, the people whom Norman Myers calls *shifted* cultivators
(to distinguish them from tribal *shifting* cultivators) move into
the forest and slash and burn their way to cultivating the poor
tropical forest soil patch by patch, until the forest is completely
destroyed and the soil degraded.[45] The shifted cultivator is
typically a peasant farmer whose own land, or that of his
ancestors, has been expropriated by government or private
landlords for cash-crop production and commercial animal-
rearing. Myers estimates that around 50 per cent of tropical
forest destruction is caused by the shifted cultivator. Whereas in
the ancient pattern of shifting cultivation, known as swidden
agriculture, indigenous forest peoples such as the Penans of
Borneo would farm a small area of forest for seven years and
then move on and allow the forest to grow back, the new shifted

cultivator exploits in a way which does not allow regrowth, while still requiring the cultivation of new plots as the poor soil becomes exhausted on old plots.[46] In many cases the shifted cultivator has been actively encouraged by governments and aid agencies. Thus the World Bank has funded schemes of transmigration of peoples in Brazil and Indonesia which have resulted in the burning of vast tracts of forest.[47] The ostensible reason for these mass transfers of people is overcrowding in places such as Java, or North East Brazil. However, the pattern of land tenure is also crucial. Subsistence farmers are deprived of access to good agricultural land by commercial interests, and forced into the forests in a desperate search for land to grow food for their families.[48]

Large-scale deforestation is not of course confined to tropical regions. Temperate boreal forests are just as much at risk from destruction and clear-cutting and their loss can lead to similar problems of soil erosion, silting of rivers, flash floods, species loss and local climate change. The great forest which stretches from California to Alaska is being clear-cut, while Canada and Scandinavia will soon have destroyed all their original forests except for small reserves. Similarly vast areas of forest in the former Soviet Union have been clear-cut of trees, and China is likely to run out of harvestable forest in the next decade. In the present century 160 million hectares of temperate forest have been clear-cut without regeneration in the Soviet Union and Canada.[49] This is equivalent to half of the uncut forests of Amazonia.

The ecology of the planet, its local, regional and even global climatic systems, are affected by deforestation on such a global scale. Trees absorb carbon dioxide and turn it into oxygen. The cutting of forests releases the carbon stored in the trees into the atmosphere, either by burning or the rotting of the wood in the forest, or by the eventual burning of the wood product after its use as paper, packaging or plywood for concrete moulding in building construction. Until the middle of this century deforestation, and the burning of forests, was the principal cause of increased levels of carbon dioxide in the atmosphere. The carbon released by logging, biomass burning and shifted cultivation is still responsible for 30 per cent of the global warming effect.

The climatic and erosion problems which followed the ancient deforestation of the Mediterranean and parts of North Africa should be a warning to humanity today.[50] Soil which lies at the bottom of the sea cannot be put back on the mountain slopes, or regions turned from arid dry heat, sandy desert or parched limestone rocks to the fertile rain-drenched climate which obtained two millennia ago. At the Earth Summit in Rio de Janeiro in 1992, 130 national leaders could not agree on a global forest convention, so powerful is the commercial tropical timber lobby, and so strong was its voice at that gathering. So-called 'sustainable management' of forests spells death to the inhabitants of the forest – wildlife, tribal peoples and the very trees themselves are threatened with extinction.[51] And yet we all play a part in the destruction of the forests and we cannot simply blame the companies which supply us with the rainforest harvest. When we choose a new kitchen, or our company, church or college a new floor or piece of furniture, we buy particle board or plywood which comes from a factory in the Philippines or Indonesia. When we buy coffee or tea, or tropical fruits, we buy them from Western companies who in turn buy them from landowners who keep millions of peasants poor and landless, who then migrate to slash and burn the forest whose loss we mourn. As Myers says, 'we all have our hands on the chainsaw, and we are wielding it with ever greater energy'.[52]

SPECIES EXTINCTION

Although much of the philosophical discussion of animal ethics, and of public concern about animal welfare, has been in relation to the hunting of animals in the wild and the treatment of animals in captivity for agricultural and scientific purposes, the destruction of species world-wide arising from deforestation, intensive agricultural practice and commercial fishing is also a matter of great ethical and ecological concern. The number of species in the world is estimated very approximately by scientists at around 30 million, of which by far the most numerous group of species is the humble beetle.[53] At the end of the second millennium, after centuries of cataloguing, scientists are still discovering new species in rainforest canopies, in coral reefs and deep channels beneath the sea, in wetlands and mangrove swamps, and even in temperate woodlands in Europe. Our inability to track down and name every species, a task given to humanity by God in the Garden of Eden according to the Genesis creation narrative, is witness to the fecundity and variety of the natural world. But this very fecundity is now threatened by human activity.

It is estimated that around 10,000 species are destroyed annually as a consequence of human activity in the natural world. This compares with an estimated natural extinction rate over the many millennia of the earth's existence of one species per year.[54] The biggest single cause of species extinction is the destruction of the rainforests of Amazonia, Central Africa and South East Asia. These areas are the richest in species diversity on the planet, and the ecosystem of the forest is fragile. Three or four hectares of rainforest in South East Asia or Central America contain more tree species than the whole of Europe or North America.[55] These trees are in turn home to thousands of species of insects, birds, epiphytic plants and reptiles. Tropical rainforests cover only 6 per cent of the earth's surface and yet contain around 90 per cent of its species. The island of Madagascar alone contained around 12,000 plant species and possibly 190,000 animal species, 60 per cent of which were unique to the island. With 93 per cent of the original forest gone, scientists estimate that more than half of the original species have disappeared.[56] Species extinction is also taking place in temperate zones, oceans and in wilderness areas far from human habitation. The intensification of agricultural practices and industrial fishing, the voracious extraction of timber and other resources from the biosphere, the effects of industrial activity and the motor car, all result in significant reductions in biological diversity.

Looked at purely anthropocentrically, the more pressing import of accelerated humanly originated species extinction may be the significance of the reduction of biodiversity for human use of the environment, for example in the quest for new pharmaceutical preparations or new genetic strains of staple foods, but in the longer term the mass extinction of species may threaten the complex interdependencies of the biotic community on which human life depends. Paul Ehrlich's metaphor of species as rivets which hold together the 'aeroplane' in which we circuit the sun, implies that the loss of species may threaten the continued existence of the biotic community: at some point so many rivets may be removed from the plane that it crashes.[57]

Individuals and species in ecosystems together make up a biotic community which represents an energy system by which the sun's warmth, and natural nutrients, are constantly taken up and recycled. Some ecologists believe that the diversity of life in rivers, seas or forests is an indicator of the health of an ecosystem.[58] The degraded river or the damaged forest experiences a loss of species diversity, and with fewer genetic resources the ecosystem is less able to renew and sustain itself through the exigencies of natural events such as droughts, and further human damage. Paul Ehrlich argues that the growing imbalance between species extinction and species creation poses a real threat in the future not only to biodiversity but to the very ecosystems on which all life depends.[59] Whole groups of species, such as the dinosaurs, have become extinct in the past, but the present array of species is built on the biological diversity of earlier periods of life on earth. As Stephen Jay Gould argues in *Wonderful Life*, many contemporary species seem to have evolved on the basis of a much larger platform of diversity in previous eras: the evolution of life on earth is what he calls 'bottom-heavy'.[60] Not all species make a significant contribution to subsequent evolutionary development, for many have been lost without biological trace in previous mass extinctions – though their fossils remain in the Burgess Shale and elsewhere. But, Gould argues, the large base-line of species in previous extinctions enabled the evolutionary development of continuing diversity. However, the size and extent of the mass extinction which is currently being brought about by human action is unprecedented and dramatically reduces the genetic base-line on which the future of life on earth depends.

The variety of contributions which the insect, plant and animal world makes to human life and survival is extraordinary and needs constantly retelling in a culture where life appears to depend more on machines and technology than on the resources of nature: the ladybirds which saved the Californian orange crop from a pernicious beetle, the weevils which pollinate Malaysian palm oil estates discovered in the forests of Cameroon in the 1980s, the sea cucumbers, clams, sharks and stingrays which promise medical benefits in the fight against cancer, the Mangrove swamps which provide rich breeding grounds for inshore tropical fish. A wild relative of corn was recently discovered in Mexico which grows perennially, which, if utilised by commercial growers, would reduce the annual ploughing of corn crops, and the associated soil erosion.[61]

Besides these anthropocentric and utilitarian arguments, we also need to be reminded of the extraordinary character of the animals and species we are destroying: the exuberance of the breaching humpback whale as it lifts its giant body out of the water, or slaps its massive tail on the water, and its ten octave songs which may last thirty minutes; the astonishingly human-like qualities of groups of chimpanzees; the peaceful nature of the mountain gorilla which Diane Fossey so intimately captured in her film footage and field notes. To dive in the warm tropical South China Sea and swim among the thousands of beautifully coloured fish and types of coral which live just a few feet under the surface in a marvellous array of patterns, shapes and colours; to see a flock of bright green and yellow parakeets take off from a tree on a Nepalese hillside and watch a great Himalayan kite circling overhead looking for its next meal; to walk through an unravaged rainforest and hear the call of lemurs, observe hornbills with their great yellow and orange beaks on perches in the branches of 200-foot rainforest trees; to watch the mists rising from the damp canopies of trees coloured green, red, grey and yellow in a bright tropical dawn, and look down at the forest floor and observe the thousands of insects involved in recycling the tree products into the fragile soil, and, through the birds that live off the insects, back into the tree tops again; to hear the enveloping harmonic chorus of cicadas and other insects and birds in the forest night: such experiences of the natural world are glorious gifts to the human senses and spirit. Biodiversity is not just an ecological principle, an economic variable or a scientific discovery – it is the astonishing exuberance of the creation itself.

POPULATION AND NATURAL RESOURCES

It is estimated that in 1650 the total human population was around 500 million, which is roughly equivalent to the population of the fifty largest cities in the world today.[62] This population was inevitably spread fairly thinly across the planet, and the impacts it made upon the commons[63] and species of the planet were relatively light. The growth rate of the population in 1650 was 0.3 per cent, which meant a doubling every 240 years. Thanks to dramatic and life-enhancing reductions in child and adult mortality because of improved sanitation, hygiene, clean water and drains, and, in the twentieth century, better medicine, the population growth rate increased to a superexponential level of 2.1 per cent by 1970, or a doubling of the population roughly every thirty years.[64] The exponential growth occurs because birth rates do not decline as mortality rates decline and so the number of people being born soon outstrips the numbers dying. In most of the countries of the industrialised North birth rates eventually fell to at or below replacement rate by the 1970s. Thus average family size in Britain is now down to 1.8. However, the drop in mortality rates occurred much faster in the countries of the South, and so the gap between death rates and birth rates is much larger than it ever was in the early industrialised countries, with the consequence that population rises in the South have been much larger than they were in the North.[65] Therefore the global population is rising in absolute terms very fast indeed.

The global rate of population increase is slowly declining, from 2.1 per cent in the late 1960s to 1.7 per cent today but the numbers of people added annually remain higher than ever because of the greatly expanded population base.[66] In 1991 the number of those born above those who died was 92 million people, which was the largest annual population rise ever.[67] The transition from low death rate and high birth rate to low death rate and low birth rate is happening very fast in some of the newly industrialising countries. Countries such as China, Thailand, Malaysia and Singapore have made this transition in less than forty years, much faster than it happened in the industrialised countries of the North. Thailand has reduced family size from 6 to 3.5 in just twenty years with a combination of improved health care, rising incomes, education and family planning.[68] Many other countries, particularly in Africa, have been unable to direct limited resources to reducing family size in this way, or prevented from doing so by the World Bank and the International Monetary Fund. Kenya has a population growth rate of 4.1 per cent, the fastest rate recorded in any nation, which means the population of Kenya will double in just seventeen years.[69] Globally, lower death rates, and birth rates which are not declining in tandem, have produced a situation where there are now around 5.6 billion individuals on the planet. Presently 90 per cent of the annual population increase is occurring in developing countries, although some Northern countries, most notably in North America, also show a still growing population, though this is partly because of immigration. Estimates of future growth vary widely from 11 to 14 billion by the year 2100. The lower figure looks less attainable than it did because there has been a slowing down in fertility decline rates since the late 1980s, owing primarily to the debt crisis and worsening terms of trade between the developed and the developing world. A key reason for this is the free market economic prescription – known as structural adjustment – which has been imposed by the World Bank and the International Monetary Fund on more than eighty debtor nations. Under structural adjustment governments are forced to reduce spending on primary health care, the provision of clean water and sewers, and food and farm subsidies. The effects of these policies have been to undermine family nutrition and health. Consequently family sizes have not reduced as parents need to

have more children to ensure some survive to adulthood.[70]
Spending on family planning services has also been cut back in
the debt crisis.

Increases in life expectancy, and reductions in child mortality, are the first and most dramatic enhancement in life
quality which modern civilisations have achieved over their
forerunners. But the consequent growth in human numbers is
regarded by many environmentalists as the single most significant factor in the environmental crisis. For 99.9 per cent of
humanity's existence there were less than 10 million people on
the planet. Ecologists argue that not only developing countries,
but developed countries such as the Netherlands, Britain and
the United States, are crowded to the point where the levels of
human activity involve systematic degradation and depletion of
natural resources such as soil, water, forests and fisheries, and
thus may be said to have exceeded what some ecologists identify
as the 'carrying capacity' of the land, by which is meant the
capacity of a particular land area, and associated commons
such as air and water, to sustain a population of humans and
domesticated animals, and their agricultural and other activities
without serious environmental degradation and without degrading the health, nutrition and quality of life experienced by
the population.[71] The concept of carrying capacity also implies
that there are physical limits to biological resources, and that
when these limits are approached certain resources become
scarce, so human activity in obtaining them becomes excessively
costly, is very damaging to the environment and often creates
enormous suffering. Many women and children in the South
walk up to eight hours a day to fetch water and wood for
washing and cooking as the land around them becomes pro-
gressively denuded of vegetation and the water table sinks.
European or Japanese fishing boats travel thousands of miles
searching for new fishing grounds as traditional fishing areas
have been over-exploited and fish stocks have dwindled. While
global food surpluses, particularly emanating from the industrial farms of the North, are very great indeed, the problems of
soil erosion, water-logging, salination and desertification mean
that there are limits to the intensity with which particular areas

of arable land can be worked, especially in semi-tropical and tropical zones. When these limits are reached in particular regions, such as the Sahel, then local food scarcity may become a real problem. Furthermore, although from 1950 to 1984 the world output of food grew 2.8 times, more than keeping up with population growth, between 1985 and 1989 there was no global increase in food production, despite continuing increases of inputs of fertilisers in the global agricultural industry.[72] Crop yields from these intensive methods may have plateaued. There may be limits to what even the most intensive technological inputs into the soil can achieve in increased output. From an environmental perspective, as we have seen, the increased yield from these intensive methods is ecologically damaging in many regions, because of soil erosion, ground-water depletion and pollution and local climate change. The United Nations Population Fund estimates that world food production can sustainably (that is without soil erosion, desertification, ground-water depletion etc.) feed around 5.5 billion people with an adequate calorific intake if everyone was on a vegetarian diet. If, however, the population derives 25 per cent of calorie intake from meat products, as North Americans and West Europeans do, then the number which can be sustainably fed reduces to around 2.8 billion.[73] The possibilities for sustainably feeding 11 billion in 2100 even with many new advances in food technology are then, at the very least, open to doubt.

A purely quantitative approach to human population interactions with environmental problems and resource availability can, however, be misleading. The critical environmental impacts of desertification, soil erosion, deforestation, loss of biodiversity, air and water pollution, ground-water depletion and global warming all relate to a range of factors which include not only population growth but patterns of material consumption, industrial production, technological development, the commercialisation of agriculture, biological resource exploitation, terms of trade between developed and developing countries and inequitable patterns of land ownership. Population is not by any means the most critical factor in these impacts. In the last 40 years the global population increased 3 times in size. But in the same period fossil fuel use rose 413 times, the global economy grew 30 times and industrial production 50 times. On some estimates humans have consumed as many goods and services since 1950 as all previous humans, and we have burnt more of the world's stored energy resources since World War II than all the energy resources used by all our predecessors.[74] It is the rise in consumption (and waste) levels amongst the richest nations in the twentieth century, and amongst rich people in poor nations, which accounts for much of the increased detrimental impact of human activity on the environment. But it remains true that these impacts are exacerbated by population pressures and so reductions in population in both North and South are highly desirable in the light of the environmental crisis.

ENVIRONMENT AND DEVELOPMENT

While many of the features of the environmental crisis would appear to originate in the actions of the industrialised and economically developed nations which are mostly located in the Northern hemisphere – ozone depletion, global warming, toxic waste and even deforestation in the tropics for the primarily Western and Japanese market in tropical timber – the impact of the collapse of ecosystems and local climate regimes is experienced most dramatically by people who live in the South, in Africa, Asia and Latin America. It is on these continents that the consequences of desertification, deforestation, soil erosion or loss of biodiversity are experienced most sharply. For the peasant farmer or the landless rural labourer in drought-ridden Africa the state of the environment is a matter of basic survival. Desertification and drought are the two biggest threats to millions of poor people in many parts of sub-Saharan Africa.[75] As Paul Harrison shows, part of the answer may be in the hands of peasant farmers, who can deploy a mix of traditional and modern methods of soil conservation, inter-cropping and animal husbandry to balance food requirements with natural ecology.[76] But, as Richard North points out, too few peasants have access to education in the right farming techniques, and too few have access to adequate areas of arable land.[77]

Another major environmental problem in the developing world is the exponential rate of urbanisation. In 1950 there were 86 million urban people in the world. In 1990 there were 1.5 billion, and many of the cities they inhabit have become major environmental disasters in themselves.[78] Mexico City, Manila, São Paulo, Calcutta, are all cities with more than 10 million inhabitants. Around 60 per cent of Third World city dwellers live in squatter areas or shanty towns, mostly without proper drainage, clean water or other environmental infrastructure. The rural hinterland of these growing megacities is severely degraded as the market for fuel wood and vegetables denudes the surrounding land. Many of these urban migrants have been forced off the land by commercial farming interests, many are environmental refugees trying to find sustenance after rural lands have been exhausted by intensive farming or overgrazing, or the food available from rivers and forests has been reduced by intensive logging activity.[79]

Industrial activities in Third World cities tend to be much less carefully regulated than industrial activities in the First World, and their environmental and human costs therefore much greater. The First World has already exported many of its dirtiest technologies to Third World cities and shanty towns where the absence of environmental regulations, or of worker unions, allow effluent to leave the factory by air or water largely untreated, and workers to be employed on very low wages and over much longer periods of time than would be acceptable in developed countries. While lack of regulation, corruption and inexperience in the use of pollution technology may all be factors in the high levels of pollution in many Third World industrial cities, it remains clear that these high levels are also a function of a global economic system where most multinational companies have their headquarters in Western cities, and their dirtiest and most labour-intensive factories in Third World cities, and where consequently their repatriated profits will be maximised.[80]

The impacts which human activity now make on land, forest,

river and ocean form a part of a global system of resource extraction and utilisation which has its origins in the period of European expansion which began with the voyages of explorers such as Christopher Columbus. The eventual conversion of tribal lands into plantations, cash-crop monocultures, mines and commercial farmlands was a process which removed millions of people from the land and has brought about levels of human malnutrition, as well as ecological degradation, which are unprecedented in human history.[81] As prime lands were expropriated for plantations and cash crops, so peasants were either forced into slavery or landless labouring or they were forced on to marginal lands. The inequitable distribution of land in many developing countries has continued, and often worsened under the actions of independent governments who degrade forests or agricultural land for quick profits, or to meet the punitive interest payments demanded by Western banks on external debt.[82]

Many of the ecological threats to land in the developing world – soil erosion, water depletion, local climate change, deforestation, over-sized megacities – originate in the problem of land tenure. The poor are forced into degrading their own environment just in order to survive. Thus the Indian rural dweller who cuts trees to sell charcoal to the nearby city for a few rupees with which to feed his children is forced into this action by inequitable land distribution. This problem has substantially worsened in the last fifteen years as the 1.3 trillion dollar debt of the Third World, much of it lent and borrowed for corrupt or environmentally destructive purposes, has forced Third World economies into increased cash crop and primary commodity production, heightening pressures on the land. The environment of indebted countries is being raided to meet payments to Western bankers under structural adjustment programmes imposed by the World Bank and the International Monetary Fund.[83]

The terms of trade as between the rich industrialised North and the commodity-oriented lands of the South exacerbate the problems of land hunger and ecological degradation in developing countries. Africa is currently a net exporter not only of coffee, tropical timber, tin and other precious metals and minerals, but of tropical fruits, cut flowers, soya, groundnuts and other products grown on land urgently needed to feed Africans. Ironically and tragically, as such commodity exports have increased to meet debt interest payments under the structural adjustment programmes of the World Bank and the IMF, the prices of many primary commodities have fallen on world markets.[84] Many years after the end of formal colonialism, Africa, Asia and Latin America remain net exporters of primary commodities and capital. The system of resource extraction in the South and capital accumulation in the North is still the basic economic context for relations between North and South. The trickle of bank credits which return as Western aid may worsen the inherent economic and ecological problems of the developing world as official aid is often utilised in prestige projects which make a significant visible impact on the environment, thus boosting the status of aid managers in their own organisations, and of Third World government ministers, while further degrading the natural environment.[85] The predilection of aid bodies and Third World governments for hydroelectric dams, such as the vast Namada dam in India, which has been universally condemned as environmentally disastrous but was largely funded by the World Bank, results in tremendous ecological damage, as well as the enforced removal of thousands more people from the land.

There is a clear conflict between the dominant model of market-driven, aid-primed industrial and agricultural development and the short-run and long-term environmental quality of many Third World countries. Already poor environmental quality in cities and rural areas causes serious problems of health and hunger, or less life-threatening but nonetheless real reductions in life quality, for many millions of people. However, as we have seen, much of the environmental degradation originates in the actions of poor and hungry people. The further intensification and commercialisation of agricultural activity combined with industrial development in the cities is said by some advocates of 'sustainable development' to be the only long-term solution to poverty and thus ultimately to

environmental problems.[86] There is, however, reason to doubt
that the paths of transnational-led Third World industrial
development and further agricultural intensification, much of it
also led by transnational seed and chemical companies, is the
solution most likely to dramatically improve the lot of the 20
per cent of the world's population who are currently hungry, or
the best solution to the environmental problems of the Third
World. The dominant development model being pressed relent-
lessly by the World Bank and the IMF on more than eighty
debtor Third World nations, pushes these countries into global
commodity and industrial markets while minimising protection
for their workers' health or longevity, or the health of their
environments. The World Bank increasingly adopts the language of sustainability in its reports, but the effects of its free
market development model can hardly be described as environmentally sustainable not least because they have increased
poverty levels in precisely those countries where poverty is so
environmentally damaging. Advocates of alternative 'green'
development argue that development can only be just, equitable and ecologically beneficent when it is a process driven
from below by the subjects of development. Ultimately the
problems of environment and development, as Bill Adams
suggests, are problems of human political economy.[87] People
need to reclaim control over their polities, their economies,
their lands and their lives. Only when models are found for
recovering this kind of community control over economics and
the environment, as I argue in detail in chapter seven below,
can we expect a better balance to be struck between human
greed and human poverty, and between human need and
ecological limits in both First and Third Worlds.

HOPE FOR THE EARTH

At the beginning of the twentieth century most of the land area
of the earth was unpolluted, its primal forests were mostly
intact, the oceans were mostly free of litter and sewage, the
rivers mostly ran free from sediment and human waste. Pollution and environmental destruction were primarily limited to

the small area of the earth's surface affected by industrial development in Northern Europe and in parts of North America. By the end of this century there is not a stretch of ocean and very few areas of forest which do not show signs of the industrial and commercial transformation of the earth into a materials bank for human exploitation. The extent of human interference and disruption of natural systems can be measured three miles above the North Pole in the loss of protective ozone, and one mile deep in the rift valleys of the ocean floor in the polluted sediments which trickle down from the waste products of modern consumerism. Students in my classes from all over the world share stories of the effects of environmental breakdown in their own regions. Monsoons or the rains no longer come in their predictable seasons, the frequency of typhoons, hurricanes and flash floods grows alarmingly, and cities in many parts of the globe have become too hot for comfort because of deforestation and local climate change. And with environmental chaos comes social chaos and anarchy.

Environmental disaster is now the biggest single cause of the movement of peoples across the globe. In parts of China land has been totally degraded by efforts to meet the absurd agricultural and iron smelting targets of the Cultural Revolution and people in their hundreds of thousands are leaving now infertile rural areas for the cities every day, to form the largest single movement of peoples in the history of Asia. In parts of Africa the land is so dry that aid agencies must sink wells thirty or forty metres to reach the water table. Ecological breakdown is also a growing cause of armed conflict as well as social anarchy. Struggles over the diminishing areas of fertile land have intensified in recent years, and land struggles continue to form the focus for civil war and resistance movements in many parts of the world.

In Britain too in the last five years a new note of social unrest has become focused on land and environmental issues. The new alliance of road protesters involving local residents, travellers and environmental activists, the increasingly strident campaigns of city dwellers against the exclusive use of the countryside for intensive farming and blood sports and the cruelty to animals involved in both kinds of activity, growing disputes over access to rural areas for travellers and walkers, all indicate a new and heightened awareness amongst the urban people of Britain about the significance of land, and their fears for what is happening to the earth. The continuing loss of wilderness, wetland and downland for motorways and intensive, monocrop agriculture in such a small and overcrowded island is opposed by more and more people whose welfare governments and landowners claim to pursue in these destructive projects. The argument that the pace of development and environmental destruction is ultimately for the benefit of humanity as a whole wears increasingly thin in a society which in the last twenty years has seen unprecedented levels of unemployment and under-employment, and levels of income inequality between land or capital owners and business managers, workers and the unemployed which are even greater than those which pertained when Karl Marx wrote the *Communist Manifesto*.

The recent growth of environmental protest amongst the poor, landless and unemployed in both the developed and the developing world indicates that environmentalism is no longer the preserve of well-educated middle-class campaigners but is increasingly a movement of dissent among all social classes against our headlong rush, under the dictates of the free market and industrial corporatism, to remake the non-human world in the homogenising forms of the monocrop, the motorway and the megalopolis. As the connections of mutual welfare between rich and poor are increasingly sundered by the unbridled pursuit of free market policies, so the assault of modern industrialism on the diversity of the natural world in the name of human progress increasingly loses its social legitimacy. The extent and range of environmental protest around the world is an extremely hopeful sign. For more than twenty years environmental campaigners, and a minority of scientists and philosophers, have been warning of the consequences of pursuing our present course. But environmental concern has frequently been dismissed as a rich person's luxury, or as the preserve of anti-progressive or even misanthropic intellectuals or hippies.[88] Today in both the North and the South there is a great groundswell of popular protest at the toxification of land, water, air and food, at the tarmacking or grassing over of forests, wetlands and highland areas, at the diversion of rivers and the pollution of coastal waters and beaches, and at the grave risks we are taking with the future of the world which our children will inherit.

Local communities in urban and rural areas, indigenous tribal groups and even the 'consumer' are increasingly resisting the bureaucratic and industrial remaking of the natural world and the unnatural and inhuman catastrophes which this remaking so often brings in its wake. While governments continue to pursue the environmentally destructive goal of economic growth at the expense of natural resource conservation, citizens from Uruguay to Finland increasingly believe that the protection of the environment, and the quality of life and human health associated with a healthy natural environment, are more important than economic growth.[89] All over the world local community groups are resisting environmental destruction of their local habitats and communities and it is this new local character of the contemporary phase of environmentalism which is perhaps its most distinctive feature. In parts of Europe and North America local communities are demanding that rivers such as the Mississippi, the Moyser and the Danube be undammed, and given back their natural meanders and flood plains so they can do the work of naturally removing pollutants and of absorbing heavy rainfall, and no longer threaten communities downstream in times of heavy rain.[90] In the Amazon, the Philippines and North India local tribal and community groups are seeking restitution through the courts for forests destroyed by commercial loggers, and an end to future logging. Local communities in Britain are confronting road-builders, quarry and open-cast mining developers, live-animal exporters and golf-course builders. In Scotland crofters and estate workers are mobilising to reclaim their land from the 'lairds' and foreign landowners who have overseen the denuding of the Caledonian forests and rich moorlands of the Scottish Highlands by subsidised sheep and deer which make Scotland's tiny number of landowners very rich at the expense of the ecology of the countryside, and its capacity to support a diversity of human occupations.

This new localism in environmental campaigning is a very hopeful sign, for some would argue that global environmentalism has produced far more rhetoric and unenforceable international regulations and treaties than it has genuine action to preserve particular local habitats and ecosystems. It also indicates a growing disaffection with national or international politics as a primary vehicle for environmental conservation. Governments and businesses increasingly use the language of the environmental movement to justify and gloss their development projects and production plans, but political debate continues to be dominated by the belief that unlimited economic growth remains the only hope for improved life quality. The only change is the recognition that this growth must be pursued in less damaging ways by the adoption of new technologies. However, the strange alliance of middle-class householders and nomadic road protesters in Britain has forced, through direct action campaigns against road-builders, a far more radical reappraisal of the great 'car-owning democracy' than has ever been proposed in the British government's own documents on sustainability. Environmental campaigners and a growing minority in the scientific and bureaucratic establishments are agreed that the priorities and values of modern industrial civilisation need much more radical change than any so far proposed by elected politicians or business leaders.

Religious groups and leaders have also become more prominent in calls for this redirection of modern civilisation. Many religious leaders see the rampant materialism and consumerism of the modern world as a sign of a deep spiritual malaise, and of a lost sense of spiritual and moral purpose in life and the cosmos. In 1943 the Christian apologist C. S. Lewis prophetically argued that the evacuation of divine meaning and purpose from the natural world would be the cause of a crisis in human relations with the non-human world: 'the stars lost their divinity as astronomy developed, and the Dying God has no place in chemical agriculture'.[91] The Muslim philosopher Seyyed Hossein Nasr argued in the 1960s that the technological domination of nature was a sign of the deep spiritual lack which modern urban humans experience in their denatured lives.[92] But Nasr also lamented that so many of the world's religions, and especially Christianity, had conformed themselves to the errors of modernism rather than critiquing the spiritual vacuity and ecological destructiveness of modern civilisation. More recently Pope John Paul II has argued that the ecological crisis is a direct consequence of human sin, of greed and of the modern tendency for instant gratification through consumerism.[93] The Pope, along with the Archbishop of Canterbury and other Christian leaders, has also attended gatherings of world religious leaders at Assisi, the birthplace of St Francis, the most radical Christian naturalist, to help co-ordinate the world's faiths in a concerted movement to conserve the natural environment against further destruction, and to alter the course of modern civilisation.

There is taking place at the end of the twentieth century an apparent revival of religious and spiritual interest. Religious fundamentalisms and new religious movements abound in every part of the world, while Christianity, Islam, Hinduism and Buddhism are undergoing dramatic revivals in many parts of the non-Western world. Even in secular Britain meditation courses and retreat centres are over-subscribed, while many young people in the West are becoming vegetarian and increasingly look to relations with the natural world, and the animal world, as a sphere of meaning and spiritual purposiveness, rejecting the 'work and spend' ethic of modern consumerism. Indeed the environmental movement in its more radical manifestations involves a deep quest for wisdom, ritual order and spiritual value in nature. It is not then simply a question of religious special pleading to suggest that the spiritual vacuum and the ecological crisis of modern civilisation are closely related.

Robin Grove-White suggests that scientific narratives of ecological decay and destruction are in themselves incapable of generating a change in human behaviour and orientation towards nature.[94] Scientific prophecies of environmental crisis do not have the motive power to change the direction of a form of civilisation which has become accustomed to courting risk and hazard as a way of life. In traditional and pre-modern societies religion is the source and legitimator of those moral values which construct the duties and responsibilities by which people order their lives, and their relationships with one another and with the non-human world. In modern Western societies we seek to order our civic life and private morals without the guidance and legitimating power of religious truth, ritual and myth, and without reference to God as the transcendent source and guarantor of goodness, beauty and wisdom. The result is that increasingly we are unwilling to recognise and affirm the moral responsibilities and duties that living together in the world entails. We are living, as Jonathan Sacks suggests, off the moral capital of our Christian forebears, but this moral capital is diminishing, as the rises in crime, violence, marital breakdown, fraud and greed in Western societies clearly attest.[95] The rising divorce rate in particular indicates that we are increasingly unwilling to allow the moral responsibilities we owe to one another and to our children to restrain our quest for personal fulfilment. Moral contracts and stable moral communities are dissolved by the modern quest for individual satisfaction, material comfort and pleasure. Similarly the duties we owe to future generations not to consume and waste and pollute the resources of the earth no longer restrain our quest for luxury and satisfaction in the present.

As Sacks also suggests, governments alone cannot make us good.[96] Moral change concerning the duties and virtues which make us better people, and which make for a more ecologically harmonious way of living, will only come about through a process of education and the adoption of moral 'habits of the heart' in communities, in families, in neighbourhood, educational and work communities, and in religious communities. This is why the activation of so many local communities around the world in environmental protest and change is such a hopeful sign. But protest without spirituality will not endure. Rebellion against one kind of establishment is no basis for a new social and moral order. The hope that we can find peace in human life and harmony with the natural world needs the anchor, the spiritual sustenance, of the religious traditions of the world, for without that transcendent reference, environmental protest is still at risk of cynicism and boredom, despondency and hopelessness.

This book is written from the conviction that only the recovery of a spiritual, moral and cosmological awareness of our place in the natural order, and of the independent ethical significance of that order, rooted in particular religious traditions, can enable our civilisation to begin to shift its priorities and its values in a more ecologically harmonious direction. The analysis of the origins of the environmental crisis in the next chapter will substantiate this conviction, for as we survey the origins and causes of the crisis in Western civilisation, we will find that the loss of a spiritual account of the situatedness of the human self in a morally significant natural order is a central feature of the crisis we currently face. The central project of this book, the location of an understanding of the moral significance of natural order in the heart of the Christian tradition, is therefore an essential element in the reorientation of modern Western societies, with their Christian inheritance, towards the ecological character of life on earth in all its beauty and diversity.

CHAPTER TWO

The origins of the environmental crisis

The precise identification of the causes of the environmental crisis is neither simple nor straightforward. A number of environmental and ethical treatises tend to rely on a single explanatory variable, though the variable differs from author to author. The ecologist Paul Ehrlich in his book *The Population Explosion* proposes over-population as the fundamental cause which needs addressing if the crisis is to be averted.[1] The environmental economists Dennis and Donella Meadows in the influential Club of Rome Report *The Limits to Growth* identify the economics of growth as the central cause of environmental over-exploitation.[2] Robin Attfield in his seminal study *The Ethics of Environmental Concern* identifies the pursuit of progress as the central feature of the modern world-view which has given rise to the environmental crisis.[3] Theodore Roszak, Edward Goldsmith and Rupert Sheldrake argue that the modern scientific method is the source of the distorted relationship between humanity and nature which has produced the crisis.[4] Some propose that the environmental crisis is basically a problem of changing cultural attitudes to the non-human world, or of the social construction of nature. Thus Lynn White in a famous article blames it on the Christian doctrine of creation, and in particular the Genesis command to dominate and subdue the earth.[5] Others blame it on 'Cartesian dualism', the disjunction between rationality and embodiment, nature and culture which is said to have originated in the philosophy of the Enlightenment. Ecofeminists such as Mary Daly or Rosemary Radford Ruether believe the problem of humanity and nature originates in gender construction and patriarchy:

40

the oppression and abuse of nature through technology are seen as symptomatic of the male tendency to dominate and control.[6] This domination tendency is located by some 'ecotheologians' in the traditional picture of a male Christian God who demands the impossible from his human subjects, who consigns them to sin and Fall and who promises redemption in some future post-material state.[7]

I shall argue in this chapter that just as the environmental crisis is complex in its nature, so its causation is also complex and multifactorial. I will propose that the roots of the crisis lie in a range of changes and social processes which together presage the beginnings of modern history, and that form of human society known as modernity, in which the human relation to nature is radically transformed. Karl Marx described the social conditions in which modernity was constructed as the experience in which 'all that is solid melts into air'. The industrial transformation of agricultural systems and land tenure patterns, of economic order, of manufacturing production and household consumption creates a radically reordered world. These transformations in the material conditions of human life effect dramatic changes in the natural environment. They also reflect and legitimate a new account of humanity's place in a cosmos increasingly perceived as devoid of moral significance or divine purpose, other than its material value to humans. The demise of traditional cosmology, and the transformation of material relations produces a new philosophical focus on the self as the locus of human identity and moral significance, and on the advancement of human comfort as the supreme goal of civilisation. The fulfilment of the individual disembedded self, set free from the fixed social roles, natural constraints and ethical authorities of the pre-modern world becomes the touchstone of the new morality of utilitarian individualism. The rise of individualism is closely associated with the quest for material fulfilment through ecologically damaging consumerism. The modern development of the global mobility of capital and of labour in industrialised societies also contributes to the disembedding of social systems of production and exchange from cultural, moral or ecological limits or moorings.[8] Global economic forces increasingly function in an abstract manner, regardless of their effects, positive or negative, on human and natural ecology. The ecological crisis calls into question fundamental features of the mobile, globalising 'juggernaut' of modernity, and its destructive effects on the stability of both human communities and natural ecosystems. The mobility, and the appetite for natural resources, of the modern global economy and the consumer society represent a systematic threat to the health of both human and natural ecologies.

THE AGRICULTURAL REVOLUTION

For 99 per cent of human history, humans were hunter-gatherers, living directly off the land, in the forest or the jungle, intervening minimally in the lives of other species and the balance of ecosystems.[9] Hunter-gatherers forage for plants and hunt animals and some of them also engage in plant growing in forest clearings. As John Bodley argues, these methods of food generation rely on a vast knowledge of plants, animals and ecosystems, and are well disposed to the delicate and limited biological resources of the often fragile regions – savannah, tropical rainforest, arid semi-desert – in which they were (and in some places still are) practised.[10] Hunter-gatherers also have a close knowledge of the inter-relationships of different animals and plants. Hunter-gatherers are, though, responsible for some ecological destruction. Fossil records indicate that American Indians caused the extinction of some large land mammals before the arrival of Europeans in the New World, and there is evidence that rainforest tribes have hunted a small number of animals to extinction. The burning of small strips or patches of forest for shifting swidden agriculture, as practised by many hunter-gatherer groups, is, some argue, also responsible for ecological degradation. However, when large areas of forest are available to relatively small groups of nomads, as was the case in most hunter-gatherer cultures until very recently, the practice has no long-term ecological impacts.[11] According to Bodley, efforts are also made to preserve rare trees and flowers.

Swiddens are typically farmed for three or four years, and then left fallow, and the forest allowed to regenerate.[12]

Hunter-gathering, mixed as it often is with swidden farming, is regarded by modern agronomists as an 'unproductive' form of agriculture, for it takes less food from the environment than the environment can provide. But, as Marshall Sahlins argues with the aid of a number of contemporary field studies, this unproductivity is inherent to the low ecological impacts of hunter-gatherers and to the large amounts of leisure time which they enjoy.[13] The hunter will not carry off all the young from a bird's nest because the birds are his neighbours and have need of life as well as his own family. The gatherer harvests only enough nuts or fruits from a bush to feed her family and neighbours, leaving some for others, or to fall to the ground as seed. Using a line or a temporary dam, groups of hunter-gatherers may catch enough fish for a night's feasting, but with no refrigerators they do not catch more than they can eat. However, in most hunter-gatherer societies there is a surprising abundance of food, much wild food is left uneaten and malnutrition is rare. This is in stark contrast to the situation of many modern tribal groups living in shrinking pockets of undisturbed forest or grassland, or removed from their natural habitat and forced to farm fixed plots, for whom malnutrition becomes a real problem.[14] Hunter-gatherers are also not prone to diseases in their natural context, as they have not acquired the animal-originated disease load of primitive agrarian cultures where humans and animals share housing. They are though extremely vulnerable to diseases on contact with modern humans and many tribes have already been extinguished for this reason. Many others have simply been driven to starvation, imprisoned or callously killed by the explorers and invaders of modern 'civilisation'.

Sahlins describes the hunter-gatherer culture as the 'original affluent society'.[15] Bodley cites a recent study comparing the Machiguenga tribe of the Amazon with the modern urban French, in which it was found that it took the French two hours' more work a day than the Machiguenga to meet their basic nutritional needs. The Machiguenga also have less work

oriented to non-food production and so they have five hours'
more leisure time for resting and visiting than the urban
French.[16] Such are the ironies of 'progress'.

In contrast to those who assert that the extinguishing of
hunter-gatherer cultures is a sure and inevitable sign of the
advancement of the human condition, Sahlins, Bodley and
others observe that modern styles of agriculture and of material
affluence may be no more conducive to the achievement of
happiness and the good life, especially for the earth's poorest
peoples, than the hunter-gatherer culture. The reductions in
life quality, and the loss of cultural, linguistic and moral goods
experienced by hunter-gatherers on reserves or in forced settlements amount in many cases to genocide.[17] This moral evil
cannot be outweighed by the economic benefits pertaining to
city dwellers or corporations from the exploitation of these last
wildernesses.

Hunter-gathering is clearly not a life-style which would be
either survivable or suitable for most modern peoples, nor
ecologically sustainable in our much altered modern environments, though the attraction of nomadism to some young
unemployed people in Britain – the so-called 'new age travellers' – indicates the enduring appeal of a life lived much closer
to the rigours and gifts of the natural world. We may, though,
have something to learn from hunter-gatherers about styles of
agriculture and artefact production which are more closely
attuned to the natural regenerative processes of the land, which
generate very little waste, and which leave more of nature's
inheritance behind for future generations.

The available archaeological and fossil evidence indicates
that the ancient move from nomadic hunter-gathering to settled
agricultural society was the occasion of the first large-scale
permanent human impacts on the natural environment.
Around 10,000 years ago new agricultural techniques were
developed in a number of locations around the world, most
notably in the Ancient Near East, though similar developments
are recorded in parts of Asia.[18] The transition of semi-nomadic
tribes into settled pastoral societies of village and town dwellers
is traced in the Bible and other ancient records of the period

from 8000 to 6000 BC. Settled agriculture then spread to Greece, the Balkans and ultimately to central Europe, while similar developments took place in Mesoamerica and China.[19] The explanations for the emergence of settled agriculture are various. One popular theory is that it emerged in response to population pressure, as the amount of land needed to sustain nomadic hunter-gatherers is arguably greater than that required for more settled forms of agriculture.

The histories of agriculture and civilisation are closely intertwined. Urban-based civilisations rely upon agricultural surplus being made available by rural dwellers to urban settlements. But, as Clive Ponting shows in his *Green History of the World*, the excessive demands of urban-based civilisations for agricultural surplus, often in order to fund or sustain large military forces, led many ancient civilisations to ruin, and turned the lands on which they relied to desert. This pattern was repeated in Mesopotamia, Mesoamerica, the Indus Valley and the Roman Empire.[20] Similar disasters have struck many areas of Africa in more recent times. Zimbabwe experienced a major agricultural collapse in the sixteenth century, while in the twentieth century there is the example of the American dust bowl experience in the 1930s, and the more recent tragedy of the Sahel in the 1980s.

When a civilisation exhausts its own soil or consumes or trades in agricultural surpluses above the capacity of its farmers, it will often seek to sustain food surpluses by territorial gains or trading advantage. Thus early modern European food abundance depended upon the expansion of the 'shadow ecology' of Europe in the colonies, as lands which came to represent Europe's ghost acreage were put into food production to feed Europe's rapidly expanding population.[21] After the voyages of Columbus and Vasco da Gama Europeans developed agricultural settlements throughout the temperate regions of the globe, in North and South America, Australasia and temperate and sub-tropical Africa.[22] The colonial extraction of agricultural surplus by and for Europeans on plantations, slave colonies and European farms, and the post-colonial extraction of surplus from Third World cash-crop economies indebted to

Western banks, has been the principal cause of ecological degradation in many parts of the world since the beginning of European colonialism. The draining of wetlands, the clear-cutting of forests, soil erosion, and latterly, high chemical inputs into the soil, all characterise the agricultural revolution which Europeans have spread around the globe, and it is the continuing impacts of European agricultural demands, for wood products, animal fodder and cash crops, and the consequent displacement of non-European subsistence farmers to poor marginal lands and forests which, as we have seen, represent the greatest threat to ecosystems and non-human species in many parts of the developing world.

European population expansion and out-migration, and the pattern of agriculture which has spread in its wake, is then a major cause of the unprecedented extent of ecological damage across the globe.[23] The demands of an expanding European population for grains, meat, wood, spices, fruits, tea, coffee, sugar and cocoa were expressed and satisfied by imperialism: by conquering traders and armies, by genocide or enslavement, by colonial rule and expropriation of non-European lands, and latterly by tariff barriers, inequitable terms of trade and indebtedness in post-colonial Third World economies. Alfred Crosby argues that ecological imperialism followed the earlier imperialisms of trade and military expansionism. Europe exported its weeds, diseases, animals, plants and peoples, and in many places the imported varieties displaced the indigenous ones.[24] A Maori in New Zealand expressed his fears of this process of displacement most percipiently: 'as the clover killed off the fern, and the European dog the Maori dog, as the Maori rat was destroyed by the Pakla (English rat), so our people also will be gradually supplanted and entailed by the Europeans'.[25]

The dispersal of European ecological influence over the globe took place in partnership with the expansion of Christianity from its origins in the Mediterranean basin to its present coverage of more than a third of the population and lands of the globe. This expansion was led by monks such as Patrick, Ninian and Columba. The influence of monasticism on the agricultural development of Catholic Europe was considerable.

The Benedictine and Cistercian monasteries had an especially profound impact on the landscape as the monks introduced many agricultural innovations, most significantly the domestication of sheep which was so to transform the pastoral landscape of Europe.[26] In England the density of monasteries was greatest in the fertile lands of East Anglia where monks drained wetlands and established an extensive pattern of monastic communities. These communities were models of sustainable farming, of self-sufficiency and self-government which reflected the Hebrew and Christian vision of natural stewardship and pastoralism.[27] As Sean McDonagh argues, this social and agricultural system reflected a spirituality of nature and land which was marked by gratitude for creation as the gift of God, and a careful quest to nurture its natural fruitfulness.[28] But at the same time the fear of wild and untamed nature is reflected in the powerful urge to order and domesticate it and to remake it for human purposes. This remaking of nature is legitimated by the growing belief in late medieval Europe that it is essentially created for human purposes.

As the monastic orders became more advanced in their agricultural techniques and amassed more lands, so their power grew, and their very success was their downfall. The Black Death, which came to Europe along trade routes from Mongolia, gave rise to serious labour shortages in many areas. This caused much monastic land to be given over to sheep-grazing, which in turn generated much more surplus wealth for the monasteries than the earlier and more diverse pattern of farming. This new wealth corrupted the monasteries, attracted the interest of the secular crown and hence was a major factor in their eventual dissolution at the Reformation. The subsequent break-up of the manorial system with the enclosure of the commons marked the final demise of monastic influence over agricultural Britain. The destruction and decay of the ecologically beneficent monastic vision of stewardship, self-government and self-sufficiency in agricultural life may be said to have paved the way for the transformation of the relations between humans and nature which took place in early modern Europe.

THE COMMODIFICATION OF NATURE

The second major factor in the origins of the environmental crisis is the development of the market economy, and the rise of a world economic system, its evolution into European industrialism and its eventual diffusion to every region on the planet. The development of an economy independent of land and human work produced a cataclysmic transformation in the human approach to nature, and to natural resources. It brought in its train a new morality which transformed human relations as dramatically as it transformed relations between humanity and nature.

The origins of the modern economic system are to be found not in the Industrial Revolution but in the high Middle Ages, in the period which Immanuel Wallerstein calls the long century from 1450–1640.[29] From ancient times until the Middle Ages society was constructed on the basis of small, largely self-sufficient units of production and exchange where land was held in common or under systems of neighbourhood tenure, and where food and the other necessities of life were shared by barter or exchange and only a very small proportion entered the cash economy at local markets.[30] Karl Polanyi argues in his classic economic history *The Great Transformation* that life, work and nature as land were connected in a relational manner in the pre-modern communities which were the units of social and economic life, and relations with nature as land were mediated through kinship and manorial structures, churches, monasteries and guilds.[31] In a similar vein, Robert Lopez argues that the common lands, open field system, strip farming and crop rotation techniques of medieval agriculture represented an ecologically benign form of agricultural organisation, and granted greater freedom and independence to the villein farmers than is sometimes allowed.[32] The contained and localised nature of the social and economic system allowed for effective ecological regulation as fields were left fallow on a regular basis, crops were rotated to replace nutrients which other crops removed, animal manure was used to fertilise the fields and minimise waste and environmental abuses, such as the deposition of cattle slurry in rivers, the biggest single source of river pollution in England today, were dealt with at village level by the imposition of fines on errant farmers. Similar traditional land management systems, where land was held in common, were the rule in every part of the cultivated earth before European colonial expansion, including the *bona* in Iran, the *zanjera* of the Philippines and the *acadia* of West Africa.[33] Although much maligned since the Enlightenment, some ecologists and historians now believe that these pre-industrial systems of agriculture and land management more effectively balanced human nutritional needs and the long-term health and diversity of cultivated ecosystems than subsequent agricultural systems.[34] G. K. Chesterton, tilting at the industrial era, argues that the peasant in these traditional agrarian societies was also a good deal happier than his modern urban counterpart, the jobbing labourer or assembly-line worker.[35]

The demise of traditional systems of common land tenure in Europe came about as a result of the conjunction of a number of factors, including climate change and new agricultural techniques such as sheep-grazing, but, according to Wallerstein, principal among the causes were the growing and competing demands of the aristocracy, royalty, church and emergent nation states for wealth and agricultural surplus.[36] The rise of the nation state in the thirteenth century in Europe, and the growth of state bureaucracies and the new standing armies, saw great demands placed upon the land and upon peasant labour. Wars between the kings and nobles of these newly defined nation states were a major cause of rising demands on feudal agriculture, in particular because of the growing expense of war after the invention of firearms. Over-consumption by a minority, straining the level of resource production in feudal agriculture, was thus, according to Wallerstein, the principal reason for its demise, and the substitution of a money-based economy.[37]

Rising commercial interests in agricultural land resulted in the enforced depopulation of rural areas in the sixteenth and seventeenth centuries and the enclosure of common lands to make way primarily for the sheep and game of the aristocracy and the new merchant classes.[38] The traditional uses of the commons for hunting, for animal-grazing and for fuel collection were denied to the peasants, many of whom were then forced to abandon their small subsistence plots which without the commons could no longer sustain a family. Many others of course were simply evicted from their rural hovels, land claims and all. According to E. P. Thompson, the Enclosures represented a war of rich against poor, involving the violent removal of subsistence peasant farmers from ancestral tenancies, commons and homes and the unprecedented location of land and social power in the new 'gentry' of England.[39] The injustices of the enforced Enclosures provoked widespread but ultimately ineffective protest. They enabled in a dramatically new way the mobilisation of the product of nature, and its trade in a market system. Transportation and communication developed to facilitate free trade between towns and regions, and between countries. Land and labour were commodified and engaged in the money economy. Traditional relations of kinship and place, and the traditional natural law ethics of Christendom, which had formerly imposed moral constraints on the use of both land and labour, were subverted. Polanyi argues that the traditional relationship between humanity and nature was therefore broken and so the natural resource demands of the growing urban culture were no longer balanced by an awareness of the limitations of soil, rivers and climate, or respect for farm animals and the creatures of the wild. The consequent disembedding of human social structures from the limits and needs of the land, and the loss of a widespread awareness of the relationality between nature and human life, is a key feature in the modern abuse of the natural world, and may also be linked to a more general demise of virtue in human relations as well as relations with nature in modern urbanised societies.[40]

The coerced wage labour of the army of rural migrants, forced into rural landlessness or urban squalor, enabled the general expansion of trade and mercantilism and was the central feature of the transformation of social relations from feudalism to capitalism in post-medieval Europe.[41] The ethical sanctions of the medieval church over buying and selling, against lending money at interest and the accumulation of profit, set the church against the great upheavals of this new economic and social system. However, the church was also implicated in the emergent trading system as a powerful land-owner and economic actor. This dominant economic role of the church was a major factor in its demise as monarchs and merchants sought to undermine the ancient privilege of ecclesiastical possessions and power. The capacity of the church to act as a restraining moral force on the emergent trading system was thus compromised by its own political and economic hegemony.[42]

Ironically, as John Hall points out, the international order of Christendom itself facilitated the emergence of capitalism, as the church's rule had created a contract culture throughout Christendom in which there was a 'hidden consensus' that contracts would be honoured.[43] The limits presented by Papal authority on the power of any one ruler or nation state in Europe also helped to constrain individual states from excessive despotism over the lives and activities of their citizens, thus facilitating the development of trade and market activity, while also helping to maintain an element of predictability in the moral and legal affairs of medieval Europe.[44] The church was also the principal economic actor through its monasteries, clergy and growing hierarchy. As it developed commercial systems of agriculture, and in particular the production of wool, the church had frequent recourse to economic exchange mechanisms which its own ethical system abjured.[45]

Over time the church's theologians sought to develop a theological account of economics which was consistent with the extent of ecclesiastical economic activity. The schoolmen developed a *rapprochement* with banking, usury and commercial activity which was, however, fiercely resisted in some quarters, and especially amongst emergent radical religious orders such as the Franciscans and the Dominicans.[46] The Franciscans maintained that private property itself was against the law of Christ, arguing, for example, that Christ did not own his own coat and therefore could not have approved of private property, and certainly would have criticised the riches and economic prowess of the church.[47] However, the Reformation in Protestant Europe helped to sweep away any final resistance of the church and the *seigneurs*, the principal bastions of the *ancien régime*, to the new political and economic developments.

In this transformation of social and economic life in Europe, changing theological and ethical attitudes to economic wealth, and to nature, played a significant role. R. H. Tawney notes that along with the demise of the common field system and manorial government went the demise of the concepts of natural justice and economic equity, and the substitution of a system of positive law which was designed to protect the enlarged properties of the new landowners: 'the law of nature had been invoked by medieval writers as a moral restraint on economic self interest'.[48] But by the seventeenth century, nature was seen in a different light, and 'had come to connote, not divine ordinance, but human appetites, and natural rights were invoked by the individualism of the age as a reason why self-interest should be given free play'.[49] Thus John Locke, like modern individualists such as Robert Nozick, argued that the state had no right to interfere in matters of property or commerce.[50] Like Tawney, Alasdair MacIntyre in *After Virtue* identifies legitimate entitlement to property, and particularly land, as the central moral problem with modern utilitarian and individualist accounts of justice. MacIntyre argues that the property owners of the modern world are the inheritors of those who violently stole the commons from the common people in the practice of enclosure which eventually spread to Scotland, Ireland and the colonies.[51] Those, like Locke and Nozick, who argue that the only legitimate role of the state in relation to human justice is to protect existing property relations, and not to redistribute wealth for the common good, ignore the history by which lands which were held in common by peasants and lords for thousands of years became the private property of certain individuals and elites, not initially through the rule of law but by the power of the gun.[52] The lack of entitlement of the descendants of these landless peasants to shelter and sustenance – such as those descendants of the victims of the

Highland Clearances who still live in urban poverty and unemployment in the vast public housing schemes around Glasgow – is then related historically to the original act of expropriation of the land. Landlessness, as I have argued elsewhere, is a problem of justice, and a problem for the poor in Britain just as much as it is in the Third World.[53] It is also an important feature in the modern alienation between urban civilisation and the non-human world.

As Tawney argues, attitudes to nature underwent a transformation around the time of the Enclosures. Protestant theologians emphasised more strongly than their medieval forebears both the fallenness of nature, and its consequent fearfulness, and they treated of nature as a resource created entirely for human purposes. Through its human use and transformation by Christian people nature might also be gradually redeemed from the effects of the Fall. Protestants sought to remove any vestige of spiritual power in the natural world, as represented in medieval Catholicism in pilgrimages to sacred places, or in festivals around sacred wells or sites of divine activity. They sought to purge the landscape of the sacred, and locate the site of God's activity entirely in the individual self. The work of salvation involved the movement of the heart and mind towards a state of grace by the inspiration of that gift of faith which, as Luther taught, alone of all God's gifts in creation, could work for a person's salvation. This inward and redemptionist shift in Protestant theology produces a doctrine of creation far more instrumentalist and secular than that of the medievals. As George Hendry argues, Luther's doctrine of creation 'reduced the whole world of nature to a repository of goods for the service of man'.[54] Similarly many Anglo-Saxon Reformation divines taught that humans had complete authority over animals and the non-human world, as Keith Thomas documents. According to one such, Richard Bentley, 'all things' were made 'principally for the benefit and pleasure of man'.[55] Thomas remarks that the central theme of many of these early modern interpreters of the Christian tradition seemed to be the supremacy of humanity and humanity's right to use the rest of the creation for any purpose that may be desired.[56] But

Thomas also argues that this changed attitude of Protestant theology was not alone enough to have generated that great transformation of relations between humanity and nature which precede the modern period. He concurs with Karl Marx that, more than religion, it was the advent of private property and the development of the money economy, what Marx called the 'great civilising influence of capital', which finally ended the 'deification of nature' and encouraged early modern Christians to abuse the natural world in a way their forebears had not.[57]

According to Max Weber, it was Protestant theological teachings which legitimated and in part inspired the new culture of mercantilism and capital, the new practices of usury, private property, the enclosure of commons and the disenfranchisement of the peasantry in the Rhinelands and in England.[58] For medievals such as Aquinas, abundance and wealth were only given to certain people by natural law so that they could succour the poor, and the poor had a natural claim to the property of the rich to meet their own urgent needs: according to natural law ethics this was not theft but lawful behaviour.[59] There was no absolute right of property in medieval ethics, and wealth and money-making were regarded until the end of the Middle Ages with great suspicion. By contrast Luther taught that all callings, whether those of the merchant or the farmer or the minister of religion were equally valid, while John Calvin taught even more radically that usury was not wrong but the natural use of money as a means of livelihood. Money should be set to work, not merely as an instrument of exchange as Aquinas, like Aristotle, had taught, but as a means for making more money for otherwise money would be idle, and this according to Calvin could not be right. As Weber argues, Calvin's doctrine of double predestination also stimulated these new attitudes to secular calling and money, for in working hard in this life, and even in acquiring wealth as the fruits of labour, the Christian could find earthly assurance that he belonged to the elect rather than the damned. In the teachings of the Puritans, and especially of their North American descendants, these ideas were transmuted into a gospel of prosperity as manifested in Benjamin Franklin's *A Way to Wealth*, which Weber extensively cites.[60]

The combination of the new money economy and the agrarian developments of late medieval and post-Reformation Europe brought about in a new way the commodification of the goods of nature. The coming of the money economy involved the abandonment of moral, ethical and religious controls over agriculture, economics, trade and relations between humans and nature. A clear indicator of this new relationship is the widespread cruelty to animals which became so prevalent in early modern Europe, cruelty which was to extend to the colonies, where animals were hunted to the verge of extinction not for food but for sport.[61] The enclosure and commodification of land is the first and most significant act in the establishment of the new money economy. The parliamentary papers at the time of the Enclosures in England indicate that the intention of these economic changes was to increase the power of government in the lives of ordinary people, to reduce them to a new subject status at the behest of state control and the power of private capital.[62] The benefits which this process may eventually have produced for many modern citizens in terms of increased longevity and affluence some hundreds of years later must be set alongside the wholesale and enforced destruction of livelihood for millions of people throughout early modern Europe, and the losses of freedom and autonomy of peasants and agricultural small-holders who, even as feudal villeins, experienced a greater measure of economic security than the under-employed inhabitants of many modern municipal housing schemes.[63] Expropriation of land by the wealthy, enforced landlessness, the loss of local autonomy and self-sufficiency, the destruction of traditional economic systems of gift, barter and exchange and of common systems of land tenure, are still the principal reasons for the continuing mass migration of rural dwellers to the impoverished shanty towns of the world's megacities in the South.[64]

The traditional vices of avarice and greed are the objects of praise in the new money economy, as Weber notes with respect to the writings of Franklin.[65] Adam Smith praised self-interest and avarice as the means by which individuals in the money economy would contribute to the good of the whole society. In his *Theory of the Moral Sentiments* he praised the transformation of nature by the accumulation of property because by it we:

> have entirely changed the whole face of the globe, have turned the rude forests of nature into agreeable and fertile plains, and made the trackless and barren ocean a new fund of subsistence. The rich are led by an invisible hand to make nearly the same distribution of the necessities of life, which would have been made had the earth been divided into equal portions among all its inhabitants.[66]

As Tawney comments, what previous civilisations regarded as vices, the advocates of the money economy praised as virtues.[67] The new money economy, the market system, made possible the untrammelled expression of these traditional vices of avarice, greed and pride in possessions by an ever larger proportion of humanity. In this freedom of ethical restraint on avarice and greed lies one of the strongest roots of the environmental crisis which is now upon us.

However, although the money economy emerged in the sixteenth century it was not until the mobilisation of technological innovations through industrialisation that the new economic system began to dramatically impact upon the natural environment of Europe and thence the rest of the world. The Enclosures might have made peasants homeless, or criminalised them as vagabonds, but the soil was still unpolluted, rivers still ran clean, and the air they breathed, at least in the countryside, was still unaffected by pollution. The first hint of the problems to come for the environment from industrialisation would have occurred as a consequence of the mining and burning of coal. Itself a prerequisite of many of the industrialised technologies of the eighteenth and nineteenth centuries, the burning of coal for domestic heating, primarily by poor town dwellers deprived of access to rural wood supplies on the former commons, was the first indication of the fouling of the nest which was soon to follow, and indeed when coal was first burnt in London it was regarded as a criminal offence as the smoke it produced was so filthy and detrimental to human health.

SCIENCE, TECHNOLOGY AND THE
MYTHOLOGY OF PROGRESS

The third major factor in the origins of the environmental crisis is the application of the technological fruits of modern scientific method through industrialism. The rise of modern science may be traced to the discoveries of Copernicus and Galileo in Christian Europe in the sixteenth century. The association between Christianity and the rise of modern science is often regarded as being more than historical coincidence as Christian belief in the rational ordering of the universe, and the predictability of nature's laws, encouraged the investigation of the regularities and underlying causative and motive structure of the natural order.[68] However, Hans Blumenberg argues that the experimental method is linked not with a view of the world as rationally ordered by God but with the ideas of medieval nominalists such as William of Ockham that the world is governed by accident and contingency rather than divine reason and purposiveness.[69] The nominalist assertion of the absolute otherness of divine rationality and the will of God denies the coherent order of the material world so that 'chance becomes the sole principle of reality'.[70] God is then superfluous to the order of the material world, which can be better explained in terms of the accidents and movements of atoms. The world thus becomes 'open' to investigation by the alchemist and the scientist whose vocation is to transform this accidental world into a world more truly at the service of human need and human desire.

Blumenberg's thesis finds empirical confirmation in the fact that the experimental method originated in the medieval alchemists' quest for gold, a 'magical' quest which it may be argued was the direct correlation of the medieval nominalist rejection of the inherently ordered and rational nature of matter. It is this same experimental method which Isaac Newton, who was both alchemist and physicist, subsequently put to work to uncover the secrets of matter and motion, and the elements of the universe. By this method he discovered and described the laws of attraction and motion, gravity and mass,

which have become the ground rules for modern physical
science. John Brooke argues that Newton's identification of
certain predictable laws in the movement of objects in the
heavens and on earth are predicated upon the idea of a world
of relative fixity and order which still reflected the earlier
Christian idea of the relation of the contingency and motion of
the world to the ordering of a rational God.[71] But Brooke also
identifies a strange mixture of the alchemical and the mechanical in Newton's view of the cosmos.[72] However, if we follow
Blumenberg we see that in fact there is no opposition between
an alchemical and a mechanical universe, for both rest on the
presupposition that the world is fundamentally made up of
matter which is governed not by reason or divine intention but
is purely the product of accident and chance, for the hidden
God of the medieval nominalists was absolutely other to the
world of matter and could not therefore be known or perceived
through the material order. This God's only clear and knowable intention and purpose with regard to the cosmos was the
creation and salvation of humanity.[73] Thus the alchemist and
the mechanicalist share the fundamental assumption of the
availability of the material world of accidents to human observation and manipulation.

In response to the development of this accidental and
mechanical cosmology in the scientific method Immanuel Kant
draws the logical conclusion in his *Critique of Pure Reason* that
knowledge of God and of the good, and scientific knowledge
based on empirical observation involved two radically different
kinds of knowing.[74] The laws of nature did not reveal to
scientific observation the purposive (teleological) activity of a
good God because a good and holy God is not apprehensible
by reasoned reflection on the nature of life or the cosmos, but
only by an act of faith in the existence of such a being. By this
means Kant hoped to disentangle science and scientific rationality from morality and religion, and so to preserve a rational
space for moral order and purposiveness within the human
mind and soul, even if this purposiveness could no longer be
identified with the order of nature and the cosmos.[75] As
Blumenberg observes, by this device Kant redirected all purpo-

sive and teleological activity in the world and nature from God to humans. Kant's transcendental criticism of reason eliminates the idea of a progressive order in the world which is guided by God. Instead the world is 'unfinished', and thus becomes for modern science and philosophy 'material at man's disposal'.[76] Kant with his deobjectification of God and morality, and Newton with his mechanistic cosmology, had forged between them a new philosophical and scientific ground for the subsequent development of an atheistic cosmology which displaced God from the cosmos, positing the world and the universe as merely the products of accident and chance, their apparent design or order simply the imputation of human perception, and their matter and natural resources awaiting the transformation of human agency and purposiveness.[77]

Modern biology and physics has confirmed this accidental character of matter and non-human life through hypotheses concerning the autogenous emergence of life from the primeval soup of gases and molecules, and hypotheses about the origin of the universe generated from infra-red recordings of light emanating from the putative dawn of space-time. This quest for origins is what Stephen Hawking ironically calls the quest to know the 'mind of God'.[78] But of course Hawking does not mean God in the sense of a pre-existent creator or spiritual being, but God as a cipher for the nature of things, and the cause of the primeval big bang which he believes set the universe on its present path of expansion and motion.

The evacuation of purposiveness and moral order from nature independent from human willing and purposiveness is therefore inherent in the world-view of modern science. To give one example, the moon is no longer conceived by most modern scientists as a heavenly body which affects the destiny of life on earth or the emotional cycles of the human psyche. It is regarded as a mere physical object which exercises gravitational pull on the tides and winds and the motion of the earth. An American mathematician has hypothesised that if we blew up the moon we could change the pattern of seasons on earth and enhance the fertility of the planet.[79] If the moon is just a physical object which exercises an at times inconvenient influence on life on the planet, then it may be argued that humans should be free to dispose of it if necessary. The idea that there may be any enduring significance, physical, spiritual or moral, in the relation of the moon to earth, in the natural path of a river or the natural contours of a coastline, is foreign to many modern scientists. Similarly, scientific ideas arose which justified the abuse of animals as these creatures were also said to lack any moral status, for they had no reasoning powers, no souls and, some argued, no sense of pleasure or pain. Descartes adopted from the Spanish physician Gomez Pereira the idea that animals were like machines, fashioned by God as automata much as humans made the complex mechanical workings of clocks.[80] Such animal machines 'do not have a mind', according to Descartes, though he believed they might still have some propensity to feel pain.[81] The moral and scientific implications of the beast-machine doctrine in respect of both animals and humans were immense. Subsequent Cartesian philosophers, though not Descartes himself, were to argue that, if animals were automata, they could have no feeling, no sensation, and therefore to dissect live animals or to abuse animals in other ways could have no moral significance as they would feel no pain. Cartesianism also anticipated modern scientific approaches to human life in the evacuation of value and purposiveness from the natural order, including the human body. The human brain is conceived by many modern scientists as an organic machine whose self-consciousness is simply a function of chemical interactions and physical sensations, and whose ensoulment is merely a cultural illusion.[82]

It is this mechanistic Cartesian approach to the natural world which is in part responsible for the abuses of nature which characterise modern civilisation. As Bryan Appleyard argues, it is a central feature of the classical scientific method to simplify and reduce reality to atoms and parts, so as to explain simple and universalisable mechanical laws which apply to the different parts of the cosmos.[83] These simple laws, such as Newton's law of gravity, turn out in time to be subject to far more complex processes, and to a range of exclusions (in the case of gravity Einstein showed that speed, time and space alter its effects in ways Newton did not imagine) but they act as simplifying generalisations without which the scientific enterprise could not be pursued. But the inter-relations between different parts of reality are often lost to the scientist whose vision is limited to one particular feature of biological or physical reality, and so the potentially harmful consequences of the scientific manipulation of one feature are often not examined in advance. More holistic, interactive and systemic scientific paradigms of life and the cosmos have, however, begun to emerge from scientific observations, such as Einstein's theory of relativity, quantum mechanics and the emphasis on the interactivity of ecosystems in early ecology which finds its supreme manifestation in James Lovelock's Gaia hypothesis, of which more below. Perhaps the supreme manifestation of these systemic approaches is chaos theory, in which all of life is said to be inter-connected in ways which are often beyond the ken of any particular scientific specialism.[84] Appleyard, like Franz Capra and others, argues that quantum mechanics is particularly problematic for the classical scientific method for its proponents have found that in certain scientific experiments the very act of observation is relationally connected to the movement of atoms or electrons which are the object of the physicist's observations.[85] But despite the ecological and metaphysical attractions of these more holistic paradigms, day-to-day science and engineering mostly continue to operate on the world as a collection of discrete systems or locales of physical, mechanical and organic activity, and as if the scientist and the object of her experiments are discrete realities, and not relationally connected. Working on the universe in bits, elements, genes, atoms, microbes or quarks, scientists reduce and reconstruct reality, both metaphorically and literally, in ways which mechanically reorder discrete parts of the natural world in order to serve particular human purposes. Hard science involves the denial of the relationality between the different parts of reality which is a feature of holistic thinking, and indeed of some versions of a Christian doctrine of creation, a point to which I shall return in subsequent chapters. Though this denial may only be a temporary suspension of belief, for the purposes of the project or experiment, nonetheless it may have a significant and powerful ecological and human down-side. Thus, for example, scientists create and set loose into nature many thousands of new chemical compounds every year. These compounds are reconstructed from different elements and molecules and then set to work as pesticides, fungicides, detergents, fuels, drugs or even chemical weapons. Many of the effects of these chemicals are individually highly beneficial to human life. The widespread use of DDT eradicated malaria from the Mediterranean and from many parts of Asia. However, the collective and long-term effects of the release of this cocktail of new substances on the totality of the environment of human and non-human life are not considered by the reductionist scientist. Their collective, or even individual, interactions with other life forms or with each other have not traditionally been part of the scientist's experimental brief. The scientist's sense of purpose or moral intention is limited to the organism, substance or function which is the object of a particular research project.

Social scientific studies of the social processes which characterise the scientific enterprise have challenged the traditional picture of the scientific quest as the objective rational search for experimentally verified truth. This picture is a long way from the reality of research communities, government and industrial funding, prized beliefs, emotional commitments, anxieties and frailties which actually provide the social, political and psychological context for the pursuit of science.[86] Like any other aspect of human culture or knowledge, science is socially constructed and value-laden, and it is through these social processes, and the *values* of domination, mechanism, production and progress that the culture of science has made such a dramatic impact on the biosphere and on the ecology of both human and non-human life. In particular modern science expresses the powerful rationalist urge to remake irrational and 'brute' nature into mechanical forms which more perfectly serve rational human purposes. Thus the strangeness, chaos, diversity and wildness of nature are eschewed by the agricultural scientist in favour of the sanitised, chemically treated, monocrop field where only the crop planted by the farmer can grow, and where even earthworms can be disposed of, poisoned by modern pesticides, as their natural function of regenerating the soil is regarded as expendable, and replaceable by fossil fuel fertilisers.

Scientists mostly avoid the ethical issues which arise from particular lines of research, arguing that it is up to society to decide how their discoveries are to be utilised. But this eschewal of ethical limits to scientific experimentation is a central feature of the emerging conflict between technological society and natural ecology, and the growing public unease at the direction of modern technology in such areas as medical technology, genetic engineering, animal husbandry and nuclear energy. The divorce between science and morality is of course the poisoned fruit of Kant's great divorce between scientific rationality and the knowledge of the good.

Through the deployment of technology, through the social processes of experimentation and observation and through the values of domination and progress, modern science is set over nature, the scientific observer over the subject of her experiment. Nature is reduced to the status of materials bank and human living space. Nature is 'available', for human expropriation and exploitation. Indeed without the application of human rationality and order, nature is perceived in the classical scientific paradigm as unproductive and meaningless. Nature is said to have no purpose other than that which humans impute to it. Early modern scientists such as Francis Bacon could speak of 'putting nature to the test' – a figure of speech for torture – in the manner of an Inquisitor helping his victim to perceive the true meaning, and error, of her thoughts. As Mary Midgley argues, the language of early modern scientists – conquest, torture, torment, woo, unveil, disrobe, forcing nature to confess 'all that lay in her most intimate recesses' – reflected a male culture of control and sexual deflowering which constructed natural resources as unproductive 'virgin' resources awaiting the remaking, and often the wasting, of modern technology and industrial natural resource use.[87] In her feminist critique of science, Carolyn Merchant argues that the 'rape' of nature and

of her 'virgin' resources are indicative of a tendency to domination and conquest which arises from the male quest for power
and control, and the male rejection of intimacy and relationality.[88] Nature is enslaved and appropriated in the reproduction of human culture and power relations and this enslavement
is related to the logic of patriarchy and Western capitalist
colonialism with its privileging of sameness, its hierarchy of
sexual and racial difference and its denial of the soul and
rationality to the non-white and the non-human.[89] The animal,
natural, embodied world is associated with the unrestrained
primitive female body, with lewdness and sexual lust in scientific
metaphors for the non-human world.[90] Nature is reconstructed
through the metaphor of hierarchy and the dualisms of mind/
body, male/female and nature/culture. Modern science in this
feminist perspective represents a social construct which legitimates the scientific quest to modify and control nature from
which so many ecological problems originate.

The role of the metaphor of hierarchy can be seen particularly clearly in the development of the theory of evolution,
which represents humanity and the primates as higher species
and birds and fish as lower species. While for Charles Darwin
his principle of natural selection was an egalitarian concept
which set humans in the context of an organic process of
natural mutation in response to the physical environment, for
Herbert Spencer and the social Darwinists the theory of evolution was used to service the idea of the superiority of human
over other forms of life, and the inevitability of the emergence
of human life as the highest form in the hierarchy of evolved
species. The social Darwinists used the idea of natural selection
as a legitimation of competitive and individualistic social
relations which in turn justified *laissez-faire* capitalism, and racist
and sexist differentiation.[91] The strong had overcome the weak
in the history of natural selection and so it was appropriate that
the same process of competitive conquest should determine
relations in human society. The same ideology was used to
legitimate the alterations and destruction of nature that
humans brought about through industrialisation and technology. The lower species and forms of life must adapt to the

demands of the highest species however destructively these demands may be expressed, as this adaptation is the principle of the evolution of life. Similar ideological tendencies are manifest in the recent work of some ecological scientists, as we saw in the last chapter. Donald Worster suggests that there is an ideological motivation in the favouring of the metaphors of competition, individualism and private enterprise in contemporary ecology, and the denial of earlier ecological insights concerning the relationality and reciprocity of species and ecosystems, reflecting the recent shift in Western societies towards a more competitive and less collective understanding of economic behaviour.[92]

Feminist and post-modernist readings of scientific metaphors such as hierarchy or competition, of the privileging of sameness and the control or subjugation of difference, represent the modern scientific world-view as a social construct which reflects the culture of patriarchal and capitalist relations in which science developed. The privileging of the human over the non-human, which is presented as the inevitable consequence of the competitive development of species, is used to justify the scientific mutation and homogenisation of the non-human world. As Descartes put it, we 'render ourselves the masters and possessors of nature', while for Francis Bacon science enables 'the power and dominion of the human race itself over the universe'.[93]

In the scientific ideas of Francis Bacon we may discern a conceptual link between medieval nominalism and Protestantism. Just as the nominalists had argued that God is absolutely beyond the world of matter and forms, which therefore may be said to await human purposiveness and ordering, so the Puritans emphasised the fallenness and total moral corruption of the natural order, which generates a moral and spiritual requirement that humans probe and remake the world, for in so doing they may call nature back to its original goodness. As Blumenberg shows, Bacon, like the Puritans, was fundamentally opposed to a teleological view of nature and of a trust in the world as it is. Misguided trust in nature's beneficence and human indolence were seen by the Puritans as the only obstacles to the progressive remaking of nature into the condition of paradise from which it had so completely fallen.[94] The scientific and industrial homogenisation and hominisation of the objects of nature thus became a spiritual enterprise in which created things at last achieved purposiveness and moral value, in service of the redemption of humans.[95] Hence scientific knowledge was seen not so much as the investigation, through the world of objects, of the divine power which orders and rules the world, but as the imposition, through theoretical curiosity, of human rationality on the world. Knowledge and rationality are no longer relationally dependent on God, and the human imposition of scientific curiosity and its technological fruits is then the inevitable and necessary precondition for progressing the welfare of humanity, for welfare and happiness are the fruits, for Bacon as for Kant, of curiosity and its product – enlightenment.[96]

With the aid of this analysis we can explain the quasi-theological claims of modern science to human salvation which are scrutinised to great effect by Mary Midgley in *Science as Salvation*, where she demonstrates the curiously other-worldly character of these claims. The modern exaltation of the purposiveness of human rationality and the denial of any inherent purposiveness in the world of matter is manifest in the frequent recourse in the writings of modern scientists to other worlds, other planets, artificial homes in space. It is also manifest in the modern scientific quest for a form of intelligent mechanical life which can replicate human rationality while overcoming the compromises which the human mind, encased in a decaying body, has to make with purposeless matter.[97] As Midgley argues, this language demonstrates the divorce between the observer and the observed, between mind and body, between scientific rationality and nature which characterises the social practices and values of much of modern science and its technological application. It is a hazardous discourse which has had very deleterious results for the body of the biosphere.

Midgley's critique also draws attention to the futurism of modern science inherent in its mythology of salvation and progress.[98] The modern scientific myth of progress holds that whatever is ancient is inevitably poorer, weaker, less fulfilling, providing less utility, less happiness than what is modern. History is said to be characterised by an inevitable progression from the 'dark ages' to the modern present and posited future. Karl Lowith claims that this belief in progress is essentially a secularised version of Jewish and Christian eschatology, in which hope in the future fulfilment of history through the return of the Messiah, or Christ, and the divine restoration of the creation after the judgement, is transformed into a humanistic futurism in which human and technological progress in history is substituted for divine action and the eschaton.[99]

The belief in progress also takes its rise from the theory of evolution, in particular social Darwinism, which sees the process of history as a process of the perfecting of the human species and of nature, and from the idealist and historicist philosophies of Hegel and Marx. And, as Richard Stivers argues, the myth of progress also relates to the deification of the scientist whose observations become total explanations of existence and purpose.[100] In eclipsing the Judeo-Christian belief in the divine teleological directedness of the cosmos and of human life, belief in progress also shifts the orientation of human life towards material progress and away from the contemplative quest for spiritual fulfilment and the related moral quest for the virtues which, as well as enhancing human relationships, were said to prepare the soul for the life of heaven.[101] Whereas traditional Christian theology involved the relativisation of the possibility of salvation in the present and emphasised the unfinished character of the human project, the modern idea of progress involves the historicist belief in the perfectibility of human life, and the proposition that each stage of history is better than its predecessor.[102] The idea of progress drives economic development and the technological transformation of the biosphere, sustaining the belief that the inhabitants of unmodernised regions, such as Bhutan or parts of Borneo, must necessarily be less happy and fulfilled than those of modernised countries who live in technologically altered environments. Progress in economic growth, or 'wealth creation', whose contemporary realisation is the consumer society with its live-to-shop philosophy, becomes the guiding *telos* of modern nation states and the global market.

But, as Krishan Kumar points out, this belief in progress has begun to turn sour in Western industrialised countries. Few people in Western countries now believe that further improvements in their quality of life are likely to come from further technological transformations of the non-human world.[103] The retreat from the belief in progress originates partly in the growing public consciousness, at least in the West, of the environmental and life-quality problems which the technological transformation of nature has brought in its wake. It also reflects a growing realisation that the possibilities for economic growth on a small planet are not infinite, and that the industrial organisation of society is increasingly unable to provide meaningful work and adequate incomes for a significant and growing proportion of the population of industrialised countries.

One of the central problems with the invention and utilisation of new industrial processes and technologies is that the possible negative human and environmental consequences are rarely assessed, or indeed assessable, in advance of their mobilisation. As Langdon Winner argues, the subjection of different areas of social life to new technologies often involves the loss of various qualities or utilities which, if we thought carefully, we might wish to preserve instead of mobilising the technology.[104] For example, the rapid transport of food and other commodities around the world often undermines the self-sufficiency and economic stability of local communities while generating other social and environmental costs in terms of noise and inconvenience for people living near main roads and airports, increases in the cost of food and increased energy costs in food production which impact negatively on human welfare and the environment. Similarly the computer-enhancement of foreign exchange markets where a trillion dollars can circle the globe in a single day, throws up sometimes devastating effects on a particular national economy, and at times threatens the economic stability of dozens of trading nations. However, once technologies are invented and mobilised on a large scale it becomes very difficult for societies to find ways of controlling them, whatever the social or environmental costs they may create. Perhaps the clearest example of the potential, and non-reversibility, of risks arising from new technology relates to the growing number of releases into the environment of genetically engineered viruses, microbes, crops and plants. No scientist can say with certainty that these new transgenic life forms will not interact with other microbes, viruses, plants or animals in ways which may threaten human health or non-human species diversity, but such is the motive power of profit that these risks are set aside in the rush to remake the very genetic code of life on earth in the image of modern intensive and productionist agriculture.[105]

Such untoward risks in the mobilisation of new technologies are an inherent feature of what Ulrich Beck has characterised as the 'risk society'. Beck argues that modern societies have embraced a calculus of technological risks which increasingly seems to threaten not only ecological breakdown but also the stability and meaningfulness of human life as well.[106] The social processes by which technology and its attendant risks have reconstructed our lives and the planet appear to be beyond the control and decision-making processes of any particular polity or even group of nation states. This is why the ecological crisis is also a crisis of modern political democracy. We have, Beck argues, to find ways in which people other than scientists, industrialists and bureaucrats can begin to express dissent, or consent, to the enormous risks which new technologies such as nuclear energy or genetic engineering represent to life on earth: 'what is important is to exploit and develop the superiority of doubt against industrial dogmatism'.[107]

Another key problem with decision-making processes in relation to new technologies and development projects is the utilitarian framework in which their value to human societies is assessed. Civil servants, politicians and scientists rely on quantitative economic measures of human welfare to estimate the social benefits which may arise from particular development projects or technologies. The supreme, but increasingly tarnished, myth of industrial society, that technological change and economic development inevitably progress human prospects and human happiness, is legitimated and sustained by this quantitative approach to moral value – utilitarianism – which sets the costs of development for particular persons and communities, and particular ecosystems, against an abstract measure of human welfare. This utilitarian abstraction of collective welfare is used in cost-benefit analysis to justify considerable moral harm arising from particular technologies or development projects for particular groups of persons, and particular ecosystems.

THE MORAL CLIMATE OF MODERNITY

The philosophy of utilitarianism is the primary moral framework for decision-making in modern societies. Frances Hutcheson's famous definition of utilitarianism as the pursuit of those actions which produce the greatest happiness for the greatest number points to the basis of utilitarian ethics in calculations of aggregate human happiness. Utilitarianism involves a numerical or quantitative equation of happiness – the more human desires that can be met, the more moral good has been created. However, where different desires or happinesses conflict utilitarianism as a quantitative account of morality is faced with serious difficulties of arbitration between such qualitatively different goods.[108] This is partly because it gives such a narrow measure of the human good that it offers almost no practical guidance to particular polities other than the bare measures of cost-benefit analysis and economic efficiency. As Charles Taylor argues, 'the refusal to define any goods other than the official one of instrumental efficacy in the search for happiness can lead to appalling destruction in a society's way of life'.[109] It is also difficult in a utilitarian perspective to calculate the likely needs of future generations and to set these against the desires of present moral agents, although some utilitarians have tried.[110] The whole schema is predicated on the basis of *measurable* happiness in the present or near future. The happiness of those not yet born is resistant to this kind of judgement.

The advent of utilitarian philosophy builds on the Kantian reconstruction of morality in the sphere of human subjectivity, and the removal of moral significance from the external order of nature and the cosmos.[111] As we have seen, the Enlightenment attempt to ground morality exclusively in human interiority reflected the philosophical and scientific evacuation of meaning and purpose from the cosmos, and the nominalist and Protestant disenchantment of nature. The cosmology of mechanism and chance removes moral value and significance from the natural order of things. Moral values are therefore conceived as human projections on the world: they are not, as Taylor puts it, 'anchored in the real', nor in the natural world which is observed by scientists.[112] David Hume therefore propounded his famous adage that an 'ought' can never be derived from an 'is'. The nature of reality, and the reality of nature, are not moral sources for the disembedded Enlightenment self. The touchstone of morality becomes instead the internal feelings of pleasure and pain, of like and dislike, which are the moral signifiers of utilitarianism. This new morality dislocates the sense of self from the natural order of the biophysical world, including the embodied character of human identity, but paradoxically, and at the same time, it generates a new focus on everyday material life as the sphere in which the self finds meaning, purpose and fulfilment.[113] This is partly because, as David Braine suggests, there is an essential kinship between the Cartesian and Kantian dualism of mental states and physical states, of values and the empirical world, of minds and bodies, and the materialism which identifies human identity exclusively with physical reality and argues for no transcendence of the self beyond the body.[114] Thus human life becomes increasingly focused on internal mental states – as the only source of real meaning and identity – and at the same time on everyday material conditions of life, for there is no life beyond this life, no progression to another world where human life is both transcended and transformed.

Thus the conditions are laid for the transformation of nature by industrialism. The denial of the teleological or moral significance of embodied, biophysical existence, which lays the world open to physical reordering for human purposes, is accompanied by a new quest for individual pleasure, and material satisfaction and meaning in everyday life, which finds a response in the myriad artefacts purveyed by the new industrial and manufacturing processes. The emergence of the consumer society in eighteenth-century England, in tandem with the new materialist philosophy of nature as machine and the new utilitarian focus on the self and on everyday life as the essential sphere of identity and meaning, may thus be more than historical coincidence. Just as the desires and pleasures of the self become central to the new utilitarian ethic, and the control over public and private morals exercised by traditional cosmology and morality diminish, so the possibilities for self-expression, individual choice and prosperity are dramatically advanced in the eighteenth century amongst the new urban classes. The colonial expansion of Britain seems to have triggered this consumer boom as cheap cottons imported from India fuelled demand in an unprecedented way for clothing and cloth in England in the 1690s.[115] A rise in consumer demand in the following century for clothes, cutlery, crockery and many other household goods was made possible by rising wages, and was met by British inventions such as Compton's mule and Watt's steam engine, which enabled the production of goods on a scale never before achieved and at a price which brought such goods within the reach of the masses. Markets in factory-made clothing were advanced by the invention of 'fashion', which necessitated changes in clothing from year to year, while markets for linen, crockery, cutlery, furniture and other household goods also rapidly expanded. Some of the most famous names in the history of consumerism originate in this period: Wedgwood, Worcester and Derby pottery, Chippendale furniture, Schofield silver. The Industrial Revolution combined with a consumer revolution so that consumption of luxuries and ownership of property of a kind confined in previous eras to a tiny minority or elite became normal for the middle classes and then the working classes as the modern revolution progressed.

There was, however, considerable resistance to the new consumer and industrial culture. Some economists believed that profligate spending and higher consumption would not generate real wealth, although Adam Smith argued that consumer demand could act as the engine of economic growth.[116] Mass consumption, and the associated excess of spending, fashion and possessions, were also thought likely to undermine public morals and civil society. Jonathan Swift said that the commonwealth should limit men's possessions and desires by law or else acquisition would 'take up their whole interest' and they would cease to do good and to contribute to the formation of the public realm.[117] A similar resistance is evident in the consumer revolution which arose in America in the late nineteenth and early twentieth century. Moralists who believed in the superiority of life lived in opposition to materialism and commerce feared that chasing after the false gods of consumerism would undermine community and the vitality of public life.[118]

The transformation of England into an industrial and consumer society in the eighteenth century has been replicated not just in North America but now on a global scale so that, as we have seen, more goods and services have been consumed in the last forty years than throughout the whole of human history. As modernisation is globalised this consumptive way of life spreads to every corner of the globe with its message that to be happy the individual must consume, and the more she consumes the happier she will be. The driver of this urge to consume is individualism and the expressivist culture which substitutes self-expression through material acquisition for moral goodness and spiritual fulfilment. Consumption and style achieve a paradigmatic status in modern culture, as the sublimation of the traditional focus of human fulfilment on moral goods and the spiritual journey from this life to the next.

Ironically, increased consumption does not necessarily equate to happiness, despite the blandishments of the acquisitive society. In one global study of happiness poor Cubans were found to be as happy as rich Americans, and reported rates of happiness and life satisfaction were remarkably similar in India and Japan, or in South and North America.[119] A North American survey indicates that despite increases in income between 1957 and 1973 the number of those who claimed to be happy actually declined over the period.[120]

Similar evidence from British Social Trends surveys points to a diminishing sense of life quality as affluence increased in the 1970s and 1980s. In Sweden Louis Harris finds that 'advances in human welfare associated with economic growth came to a halt in the mid-1960s while alienation, boredom at work, mental illness, social tension, suicides, alcoholism and loneliness kept increasing'.[121]

Studies of happiness and life satisfaction point to a lack of correlation between affluence and happiness. In a major social study of happiness, Michael Argyle finds that marriage, social and sexual relationships, friends, children, satisfying work and creative leisure all rank above income and affluence as indicators of happiness and fulfilment.[122] Argyle also found that increases in life satisfaction related to rates of pay or housing depend more on comparisons with what other people have, and with a person's past experience, than on actual amounts of money. The very poor are unhappy in any country. But this explains why levels of reported unhappiness between rich and poor countries are comparable. Once basic needs are met, a comfort threshold is reached and a degree of economic security has been achieved, increased affluence produces only marginal increases in human happiness or life satisfaction, and may often have as many negative as positive effects on the true sources of human happiness. Socio-psychological evidence of the weak relationship between affluence and happiness challenges the common-sense assumption that people are happier when they have better houses, better cars, more foreign holidays and more food and drink. According to peoples' own self-reporting of their state of life satisfaction, the essential factors for happiness are the company of other people, and satisfying work and leisure.[123] Activity in the market may act as a compensation for those who are not doing well in these non-monetary sources of happiness. Such people may labour under the impression that if they do well in the market they will achieve happiness.[124] The market may then act as a temptation or distraction from true sources of human happiness and value. But the whole process of modernisation and the quest for economic growth is predicated on the assumption that people are happier when they have higher incomes, and consume more material goods and services.

Ironically, the quest for rising affluence and economic growth has had significant impacts on non-material sources of happiness, and particularly on social relationships. Liberal Western democracies treat the volume of goods produced as a barometer of national health even when economic growth ceases to produce the social goods which actually increase the quality of life and the happiness of their citizens. Technological change in the pursuit of lower production costs has thrown many people out of work, the source of greatest life satisfaction for many people. At the same time affluence and increased personal mobility have contributed to a decline in community and family stability, rising divorce rates and increasing social anomie. The quest for economic growth introduces commercial considerations into more and more areas of human social interaction. As Fred Hirsch argues, the effect of this is that benefits or utilities previously derived from the social domain, from give and take with neighbours, friends or relatives, become marketised even where the market may not be as effective at meeting needs as non-commercial forms of social interaction.[125] The decline of public provision in health, education and transport in the United States and Britain in the last twenty years, and the increasing levels of personal and property security which rising anomie, crime and violence necessitate, are both related to the commercialisation dynamic. As more and more goods are privatised, social goods and norms of behaviour – trust, neighbourliness, non-violence, mutual regard and care – diminish.

There is a growing awareness that affluent societies tend to be corrosive of communal and personal ties and as these disappear so the traditional restraints on human conduct are undermined. Galbraith's prediction of 'private affluence and public squalor' has come to characterise the social ecology of many modernised societies.[126] Long before Galbraith, Alex de Tocqueville in his *Democracy in America* predicted that materialism would ultimately come to undermine democracy as people pursued private comfort and the enervating distractions of their acquisitive desires at the expense of their own peace of mind, and the moral fabric of society itself.[127] He feared that people caught up by covetousness would no longer cultivate those public goods such as charity, honesty and religion without which societies would spiral into a vicious decline. The removal of moral constraints on covetousness and material consumption was the precondition for the emergence of the dynamo of consumption and industrial production which produced the wealth of nations on which Adam Smith theorised in the early modern period. However, the fears of Swift, de Tocqueville and indeed of Adam Smith himself that the consequent exaltation of self-interest and individual desire would undermine the basis for virtue and the common pursuit of shared social goals would seem to have been realised. As Francis Fukuyama observes, stable democracies require sanction and consent which arose historically from pre-modern moral values and religious ideals. As moral values and religious ideals are eroded in the context of the unbridled pursuit of individual desire, so the basis for consent, trust and the other public goods on which complex social systems rely is also lost.[128] Analogously, as modern capitalist democracies have pursued the utilitarian philosophy of raising the satisfaction of (acquisitive) desire to the central goal of social life, the basis for the common good, for collective action, civic virtue and the very consent to common social goals on which these societies depend has been undermined.[129] Thus the very values which capitalism requires for wealth creation, such as the work ethic and mutual trust between economic actors, may be undermined by the exclusive focus of capitalist societies on the processes of wealth generation.[130] As Alasdair MacIntyre argues, the core moral paradigm of modern culture, utilitarianism, is parasitic on moral goods, virtues and habits which in turn derived from the religious traditions of Western culture, and especially Christianity.[131] But the parasite overruns and destroys the predecessor culture, and moral virtues and habits which are essential to human sociality, and to the preservation of the non-human world, are eventually discarded or lost.[132]

MODERNITY AND ECOLOGY IN CONFLICT

The changes in the material conditions of human life, including land tenure, economic exchange, industrial production and consumption, which presage and characterise modernity are, as we have seen, accompanied by significant changes in the metaphysical, theological and moral conceptualisation of the cosmic context of human life and the nature of the self and society. These changes involved the removal of God from the human vision of the cosmos, of time and space, of exchange relations, of persons in community, and of the end of human life itself. They also represented a new focus on the human self, and on material fulfilment as the goal of human life.

At the birth of modernity, the money economy is substituted for the traditional economy of barter and exchange, and the abstract spirit of the money economy begins to displace the natural and revealed laws of the divine spirit which guided exchange relations and productive processes in pre-modern societies. In pre-modern Europe, land and work were seen as part of God's creation ordinance and as properly subject to objective and religiously inspired ethical standards. Nature was conceived by the monastic agriculturist as gift not property, for land belonged absolutely to God not humans. Similarly time, like space, was conceived before modernity as God's time. The offices of prayer governed the monastic agriculturalist's day, and together with holy days and Sundays, set a pattern of work, contemplation and recreation which regulated human work and economy. Thus, for example, usury was wrong not least because the usurer's money acquired interest on the Sabbath and this was contrary to God's law. But usury was also wrong because it allowed money debt to become an ordering principle of human relations, and this hegemony of debt was contrary to natural law and natural justice in which each member of society had a natural right to meet the needs of his own household by his own labour. Relations between persons and their real human needs were prior to the abstract relations of the money economy in pre-modern societies.

According to Anthony Giddens, the crucial distinction

between traditional societies and modern societies is the spatial distancing and abstraction of human relations which is enabled by the new power of money. Drawing on Georg Simmel's *Philosophy of Money* Giddens argues that money 'is a means of bracketing time and so of lifting transactions out of particular milieux of exchange ... money provides for the enactment of transactions between agents widely separated in time and space'.[133] Money has the effect of disembedding human social life from naturally ordered space and time. It creates a new concept of space and time which is as abstract from the natural order of land and seasons, night and day, as digits in a computer database, but whose abstract power is exercised in a totalising way over the lives of people for whom those digits are a debt incurred by their household or their government.[134] By this abstractive force of money, power in human affairs is concentrated in the modern world in the hands of those who have the most money, typically large corporations, banks and institutional investors. The new mobility and concentration of social power as money dissolves traditional sources of authority and mechanisms for the shared exercise of power within moral constraints, as represented by tribal and family groups, by communities of place including villages and small towns and by religious communities.

The new money economy which is born in the late Middle Ages, and ultimately gives rise to the global form of modernity, has the effect of disembedding human agency in productive work and exchange from local communities of place, and so of disembedding material production and money transactions from natural order and ecological constraints in particular places. Money, commodity, dissolves traditional time–space relations, and it dissolves traditional ethical obligations of neighbourliness, justice and care between persons, and between humans and the non-human world. Thus the violence of the sixteenth- and seventeenth-century Enclosures which continues until today amongst indigenous peoples, is an inevitable pre-cursor of the violence of the industrial assault on the natural order, and is intrinsically related to the nature of the money economy, and its disembedding effects on human community, human agency and the experience of the self. The self is wrested from its location in a divinely ordered cosmos, and from ethical and ritual obligations to other humans and to non-human forms of life, by the abstract power of money.

In a theological deconstruction of the money economy, Douglas Meeks argues that the money economy substitutes for divine relationality the idol of money as the fundamental principle of human relationality and as the primary mode of relationship between persons, and between persons and nature.[135] Money displaces God as the ordering force or guiding spirit of modern relations of exchange and of modern culture. The modern industrial economy operates independently of divine, ethical, personal or ecological constraints. Money measures wealth in units of exchange which may be maximised by the destruction of other people's livelihood. The corporate buy-out of a bicycle workshop or the felling of a rainforest both add digits to the abstract money economy while destroying the real livelihood of existing persons who depend on the cycle workshop or the rainforest to feed their families. Modern economics abstracts acquisition and wealth creation from social relations because it uses false measures of human welfare. Growing numbers of destitute homeless people in contemporary Britain and the United States represent a diminishment of life quality for both rich and poor, but their homelessness is partly a function of the increased property, and numbers of houses, owned by affluent people in both these countries. However, the owners of this new wealth do not consider the homeless as having a claim upon them even though they may have three houses and the poor none. This denial of relationality, and of interaction between wealth and poverty, is a function of the abstraction of money economies, as well as the abstraction of modern calculations of utility and welfare.

There is a similar denial of relationality in modern economics and industrialism in respect of the natural order. Environmentalists argue that the modern money economy operates regardless of natural ecological constraints because its measures of wealth and of exchange relations are abstracted from natural ecological systems.[136] The spatial abstraction of modern economics is so extreme that even were all the rainforests to disappear and sea levels to rise two feet, and the climate warm by four degrees, and large parts of the world become uninhabitable, individuals and companies who had burnt the energy or consumed the forests in industrial production would still be reckoned wealthy in economic parlance. Industrialism commodifies nature and treats ecosystems as materials banks, pollution sinks or productivity zones. Nature only has value in an industrial economy in terms of its transformation from its wild state to its productive or polluted state.

Urbanised living, which is not confined to cities, also contributes to the modern denial of relationality between human life and the natural world, for it involves the fabrication of life around mechanical and technological rather than natural cycles. This brings freedom from dependency on natural seasons, natural light or heat sources. But at the same time it brings a new kind of dependency on industrialised systems of power generation and food production and transportation. Paradoxically, even modern nature conservation can have this distancing and transforming effect. Wilderness reserves or game parks are as artificial in their construction of relations between humans and nature as monoculture pine forests or wheat prairies because indigenous peoples are often excluded from these 'protected' parts of the non-human world which they have respected and preserved and lived off for thousands of years. Modern urban-based nation states have lost this primal ability to inhabit fragile ecosystems without destroying them and so all human life is viewed as a threat to the national park or game reserve, which are preserved in parts of Africa and Asia exclusively for the monied and controlled tourist and the professional conservationist. Natural relationality between humans and the non-human world is denied even to the indigenous peoples for whom this relationality remains fundamental to their culture and life-style.

Ecological criticism of capitalism and industrialism is not new. Karl Marx criticised industrialism for its ecological effects, but he nonetheless believed that the industrial transformation of nature would ultimately advance human welfare and benefit by bringing to an end human poverty and class divisions, and by giving material abundance to all.[137] Thomas Malthus believed, unlike Marx, that the earth's resources were not infinite and would not sustain indefinitely the expanding populations and resource consumption of early modern Europe and its colonies.[138] The growth of international conflicts over limited natural resources such as oil, water, fish and forests in the late twentieth century indicates that Malthus rather than Marx was the more percipient. The fish in the sea, the soil on the land and the timber in the forest are limited natural resources, as is the capacity of the earth's atmosphere to absorb waste heat from industrial and energy production. Industrial fishing, forestry or farming ultimately threaten the sources of human food and protein as well as destroying the richness and diversity of the non-human world.

But of course Marx and Malthus were both in some senses right. Capitalism, technology and industrialism have brought a material standard of living far above that of medieval peasants within reach of millions of people. The experience of infant mortality, a constant eventuality for pre-modern families, is now largely confined to the poor of the Third World while even in the poorest countries in the world life expectancy for those who survive childhood has advanced from forty to fifty or sixty years, and to seventy or eighty years in the richest countries. However, the exclusion of indigenous peoples from their ancestral lands by the processes of modernisation initially involves increases in mortality rates as well as denials of basic human freedoms and rights. The subsequent reductions in mortality rates for shifted cultivators and squatter dwellers must be offset against these initial increases. In many cases indigenous peoples simply do not survive this transition. They become subject to diseases to which they have no resistance and to social processes which deny them traditional sources of nutrition and identity.[139] In many parts of contemporary Africa the transition to modernity now appears to be operating in reverse and indices of health and life quality are actually declining. African students of mine are increasingly questioning the need for their people in rural areas to become involved in a culture of modernisation which generates artificial material needs while destroying traditional African village culture, and often producing a poorer life quality even on the narrowest of health indices.

Indigenous pre-modern peoples lived a life of material sufficiency but their wealth in human goods – communal feasting, leisure time, ritual, play and sheer joy – far exceeded the availability of these goods in many sectors of modern societies. The very life qualities which modernisation tends to corrode or reduce – long-term relationships, stable families, communities of place, meaningful leisure, co-operative games, religious rituals, care for the local environment – are those which so-called primitive cultures have in abundance. Modern problems of meaninglessness, stress, employment insecurity and the diseases of affluence such as heart disease are also almost unknown in many traditional societies.

One of the greatest ironies is that the Europeans who first encountered indigenous cultures criticised them as lazy and feckless, immoral and ignoble. In eighteenth-century Malaya, British missionaries and traders criticised the 'lazy' Malay peasants who planted rice once a year and watched it grow, plucked fruits from the trees and fished in the sea or the river but otherwise spent a good deal of time resting, playing with their children, praying at the mosque, spinning tops and flying kites.[140] Today in modernised Malaysia industrialised rice farmers plant rice twice a year, fruit is tended in agri-business plantations and fish is industrially trawled from the ocean. People increasingly live in traffic-ridden and polluted towns and cities, though their grandparents may remain in the villages. In modern Malaysia time is at a premium; most people work six days a week in factories and offices, and return to the village only for the most significant of the annual religious festivals. But advertisements and the tourist industry portray the life of the village, and the life of leisure as the icons of all this modern productive activity: the visit to the village, the sun-bed by the pool, the cocktail under the palm tree, the tourist in her hammock are the advertising images of leisure and indolence purveyed as the goal of those who succeed in the industrial rat race. But it was the abundance of such images of indolence in pre-modern Malaya which was most criticised by the Europeans who first sought to drag the Malays into the modern world.[141]

The money economy and industrialism have together generated a social form – modernity – which is dedicated to the systematic transformation of human relations with nature. Modernity substitutes material wealth and globalised Western technology and culture for human community, ecological richness and local knowledge. And yet the globalising of the principal features of Western culture and life-style – packaged food, domestic machines, electronic entertainment and private automobiles – not only undermines human life qualities such as community and stable families, but also may presage ecological disaster for the planet.

Alongside the demise of human and natural ecology, modernity has also proved inimical to religion. The disembedding of people from nature and community by the money economy and the industrialisation of food, work and leisure also reflects and enhances the disembedding of human consciousness and community from the sacred cosmos. The world as portrayed by modern science and industrialism is seen primarily as the domain of humans to transform and dispose in the service of human welfare and the progress of economic development and modernity across the globe. It is therefore rather curious that Western environmentalists have blamed religion, and in particular Christianity, for the environmental crisis. Many environmentalists have accepted Lynn White's argument that biblical teaching about creation, by distancing God from nature, despiritualises nature and makes it available for technological and industrial transformation.[142] I shall explore below in more detail the significance of the Christian theology of creation for the ethical valuation of nature, but for now suffice it to say that the rise of instrumental views of nature has gone hand in hand with the demise of the traditional Christian view of creation as the sphere of God's providential ordering, and with the gradual secularisation of European civilisation which began at the close of the Middle Ages and reaches its nadir in secularised modernity.

Wherever secular modernity encounters traditional culture and religion, it tends to disrupt and corrode harmonious human relations with nature, and the religious sensibilities and rituals by which these relations were traditionally sustained. This happened after the Reformation in Europe when attitudes to money, trade, land and work were secularised and it continues today in the assault of modernity on the local religions and cultures of primal peoples. The traditional religious world-view of the Middle Ages tended to preserve the natural world from excessive human interference. Religious rituals were closely tied to natural cycles and seasons, and were often perceived as contributing to the fertility and beneficence of both divine–human relations and relations between humans and their animal and plant neighbours. This conserving function of religion may be seen as much in the rituals and offices of the medieval Cistercian or Benedictine monastery, based as they were on the Hebrew Psalms with their powerful nature imagery, as in the rituals of the African Nuer or Australian aboriginals.

However, Lynn White was not entirely wrong to identify the historic roots of the ecological crisis with elements of Christian teaching and influence, for as we have seen, the end of the Middle Ages marked the emergence of a new humanocentric type of European religion which sustained a more instrumentalist perspective on nature, and accompanied the rise of early modern science with its gradual evacuation of divine significance and purposiveness from the cosmos. This new orientation of Christianity also generated the Protestant work ethic, which in turn legitimated the relations of the money economy which were themselves the precursors of the industrial transformation of nature. Protestant theology focused religious concern on human inwardness and the redemption of the individual soul. Creation was increasingly seen as fallen and as marginal to the primary will of God, which was to save humans from perdition. The principal purpose of creation was to serve humans in their redemptive quest, and so gradually the religious and ethical constraints on land ownership and use, on trade in agricultural commodities and on usury were eroded. The world and the economy of the earth were for humans to order for their own purposes, and God was increasingly excluded from the cosmos, and displaced from the central goals and ethical values of the civilisation which succeeded medieval Christendom.

The connection between traditional religion and respect for the order of nature is axiomatic in most non-Western cultures. This is evidenced in the fact that religion remains the primary source of identity and meaning in the non-Western world and so it is the catalyst of most rural and much urban protest at ecological destruction. The ethical values of many of the world's religions encapsulate a deep primal respect and reverence for the natural order, and hence they help to sustain human social practices which recognise its limits and preserve its self-renewing capacities. In contrast, the more secular character of Western environmentalism reflects the Romantic turn of Enlightenment philosophy and culture towards nature as the source of human purpose and meaning, in a universe devoid of divine presence or moral purposiveness. It is from the Romantic quest for aesthetic value and moral purposiveness in nature, without divine warrant, that ecological thought emerges. In the next chapter we will explore the implications for environmentalism of this philosophical and cultural turn to nature. As with the inward turn to the self we may find that the turn to nature is also incapable of providing a resolution for our contemporary moral and ecological dilemmas.

CHAPTER THREE

The turn to nature

For I have learned
To look on nature, not as in the hour
Of thoughtless youth; but hearing often-times
The still, sad music of humanity,
Nor harsh nor grating, though of ample power
To chasten and subdue. And I have felt
A presence that disturbs me with the joy
Of elevated thoughts; a sense sublime
Of something far more deeply interfused,
Whose dwelling is the light of setting suns,
And the round ocean and the living air,
And the blue sky, and in the mind of man:
A motion and a spirit, that impels
All thinking things, all objects of all thought,
And rolls through all things. Therefore am I still
A lover of the meadows and the woods,
And mountains; and of all that we behold
From this green earth . . .
        . . . well pleased to recognise
In nature and the language of the sense
The anchor of my purest thoughts, the nurse,
The guide, the guardian of my heart, and soul
Of all my moral being.[1]

Wordsworth's poetry is perhaps the best exemplar in English literature of the turn to nature in European thought which accompanies the rise of humanism and modern science, industrialisation and consumerism. We see in *Tintern Abbey* how nature has become for Wordsworth the source of moral value and spiritual awareness. In another poem, *Peter Bell*, Wordsworth seeks to show that nature can take the place of the Bible and the supernatural as the source of social and moral control for a people who had lost touch with the governing and guiding religious sources of an earlier age.[2] The Romantic reaction to Enlightenment humanism and deism which began in the eighteenth century issues in a range of responses where nature becomes the source of goodness and virtue, while evil and conflict are identified with wrong human choices and societal tendencies.[3] As Charles Taylor argues, it is estrangement from nature, not from God, which for Rousseau and Wordsworth is the source of discontent and of the troubles of the times.[4] Nature also symbolises the spiritual unity of all things in which humans are united with the cosmos, the 'presence that disturbs', 'a sense sublime', 'of something far more deeply interfused, whose dwelling is the light of setting suns'.[5] These two themes of nature as guide and moral source, and of nature as representing an ultimate unity or community of being which transcends human individuality, are both influential in the development of ecological thinking.

While nature Romanticism may be seen primarily as a response or reaction to the humanistic, mechanistic and deistic tendencies of philosophy and science in the eighteenth century, there are also significant connections between humanism and scientism, and the Romantic response. The emphasis on the individual as the site of spiritual awareness mediated through nature is of a piece with the individualism of Enlightenment humanism, as Taylor demonstrates.[6] The individual as artist or scientific recreator of nature, as well as the individual as sensual receptor of the natural world, becomes the agent of the eternal in the temporal; the individual becomes the Creator.[7] The links between art and the turn to nature are evident in the aesthetic philosophy of John Ruskin and in the increasing popularity of nature painting which takes over from traditional depictions of classical or biblical themes and stories in the art of the period. Eugene Hargrove argues that the rise of landscape painting, and the fashion for detailed sketching, drawing and painting of animals, birds and geological features both indicate this aesthetic shift towards natural beauty and order as the source of creative and artistic inspiration, as well as of moral virtue.[8]

Similarly the increasing fashion for informal gardens and landscaping in the eighteenth and nineteenth centuries, which eventually developed into the aesthetic appreciation of wilderness, especially in North America, is indicative of changing aesthetic approaches to nature which reflect and feed the Romantic and conservationist traditions.

Another source of this changing attitude was natural science itself. Hargrove identifies an interaction between scientific and artistic circles. Many of the observations of the eighteenth-century poets and the landscape painters were scientific in character. As scientists, looking for rational laws and regularities, devoted their attention to observing the objects of nature, part of their evaluation of what they saw inevitably related to the aesthetic.[9] Whether through scientific sketches and accounts of landscapes and animals, or through the collection of strange flora and fauna and their placement in botanical gardens or natural history museums, natural science gave rise to a new public interest in nature. Beauty and unadorned nature were identified and people increasingly came to admire nature in its wild state.[10] Instead of the traditional fear of the dark forest or the wild jungle or desert, nineteenth-century natural science, art and literature evinced a fascination and even an identification with the 'vernal wood' and the verdant jungle which would have been quite novel in previous centuries.[11] This new appreciation for the beauty or sublimity of nature means that attributes that were exclusively ascribed to God by nominalists or Puritans are again identified with nature.[12]

The Romantic approach to nature issued in the establishment of voluntary societies and trusts for the protection and preservation of areas of great natural beauty, such as the Lake District in North West England, by Romantic exponents such as Ruskin and Wordsworth. At the same time in the writings of Emerson, Thoreau and John Muir the conservation movement was born in North America. Its first public achievement was in the campaigns to preserve the great wildernesses of Yosemite, Yellowstone and the Grand Canyon from forestry, quarrying and hydroelectric developments, through the device of making them into protected national parks.[13]

The Romantic and aesthetic appreciation of nature may have been linked with the early scientific perspective of botanists, biologists and geologists as well as the new aesthetics of the natural world.[14] It was also linked to moral and religious sentiments and ideas. Keith Thomas traces a growing domestic compassion for animals, and a concern for the preservation of wildlife from the Middle Ages to the modern period which ironically accompanies the increasingly harsh treatment of animals in laboratory experiments.[15] Animals were regarded by Francis of Assisi as creatures with a moral status before God not much different from humans. By the seventeenth and eighteenth centuries this same attitude is reflected in increasing concern at the depredations animals suffered in the preparation of meat for human consumption. Animals were sometimes described as moral creatures with the same rights as humans by philosophers of the period. The origins of the contemporary concern for animal rights, and the concern for the preservation of threatened species, may again be traced to this period. Thus John Bulwer questions whether it is lawful for humans to eradicate any species because 'this were taking away one link of God's chain, one note of his harmony'.[16]

The period of the rise of the Romantic movement is then characterised by two contrasting trends. Nature is increasingly subject to instrumentalist exploitation under the demands of European population expansion, industrialisation, consumerism and imperialism. And yet at the same time the changes which human society was visiting on nature evoked strong protest as philosophers, poets and ordinary people increasingly came to regard the natural world as a source of beauty, pleasure and moral guidance. This quest for moral significance in, and emotional identity with, nature is also linked to the demise of theism and the loss of a sacred cosmos. As God and creation are pushed apart by the rise of modern science, so there is a correlative need to invest the cosmos with a new kind of meaning, not provided by God or Christian revelation, but by an account of the independent beauty and moral significance of the natural order.

ENVIRONMENTAL ETHICS: CONSEQUENTIALIST
APPROACHES

The Romantic quest for moral value in the non-human world is taken up in a more disciplined way in the recent development of environmental ethics, which has been sponsored by moral philosophers and environmentalists. The most prevalent style of environmental ethics may be described as consequentialist. Consequentialism, as its name implies, involves the estimation of the rightness or wrongness of a particular action from the consequences which follow from the action, and entails no claims concerning the intrinsic goodness or badness of any particular action or type of action. It locates value in the effects of actions on those who may be considered moral agents. Consequentialist approaches mostly rely on the utilitarian identification of moral agency with persons, and their moral welfare with experiences of pleasure and pain. Straightforward humanocentric and utilitarian approaches to environmental decision-making are the standard form of moral argument deployed in government and inter-governmental reports on the environment such as the Bruntland Report *Our Common Future* and *Agenda 21*, the report of the Rio Earth Summit. This approach is also found in scientific resource management approaches to environmental problems, and in environmental impact assessment reports. The environmental costs of a particular development project or programme for certain persons, and for non-human life and ecosystems, are set against the benefits to other persons in this approach. Thus in the case of a proposed hydroelectric dam in Sarawak, Borneo, there are six thousand tribal people whose lands and homes will be flooded as a consequence of the dam being built. Thousands of individual trees, birds, mammals and insects will similarly be either displaced or killed by the artificial inundation. But two thousand miles away there will be people living in cities in West Malaysia whose electricity demands will be partially met by the dam, who will be able to burn lights in the night, run refrigerators to cool food in the tropical heat, and enjoy a cooler air-conditioned environment in their offices and homes.

The dam may mean that electricity is cheaper for consumers, it may mean that some people have access to electric power for the first time because of this lower cost, with all the enhancements to human comfort which it will enable. Humanocentric cost-benefit approaches will thus rely on the enhancement of human welfare, the increase of pleasure over pain, to offset the environmental and human costs of nature-destructive human activity.

The core problem with consequentialist and utilitarian moral arguments is that, although they are putatively focused on the welfare of moral individuals, the way in which decisions about resource use are made in cost-benefit analysis is actually, as we have seen, to aggregate the sum of costs and benefits arising from a particular development project, rather than to focus on its effects upon the particular individuals whose lives may be most dramatically affected by it, such as the tribal peoples whose villages lie under the water level to be created by a new dam. The focus of consequentialist and utilitarian moral arguments on the moral individual may then in fact be a logical fiction. As Mark Sagoff argues, a political community governed by utilitarian principles will tend not to treat individual persons as moral ends, but will rather subjugate individual interests to an aggregate of social welfare.[17] Thus in modern states, both democratic and totalitarian, utilitarian styles of consequentialism are frequently used in totalising ways which infringe significantly on the moral welfare of particular individuals or minority groups, by destroying benefits which they derive from their local environment.

The failure of utilitarianism in practice to effectively locate moral value in individuals may be a consequence of its primarily procedural location of moral value. Particular actions are measured in terms of their procedural consequences for an aggregate of human persons, but this quantitative measure of moral value is highly elusive in practice because of the narrow definition of moral goods – pleasure and pain – which utilitarianism allows. Happiness, pleasure, even pain and discomfort, are not easy to define or measure. Pain and discomfort thresholds vary between individuals, as indeed do capacities for happiness and joy in different circumstances. Pleasure and pain, welfare and discomfort, are inherently subjective states, agreement about which is collectively elusive.[18] Utility – the utilitarian location of moral value – is thus inherently hard to define. One person's utility is another person's disutility. The rational moderation of different people's needs and happinesses by social institutions is a prerequisite for the societal application of utilitarianism. Arbitrating between utilities and disutilities is the business of modern bureaucracies, legal systems and economic markets. But, as we have seen, in practice these institutions have not been effective in moderating interests of groups that are disparate in levels of wealth or power, or disparate in space or time, nor in giving due place to non-human environmental goods.

Alasdair MacIntyre argues that the exclusive focus of utilitarianism on the subjective notion of pleasure or happiness is itself the principal cause for the slide of morality into subjectivism – 'I want this, you want the opposite and we are both right' – and the difficulties modern societies have in reaching agreement on significant moral concerns such as medical technology and environmental issues, hence the increasingly conflictual and even violent nature of disputes over abortion, animal rights, land use, ocean fishing and development projects.[19]

This tendency towards contemporary moral disagreement is again the consequence of the exclusive modern focus on aggregate human utility as the arbiter of moral decisions, which provides an inadequate framework for the protection of the dignity of particular human persons, communities or environmental goods from technological invasion. Utilitarianism is also incapable of providing an effective account of the moral interests of non-sentient life, of ecosystems or of the moral significance of the environment and the biosphere, because it relies on the subjective sensations or feelings of moral actors, or groups of actors, rather than on any objective order of things apart from subjective consciousness, and human valuing. This is why I shall argue in subsequent chapters that the resolution of the environmental crisis requires the rediscovery of the existence of value and moral significance in the objective order of the world prior to human acts of valuing, an independence which Western theists have traditionally located in the original act of divine beneficence in the creation of the world, and in the valuing of the creation by the creator God. Without a recovery of this traditional recognition of the moral order and purposiveness of the world, prior to its processing by human perception, I do not believe it will be possible for modern societies ultimately to reduce their impacts upon the ecological integrity of the non-human world.

Despite the problems associated with consequentialist utilitarianism, it remains the dominant modern moral paradigm and a number of environmental philosophers have sought to enhance and adapt utilitarian and consequentialist styles of ethical argument, rather than propound new styles, or, as I propose, repristinating more ancient ones, to resolve environmental conflicts and problems. Peter Singer was the first environmental philosopher to develop a systematic case for extending utilitarian arguments to non-human life in his book *Animal Liberation*, which soon became a seminal text in the animal liberation movement.[20] Singer develops an argument for the recognition of the moral interests of animals by means of the classic utilitarian identification of moral good with the avoidance of pain. Since scientists now agree that animals can feel pain, a consistent utilitarian will therefore consider the moral interests of sensate animals as well as of sensate humans in the estimate of aggregate welfare, and will therefore avoid subjecting them to pain, in laboratory experiments, in factory farming or for any other human purpose. Singer coins the term 'speciesism' to refer to the prejudice against animals in human society, a prejudice which he compares with racism and sexism. He argues that, as with racism and sexism, the ethically consistent position is to abolish the absolute moral boundary between humans and animals: 'we should give the same respect to the lives of animals as we give to the lives of humans'.[21] There are therefore occasions when, if we had to choose between, for example, extending the life of a seriously senile person and the life of a non-human primate such as a chimpanzee, with, arguably, a greater level of self-awareness, and a greater capacity for meaningful relations than the senile person, that we should favour the chimp over the human. A clear example of such a choice would be in the case of the use of the heart valve of a healthy young pig in a transplant operation to treat a heart-valve dysfunction in a senile person. Singer's position would mean that killing the pig for the treatment of the human is unjustified. His approach is clear and concisely summed up in the following statement: animals and humans are, at respective levels of consciousness, to be treated equally.

Singer's utilitarian focus on the enormous increases in animal pain arising from the scientific and industrial techniques of modern civilisation has been taken up in the animal liberation movement, where the pain caused to laboratory animals, to foxes and deer in hunting, and, to a lesser extent, to animals and birds in factory farming and live transportation systems, has become one of the defining moral issues for many people in modern democracies, and especially in Britain. However, the reliance of animal liberationists on utilitarian ethics produces a negative and combative tone in the movement's moral vision which seems well suited to protest and indignity, and which in the extremes of the movement is often expressed in acts of violence against scientists, hunters or farmers, which seem to evidence a lack of moral consistency to say the least. But as we have seen, utilitarianism is far better at fuelling incommensurable moral disagreements than at generating a positive moral vision of those goods and goals which might redirect modern civilisation towards greater kindness and gentleness in its treatment of animals, and greater respect and care for human persons disadvantaged by the exigencies of modern industrial development. It is the inability of utilitarianism to provide a convincing account of human community which is the principal reason for the weaknesses of utilitarian approaches to environmental ethics. The focus on individual sentiency offers no basis for an understanding of the nature of the community and totality of life forms, sentient and non-sentient, in which both human and non-human flourishing is experienced. Furthermore, the use of sentiency as the arbiter of moral value does not allow the utilitarian to ascribe moral significance to non-sentient life forms. At the same time the focus on pain as the key moral problem in relation to the environment distorts the human vision of the biotic community, which does indeed involve pain and suffering as well as flourishing and fulfilment. But it may be argued that the balance of flourishing and pain in the life of an animal hunted and killed by another animal, or by a human with a rifle, is simply part of the functioning of the natural order, and that a world in which there is no predation, no hunting, no eating of one species by another, is inconceivable. As Singer says, the natural occurrence of predation cannot provide support for human cruelty to animals,[22] but it may help us to set the pain an animal experiences at the end of its life in the perspective of the whole life of the beast. After all humans also often die in pain, but a painful death does not undermine the value of a good life. We should certainly try to minimise pain in the human treatment of live animals, but that we should cease to use animals for any human purposes would seem to be an unnatural moral position which contradicts not only the whole history of the human relationship with the non-human world, but the reality of predation and of the food chain in the non-human world. Finally Singer's version of utilitarianism raises a further problem in relation to the ethics of human life, and this is the danger of cheapening the life of human beings in a world where animals are put to death or subjected to great pain for trivial reasons such as cosmetic testing. While Singer certainly recognises this problem, he does not seem to give an adequate answer to it.[23]

In his seminal work *The Ethics of Environmental Concern*, Robin Attfield, like Singer, adopts a consequentialist framework but he shifts the basis for measuring utility in non-human life from the sense of pleasure and pain to other features of living organisms, including their 'capacities for growth, respiration, self-preservation and reproduction' which are 'common to plants and sentient organisms', and by this means attempts to overcome some of the difficulties raised by Singer's reliance on sentiency as the principal determinant of moral significance in human and non-human life.[24] On the basis of this richer account of life experience, Attfield finds intrinsic value in the flourishing of individual non-sensate life forms, and rejects positions which hold that intrinsic value is only present where there is consciousness. But he also rejects the extension of intrinsic value to collectivities or wholes such as the biosphere, ecosystems or habitats such as forests, oceans and mountains, which many environmental ethicists advance. According to Attfield, actions which have the consequence of harming non-human organisms without correlatively achieving significant and balancing human goods through this damage, such as the prevention of human hunger or disease, are morally wrong and to be avoided. Whereas Singer simply develops consequentialist utilitarianism in the direction of an animal ethic, Attfield demonstrates the considerable resources that an ecologically revised consequentialist ethic presents for the moral valuation of all forms of organic life, with his separation of moral value from sentience. By this means he distances himself from utilitarian versions of consequentialism. He also supplements his basically consequentialist arguments with some elements of a deontological approach, with his theory of intrinsic value.[25] Attfield's approach also goes some way to giving moral considerability to ecosytems, even if only of a dependent variety, for if an ecosytem is sufficiently harmed so as to have consequences for the flourishing of large numbers of its inhabitants, then this is a moral wrong which is to be avoided unless it is outweighed by some greater human good. Attfield resists the idea that the environmental crisis has arisen because of fundamental flaws in the modern Western ethical tradition. He defends the Western traditions of moral individualism and utilitarianism from ecological polemic. If we rightly value the moral interests of present and future individual persons, and balance these with the more limited moral interests of individual animals, we can generate an attitude of respect and of care for nature which can reverse the ecologically destructive tendencies of modern civilisation. There is no need to ascribe moral value to ecosystems or communities of species being as deep ecologists do.[26] An adequate response to the environmental crisis can be developed by the more consistent application of the Western moral tradition, and in particular the core utilitarian and consequentialist principle of the quest for the maximisation of welfare to human decisions about natural resources. Again, though, Attfield's position is subject to the fundamental inconsistencies and problems already adduced with respect to more explicitly utilitarian styles of consequentialism, and not least the failure of the aggregate measures of welfare deployed in consequentialist cost-benefit approaches to environmental resource use, which he seems to favour, to truly respect individuals, either human persons, or individual species, or to value independently of sentient individuals ecosystems and environmental commons such as oceans and air.[27]

ENVIRONMENTAL ETHICS: DEONTOLOGICAL APPROACHES

In the light of the weaknesses of consequentialist moral arguments, some environmental ethicists have developed various forms of deontological argument for environmental values. Deontological approaches to ethics are characterised by the attempt to establish the moral validity or goodness of an action independently of its consequences. According to Immanuel Kant, who first fully enunciated the modern deontological approach, an action is right because it represents goodness, a universal property which can be identified by all rational minds. Goodness just *is*. Right actions are not right because God says they are, or because we find their consequences acceptable or even pleasurable. They are right independent of human or divine volition and independent of their consequences. Kant seeks to ground morality in a self-evident rational principle – what he calls the categorical imperative or the supreme principle of morality – whose universal truth and applicability rely neither on human perception or desire, nor on changing contexts.[28] I will illustrate this approach by a story. If I were to go along to my local park and cut down a tree for firewood I would be stealing part of a publicly owned asset, removing a home for birds and beetles and other living things and destroying an object of pleasure for hundreds of my city-dwelling neighbours. If everyone were to behave as I had done then there would be no parks, no public places worth visiting.

We may then universalise from this story to a general maxim or rule about moral behaviour which everyone can agree on: stealing trees from public parks is always wrong.

This approach to ethics, because it seems to depend less on human perception or desire, lends itself rather better than consequentialism to a moral consideration of duties owed to animals and the non-human world, and especially to non-sentient aspects of the natural world such as trees and mountains. Eugene Hargrove proposes an aesthetic version of deontology, though he calls his version an *ontological* argument.[29] According to Hargrove, humans universally recognise a duty to preserve aesthetic beauty in art objects. This duty to preserve beauty in art legitimates the duty to preserve beauty in nature.[30] The duty to preserve nature also relates to the ontological status of nature as being, life, which exists, unlike art objects, prior to human intervention and without human volition. The first step in Hargrove's argument is that humans have a duty to promote and preserve goodness. Moral goodness is then identified with beauty, both artistic and natural. Natural beauty, Hargrove concludes, pre-exists human art and therefore humans have a greater duty to preserve natural beauty than they do aesthetic works of art.[31] There is a beguiling simplicity and elegance to Hargrove's position, and it also draws on a long strain of reflection on the beauty, and hence the value, of nature in Western culture which goes back at least as far as the Hebrew Psalms. However, the exclusive ontological focus on beauty in this approach is not without its problems. Does the identity of goodness and beauty mean that beautiful people are more moral than ugly people? How do we decide where there is a conflict between the maintenance or creation of a beautiful art object and the continued existence of a beautiful natural object such as the tree from which a work of wood sculpture is shaped, or with which a cathedral roof restored? Is unformed, uncreated, pre-existent beauty always to be preferred to human creativity and altered nature? What happens when there is a conflict between pre-existent natural beauty and a need to feed existent beautiful people?

Another approach to deontological environmental ethics is

that of rights ethics. While some contemporary utilitarians try to hold the concept of rights in tension with the core principle of utilitarianism, there are a number of reasons for supposing that the discourses of rights and of utility point to different, and mutually incompatible, ethical paradigms. As Kieran Cronin argues, early utilitarians identified an inherent contradiction between the assertion of inalienable moral rights, as distinct from legal rights, and the pursuit of the principle of the maximisation of utility.[32]

The basis for the assertion that all persons have rights is said to be that all individuals have inherent value. To say that this value *inheres* in them is to say that it is independent of their desires or perceptions or the utility that they experience. It just *is*.[33] Because individuals, whether rich or poor, beautiful or ugly, intelligent or foolish, all have this inherent value, all humans have moral rights which it is usually wrong for states or groups or other individuals to deny or abrogate even if the consequences for other groups of persons may be an enhancement of their pleasure or welfare. The concept of rights implies duties which correlate to these rights. These duties rest upon the reciprocal recognition of the existence of another's rights. Rights are also necessarily universal. If I have certain rights by virtue of my being human, then every other human must have these rights also. However, some varieties of human have more claim to recognition of their rights than others. To take an obvious example, human foetuses which are less than twenty weeks in gestation have fewer rights in most societies than full-term babies. Infants, young children and the mentally impaired have fewer rights in most societies than do adults.

Animal rights philosophers and activists have sought to appropriate the language of rights in the context of the modern abuse of animals in factory farms and laboratory experiments, and in relation to the destruction or erosion of natural habitats which threaten the flourishing of sensate mammals such as gibbons or whales. Tom Regan in *The Case for Animal Rights* proposes that all mammalian life forms have inherent value because of their experiences of sentience including pleasure, joy, pain, a sense of identity, memory, a sense of the future and potential for fulfilment, experiences which are parallel, if not of the same quality, to aspects of human consciousness.[34] These characteristics may not make them moral agents but animals can legitimately be said to be what Regan calls subjects-of-a-life. As such subjects-of-a-life mammals have the same rights as human moral *patients* who suffer when treated immorally and flourish when treated morally, but are not themselves morally responsible.[35] As moral patients mammals merit the same respect accorded to moral patients in human society such as human infants, children and the mentally ill. Consequently the duties owed to animals are almost indistinguishable in Regan's view from the duties owed to other humans. This means of course that animals are owed the same duty as humans not to be harmed. This in turn means that the hunting and trapping of animals, the rearing of animals for food production, the use of animals in laboratory experiments and the eating of meat in any form are all wrong, as morally wrong as killing or eating humans.[36]

Regan's argument is attractive in its lack of ambiguity. Like Singer, Regan believes humans must abandon all forms of animal husbandry, hunting or meat-eating. But Regan's argument is based on a deontological moral claim for the inherent value of all sensate life forms. There are elements in Regan's approach which are of value in the reconstruction of a Christian environmental ethic, and particularly his emphasis on the need to avoid cruelty to animals in any form, which resonates with similar prohibitions in the Hebrew Bible. However, the emphasis on sentience as the determinator of moral significance does not address the problems associated with human environmental impacts on non-sentient parts, and wholes, of the non-human world. Similarly, as I observed in relation to Singer, the exclusive emphasis on sentient individuals, and the prohibition on hunting or meat-eating by humans, seems inconsistent with the fact that predatory behaviour is a key feature of the natural order, that animals will continue to eat other animals even if humans stop. It may be argued that the suffering of a gazelle at the paws and teeth of a lion is greater than that of a red deer shot by a skilled hunter. Indeed where humans stop hunting certain kinds of mammal – for example the elephant or the red deer – these animals can wreak as much damage as careless humans on their natural environment. New protection for elephants in parts of Africa has led to environmental devastation and serious conflict between humans, elephants and other animals in Kenya and Zimbabwe. Similarly the uncontrolled spread of red deer in the Cairngorms in Scotland results in overgrazing and hillside erosion.

Many environmental ethicists argue that there is no inherent injustice or immorality in animals preying on animals, or in humans hunting and killing animals for food.[37] The moral problem is not in the eating of animals but in the avoidance of unnecessary cruelty, indignity and pain. The harm done to animals and birds in modern methods of factory farming and intensive rearing is undoubtedly great and of moral significance, even if we do not adopt a rights approach to the moral status of non-human life. The raising of chickens, pigs or veal calves in spaces which allow no room for movement, and the chemically and genetically altered environment which farm animals increasingly inhabit, all are indicators of unnecessary suffering, and of the denial of any possibility of life quality for most intensively reared farm animals. Similarly the trade in and abuse of millions of animals in laboratory experiments, for human entertainment and in circuses or zoos, is undoubtedly a moral evil which is clearly contrary to injunctions against cruelty to animals in much of the Western ethical tradition, and a further symptom of the modern commodification and reduction of nature to the status of materials bank or 'cash cow'. Furthermore a major cause of global warming and of soil erosion, two of the most significant features of the environmental crisis, is the sheer number of cows and other domestic animals kept by modern farmers, and the deleterious environmental impacts of modern methods of intensive animal husbandry: overcropping by domestic animals is a major cause of desertification and soil erosion. The methane emitted by the billions of cattle in the world is one of the largest sources of the enhancement of the greenhouse effect, and the effluent from intensive animal rearing represents a serious pollution problem.

Reductions in meat-eating and in the quantity of animals kept by humans for food would then seem to be prerequisites for addressing central features of the environmental crisis.

However, we should also recall that the keeping or hunting of chickens, rabbits or fish provides a vital source of protein for many of the world's poorest people. The earliest forms of human civilisation – hunter-gatherer societies – depended on a daily diet of vegetables, fruits, nuts and berries enriched by occasional hunted animals and fish. These forms of society were not normally vegetarian and yet they preserved the balance between human needs and the flourishing of other animals and species.

One of the principal weaknesses of the rights approach for environmental ethics is that it is difficult, as Regan acknowledges, to extend moral claims based on the concept of subject-of-a-life to non-mammalian species such as earthworms or non-sentient species such as trees, although Christopher Stone attempts to extend rights language to non-sentient life in his *Should Trees Have Standing?*[38] However, the central problem with an exclusive reliance on the language of rights in relation to environmental issues is that rights ethicists can give no moral value to collectivities or communities of life, such as ecosystems or the biosphere. This lacuna reflects the fact that rhetoric about rights tends to privilege competition over co-operation, individuals over collectivities and moral claims over moral relationships and responsibilities.[39] While, as MacIntyre argues, demands for the recognition of rights may fuel the often incommensurable moral demands of modern protest movements, not least the animal rights movement, it is less clear that rights ethics can provide a coherent account of how individuals actually live together in moral and indeed in ecological communities.[40] Feminists, such as Carol Gilligan in her justly celebrated book *In a Different Voice*, argue that the competitive and individualistic vision of the human condition, and the condition of the natural order which sustains and is legitimated by both utilitarian and rights ethics, reflect a bias towards male moral experience. Gilligan contends that women's moral experience points instead to the situatedness of ethical values and behaviour in patterns of relationality, intimacy, connectivity, community and care.⁴¹ Feminists claim that the emphasis on connectivity and care which emerges from a more relational account of ethical behaviour represents a more effective ethic for overcoming the alienation between human and non-human life than the atomistic ethic of rights, a claim which we shall examine in more detail in the next section.

A third kind of deontological environmental ethic is that associated with the concept of intrinsic value which, as we have seen, is also utilised by consequentialists such as Attfield. According to Holmes Rolston the concept of intrinsic value proceeds from an account of the independent existence and purposiveness, the *telos,* of organisms and collectivities of organisms rather than from human perception.⁴² The objective reality of biological life, its existence, creativity and evolution, independent of human knowing or willing, forms an alternative base than sentience for the recognition of the value of non-human life. Although programmed genetically, chemically and instinctively, organisms even as basic as plankton or mudslappers represent the independent and self-propelling character of life itself. Rolston is therefore critical of those environmental ethicists who identify moral value in nature exclusively with human perception or imputations of value, and those who only value species or forms of life which come close to human experiences of value – beings which experience subjectivity or sentience analogous to human consciousness. In contrast to Regan's subject-of-a-life, Rolston deploys the notion of object-with-will to refer to the objective, autonomous, self-impelled character of all organic life forms. As we have seen, intrinsic value is presented by Hargrove as value which humans confer upon natural objects or organisms as in 'beauty is in the eye of the beholder'. By contrast Rolston proposes that value resides in the object-with-will entirely independently of human perception or value conferral. In this way he defends the genuine otherness of natural objects, and the claims of the other – whether mammal, plant or micro-organism – to flourishing. Rolston's approach to intrinsic value, unlike that of Attfield, also allows him to give objective moral value to biological collectivities such as ecosystems, species and the biosphere as well as to individual life forms. This also means that Rolston, unlike Regan, Singer or Attfield, can generate a coherent moral argument for the preservation of particular species as providing the genetic and biological context in which individual life forms emerge.[43] Similarly, ecosystems and the biosphere itself have moral considerability which is more than the interests of the living parts which inhabit them, for again they may be said to express the *telos* of producing and maintaining a certain number of life forms.[44]

Having established to his own satisfaction the intrinsic – that is external to human perception – value of nature, Rolston goes on to develop a gradient or hierarchy of value by which we may discern between different goods in making decisions about environmental use. His gradient is informed by the idea that the characteristics of different life forms add value to those which manifest a richer character. Thus a monitor lizard is more valuable than a microbe. Therefore in assessing human decisions about environmental use, the goods created for the forms of life with highest value by the destruction of a natural resource must be weighed against the loss of goods which is occasioned for plants, animals and ecosystems. Rolston believes the concept of intrinsic value is capable of providing principles for evaluating decisions about environmental resource use and management by assessing the duties and claims of different levels of value from the micro-organism to the human.[45] In this way Rolston distances himself from biocentric positions which identify value with all living forms equally, and so give no basis for deciding between different courses of action and the balance between human needs and the existence of other life forms.[46]

Rolston provides one of the most carefully nuanced approaches to the ethics of human duties to nature and the intrinsic moral value of the natural world. His combination of deontological and consequentialist arguments, and his recognition of the moral significance of both individual lives and of living collectivities, seem to resolve a number of the problems associated with approaches which rely more on utilitarian and consequentialist approaches to the ethics of the environment. However, his approach to environmental decision-making, while innovative and insightful, does not address many of the factors identified in chapter two above in the alienation between modern civilisation and the natural world. And this is a criticism which may be made in relation to both the consequentialist and deontological positions which I have briefly surveyed. As we have seen, the ecological destruction which is taking place in many parts of the world is intricately connected to the social and technical processes of modern industrialism and capitalism, and to the human injustices of landlessness, enforced migrancy, malnutrition and poverty, to which these processes often give rise. These processes were in turn legitimated by and productive of an account of the meaning and value of human life which was increasingly detached from the moral order of the natural world. This detachment was also a function of the gradual demise of a religious world-view and the rise of modern scientific cosmology. Accounts of the rights or intrinsic value of aspects of the natural world which do not also address these fundamental ideological, moral and social aspects of the environmental crisis may not therefore be sufficient to produce the ecological reorientation of modern societies which the crisis seems to require. As we have seen, modern civilisation manages to combine a very high valuation of aspects of the non-human world, and especially sensate animals, with an unprecedented degree of cruelty to these self-same animals, and with environmental impacts arising from the material and economic processes of modernity which are global in their scale and consequences. It is not clear that the extension of modern ethical discourses to incorporate the utility or rights or intrinsic value of nature will alone generate the resources for the radical reform of the moral and spiritual world-view of modern humans, and the material processes of modern human life, which the environmental crisis seems to require.

ECOCENTRIC ETHICS

Ecocentric approaches to environmental ethics seek to address both issues of ecosystem flourishing, and the underlying spiritual and moral problems which are indicated by the modern human alienation from nature, through an emphasis on the total integrity of the land, and on the moral significance of ecosystems considered as total communities of interdependent life including both humans and non-humans. Aldo Leopold in his classic *A Sand Country Almanac* drew on his experience as a part-time forester and developed a land ethic which is constructed with the aid of ecological insights about the community of life on the land.[47] He argues that ecosystems represent communities of being characterised by competition and co-operation between their diverse parts. The energy flows and nutritional cycles through which the community is sustained have an ethical significance, for by them the diversity of life and the health of each ecosystem are maintained, and therefore humans have duties of conservation in relation to the different parts of each ecosystem from micro-organism, soil, hillside or river-bed to plants and predatory animals.[48] Leopold contrasts violent conquest of the land and invasive farming techniques with 'biotic respect', and the economic commodification of nature with a larger concern for the total ecological and aesthetic value of land. The land ethic is encapsulated in the following statement: 'A thing is right when it tends to preserve the integrity, stability, and beauty of the biotic community. It is wrong when it tends otherwise.'[49]

Leopold's land ethic emphasises the moral significance of the whole, of the community of all life, rather than the moral significance and rights of individual sensate beings within the whole, and this creates a human ecological duty to seek to preserve the integrity and balance of the biotic community or to restore it where human activity has undermined it. Thus advocates of the land ethic argue that the place of predators must be preserved as much as any other species. As we have seen, one of the principal problems of land management in certain areas stems from the reduction or elimination of natural predators such as wolves or lions and the consequent destructive over-population of forest or wilderness areas by such species as elk or deer. The humanly originated loss of these predators creates, according to the land ethic, an ethical duty to limit numbers of destructive species which no longer have natural predators. Advocates of the land ethic would also argue that we have a duty to reintroduce species which in a less ecologically sensitive age were eliminated by the hunter and the farmer. Wolves are now being reintroduced to parts of North America whence they had been eradicated, and some conservationists have argued that the wolf should similarly be reintroduced into Scotland. The principal duty for humans, according to the land ethic, is to preserve the balance of species because moral value is attached to the balanced functioning of the ecosystem rather than to particular individual animals or plants within the ecosystem. Humans therefore also have a duty to limit their own numbers, for excess human numbers occasion the most significant ecological imbalances.[50] Leopold argues that less intensive use of agricultural land, and organic farming methods, are also to be preferred, because these approaches will foster soils and ecosystems characterised by greater biological diversity and which are then more capable of self-renewal.[51]

According to the land ethic, moral duties arise from the communal and systemic character of biotic life in just the same way as certain kinds of moral duties may be said to arise from the nature of human community. As Baird Callicott argues, value in the land ethic is not located in the individual parts but in the good of the whole, in the flourishing of the biotic community and in the balance of all its parts.[52] In opposition to utilitarian or rights ethics, advocates of the land ethic place greater emphasis on the moral significance and preservation of the integrity of the land, and biotic communities, than on the ethical value of particular persons or particular animals. Thus Garrett Hardin argues that wilderness should be preserved by the exclusion of roads and mechanical intrusions of any kind, even including the helicopter of a mountain rescue service. The preservation of the integrity of wilderness takes precedence over the threatened life of an individual fallen mountaineer.[53]

Advocates of the land ethic, such as Callicott, also accept the biological value and significance of pain as part of the natural information system. Instead of making the exclusion of pain the principal ethical aim, and extending this to animals, *pace* utilitarians and animal rightists, advocates of the land ethic locate ethical value in the integrity of the whole natural community, including non-sensate plants or soil as well as animals and humans. Predators cause pain to their prey. The land ethic does not deny this natural behaviour as it is an intrinsic feature of the ecological balance of species. Instead advocates of the land ethic seek to restore the balance between predator and prey, human and non-human in the quest for the wholeness of the system. The application of the land ethic would then involve a reappraisal of the demands of human civilisation on the non-human world and require the moderation of human demands for comfort, pleasure and even the absence of pain when this is at the expense of the integrity of the biotic community. Neither pain nor its absence but the ecological integrity of biotic communities provides the central fact of moral significance for Leopold.

Leopold's emphasis on the inherent integrity of land has a number of resonances with the Hebrew and Christian tradition. The land plays a central role in Hebrew theology and ethics, as we shall see in chapter five below. Land is gifted by God to his people to tend and nurture, but not to own outright or to exploit to ruin. In the earliest Christian traditions the emphasis on land as, in some senses, sacred space is etherealised and detached from the holy land of Israel, and the new people of God, dispersed throughout the Mediterranean region, become the locus of God's saving grace and power.[54] But the emphasis on land returns as the church begins to acquire land and property, and becomes still more central with the emergence of Christendom and of monasticism. The monastic quest for the spiritual life in the desert, and the later formation of agricultural communities around the monasteries in medieval Europe, resonates with Hebrew attitudes to nature, land and wilderness.[55] Leopold and Callicott also emphasise the moral interactivity of human and non-human life in the collectivity of the biosphere, and the moral power of nature to mould and shape human life in ways which are conducive both of human flourishing and of ecosystem flourishing. Again, there are significant parallels with the interactive and relational ethic of the people of God and the land which I argue below may be found in the Hebrew Bible.

However, the ecocentric ethical priority which the land ethic gives to the stability of ecosystems is not consistent with a Hebrew and Christian ethic, for it seems to locate moral value primarily in the biotic community of the land. As I shall argue below, the land community is given distinctive moral value in the Hebrew tradition, but this moral value is fundamentally linked to the human moral and social order. When human life manifests those moral characteristics or virtues which are affirmed in the Torah, and reaffirmed in the ethics of Jesus – love for God and neighbour, fidelity, justice, prudence – then the land flourishes. When on the other hand injustice reigns and traditional communal obligations to God, family, ancestors, children and neighbours are disregarded, then, according to the Hebrew Bible, the land suffers. As we have seen, the experience of the Enclosures in early modern Europe, and in the contemporary Third World, confirms this. When the Highlanders of Scotland were removed from their ancestral lands, within a hundred years the land was denuded of trees by the grazing of too many sheep and deer. Reductions in the diversity and cover of vegetation resulted in substantial erosion on hillsides, in periodic floods on estuarial land and in local climate change. Similarly in contemporary Amazonia when the Yanomami, who have preserved the forests for millennia, are removed from the land by loggers, ranchers, iron smelters and gold panners, the astonishing diversity of the rainforest is rapidly lost.[56]

Human injustice, the subversion of human communities of mutuality and care, and disregard for ancestral claims on lands and the natural inheritance of children, frequently precede ecological devastation. In the first instance, the problems do not originate in a disrespect for the integrity and stability of ecosystems but in the break-up of human communities and traditions which, in many cases for millennia, have developed patterns of human habitat which have preserved the balance of species. The environmental crisis requires then a new ethic of human and social relations which addresses human injustice, and the self-interested pursuit of material gain at the expense of traditional communities of place and land and of the spiritual orientation of human life towards God and the transcendent, of which materialism is so corrosive.[57] If the systematic assault on traditional human communities which precedes the transformation of land into commodity is not first addressed, an ecocentric ethic which emphasises the primary moral significance of land and ecosystems will literally find no space in the world where it may be expressed, except perhaps in limited parklands or small ecological reserves of the kind Leopold himself owned. As I will argue in chapter seven, the recovery of a right relation between human flourishing and ecosystem flourishing in countries where land has already been completely expropriated as a commercial commodity will involve a new approach to human community and patterns of human settlement, and a recognition of the inherent relationship between the flourishing of human moral communities and their location in, and nurture of, particular ecological contexts.

James Lovelock's Gaia hypothesis extends the systemic ecocentric idea embodied in the land ethic into the realm of the molecular chemical structure and processes of the planet. In Lovelock's biochemical model the earth, or Gaia, is conceived as a whole living organism and a self-regulating system manifesting qualities of intelligence which maintain a homeostatic state favourable to the development and maintenance of a biosphere suitable for complex life.[58] While Lovelock denies that his model makes of the earth a teleological system, nonetheless the Gaia hypothesis combines elements of holistic as well as modern scientific reductionist thought. It represents the planet as self-organising and apparently purposive in the sense that the inherent tendencies of entropy to decay – characterised by the second law of thermodynamics – are overcome by Gaia whose 'unconscious goal is a planet fit for life'.[59] Lovelock suggests that the Gaia hypothesis represents the scientific recognition of the ancient belief that the earth is a living entity. The self-organising tendency of Gaia means that Gaia is alive, a kind of immanent mind within the processes and pathways of the earth which may be functionally comparable to the traditional idea of God as sustainer of the life of the cosmos, though Lovelock rejects any theistic interpretations of his hypothesis.[60]

Lovelock argues that as our influence on Gaia grows, so does our responsibility for Gaian processes.[61] The extension of human activity to every corner of the globe means that human interference in the processes of Gaia, especially in the most fragile regions such as the tropics, may undermine the capacity of Gaia to maintain suitable life conditions for humans and other oxygen-breathing mammals, though Gaia herself will find some way of adapting to these new conditions, even if humans do not. In addition to the extension in human numbers, Lovelock suggests that a principal cause of our heedless destruction of the earth is that modern urban humans, and especially scientists, are out of touch with the natural world. Living in the city, conducting experiments in laboratories, modern scientists and their principal beneficiaries, urban humans, have forgotten their dependence upon natural systems and their place within them.

The Gaia hypothesis is suggestive of a democratic planetary egalitarianism which conceives of humans as partners with natural and planetary forces rather than as owners, tenants, guardians or managers. Thus for example, because scientists are still unable to predict what effect the destruction of the tropical forests will have on the world's climates, waters and organic and chemical pathways, we would be wise to see ourselves as parts or subjects of the systems and processes of Gaia, rather than controllers or managers of Gaia. Like Leopold and Callicott, Lovelock therefore suggests that humans must seek to limit the impacts of their own demographic growth, of technological innovation and of the agricultural practices of monocropping and intensive livestock management which are radically changing the surface of the earth and its climate systems.

As with the land ethic, the Gaia hypothesis resonates in some significant ways with the ecological account of the Hebrew and Christian ethical tradition which I develop below. In particular the emphasis on the interactivity of all earth systems – climate, atmosphere, oceans, rivers, land – and the relationality of these systems to human activity is also a fundamental feature of the cosmology of the Hebrew Bible, as I will argue in chapter 5.[62] The order and stability of climate, the predictability of rains and sunshine, the boundaries which prevent the oceans and rivers from flooding and the vegetation which keeps the plains from turning to desert, all of these are fundamentally related, according to the Hebrew Bible, to the providential ordering of the creation for human and animal flourishing. When human society becomes radically unequal and unjust, and abandons the moral law, then the laws of nature are also disrupted; the rains fail, the rivers dry up, the plains turn to desert and the mountains turn to harsh rock.

But the Hebrew emphasis on the moral and biological centrality of human life and community to the purposes of God for the cosmos is of course inconsistent with Lovelock's Gaia hypothesis. Lovelock suggests that Gaia may throw off the human race, rather as a disease-ravaged body finally throws off a particularly invasive organism.[63] Whatever humans may do to the earth, even rendering it unfit for primates, Gaia herself will survive. This kind of extreme ecocentrism is clearly inconsistent with a Hebrew and Christian approach which regards human life as closest in form and purpose to the life of God, and which therefore places supreme moral value on human persons and communities.

Equally an overly mystical and holistic emphasis on the unity and spiritual oneness of all life, which is a feature of the adoption of the Gaia hypothesis by deep ecologists such as Freya Matthews and ecotheologians such as Matthew Fox, though not of Lovelock's own thinking, can seriously distort and subvert the real differences between human and non-human life, and reduce the extraordinary diversity of different parts of the globe to a universalising, mystical oneness.[64] The world is conceived as an all-embracing pantheistic Self or Whole by deep ecologists such as Matthews, but, as Val Plumwood argues, this kind of pantheistic universalism masks the genuine otherness of human and non-human life, and may actually foster the further homogenisation of nature after purely human purposes, and the consequent reductions in the diversity of life.[65] Gaian pantheism, or panentheism as Matthew Fox calls it,[66] encourages us to experience oneness and love for the world as a total concept, but in so doing this approach is in danger of erasing the particularity of place and ecosystem, the diversity of life, the distinctiveness of traditional human cultures and the moral and ecological life strategies such cultures have developed over time to preserve the land in balance with human needs. Imagining the world as one, we remake nature in an anthropomorphic image, and after our needs, and so destroy its very difference from human life. As Plumwood argues, Gaia often takes the place of God in modern ecological mysticisms but the Gaian goddess robs particular life forms of 'their own measure of significance and agency'.[67] In this respect the pantheistic offshoots of the Gaia hypothesis differ radically from the traditional Christian understanding of God as Trinity and of the relationship of God to the cosmos. As Colin Gunton argues, the Christian recognition of the inherent diversity of being and relationality within the divine life guards against the tendencies of ecological pantheism to suppress the diversity of the many into the one, a tendency which, far from reversing the homogenising and destructive tendencies of modern culture towards nature, may simply legitimate them.[68]

The deep ecological philosophy, or 'ecosophy', of Arne Naess has elements in common with the land ethic and the Gaia hypothesis but differs in orientation from them in the place that Naess gives to human consciousness and human community.[69] Naess proposes that a central cause of the modern problem with nature is the atomistic conception of the self which predominates in Western philosophy. The growing moral failure of modern individuals to identify their interests with other living beings, human and non-human, subverts ecological order. Naess believes that we will only reorder our behaviour with respect to the biosphere of which we are a part when we reconceive human self-interest in ecological terms. This reconception of self-fulfilment involves a rejection of utilitarian individualism. Naess proposes that instead of the utilitarian quest for the maximal realisation of individual welfare, typically cashed out in the self-interested quest for material affluence, human self-interest would be better served by the maximisation of the possible relationships which each individual experiences both with other humans and with the diversity of ecological life. Instead of the utilitarian emphasis on the absence of pain, individuals and societies should pursue the positive qualities of personal engagement and mutual dependence.

Naess uses the analogy of mountain-climbing to illustrate his argument. Mountaineering is dangerous and often painful, but happiness in mountain-climbing relates to that inner glow which comes through the experiences of risk and pain of the climb, in reaching the peak of a mountain, in experiencing a beautiful view, in participation in wilderness and the peace of the mountain and in the satisfaction of a strenuous climb completed. These experiences in mountain-walking represent happiness and also its relation to pain in a qualitative manner which contrasts with quantitative utilitarian measures of happiness and pain.[70] Self-realisation involves reaching for an ultimate goal or good which is not just ego-satisfaction. This reaching for the beyond will involve sharing joy and pain with others, both other human individuals and ultimately 'all life forms'.[71] Benevolent and beautiful actions towards other selves, and nature, thus follow as concomitants of the quest for the true self, and of a revised conception of the interests of the self. In emphasising relational self-realisation as the essence of the good life of persons, Naess rejects both the utilitarian humanocentric position and ecocentric positions which oppose human fulfilment and the diversity of nature. In a true quest for the quality of life in which the maximisation of human relational goods are the central aim of social systems and of individual life plans, nature will not be over-exploited. Instead human interdependence upon nature will increasingly become explicit and valued.

Again, there are considerable parallels between Naess's programme and the attempts I make below to construct a Christian environmental ethic, not least his emphasis on the moral and spiritual significance of relationships as the fulcrum of human flourishing. However, Naess's deep ecology suffers from the same problem we have encountered in other mystical styles of ecocentric ethics, and this is the emphasis on self-realisation and the extension of the self to the Whole of nature. Naess proposes that this extension of the self means that the quest for individual fulfilment, and the modern exaltation of self-interest to a virtue, can be accommodated in an ecological world-view, for by caring for the interests of nature, one is caring for the self. However, as Plumwood argues, this approach undermines the real differences that there are between human selves and the non-human world.[72] And furthermore it presents the ethical quest as a quest for oneness, for identity with the whole, and as the attempt to conceive of the other as incorporated into the self. Instead of recognising the interactive limits on self-fulfilment presented by the existence of the other, Naess seems to propose incorporating the other into self, thus allowing for the focus on individual self-fulfilment of much modern philosophy and culture to go unchallenged. But this motif of incorporation, or self-extension, is not so much an escape from a false consciousness about nature as the rationalisation of the remaking of nature in the image of the individuated human self. As with other versions of deep ecology, such as Freya Matthew's ecological self, Naess's conception of the extension of the self into nature still appears to involve the collapse of difference into sameness, the colonisation of other as self, or, as Gunton puts it, the dissolution of the many into the one.[73]

Plumwood argues that the resolution of the environmental crisis will not be resolved by the adaptation of existing philosophical systems in the modern rationalist styles of Western philosophy, such as those proposed by the various advocates of environmental ethics I have briefly surveyed, nor the adoption of a more mystical style of monistic identification with the whole which is characteristic of many deep ecologists and ecofeminists. Instead Plumwood develops the notions of the relational self and the relational society as the keys to restoring more harmonious relations between humans and the non-human world, and she links this approach with the Western tradition of virtue ethics, and the moral traditions and practices of primal societies.[74] In this approach I believe Plumwood comes closer than the other ethicists we have surveyed to the account of the relationality of God, humanity and nature which I shall argue is characteristic of the Hebrew Bible and of the natural law ethic of Christian tradition.

THE RELATIONAL SELF AND ECOLOGICAL VIRTUE

A number of anthropological studies of tribal and indigenous cultures indicate that human relationships with nature, and the conservation of the environment are linked with kinship and community patterns, and with social arrangements and rituals whereby the mutual health of particular human communities and particular ecosystems is sustained and preserved.[75] Edward Goldsmith argues that in indigenous cultures people preserved their environment because their settlement patterns, their technology, agriculture and economy were small and because they were relationally engaged with the limits and constraints of the natural environment.[76] In large settlements, and cities, human culture looses the relationality with nature which characterises the small tribal settlement.[77] Similarly the abstractive power, mobility and growing size of the cash economy undermines the relationality of primitive human exchange and the biological limits imposed on local exchange activity by the constraints of local ecosystems.[78] Human life in small settlements or communities is characterised by a much greater degree of personal interaction and relationality than it is in larger, more anonymous cities. Thus in small tribal settlements relationality with both nature and with other persons is an essential feature of human experience. Persons are known to other persons, and the land, its rivers, streams, animals, trees and vegetation are known to the human communities which live amongst them, and are nurtured by them.

According to Plumwood, the relational character of primitive human communities and social systems is a universal feature of the human moral life but one which is distorted or obscured in modern culture. Whereas modern rationalist accounts of ethics, and modern economic and political practices, are organised around individual self-interest as the primary driver of human identity and social interaction, Plumwood, like Carol Gilligan and other feminist philosophers, argues that the moral consciousness of at least one half of modern humanity, women, and also of primal peoples, is characterised by relationality, connectivity and care rather than atomistic individualism and self-interest.[79] This is why, when Western rationalist and individualist ethical frameworks treat of women's psychological development, or of environmentally beneficent indigenous cultures, both women and indigenous people are usually found to be ethically deficient, for it is said that they lack a clear sense of the separate identity, and ethical rights, of the individual, and the ethical rules required to restrain individualism.[80]

The ethnocentricity and the gender differentiation of Western moral consciousness originates, according to Gilligan, in the structure of the family and in the differentiation of public and private spheres in modern patriarchal societies.[81] Where women do most of the child-rearing, women retain an ethical preference for relationality and care because they continue as adults to identify with the maternal environment. Men on the other hand must distinguish themselves from their early maternal environment in order to establish their male identity in the public world, and this is why they tend to acquire a more individuated sense of self, and an ethic which emphasises self-interest and the rights of the individual rather than relationality and care.[82]

Feminist approaches to ethics point to the situatedness of ethical discourse and behaviour in patterns of relationality, intimacy, connectivity, community and care. They contrast this approach with the universalising and rationalistic tendencies of the modern Western moral tradition which, as Zygmunt Bauman also argues, eschews the normal human discourses of love and care, reciprocity, emotional attachment and familial concern in the quest for a logical, abstract and universal moral discourse of contracts and absolute norms and responsibilities.[83] Instead of regarding normal human moral preferences for family members, neighbours and the local community as ethically problematic, feminists seek to build out from these particular and personal attachments an ethic of care and respect for persons which validates difference and otherness on the basis of a firm sense of the moral significance of personal, familial and local identities and attachments.[84]

The ethic of connectivity and care which emerges from a feminist account of ethical behaviour, and from studies of the moral life of indigenous peoples, also represents a much more effective ethic for overcoming the alienation between humans and nature than the atomistic ethic of individual rights or the categorical imperative of reasoned self-interest, guided by the liberal state or the market's hidden hand, towards an abstract maximisation of aggregate welfare. As Plumwood argues, the feminist account of the moral life 'treats ethical relations as an expression of identity, for example, maternal care as an expression of self-in-relationships, rather than as the discarding, containment or generalisation of a self viewed as self-interested and non-relational'.[85] Thus the attempt of Naess and other deep ecologists to found an environmental ethic on self-interest is shown to be unnecessary. Rather we should allow the relational character of the ethical consciousness of primal peoples, of women, a character which is also of course often expressed by men, and retained in many communities of place and of worship in the West, to reform the Western rationalist account of ethics as the engagement of individuated and competing selves. This relational account of the self involves a rejection of rationalist and market-economic appeals to self-interest as the central denominator of human identity. It involves an ethical validation of the ecological attachments of indigenous peoples, and of local communities of place when they seek to oppose oil-drilling, open-cast mining, motorway extensions, toxic or nuclear waste dumps, rubbish incinerators, waste outfalls from chemical plants into estuaries or air or the polluting effects of the car, in *their* localities, and on *their* land. These local protests against environmental degradation are dismissed and resisted by governments as 'nimbyism', 'not in my back yard-ism'. In the name of universal welfare indigenous peoples are uprooted, communities in the way of a motorway or near a chemical plant are ignored, bought off or even terrorised.[86] But if every community effectively defended its back yard from environmental pollution and destruction, then we would be on the way to a solution to many features of the environmental crisis. And of course all over the world, environmental nimbyism is taking root, as people no longer trust the universalising ethic of the trader, the miner, the accountant, the planner and the government lawyer to protect their local environment.

Some deep ecologists, like most modern moral philosophers, regard personal and partial attachments to particular pieces of land as problematic, as corrupting and self-interested. Thus the deep ecologist Warwick Fox, in his clear exposition of deep ecology *Towards a Transpersonal Ecology*, argues that personally based identification with family and local community and with particular parts of nature known through personal contact are not helpful in preventing ecological abuse and may even be harmful.[87] Instead Fox commends, like Naess, an identification with the whole which is ontological and cosmological, or, in Fox's term, transpersonal. This identification is linked to a pantheistic philosophy mediated through the thought of Spinoza and Gandhi, and to Eastern religious monism which conceives of all beings as essentially One. In Eastern religious philosophy the One may be identified with an ultimate divine principle such as the Buddhist 'Om'. In Western deep ecology Nature is constructed as the One.[88] But this denigration of personal identification and of the spatial as well as personal elements in the construction of human identity evades a fundamental issue in environmental destruction and this is the abstract and distant character of the forces which bring this destruction about. In environmental history the destruction of traditional peoples and their cultures of care for the earth, and the destruction of particular lands and regions of the earth which they inhabit, is mostly associated with colonial traders far from their own lands, with multinationals based thousands of miles away in Wall Street or the City of London and with national governments based in the distant metropolis, who plunder and destroy the ancestral lands of particular indigenous peoples in the name of the greater good, or of stockholders or

voters far away from the destruction. The monistic conception
of the cosmos as a whole is very close, in its degree of
abstraction from the relational and personal character of
human life and traditional interactions with nature, to the
abstract forces mobilised in the global money economy. The
conception of the world as a whole, as one, may not in fact
encourage the love and care of particular parts of the earth
nearly as well as the personal identification of persons whose
very identity and moral orientation has been formed in relation
to a particular river adjacent to the family home, or to the
mountains, fields or forests in which they walked as children. As
Plumwood argues, the monistic and universalising tendencies of
Naess's deep ecology and Fox's transpersonal ecology is a
reflection of the Western rationalist construction of ethics as a
universal and impartial discourse which is essentially opposed
to the particular.[89]

Feminist philosophers and a growing number of anthropologists argue that indigenous communities for many millennia
successfully balanced human settlement and agriculture with
care for their local environment because they treated it relationally, as in some essential way a part of their particular
moral world. As we have seen, when colonial travellers and
traders encountered many of the diverse agricultural, medical
and ritual practices of indigenous peoples they typically dismissed them as primitive and even as harmful to human health
and the environment. Only now, with more systematic study of
the local knowledge of indigenous peoples, are anthropologists
and agronomists slowly awakening to the ecological wisdom
that traditional cultures actually displayed in relation to their
local environments.[90]

The feminist account of the relational character of ethics,
and of the ecological and ethical significance of particular parts
of nature to particular peoples, not only meshes with anthropological accounts of local ecological knowledge, and with the
growth of community-based resistance to environmental destruction, but also resonates powerfully with beliefs and values
concerning land and human community which we find in many
religious traditions, including, as I shall argue in the next two

chapters, the Hebrew Bible, and the Christian tradition. The Hebrews treated of the land as part of their ethical, covenanted community. Their laws and prophets charged them to respect the land, and to recognise moral constraints on its use, because they understood that it was given to them as gift. There is in the Hebrew Bible a deep relationality between the calling of the people of God to live justly and morally and the fertility and goodness of the land. The Christian doctrine of the Trinitarian Creator is also associated with a relational account of humanity and creation.[91] The emphasis on love of neighbour in both Hebrew and Christian traditions is also an important corrective to the universalising features of modern rationalist ethical discourse, and of ecological monism. As the writer of the Epistle to John argues, it is doubtful that a person can be said to love God if he or she does not love her neighbours in a particular worshipping community.[92] Furthermore the Christian natural law tradition locates moral value in a relational account of the common good of humans, non-humans and the cosmos, and in the quest for the diversity of human and non-human goods in particular moral communities where the virtues of justice, compassion and prudence are generated and sustained. It is my intention to demonstrate below that both the primal moral world-view of the Hebrew Bible, and the natural law and virtue ethics traditions of the Christian religion, support a relational account of the nature of the human self and of the interaction of divine, human and non-human life. The anti-relational economic ethic of the pursuit of self-interest, and the rationalist ethic of utilitarian individualism both ignore this relationality in the structure of life on earth. They also fail to generate an account of the rich range of moral goods of human and non-human life which can never be adequately sustained by nation states, and even less by global economic forces, without the moral base of communities of care and nurture in which the virtues of love, justice, temperance and prudence are fostered and sustained.

Alasdair MacIntyre in *After Virtue* locates his account of human moral goods, and of moral qualities or virtues, in the context of the particularity of specific religious traditions and cultural identities.[93] Like Plumwood and Gilligan, he criticises the location of the fulcrum of morality in the conception of the individuated modern self and the reasoning powers of the mind, arguing instead that it is the self in relationship to other persons, social roles and communities, and in the context of particular moral duties and responsibilities, which is at the heart of the conception of the human moral life in all predecessor cultures to modernity. On MacIntyre's account, as on Plumwood's, the recovery of a non-instrumentalist regard both for persons and for non-human life and ecosystems will then involve the recovery of an emphasis on the experiences of mutuality, reciprocity, compassion, care and above all justice, which have traditionally been affirmed as the fundamental moral qualities or virtues in most primal communities and in most pre-modern religious traditions including Judaism and Christianity. MacIntyre argues that it was precisely the virtues of care for and attentiveness towards nature which characterised the agricultural communities of rural England before the cataclysm of the Enclosures. He cites with approval William Cobbett, who observed at the end of the pre-modern era that the agricultural small-holder was the archetype of virtue: 'If the cultivators of the land be not, generally speaking, the most virtuous and most happy of mankind, there must be something at work in the community to counteract the operations of nature.'[94] The 'something at work' was of course the commodification of land after the Enclosures and the new and widespread economic practice of usury 'inflicted on society by an individualistic economy and market in which land, labour and money itself have all been transformed into commodities'.[95]

The reversal of the environmental crisis will not come about simply by a change in our conception of nature, or by the relocation of value in the natural world alone, as proposed by many of the advocates of environmental ethics we have briefly surveyed in this chapter. It will only come about when we recover a deeper sense for the relationality of human life to particular ecosystems and parts of the biosphere, and where communities of place foster those virtues of justice and compassion, of care and respect for life, human and non-human, of temperance and prudence in our appetites and desires, which characterise to this day many of those surviving indigenous communities on the last frontiers of the juggernaut of modernity, and which are associated with the pre-modern religious traditions of East and West, North and South. It is these very virtues in human communities which have been so systematically eroded by the disembedding and dissolving power of mobile economic forces blindly driven by the modern ethic of self-interest. As Plumwood argues, the capacity to experience sympathy and care for non-human life, and for a non-sensate mountain or a river, is a true indicator of moral character, and equally the vandalistic spirit of wanton destruction of natural beauty or cruelty to animals is its converse.[96] But the virtues of justice, care and compassion can only be generated where children experience nurture in stable families and settled communities, and where social and economic forces do not fragment and destabilise these traditional environments of nurture.

An ecological approach to virtue ethics will also involve the recognition of the contribution of particular places and parts of nature to the formation of human moral identity, dignity and purposiveness, and the correlative moral care of these natural environments. As Plumwood, like Rolston, argues, an ecological virtue ethics will involve the nurturing and befriending of particular places in the natural world, and of particular plants and species, as essential parts of the environment of networks and relationships which together construct human identity and the virtues.[97] In the religious traditions which formed the predecessor culture of Western modernity, there is no better exemplar of this conception of the relational community of land and people, and the virtues which this community generates, than the primal ethic and world-view of the Hebrew Bible. But before turning to an exploration of this world-view, which will be the starting point for my own endeavour to construct a Christian environmental ethic, it is important that we consider the responses to the environmental crisis which have emerged in the developing tradition of Christian ecotheology in tandem with the philosophical and environmentalist traditions reviewed in this chapter.

CHAPTER FOUR

The flowering of ecotheology

The popular characterisation of Christianity as an anti-ecological religion is often exemplified in the putative weakness of the Christian response to environmental crisis.[1] However, as I engaged with parts of the enormous literature arising from Christian reflections on environmental issues in preparing this book, it became clear to me that, both in its early origins – writings on the environmental crisis of modern civilisation by evangelicals such as Francis Schaeffer and Basilea Schlink date back to the late sixties – and in its size and ecumenicity, the Christian response is at least as significant as that which characterises the response of humanists, and of modern philosophers in particular, such as those reviewed in the last chapter.[2] Like the philosophical response to environmental crisis, the Christian response is characterised by a range of polarities or antitheses, but these polarities do not simply coincide with those explored in the previous chapter, though there are points of similarity, particularly in relation to ecocentric approaches. I have therefore chosen three headings, humanocentric, theocentric and ecocentric, under which to attempt to characterise the various positions taken up by Christian theologians and ethicists writing on environmental themes. These positions it must be said are often less hard fought than those of the philosophers, and perhaps less hard won also. It will therefore be evident that a number of authors might at times be described as humanocentric, and at other times as theocentric, and even at times ecocentric. But the fluidity of the categories does not I hope detract too much from their heuristic and typological value.

HUMANOCENTRIC APPROACHES

The writings of the Catholic theologian Teilhard de Chardin offer perhaps the most systematic statement of a humanocentric and progressive style of theology which recast the ethics of the human relations with creation in the context of the progressive hominisation of the natural world. Teilhard argues that humanity is the highest form of the evolution of life in the universe and that the unfolding of life is crowned by the emergence of this supremely conscious being.[3] It is humanity's destiny to turn the universe and nature into a more conscious and humanly beneficent place, and to reorder the natural world in order to 'think out again the instinctive impulses of nature so as to perfect them'.[4] Teilhard represents the process by which we will achieve this as the 'self-totalisation' of human consciousness which will through science, technology and research come to encapsulate the whole 'noosphere' and influence the evolution of all subsequent life on earth. Teilhard views the changes which the expansion in human population and technological adaptation are effecting on the earth in an entirely positive light. For Teilhard the hominisation and homogenisation of the earth by the machine and through the expansion of human numbers and new technological powers over nature is a cause for celebration: 'how can we fail to discern in the simultaneous rise of Society, the Machine and Thought, the threefold tide that is bearing us upwards, the essential and primordial process of Life itself – I mean the infolding of Cosmic matter upon itself, whereby ever-increasing unity, accompanied by ever-heightened awareness, is achieved by ever more complicated structural arrangements?'[5] Teilhard is in no doubt that human life is changing the face of the earth and of nature but he celebrates this change as the maximisation of human consciousness over the physical and biological forms of the cosmos. And this consummation of human consciousness is also a Christological event for it is the precondition for the final eschatological establishment of the Kingdom of God on earth. For a Christian who believes in this Christological shaping of the *techne* of modern humanity 'the eventual biological success of Man on Earth is not merely a probability but a certainty'.[6]

Teilhard's optimism and progressivism in relation to the mechanistic age, his total marriage of science and faith, earned him both considerable praise, and criticism, criticism not least from a Catholic establishment who viewed these same developments with much more suspicion. More recent Catholic ecological theologians, most notably Thomas Berry and Sean McDonagh, have sought to build on Teilhard's evolutionary and optimistic theology, but to carry it in a more environmental direction.[7] Thus in his book *To Care for the Earth* McDonagh expounds the Teilhardian creation story of the evolutionary emergence of consciousness as the purpose of the universe, and argues that this new story sets human technological interference in an important new light.[8] If human consciousness is the supreme event of evolutionary development, it has nonetheless occurred very late in the time of the universe and the lateness of our emergence into the cosmos should make us particularly careful about making great changes to the structures of life.[9] McDonagh thus draws entirely the opposite conclusions to Teilhard about the hominisation of the planet, whose extent for Teilhard is the sign of the approaching parousia. These contrary conclusions reveal a deep ambiguity within Teilhard's overall schema. To what extent are we justified in taking this excessively optimistic and human-centred view of the evolutionary process? Are humans capable of being in control of the subsequent evolution of life on earth as Teilhard claims? And even if humans are truly the meaningful and purposive centre of the universe, it may still be argued that the degree of self-totalisation which we are currently visiting on the planet may ultimately be as bad for future humans as it is for non-human life.

A far more critical picture of the modern human relation to nature is painted by Francis Schaeffer, the North American evangelical theologian, in his *Pollution and the Death of Man*, which was written in 1970 at least partly as a response to Lynn White's famous attack on Christianity in the essay 'The Historic Roots of our Ecologic Crisis'.[10] Schaeffer argues that Lynn

White is wrong to blame Christianity's teaching about the dominion of humanity, and its desacralised doctrine of the material creation, for the ecological crisis, and that the pantheistic and humanistic alternatives to these traditional Christian doctrines are much more ecologically problematic. Instead Schaeffer proposes that it is a central affirmation of the Christian doctrine of theistic creation out of nothing that all things are equal in their origins. Everything – humans, trees, mountains – originates from nothing, except God who made the world from nothing. However, humans are distinguished from plants and animals because they are personal, because they are made in the image of God who is also personal. The distinctiveness of personality relates to both intellect and consciousness, which mark off humans from trees or animals, and is the reason for the human dominion over the natural order.[11] But according to the biblical idea of covenant this dominion still involves the recognition of the distinctive integrity and order of each aspect of creation, both personal and impersonal. The incarnation and resurrection of Christ show that God loves material and embodied reality as well as intellect and consciousness, and hence God loves trees and not just persons.[12] The responsibility of humans for creation is properly described as dominion, but, because of the effects of the Fall, the human dominion over nature has been exercised in sinful and corrupt ways. However, Christians are called to be a redeemed people, and also to participate in the redemption of the fallen world. This means that Christians can act to heal the world of sin through acts of love and care for one another and for the non-human world. Thus Christians have a responsibility to value each aspect and order of creation: when chopping down a tree, we should remember it is not just created for human purposes but has an independent value. We should not then waste the product of the tree, and we should not cut down trees needlessly. In conclusion Schaeffer, who established a Christian community called L'Abri in a beautiful Swiss mountain village, emphasises that we are called to treat nature personally, including those orders of the creation such as alpine flowers and mountains which are not personal.[13]

Schaeffer's representation of the integrity of the non-human world anticipates the idea of the intrinsic value of nature advocated by many deep ecologists, even though his conclusions about environmental management may now be considered rather conservative. But he grounds this intrinsic value not in human recognition, nor in human observations of nature, but in the fact that nature is God's handiwork. Nature has value because God made it good and beautiful and further because it is the intention of God to restore not only humanity to full relationality with divinity, but also the natural order.[14] In this location of value in God and not in human acts of valuing, Schaeffer may be more theocentric than humanocentric, even though his conclusions about human actions in relation to nature, and his strong advocacy of human dominion, argue for a more humanocentric orientation in his work.

Schaeffer's writing on pollution and environmental issues is highly significant, for many in the Reformed and conservative evangelical churches continue to dismiss the modern concern for nature and the environmental movement as at best an irrelevance to the only issue of any real import to Christians – the salvation of humanity – and at worst a pagan subversion of Christian culture and civilisation. However, there is now a growing body of writing in the evangelical and Reformed traditions which argues, like Schaeffer, that the environment is deeply marred by the Fall, but that it remains God's good gift to humanity, a gift held in trust, which trust does not permit or legitimate human destruction and abuse of the non-human world. Schaeffer's argument that the abuse of nature by humans is a consequence of the Fall is also taken up by these writers. The alienation between God and humans which is the first effect of the Fall is reflected in alienation between humans and the natural world.[15] Finally and perhaps most significantly of all, the intrinsic valuation of the non-human as God's handiwork is a theme taken up in numerous subsequent writings of a Reformed, Catholic and liberal hue.[16]

Stewardship is a central theme of much humanocentric Christian writing on environmental themes and environmental ethics.[17] It is defended with considerable cogency by Robin

Attfield. Like Schaeffer he argues, against Lynn White, that neither the Hebrew and Christian doctrine of creation, with its separation of creation from creator, nor the concept of human dominion over nature, involve a purely instrumentalist vision of nature which legitimates ecological plunder, because the role of humans with respect to nature is ordered by the metaphor of stewardship through which the Genesis creation accounts describe the human–nature relationship.[18] The tradition of stewardship legitimates the reordering of the non-human world in the interests of human welfare provided this is balanced with a sufficient regard for obligations to conserve the natural world, to protect the moral interests of wild and domesticated animals and to regard the interests of future generations as well as those of presently existing persons.

However, stewardship is a highly problematic notion in ecological terms. The fundamental problem with this metaphor is the implication that humans are effectively in control of nature, its managers or, as Heidegger prefers, its guardians. And yet so much of recent environmental history teaches us that we are not in fact in control of the biosphere. Climate, oceans, ecosystems are all affected dramatically by human actions but these actions frequently produce consequences which were entirely unforeseen by their human progenitors. As Laurence Osborn argues, it may be that stewardship is also unhelpful precisely because of the idea of a steward caring for his master's property.[19] Human experience teaches us that this kind of master–servant relationship is not so likely to produce care and responsibility as a more participative sense of shared responsibility. This does not mean that individual ownership is the only effective means for human preservation of the non-human world, for I argued above that it was the commodification of land ownership with the demise of traditional and communal systems of land tenure which was a crucial event in the origins of the environmental crisis. But instead of stewards of nature we might be better advised to imagine ourselves as members of the community of life which includes humans and non-humans. I will argue in subsequent chapters that a more important metaphor in the Hebrew Bible for humanity's relationship with nature is that of covenant, in which humanity as the people of God and nature as the Promised Land are both represented as members of the covenant community which God establishes with Moses and his descendants.

This metaphor of covenant is taken up in the reflections of the World Council of Churches on environmental issues emanating from a programme established after the Vancouver Assembly in 1983 under the heading Justice, Peace and the Integrity of Creation. A process of international, national and regional conferences was concluded with the issuing of a covenant for the Justice, Peace and Integrity of Creation (JPIC) in 1990 to which member churches of the WCC were called to commit themselves.[20] The covenant emphasises that the creation is the gift of God, and this good gift is being destroyed by the interwoven threats of injustice for the world's poor, violence, genocide, the denial of human rights and the degradation of the environment. Against these threats the covenant affirms that the world belongs to God and so human power is only to be exercised in relation to God's purposes for justice and peace in the world; that God has a particular love for the poor and the vulnerable, including children; that God is opposed to all forms of racism, sexism and classism. In relation to the environmental crisis, two aspects of the covenant are particularly significant. The first is the affirmation in its seventh part of the integrity and intrinsic value of ecosystems and commons, including land, waters, air, forests, mountains and living creatures. It consequently eschews all attempts to treat God's handiwork in creation as merely resources for human exploitation, which are seen as denials of its inherent value. The most distinctive feature of the covenant is the linkage between this understanding of the integrity of creation and human social order: 'The integrity of creation has a social aspect which we recognize as peace with justice, and an ecological aspect which we recognize in the self-renewing, sustainable character of natural eco-systems.'[21] This recognition of the interaction of the divine and human quest for justice and peace, and the self-renewing capacities of ecosystems is then taken up in the eighth affirmation, which links human poverty and injustice, and especially the oppression of indigenous peoples and poor farmers with the degradation of the land and the waters of the earth. Affirming that the land belongs to God, the covenant resists modern attempts to treat all land merely as a marketable commodity, and resists the related threats to the land rights, cultures and spiritualities of the world's indigenous peoples, peasants and poor farmers, and to wild creatures which are also left no space to live. This emphasis on the interaction of human injustice and ecological integrity is also central to the project I am pursuing in this book. As I will argue in the following chapter, this linkage takes its rise from central features of the covenant between God, humans and nature witnessed to in the Hebrew Bible.

The metaphor of priesthood is advanced by Orthodox theologians as more appropriate than that of steward for the human relation to, and responsibility for, creation. Thus in his *Rape of Man and Nature*, Philip Sherrard proposes that 'man is the mediator between heaven and earth, God and His creation' and that it is 'only through man fulfilling his role as mediator between God and the world that the world itself can fulfil its destiny and be transfigured in the light of the presence of God'.[22] In this role 'man' may be described as the priest of God, offering the world to God in praise and worship. But because of the Fall, humans are alienated from the source of their own flourishing, and the true ground of being, which is the Divine Logos, who is Christ. This alienation manifests itself in a particularly dehumanising and ecologically destructive form in the culture of modern science. According to Sherrard, modern science has obscured the essential orientation of humanity towards the transcendent God, and the scientist has taken the place of the priest, bringing to birth a new kind of society oriented to consumerism rather than to the eucharistic worship of God, in which human life and the environment are transfigured by the processes and icons of mechanistic production rather than by the icon of the perfected humanity of the incarnate Christ.[23] Modern science dehumanises humans because it desanctifies nature; the spiritual significance of the created order has been lost for modern humans who believe it to be driven by blind forces and not by personality or grace.[24] In response to this desanctification, Sherrard insists that the Greek Fathers of the church regarded the material world through the prism of the incarnation. Because God is manifest in Christ, we can see that there is no unbridgeable gulf between God and creation but rather spirit and matter may be said to be the 'self-expression of the divine, and the divine as totally present within it'.[25] Sherrard draws an analogy with the Christian sacraments: 'the created world is God's sacrament of Himself to Himself and His creatures: it is the means whereby He is what He is'.[26]

Sherrard's most recent book *Human Image: World Image* takes further his trenchant critique and rejection of modern scientific cosmology in all its forms, and all its discoveries, and contains further reflections on the idea of the Logos as the underlying order of creation, and on the themes of the priesthood of humanity in creation and nature as sacrament.[27] In the antithetical dialectic between science and theology, and the roles of scientist and priest, we can perhaps see the fundamental problem with Sherrard's vision, for his understanding of humanity's priestly mediation between God and creation is but a theological mirror-image of the modern ideology of science as salvation. He rightly challenges the atheistic and salvific claims of modern science, the consequent turning away of modern civilisation from the worship and praise of God, and the consequent denial of the divine origins and spiritual significance of natural order. However, it is doubtful that his humanocentric concept of humanity's priesthood in relation to created order, and his total rejection of the value of empirical observation of the world as a means to understanding this order, is productive of an environmental ethic which allows nature apart from human purposes the space to *be*. As I will argue in subsequent chapters it is precisely the modern scientific method of empirical observation, applied with true ethological consistency to animal sociality and organic connections in the non-human world, which allows us to dare to believe that the non-human world, as well as human society, still contains within it marks of the moral order, as well as the physical design, of the creator God who first affirmed its goodness.

The Orthodox Bishop of Delhi, Paulos Gregorios, argues that the ethical problems of the environmental crisis and the technological domination of the natural world can only be resolved when modern humans learn to balance 'mystery and mastery'.[28] The mystery is the recognition of the salvific effects of Christ's incarnation as a material being, and his sacrifice on the cross, for both human life and the whole creation. In the incarnation Christ becomes part of the created order and in his sacrifice on the cross Christ lifts up the creation to God. Humanity has then a special vocation as the 'priest of creation, as the mediator through whom God manifests himself to creation and redeems it'. Humanity is set apart from the rest of creation by this vocation and participation in the 'eternal priesthood of Christ'.[29] Thus Gregorios affirms humanity's lordship or dominion over creation, and further that it is through technology that we express our God-given dominion or 'mastery' over nature by 'humanizing the world of matter in time-space', thereby 'extending the human body to envelop the whole universe. But that humanizing and extension, if it is to be salvific, must find its proper culmination in man's offering of himself and the universe to God in love.'[30]

Gregorios, like Sherrard, goes on to argue that this priestly vision, with its deeply spiritual view of matter, represents a challenge to the order of ethical values which modern techno-centric economic development represents. He proposes a new pattern of civilisation in which the values of acquisitiveness and aggressiveness are replaced with a more participative social order in which the concern for justice and for the environment will converge.[31] However, it is clear from Gregorios' reflections on humanisation that, perhaps even more than stewardship, the concept of humanity's priestly role in relation to creation is deeply humanocentric and seems to encourage the remaking and hominisation of the whole biosphere in the human image and for the needs of the human body. Nature or creation by this metaphor is denied any independent or intrinsic value. Its value is instrumental and can in no sense be said to reside in and for itself. The metaphor elides or misses the extraordinary difference and otherness of life which is not human and not God, and the potential for non-human life, albeit partially obscured by the Fall, and for nature, like humanity, to render praise to God in its beauty and order. In the Orthodox view nature can only reveal God to humanity, and await its transformation into a human and priestly offering back to God the creator.

Pope John Paul II echoes elements of the Orthodox approach, as presented by Gregorios, in his 1989 encyclical *Sollicitudo Rei Socialis* on human development. He argues that the development of human life through economic and technological progress must be tempered and ordered by a new moral concern both for justice and for ecological limits.[32] Modern human development is threatened both by super-development, characterised by an excess of material goods and enslavement to possessions, and by underdevelopment, the converse of super-development, where so many people do not have the means to meet their basic biological needs. The disorder of super-development and underdevelopment can only be challenged by the recognition of the spiritual as well as material nature of human life, and the directedness of human life towards divine transcendence and human immortality. The quest for development remains nonetheless a divinely given vocation to dominate and transform the world so as to improve the human situation and condition. But the effects of immoral development endanger the order of creation as industrial pollution threatens human health and life quality. In recognition of the ecological problem, the Pope argues firstly that we must not view created things from a purely economic viewpoint, but rather, 'the nature of each being must be respected for itself and in its relationship with the rest of the created order.'[33] Secondly we must recognise that there are limits to biological resources, and if we simply use them at will, 'as if we were their lords and masters', we endanger both our own lives and those of future generations. Finally the Pope suggests that in our dealings with the natural world we should respect the biological and moral laws which are inherent in its nature.[34]

The most extensive Papal utterance on environmental questions is Pope John Paul II's message on the World Day of Peace in January 1990 entitled *Peace with God the Creator, Peace with All of Creation*.[35] In this message he argues, like Schaeffer, that the origin of the environmental crisis is original sin. Adam and Eve were given dominion over the earth but because they chose to sin they undermined its created harmony and rebelled against the creator's plan.[36] It is not humanity's vocation to dominate the earth which is at fault however, for according to Genesis this vocation always had limits, hence the command not to eat of the fruit of the tree. But humanity's rebellion against God turns just domination into environmental destruction. However, in Christ, the Pope argues, the creation is redeemed and restored, just as humanity is redeemed and restored. The extent of environmental destruction in modern civilisation is a consequence of spiritual ignorance, or a wilful turning away, from these redemptive and restorative events. Because so many modern humans have ceased to recognise the effects of original and personal sin, they have adopted the idols and instant gratification of consumerism. Respect for life and especially human life, issues from believing that there is a God and that 'there is an order in the universe which must be respected, and that the human person, endowed with the capability of choosing freely, has a grave responsibility to preserve this order for the well-being of future generations'.[37]

This Papal message is the fullest expression, at the time of writing, of a contemporary Vatican view on the ecological problem. It is deeply humanocentric but the judgement concerning the significance of a prior order in the creation, and the human duty to preserve this order, if only for future generations, is nonetheless a significant one, and the concept of created order is one which I will develop further in this book, though in a less humanocentric direction. However, subsequent Papal encyclicals on ethical issues, notably *Veritatis Splendor*, and *Evangelium Vitae*, indicate that the humanocentrism of the modern Vatican remains ecologically problematic, for at least two reasons.

Firstly the Vatican remains implacably opposed to any form

of artificial birth control, which is described in *Veritatis Splendor* as intrinsically evil, a remarkably strong condemnation in the light of the silence of the encyclical on so many more obviously evil tendencies in modern civilisation.[38] This opposition has tremendous implications for human population growth, especially in majority Catholic countries in the Third World, where, unlike in Italy or Poland, the population is still growing rapidly, and where less educated Catholic believers are less likely to resist Papal teaching and the exhortation of their parish priests on grounds of conscience.

Secondly the moral presuppositions on which the Pope relies in his encyclicals are exclusively focused on respect for human life, and the priority of human moral goods. Thus in *Evangelium Vitae* the Pope speaks of humanity's dominion over and responsibility for all life, and of the biblical respect for the 'great good of life, of every life', but only human life has sacred significance.[39] Thus only human life is the object of the revealed moral law, and of the moral laws of the church and civil society. Amidst the many ringing condemnations of the failure of these laws in modern societies to protect the human embryo or the unborn child there is no single reference to the immoral treatment and loss of dignity which so many millions of farm animals and birds experience, also at the hands of modern technology, and which technology is visiting on all forms of life throughout the created order. This encyclical, with its powerful theological and ethical argument for the value of human life against the dehumanising tendencies of modern technology and modern society, is a powerful reminder of the limited ecological vision of the present Pope and his advisers.[40] We can of course account for this in historical terms for there is little evidence in the recent past of modern Catholicism attending to ecological issues. However, it is in the reliance on a humanocentric account of natural law in *Veritatis Splendor* that I believe the answer to this ecological unconcern is to be found. Although, as I shall go on to argue, the pre-modern natural law tradition involved a deep understanding of the moral significance of created order, and of all the orders of life from material to animal as well as human, the Papal concept of natural law and of the moral goods which this law advances, prevents the recognition of any intrinsic moral goods, or moral value, in the non-human created order. This deeply humanocentric interpretation of the Christian tradition of natural law reflects the Papal reliance on a modern philosophical revision of this tradition, and in particular on the work of John Finnis and Germain Grisez, both of whom accept without challenge the divorce between natural order and moral order of modern scientific cosmology and modern moral philosophy.[41] In the remainder of this book I intend to argue that natural law, which is a central feature of the Christian moral tradition, actually provides significant resources for an ethical response to the environmental crisis of modern civilisation, but only if the humanocentric revision of this tradition by Finnis, Grisez and the Vatican is rejected in favour of an ecologically informed reappropriation of the pre-Enlightenment natural law tradition, focused as it was not just on human life and human moral goods but on the moral significance and moral goods of the natural created order.

Finally under this heading of humanocentric approaches I want to consider the writings of Rosemary Radford Ruether. It is perhaps part of the richness of her theology that it is not at all obvious under which heading to place her contribution, for she does indeed seem to combine rather more than most theologians, elements from all three styles of approach to which my headings point. However, I think we are justified in considering Ruether's ecofeminist theology as humanocentric because she constructs her ecological theology on the basis not of a new account of nature, nor a new account of God, but of her critique of patriarchy and the ecofeminist account of the normative significance of the experience of women for human relations with the non-human world. Her recent book *Gaia and God* provides the most extensive and systematic account of her views, and she commences by affirming the ecofeminist judgement that the oppression of nature and the oppression of women have a common root in the patriarchal structures of Western societies.[42] The answer to the oppression of both women and nature is a new human social order which eschews domination and instead is characterised by relationships between men and women, between races, and social classes, of love and justice.

The domination of women is linked, Ruether argues, with the idea of a male monotheistic God who is separated from the creation. Women are construed in patriarchal cultures as closer to the earth, because of menstruation and child-bearing, while men are construed as being more ensouled and godlike. The answer to this problem is not though simply to replace the male transcendent God with an immanent female Goddess. Ruether argues that in any case patriarchal religion has by no means simply fostered attitudes of oppression towards women and nature. At least in their struggles against injustice and evil, the prophets, apostles and saints of the Hebrew and Christian traditions may be said to have represented both the interests of oppressed women and oppressed nature as well as of men. Ruether finds the roots of the oppression of women and of nature in Western culture in what she identifies as the Platonic denigration of the body, and Platonism's pessimism about the possibility of material embodied life achieving goodness.[43] This Platonic pessimism is translated by Augustine into a disembodied asceticism and a patriarchal assertion of the necessity of male power and control over the body and society represented through military power and state control. The consequent ideology of male domination is reiterated in the medieval fear of the power of women, in the witch-hunts of the Reformation and in the urge to dominate and tame the wild forests and animals of the natural order in both Catholic and Protestant Europe.[44] The ascetic fear of the body and of nature is mediated in Reformation theology to the cosmology of early modern science, which further entrenched the dualism between nature and humanity, bodies and spirit, animals and women encapsulated in Cartesianism, and in the Newtonian evacuation of God from the cosmos. The recovery of a non-oppressive religion of 'earth healing' will then involve the attempt to overcome the divorce between spirit and matter, between God and cosmos, reason and organism, science and religion. But, Ruether argues, a changed ideology will be of no practical or ethical use if it does not also involve a new set of relations and social structures in which oppression, domination and deceit are replaced by love, participation, truthfulness and justice.

Ruether then explores a number of attempts to heal the dualisms which she identifies at the root of the modern problem with nature, and she is drawn to two approaches, the first being the tradition of covenant between God, humanity and the natural order. At the heart of the Hebraic covenant tradition Ruether finds an inter-connection between human history and nature which is represented by the inter-connection between human justice and the fertility and goodness of the land described in the Psalms and the Prophets. Hebrew thinking links God and humanity to the natural order through the concept of the gift of the land. But if Israel pollutes the land then God's blessing on Israel will be removed. The Hebraic covenant in other words attests to a relationality between human social order, divine blessing and the goodness of the land.[45] This first strand in Ruether's thinking is one that I shall also explore more fully in the following chapters, and seek to appropriate in the construction of an environmental ethic which is grounded both in this biblical covenantal tradition and in traditional Christian theism.

It is in relation to traditional Christian theism that we find Ruether being much more radical, and ecocentric. The second strand in Ruether's ecotheology, which she describes as the sacramental tradition, is much influenced by the accounts of Teilhard, and of the process theologians, of the ubiquity of consciousness in all orders of life in the cosmos from humans and mammals to fish, plants and even sub-atomic particles.[46] Drawing on the insights of process thinkers, and the modern science of quantum mechanics, Ruether argues that all physical reality, right down to the macroscopic level, is characterised by inter-connectedness and relationality, 'and thus what we have traditionally called "God", the "mind", or rational pattern holding all things together, and what we have called "matter", the "ground" of physical objects, come together'.[47] This coming together means that the ancient and modern dualisms are overcome and we can once again see ourselves as humans, body and soul, as parts of an inter-connected whole from which we cannot abstract ourselves by some rational or technological device. Again drawing on process insights, Ruether argues that consciousness itself is not distinctive to human life but that different kinds of consciousness or interiority are experienced at every level of material existence from mammalian life to the energy events of atomic structures.[48] As a result of this aware-ness, an ecological spirituality will be awakened to human kinship with all organic life, but at the same time it will continue to affirm the centrality of personal being, and the recognition that ecological destruction can only be reversed when the lives and societies of human persons are reordered by compassion for all other persons, and for every living thing.[49]

The ethic which issues from this 'sacramental' cosmology, and the revised theology of covenant, is fundamentally an ethic of equity, equity between men and women, between races and nations and between human and non-human species.[50] Ruether argues that human societies need to be restructured by a 'biophilic mutuality' which reverses the trend of technological exploitation of the natural world. She proposes a number of quite specific initiatives to effect this reversal, such as the phasing out of the use of non-renewable energy sources, increases in mechanical efficiency – for example the abolition of the inefficient private car in transportation systems – and the reinvention of local communities in which land, species and natural resources are more effectively conserved and more equitably shared. The new ecological society will also be a society in which male individualism and egocentric power is transformed by the feminine awareness of inter-connectedness and relationality. Above all Ruether suggests we need to reaffirm the vital role of local communities in which the bio-sphere is locally valued and nurtured, and the global trends of militarism and multinational domination are resisted and re-versed.[51]

There are many valuable insights in Ruether's ecotheology. She attempts to conserve much of the Christian tradition from the excessive deconstructionism of much feminist criticism, and at the same time to seek out the potential of biblical, doctrinal and liturgical traditions – particularly the sacraments – for an ecologically restored theology. In her biblical reflections on covenant in the Bible, in her attentiveness to ecological insights about the interdependence of life on earth and in her understanding of the ambiguities of sin and evil in both nature and humanness, Ruether is much closer to the Christian tradition than many other ecofeminists who prefer to abandon central tenets of the faith rather than seek to revise the faith in the light of modern threats to the created order.[52] Alongside these more traditional themes and emphases, she also embraces some of the central tenets of process theism and of biocentric egalitarianism, without exploring the full implications of these for more traditional and biblical versions of Christian theism. But in her practical ethical conclusions Ruether clearly envisages that humans will continue to use nature instrumentally to meet human needs, to overcome poverty, to provide not only food and shelter and warmth but also cultural richness and indeed resources for ritual and religious celebration. It is then clear that her values and priorities are closer to the covenantal tradition which she expounds at the heart of the book, revised by her appropriation of modern feminism, rather than by a biocentric or ecocentric egalitarianism.

THEOCENTRIC APPROACHES

The primary candidate for a theocentric approach to environmental theology must surely be Jürgen Moltmann's pioneering ecological theology *God in Creation*, and his subsequent volume on related themes *The Spirit of Life*.[53] The central theme of these volumes is that God as Spirit is indeed *in* creation; he inhabits the world of matter and ecosystems, plants and birds, animals and humans. But this immanence does not mean that God is entirely identified with the creation, for God as Trinity is both related to the creation as Son and Spirit, and distinguished from the creation as Father.[54] This pneumatological cosmology is counterposed with the mechanistic cosmology of modern science, but it can also help to elucidate less mechanistic and more developmental and holistic understandings of life on earth. Thus the immanent Spirit can be said to work through matter and organic life creating new possibilities of being, and at the same time the Spirit is the holistic principle which creates and harmonises the interactions of life forms into a community of life.[55] The Spirit is then both the principle of individuation and of differentiation guaranteeing the ontological significance of the myriad life forms in the cosmos, and their relationality to the one holy and transcendent God.

Moltmann seeks to ground an ecological valuation of nature then in a revised doctrine of God, a revision which he justifies with numerous biblical and patristic references. There are many other significant themes in his work, some more speculative and much criticised, others equally well grounded in Christian tradition and in ecological insight, and particularly his elaboration of the Sabbath as the crown and final destiny of creation. Moltmann develops the theme of the Sabbath in the Hebrew Bible and argues that from the first Sabbath the creation is perceived as being on the way to redemption and completion, and is only completed in the rest of God on the seventh day, a redeeming rest which blesses and hallows the work of creation.[56] This Sabbath hallowing is affirmed in the Sabbath laws of Israel and the Jubilee commands requiring that the people of God allow the land and their farm animals to rest as well as taking rest themselves, and in the resurrection of Christ on the Lord's Day, the Christian Sabbath or Sunday, for the resurrection anticipates the final redemption and completion of creation at the eschaton.[57]

Moltmann's theological insights are a rich source of ecological theology. They are however not without problems, as his critics have argued. In relation to environmental ethics, not least of the problems is how we can construct a theory of values in creation and the environment when according to Moltmann's avowed 'panentheism' God as Spirit is in everything including presumably the smallpox virus and the louse. Moltmann comes very close to biocentrism in his way of stating the relation of the Spirit to life on earth, though at other times he sounds equally humanocentric.[58] Another danger with Moltmann's approach is his tendency to overvalue the dynamic and changing character of the cosmos, to overstate the orientation of the destiny and time of humanity and nature to the future and thus to devalue, as most moderns do, both the past and present as past and passing moments on the way to the future. This future orientation reflects Moltmann's reliance on progressive modern philosophers such as Bloch and Hegel, whose philosophies of progress are, as I argued above, deeply implicated in the roots of the ecological crisis of modern civilisation which always restlessly prefers change to stasis, and reorders the non-human world under the presumption of progress even where the reordered world may at times represent a regress in terms of the richness of non-human life and even in terms of the richness of human goods.

A more traditional approach to a theocentric ecological theology and ethics is that developed by James Nash in his book *Loving Nature*. Nash argues that the intrinsic value of the creation is established by its original and ongoing relationality to the creator God who loves all the objects of the creation, from stars to starfish, who gifts the world to all living creatures and not just to humans and whose redemptive purposes include not only human life but the earth itself.[59] Nash goes on to argue that the whole creation is therefore a locus for communion between God and humans and a means of grace which may be described as sacred and sacramental, and that the primary mode of relationality between God and the creation remains that of love. In the incarnation God makes this love for matter and creatures and humans fully and materially known by becoming a body and a person. Christian ecological responsibility may then be most appropriately described in terms of the generosity and grace of divine love, which characterises all God's relations with the earth, and of which all human acts of loving are a reflection. Nash considers the kinds of action which emanate from an ecological ethic of love and these include: beneficence to wild creatures, and Christian activism to clean up the environment; esteeming the otherness of non-human creatures as having a legitimacy independent of human identity; humility in the face of the awesome beauty and diversity of life and the cosmos, receptivity to the interdependence of all life and the nurture of life and ecosystems beyond their utility to humans; and justice which includes not only recognition of the rights of humans but also of the inherent though relative rights of non-human life. These relative rights to life and dignity may only be overridden for just human causes including the satisfaction of proper human needs, both biological and cultural.

Nash's approach to ecological love is reminiscent in some ways of E. O. Wilson's idea of biophilia, but Nash's conception of love for nature is rooted not in the ecological explorations of Wilson, but in an understanding of divine love, and the centrality of divine love and intentionality to the purposes of the cosmos as well as to human life.[60] Nash identifies this understanding of ecological love and relationality as the 'theocentric kinship of all creation', a kinship in which the moral and relational interdependence of all orders of life in the cosmos is affirmed.[61]

The value of Nash's approach to ecological ethics is that it is deeply theological. He generates a Christian environmental ethic, and an account of the political implications of this ethic, from a wide-ranging exploration of the ecological implications of Christian doctrines from God and creation to sacraments and the eschaton. There is, however, a certain lack of system in Nash's approach which manifests in an unwillingness systematically to critique the real roots of the ecological crisis in modern civilisation, or to generate a systematic account of an environmental ethic which makes linkages between the attitudes of love for nature and its intrinsic value and the actual procedures and processes of modern human social and economic life. Nash develops a number of ecological 'middle axioms' but these mediating principles are not given much flesh in terms of alternative political, economic and social models. His book remains, though, one of the clearest attempts to outline a Christian approach to environmental ethics.

A number of Christian theologians writing on environmental problems have, like Nash, proposed that the earth is a sacrament of the divine, a means of grace. This approach which we have already encountered in the modern Orthodox tradition, seems to arise there less in response to environmental crisis than as an alternative to the mechanistic cosmology of modern science.[62] But the sacramental approach also seems to appeal to the scientifically trained theologian, as we see it taken up by both Arthur Peacocke and John Habgood.[63] These Anglican theologians point to the incarnational significance of a sacramental approach to matter and life. According to Peacocke, the incarnation reveals God's 'pattern of activity' towards all matter and created things, a purposive pattern of redemption, so that the world of matter can be said both to express the mind of God and be the means by which God achieves his redemptive purposes for both humanity and nature.[64] The enormous value of a sacramental approach, as Habgood points out, is that it makes of every Sunday eucharist a powerful ecological parable of the capacity of matter itself to be redolent of the redemptive purposes of God for the creation and to mediate God's grace to the eucharistic participants. The transformation of bread and wine into elements which mediate the presence of Christ is a reiteration of the potential of all material existence to reveal God's grace.[65]

Stephen Clark in his *How to Think About the Earth* also makes the case for a sacramental and theistic approach to ecological issues, arguing, like other sacramentalists, that God is embodied in the creation as Spirit, and that the incarnation confirms the divine and graced potential of all material and embodied life.[66] The most distinctive feature of Clark's approach is his exploration of the Christian doctrine of atonement which he finds has a number of implications for a Christian approach to nature. Firstly through the death of Christ our debts to creation, to animals and trees as well as to people against whom we have sinned, are paid, and we are liberated from guilt. Instead of guilt and shame at the degradation of the earth we are given a new view of a creation restored by atonement which may help us to harm and waste less of the non-human world.[67] Secondly the recognition of the need and appropriateness of judgement on evil reminds us of the seriousness of evil, both as it damages humans and non-humans. This recognition in itself may help to encourage us to change our ways; to forgive our debts, as ours have been forgiven, not least debts from Third to First World, and to demand less, especially less wealth, from others and from nature. Clark affirms that beyond judgement there is a new order of life and peace, and that this new order is implicit in the act of atonement. The new heaven and the new earth are not simply a metaphorical dream but a firm Christian expectation that the God who raised Christ from the dead will one day also transform the earth, and restore the polluted and ravaged land.[68] Like Nash, Clark demonstrates the riches that there are in the mainstream Christian tradition for an ecological theology, though, again like Nash, Clark resists the more radical rereading of Western Christian thought of many deep ecologists and ecotheologians.

Finally under this heading I will consider the writings of Andrew Linzey whose first book *Animal Rights* was a pioneering work on animal rights and welfare from a theological perspective, published in the same year as Tom Regan's *The Case for Animal Rights*.[69] However, having rehearsed earlier some of the issues concerning animal rights, I want at this point to consider Linzey's more recent work, and in particular his desire to find a more theological, and theocentric, way of expressing the moral value of animals other than the language of rights. In his *Christianity and the Rights of Animals* Linzey argues that the key to the recognition of the independent moral value of the creation lies in our doctrine of God as the generous creator who values all that is created.[70] We will only be able to reorient ourselves from our modern anthropocentric abuse of the non-human world when we have allowed our horizons to be set by a more God-centred or theocentric vision of life. This God-centredness is the product of daily spiritual practice, and not least of contemplation on the beauty of the creation, and will bring to us a love and sensitivity towards all that God values.[71] Linzey then explores the concept of covenant in the Hebrew Bible, observing that the covenant community included not just humans but animals as well, and that the redemption which the covenant promises to humans is also promised to sentient animals which are also enlivened by the Spirit, and may in this sense be said to have souls much as humans do.[72] Thus the modern love of animals, and the moral recognition of their rights, is not sentimentality but a sign of holiness and grace, for in Christian history it was saints such as St Antony and St Francis who from the depths of their love for God came also to love deeply the animals amongst whom they lived.[73]

To this theocentric perspective Linzey attempts to wed his earlier emphasis on the rights of animals, which now become 'theos-rights'. It is because all creatures are Spirit-filled individuals that we can affirm that they have rights, for these rights rest upon the 'objective right of God in creation'.[74] Against Tom Regan, Linzey argues that these rights of animals are not reliant on any inherent features of the animals themselves, but simply depend on their status as the living, breathing creatures who are enlivened by the Spirit of God. Linzey recognises that this approach might leave him open to the charge of mammalocentrism.[75] However, his earlier reflections on the significance of God's valuation of all creatures, including birds, fishes and perhaps even plants, allow him to argue that his position is broader than that of utilitarians and animal rightists whose prime environmental concerns remain those of the pain and suffering caused to individual animals, for even slugs and earthworms may still evince from us a duty of respect – it is simply that because they are not ensouled, they do not have rights. The rights of individual sentient animals remain Linzey's prime concern, but there are within his theology elements of a broader environmental ethic, elements which are also hinted at in his most recent work *Animal Theology*.[76]

ECOCENTRIC APPROACHES

In 1972 John B. Cobb wrote a path-breaking book on Christianity and the ecological crisis entitled *Is it Too Late?*[77] The book is significant not just because it is one of the earliest texts of Christian ecotheology, but because it establishes a new ecotheological paradigm which has been highly influential amongst most North American ecological theologians of a liberal theological persuasion, both Catholic and Protestant. This new paradigm reflects the influence of the scientific philosophy of Alfred North Whitehead and his interpreter

Charles Hartshorne and has come to be known as process theology.

Cobb finds the roots of the ecological crisis in modern philosophical and theological attitudes to nature which, as I have also argued above, represent nature as an essentially material realm from which nothing may be learnt of any moral or spiritual or metaphysical significance. This modern dualism between God and nature is also mirrored by a dualism between humanity and nature which, Cobb argues, we must overcome if we are to address the crisis. We are most likely to be able to do this by reconceiving human history and the history of nature as an essential unity.[78] Humans are a part of evolutionary history and we should therefore imbue the matter, organisms and life forms from which we have evolved with intrinsic value, for these sub-human elements, living and non-living, existed '*in* themselves as something *for* themselves'.[79] This 'evolutionary philosophy' represents a challenge to what Cobb calls the humanocentrism of the 'dominant philosophy' because it emphasises the incipient purposiveness of all life, non-conscious and conscious, whereas modern philosophy only recognises human consciousness as the source of value and genuine moral purposiveness, and regards the rest as brute matter or mechanism.

Cobb goes on to expound the roots of this new approach to nature in the new organic and evolutionary philosophy of Whitehead who argued that the world was and had always been characterised by a process of being in becoming, and that each stage of life, each new event in the evolutionary process has intrinsic value, and particularly those events which add to the harmony, intensity and diversity of the world.[80] Each event in the past is organically related to life as it is now experienced, and events and life forms in the present are also relationally connected in the total environment which is life. So instead of human experience, and especially reason, being that which is the measure of all things, as humanocentric philosophers would have it, it is the degree of richness of each event in the evolutionary process which is the measure of all things. The events in this process are guided by God, at every point. God is *in* every event, is affected by, suffers or is enriched in all that happens, and coerces and compels the processes of life in certain directions.[81] This approach involves a very different understanding of God from the transcendent God of Christian tradition, as Cobb recognises. We might, he says, be better to abandon the word God and speak instead 'of Life, of Nature, or of Creative Process. Perhaps we should speak of the Word or of Christ, since the everywhere active, suffering, persuading, life-giving reality who emerges from Whitehead's analysis is recognised by him as manifest in a peculiar way in Jesus.'[82]

Cobb's embryonic exposition of the ecological value of process theology is developed in greater detail in subsequent works, and by other authors, but its essential insights are clearly and concisely advanced in *Is it Too Late?* The later book which he writes with the biologist Charles Birch, *Liberating Life*, clarifies the position with respect to the relationship between God and life, with its explicit statement that Life may be called God, and its argument that God and the world – by which is meant the universe – are coterminous because 'God includes the world' and 'there is no God apart from some world'.[83] It also clarifies the ethical procedure which follows from process theology for although intrinsic value is located ubiquitously in all events which contribute to the life process, nonetheless certain of these events lead to, or are imbued with, richer and more intense possibilities than others. For this reason the organic, relational life of the cell is to be preferred to simple atoms and molecules, and an organic universe to an inorganic one, and the richness of human and mammalian subjectivity is to be preferred to the subjectivity of the cell or the plant.[84]

Cobb's ecotheology is a rich brew and there are many sub-themes and alternative pathways which supplement the central paradigm. However, it will be clear from even this brief exposition that Cobb's approach is a dramatic departure from traditional Christian theism, and has much in common with the holistic, mystical and ecocentric deep ecologies which we explored in the last chapter. At some other points in the present book we will return to a more recent work of Cobb, written with the economist Herman Daly, *For the Common Good*, which has many valuable insights about the economic and political implications of ecological crisis.[85] But there is some doubt that these insights depend in any systematic way on the process theology of Cobb, whose almost total identification of life and the universe with the being of God is subject to the same criticisms made in the last chapter concerning the homogenising and totalising tendencies of some versions of deep ecology, while it also poses grave problems for Christian theism. The ecological advantages of a suffering and living God who is wholly immanent in the world are clearly that such a God is diminished when species are extinguished, is harmed when the oceans and the air which sustain life are polluted and suffers when animals are subjected to terrible pain in laboratories or in cruel factory farming systems. However, equally, as Clark points out, such an immanent suffering God is also by definition a God who is the progenitor of all this evil and suffering.[86] A God who is totally identified with all life is a God who commits a tremendous amount of evil, including not only natural evils such as parasitism but also human evils such as genocide, vivisection and species extinction. The problems for theodicy are surely greater than the problems of historic Christian theism, for the traditional Christian belief that humanity and the world are in some ways corrupted by the Fall means that we can see that natural evil and humanly originated evil were not a part of God's original good will and design of the cosmos. Furthermore, process theology may be no more environmentally beneficent than the technocentrism and humanocentrism of the 'dominant philosophy', for by eliding the genuine difference or otherness between humans and nonhumans, plants, cells and atoms, as well as between God and that which is not God, process theology, like Naess's deep ecology, seems to present a homogenising view of the natural world which may simply encourage its further hominisation, for it undermines the legitimate difference and otherness of the different orders of matter and life in the cosmos.

Jay B. McDaniel defends process theology against the charge of inadequate theodicy in his *Of God and Pelicans*, in which he specifically addresses the moral problem of natural evil and predation by positing that the life process, and the series of events which, according to Whitehead, constitute this process, are not entirely under God's domain or control.[87] According to McDaniel the events which make up the evolutionary process are inherently creative and spontaneous; there is a creativity in matter and in life which is not predetermined or ordered by God.[88] This independence of matter and life from God is inherent in the original chaos of energies from which God fashioned the world. God creates order out of this chaos, but the universe, and each individual energy event, retain the possibility of novelty, and hence of choosing a harmonic or a discordant path. God's intention for all matter and life is relational harmony and integration but this intention is only an offer of possibilities. The creatures themselves – from atoms and cells to mammals and humans – must make the choice of which possibility to take up.[89] God was unable to prevent animals and humans from evolving in ways which led them, at times, to cause pain to one another, because of a 'necessary correlation' in the very nature of life between the capacity for intrinsic good and the capacity for intrinsic evil.[90] However, at this point it becomes clear that this is not so much a resolution of the problem of evil as its dissipation into a new kind of metaphysical dualism in which God and the cosmos, good and evil, are posited as growing and developing side-by-side, mutually interpenetrating each other, and indeed at times apparently coterminous with each other. It is indeed strangely reminiscent of the early Christian Gnosticism in which matter was regarded as both inherently evil and beyond redemption, hence the Docetic tendency to disallow the embodiment of God in the human person Jesus Christ. Redemption in McDaniel's schema is also a long way from a traditional Christian understanding of it. The redemption of humans and sensate non-humans from experiences of pain or frustration will only come about when enough creatures, though evolved to a point where they are free to diverge from divine aims, nonetheless choose to respond to 'the divine lure' of redemption. Just as we are in McDaniel's terms co-creators with God, we must also become co-redeemers if the world is to be transformed from a realm in which some pelican chicks invariably die in pain, and in which humans inflict pain and suffering on animals and drive species to extinction.[91] Again the departure from Christian orthodoxy here is so dramatic as hardly to need stating. The problem with this kind of ecotheology is that it departs so far from a recognisable Christian theism as to be hardly recognisable as Christian belief.

McDaniel, though, argues that such radical adaptation of Christian belief is required both by evolutionary theory, and by the nature of the ecological crisis, and he goes on to develop an account of environmental values consistent with his exposition of process theology. He proposes that animals in particular have rights and intrinsic value along with humans, but unlike Linzey he argues that these rights are independent of God's ascription of value or rights to the creation, just as they are independent from God's ordering will in the events which make up the life process of which they are a part. God is not so much the origin of values and rights in the natural world as the one who lures or 'beckons us into a respect for those rights'.[92] This non-theistic origination of rights is very similar, as McDaniel acknowledges, to Regan's deontological case for animal rights: they simply *are* because of the intrinsic nature of animal life. But McDaniel goes beyond Regan in ascribing values beyond sentient life to 'all of nature's existents – from plants and bacteria to rivers and stars'.[93] However, it is still possible to value a dog more than its parasitic ringworm for the dog has more strength of psyche – more soul – than the parasite. Finally McDaniel enunciates his principle of ordering values with reference to the Whiteheadian notion of the degrees of harmony and intensity or richness that different life events, and different originators of these events, manifest. Thus human experience, being the most intense and potentially most harmonious form of consciousness, is the most valuable, while animal experience is derivatively valuable but less so than human consciousness, and multi-cell organic life is more valuable than single-cell life and so on. McDaniel's statement of a process derived environmental ethic is clear and concise. It leaves, however, a number of problems, both for the traditional Christian theist, and the environmental ethicist. Since value is identified with harmony and richness, rather than with, say, the being of God, or the nature of personhood, McDaniel's approach leaves open the possibility that human life may not be the most valuable kind of life in all circumstances: it is quite possible, for example, to imagine a group of dolphins or elephants who have a richer emotional life, and a more harmonious set of social relations, than some groups of humans who through disability, senility or plain evil, manifest neither the compassion of the weeping elephant, nor the communicative richness of the chattering dolphin.[94] Why, given this possibility, should we value the human group over the animal group on McDaniel's value theory? Another key moral problem with McDaniel's approach concerns the origin of the compassion and empathy towards the expression of which, he argues, God lures all life. By his own admission, in the nature of things good and evil are equally present in the order of the cosmos. There is no fundamental ontological or metaphysical priority of the one over the other. If this is the case, what grounds do we have for hoping that humans can ever, as a species, become more empathetic towards the non-human world, with its inferior intensities and harmonies? The traditional Christian view of the Trinitarian God sustains hope in the triumph of good over evil, firstly because the original order of life, which is still perceptible though obscured in the world, is a fundamentally good and moral order, and secondly because this original goodness is affirmed in the triumph of good over evil in the death and resurrection of Christ who is of the Trinitarian God. Our hope that humans may be better does not then rest solely on incipient human qualities but also on the original order of creation, and the restoration of that order through the infusion of divine grace into human life which begins in the Christ events, and which is sustained, though never fully realised, in life in the Spirit. Though McDaniel often uses Christic and redemptionist language it is clear that his use of such language does not have this traditional Christian import. And this leaves us, many Christians would argue, without hope that good will triumph over evil, and that the world will indeed be redeemed and restored in the

good purposes of God who is not only *in* all, but *over* all in
traditional Christian theism.

The mention of original goodness in the last paragraph
brings us to the ecotheology of the former Dominican theologian Matthew Fox, whose elaboration of a 'creation spirituality'
develops the implications of process theism in an even more
avowedly revisionist, and pantheist, direction.[95] *Original Blessing*
is the title of Fox's major treatise on creation spirituality and
the title points to its primary theme, which is that the creation
was characterised in the beginning by the blessing of God on all
that came to life, and this blessing remains paradigmatic for the
nature of both human and non-human life on earth.[96] He
argues that our modern abuse of the environment derives at
least partly from the Christian desacralisation of nature, which
is closely related to the Augustinian doctrine of original sin:
'original sin grew to become the starting point for Western
religion's flight from nature, creation, and the God of creation'.[97] The doctrine of original sin represented creation and
human life as inherently sinful, and human sexuality and the
body as morally suspect. The consequence was that the original
biblical teaching of the goodness of creation and of embodied
life, human and non-human, was obscured in post-Augustinian
theology, and that pleasure, desire and sensual love were
regarded with deep suspicion, and the fertility and beauty of
creation were no longer seen as agents or means of divine
grace. Fox proposes that the primary Christian doctrine with
regard to creation and life is not original sin but original
blessing. The doctrine of original blessing encourages us to take
pleasure in our bodies, and in the earthiness and fertility of
creation: it releases in us the power of Eros and fertility both to
order our own lives without the directing power of priests and
prelates who, under the doctrine of original sin, seek to gain
control over the lives of the faithful, and to reorder our relations
with nature so as to participate in its cosmic harmony, beauty
and justice.[98] Participation in the original blessing and justice
of creation is the key to human fulfilment. Humans are not
called to transform nature but rather to integrate their life and
society into the prior order and harmony of the cosmos.[99]

Fox rejects what he calls 'fall/redemption' theology because of its false dualism between subject and object, human and non-human, body and soul, God and nature, blessing and sin. Instead of dualism Fox proposes relationality, balance, harmony, blessing, as the deep structure of the cosmos and of human life. However, Fox is still left with the problem of human evil, and of natural evil. He resolves this problem with a new kind of dualism, or as he prefers, dialectic,[100] one with which we are already familiar from process theology, between good and evil, harmony and disharmony, life and death, pleasure and pain: these are all equal options created by God for the creation to follow in all its parts. Fox identifies these options with the two paths of creation spirituality which he calls the Via Positiva and the Via Negativa. The Via Positiva emphasises blessing, awe, harmony, fertility, pleasure, beauty. The Via Negativa recognises and affirms the reality of pain, suffering, nothingness and death. These negative experiences are the shadow-side of God and of original blessing: God is both light and darkness, the creator of blessing and of nothingness.[101] We are conceived in the dark, and the creation is birthed in the dark heart of God. We are called then to 'dare the dark', to embrace nothingness and pain as redemptive experiences and energies.[102] Redemption for Fox involves then the balancing of these two ways, the light and the dark. We have, like the Wikkan goddess worshippers to whom Fox often refers, to learn to dance the circle of life, to weave the web which catches both the sensual lure of erotic desire and pleasure and the sensual stimulant and energy of pain.[103] The death of Christ points the way to this redemptive balance of the positive and negative pathways by teaching us that the fear of death is to be embraced rather than eschewed.[104]

This new theology is of course an even more explicit departure from traditional Christian theism than the process theologies of Cobb and McDaniel. The theological problems are numerous and yet there are many profound insights in Fox's rereading of the tradition which a more traditional ecological theology might also draw upon. These include his emphasis on the original goodness of created order, a goodness which is not wholly destroyed by the reality of sin, although of course in Fox's system the value of this affirmation of original goodness is somewhat eclipsed by his conception of the equal and negative power of non-being, nothingness, darkness and evil. Fox's affirmation of embodiment and sexuality, and the links between human embodiment and fertility and the embodiment and fecundity of the natural order, is also an important counterbalance to the tendency of the Christian tradition in both East and West to regard the body and sexual activity in particular with some suspicion. Finally the affirmation of sheer joy, pleasure and praise in the wonder, fertility and diversity of creation is a powerful corrective to the distorting orientation of so much Christian worship and doctrine towards the corrupting potential of natural instincts, and the joyless suspicion of pleasure in much moral exhortation. However, for traditional Christian theism Fox's theology presents serious and fundamental problems: the duality of good and evil which is read into the being of God; the location of redemption in the balancing of these tendencies in human and non-human life rather than in the redeeming of humanity and nature in the life, death and resurrection of Christ; the adulation of erotic power as exemplified in the frequent references to the writings of Starhawk and Wikkan ritual and belief with their embrace of eroticism and pain, and their worship of the elements as representations of God; and finally the sacralisation of the created order as the body of God. Fox's pantheism, like that of McDaniel, reduces God to an almost entirely immanent being whose identity with the cosmos is so complete that we cannot distinguish his good will for creation and human life from the occurrence of so much evil and suffering.

The environmental ethic which issues from Fox's creation spirituality is primarily an aesthetic ethic, reflecting once again the influence of Whitehead.[105] Human creativity is the evidence of the image of God in us, and we are charged as co-creators to evoke in artistic and creative achievement the perfections of harmony which are around us in the natural order.[106] Through disciplines which are directed towards this aesthetic recreation of harmony – painting, meditation, gardening, furniture-making, child-rearing, music-making – we will acquire a truer sense for what is valuable in the created order and in human life. Fox develops a theory of human work in which he argues that work is primarily oriented to aesthetics rather than economics and that true work involves the transformation of the world towards a greater harmony and beauty. He also emphasises the significance of what he calls erotic justice, by which he seems to mean compassion, particularly between First World and Third World peoples.[107] Again, traditional Western theism is said to be at fault here, for its notion of justice is cold and distancing. Instead we need an immanent justice which identifies with the victim, which remakes the broken chain of relationships against the distancing and unjust processes of global warfare and global capitalism. Fox's aesthetic value theory is rarely explicit though about precise environmental issues and conflicts, or about the relative rights of different orders of life. The sweep of his writing is towards the harmonic oneness and relationality of all things. The ethical problems with this approach are again similar to those already rehearsed in relation to process theology and some versions of deep ecological holism.

The ecotheological tradition of panentheism, represented by Fox, Cobb and McDaniel, finds perhaps its most explicit advocacy amongst those, mostly feminist, theologians who propose that the most effective cosmological model for our ecologically endangered times is to conceive of the world as the body of God. Grace Jantzen in *God's World, God's Body* argues that we need to resacralise the world of matter against that tendency in the Western Christian tradition to oppose divine being and material substance. God in Jantzen's view *is* matter and bodies.[108] Identifying the material world as God's body, she rejects the traditional Christian dualism between an eternal, immaterial, invisible, timeless God and the contingent, material, embodied cosmos: 'the model of the universe as God's body helps to do justice to the beauty and value of nature'.[109]

Sally McFague in *The Body of God* proposes that the metaphor of embodiment is the most effective model for the ecological revisioning of relationship between God and the world in

Christian thought, but she differentiates her position from the more thoroughgoing materialistic immanentism of Jantzen.[110] However, although she argues that her proposal is analogical and metaphorical, and that she is not actually describing God as having a body,[111] she nonetheless goes on to argue that both God's immanence *and* transcendence can best be conceived as being embodied in the world: God is an 'embodied spirit', the 'inspirited body of the entire universe'.[112] This model is adopted because it coheres with and sustains an organic model of the world in which all the parts of the world are relationally inter-connected, and, McFague argues, to conceive of the world in this way is more likely to produce ecological respect for the environment than a cosmology which conceives of the world, and bodies, mechanistically, and God as being outside of and distant from the material and embodied cosmos.[113]

This new ecological theology of God's embodiment issues in an understanding of sin as not so much our rebellion against God as our refusal to 'stay in our place, to recognize our proper limits so that other individuals of our species as well as other species can also have needed space'.[114] Ecological sin causes us to devalue and harm animals and inanimate nature; it also causes us to refuse to appreciate the difference from us which animals and inanimate nature represent. The recognition of the legitimate otherness of nature should lead us to restrain our demands and our wants so as to allow the non-human space to be. But McFague also argues that our respect for nature will evolve further when we come to value nature as a whole by extending our self-definition, as Naess also suggests, to incorporate not only family and friends, and not only animals, but the whole planet.[115] She wants in fact to argue both for the affirmation of difference and of holistic self-extension and identity. However, her model of the earth as the body of God runs the danger of all pantheistic and monistic systems of removing the transcendent ontological ground of difference and conceiving the whole, and its various parts, as extensions of the God/self to which we all belong.

Again, as with McDaniel and Cobb, McFague's ethical orientation is towards the aesthetic: 'if God is physical, then the aesthetic and the ethical unite',[116] for the vision of the world as the body of God encourages us above all to praise the beauty of this body, and to nurture its wholeness and harmony in a more ecological life-style. This life-style will be characterised by the recognition of the biological needs of 'other life-forms, and not just human ones', the need to 'allow space for other species', the human vocation to nurture life and in particular to identify with the oppressed of the earth, including the 'new poor' which is nature: 'a shift in paradigm from the modern construct to the organic one involves decentering our species individually and collectively in terms of both numbers and life-style and recentering us as the species responsible for helping the rich, varied, interdependent community of individuals of many species to continue'.[117] Finally, McFague concludes, the embodiment of God is rightly conceived as an embodiment in every particular body in nature from bears to rainforests. This recognition means we must not use nature instrumentally, as a means to an end. Instead we should ascribe intrinsic worth to every creature.[118]

McFague thus tries to combine aspects of an individualistic and a collective environmental ethic, and attempts to nuance the monistic tendencies of her pantheistic and holistic metaphor of the body of God. But as with other pantheistic and holistic approaches, McFague's ecological theology seems to offer few practical glimpses of how we might actually discern between the needs of different species and organisms, given her intrinsic valuation of every living and even inanimate particular as God-breathed and inspired. Nor does she give us a clear account of how we might understand natural evils such as predation.[119]

Like Fox, McDaniel and Cobb, McFague compromises or abandons central elements of Christian theism in her ecological theology in the hope that her new pantheistic metaphor of the relation of God and the world will inspire a new more ecologically friendly civilisation, and yet she actually offers little evidence for this belief. Why should a monistic cosmos which is identified with God lead us to respect the vulnerable more than the powerful? If God is identified with life so completely then does it not follow that, since the human species has come to dominate and hominise the planet, that God has done this as well, as indeed Teilhard argues? Does God catch a cold when we catch a cold? Is God in the atoms which were split apart by a nuclear bomb on Mururoa Atoll as I wrote this chapter? The answer according to McFague is that whatever happens, 'happens to God also and not just to us'.[120] But this leaves too many questions begging. I suspect that she does not press the logical problems very far because she claims that her theory is analogical.[121] However, in this case, one wonders of what elements might it actually be true to say, in relation to her metaphor, 'God is really in *this*.' Christians have usually affirmed this of the incarnate Christ, and to a lesser extent of the elements of the eucharist. Is God *more* embodied in Christ than s/he is in my body, or the body of a bear or an elephant? If God is no more truly in Christ than s/he is in the elephant, then what grounds do we have for discerning between what is God and what is not God, and hence what is God's will and what is not. The answer is not clarified by the simple claim that all religious language is analogical. Environmental philosophers do not resort to this linguistic sleight of hand. Why then should ecotheologians?

The traditional Christian answer is of course that the revelation of the scriptures, and the revelation of Christ, are both means by which God directly addresses humanity, and not only in metaphor. Killing people is wrong, cruelty to animals is wrong, not because these acts are ugly, nor just because of their consequences, but because they are opposed to God's mind, God's revealed and incarnated will. Christians, like Jews and indeed many other religionists, have also mostly affirmed that moral guidance may be had from the created order, in addition to the revelation of God in the Bible and in Christ. But for McFague, as for McDaniel, Fox and others, the order of creation as described by modern science is so deeply morally flawed that we dare not read the mind of God from it. As McFague herself says, ecotheological pantheism is a radical attempt to combine the anti-teleological world-view of modern science with a version of theism.[122] However, as I have argued above, this post-Enlightenment divorce between teleology and physical reality, between the physical reality of the cosmos and the good purposes of God for the creation, between created order and moral order, is precisely and centrally related to the roots of our modern problem with the natural order. It is because we no longer regard the world as morally ordered that we treat it as we do. Perhaps, though, this explains why we find pantheists such as Fox and McFague avoiding discussion of the real moral conflicts which living together in a physical universe actually raise, because there is according to their dialectical pantheism of good and evil, pleasure and pain, no clear direction towards the good, or the goods, to be gained by a closer scrutiny of the created order. The irony is that whereas secular environmental philosophers such as Holmes Rolston and Val Plumwood are prepared to discuss a hierarchy of value and moral goods on the basis of their reading of value in the natural order, we find the more radical ecotheologians stepping around this territory precisely because their analogical language does not permit of these kinds of discrimination between what is actually, truly, right and wrong.

CONCLUSION

As I argued at the commencement of this chapter, the complete identification of the evolutionary history of life on the planet, including human life and history, and the purposes and intentions of God for the cosmos which we find in ecological pantheism, whether that of Teilhard, Cobb, Fox or McFague, has as much potential for a humanocentric as for an ecocentric perspective, as well as producing a whole range of philosophical and moral problems in relation to traditional Christian theism, and in relation to environmental values. It is in any case unclear that 'non-dualist' or monist accounts of a sacralised nature necessarily produce a greater respect for nature. Most modern Japanese hold to one or other variety of Shintoism, which has just such a monistic perspective on nature, identifying the gods of Shinto belief with particular features of the natural order, and yet Japan as a nation is one of the most ecologically rapacious in the modern world. Despite their love for the formal Japanese garden, Japanese industrialists and consumers throw away every year whole forests of teak, merbau and mahogany as disposable chopsticks or disposable concrete mouldings in the construction industry, while within Japan the mercury poisoning of rivers and oceans, or animal welfare issues, attract very limited environmental protest.[123]

The new ecotheological pantheistic orthodoxy, so popular amongst North American theologians, can drive us either to the optimistic adulation of human progress and the anthropogenic homogenisation of the non-human world such as we find in Teilhard or to the deep ecological sentiments of Fox or McFague. The reason for this moral and ecological ambiguity in pantheism is precisely because, as we have seen, it offers no grounds for distinguishing the being of God from the life of creation, and therefore seems to offer no philosophically defensible account of moral evil. But the environmental crisis is rooted in moral evil and human guilt, and in the turning away of modern human civilisation from God's order and redemptive purposes for the world and human life. The destruction of the non-human world is a consequence of sinful individual actions and of structural sin in the social processes which together produce environmental destruction, as Schaeffer argued twenty-five years ago and as Ruether argues with great clarity in *Gaia and God*.[124] While Fox claims that his pantheist creation spirituality offers the only hope for ecological redemption, we should recall that cultures which share this deeply naturalistic picture of God or the gods often account for ecological disaster and other evils as the will of God, as fate or *karma*, and therefore as features of reality which it is futile to resist. This may help to explain why there is less public protest and resistance to ecological destruction in Japan than in countries with a less monistic view of the non-human world such as Germany or the Netherlands.[125] It is quite possible that resistance strategies towards environmental abuse, and other forms of human evil, may actually be undermined by the demise of the categories of sin and moral evil in ecological pantheism.

In what follows it is my intention to demonstrate that the siren calls for the remaking of Christian belief by many ecotheologians in the light of the environmental crisis, and the rejection of central elements of Christian theism which are held to be at fault, have not only misrepresented the Christian tradition, but have also obscured the potential of essential features of the Christian theological and moral tradition to reorient modern Western and Christian-influenced civilisation towards a more harmonious relationship with the non-human world. I will argue that more traditional interpretations of the doctrines of creation, Trinity, incarnation, redemption and eschatology can in fact provide us with a powerful model of embodied human life, and of self-in-relation, which challenges the atomistic and denatured self of post-Enlightenment utilitarian individualism, and which has the potential to reorientate the modern human project of economic development towards the preservation of central moral goods in human life including sociality and community, and towards the recognition, and conservation, of related moral goods which may be identified in the natural order. I intend also to begin to indicate how we might arrive at a more precise ordering of human and non-human goods and values from moral resources within the Christian tradition – and particularly the natural law tradition – than the vaguely egalitarian value theory which is associated with Christian ecocentrism.

In the next chapter I will propose that a relational and ecological account of the human self-in-relation and of the non-human world is suggested by an anthropologically informed reading of attitudes to the created order and the relationality of human moral and social practices with nature which we find in the Hebrew Bible. In chapter six I will then pursue this theme of relationality through the Christian tradition by an exploration of the ecological implications of the incarnation and resurrection of Christ, the Christian doctrine of the Trinity and the last things. I will then seek to outline an environmental ethic which draws on insights about the relational character of created order and the moral life which we may find in the Jewish and Christian tradition of natural law. In the final chapter I will pursue the implications of this natural law approach to environmental ethics for contemporary political and economic practices.

CHAPTER FIVE

The order of creation

In this chapter I intend to demonstrate that the Hebrew Bible, which is central to the religious traditions of Judaism and Christianity, presents the non-human world as a created order which is redolent of the purposes and providence of the creator God, though it is ontologically distinct from the being of God. The purposive order of the cosmos reflects the will and design of the creator. But this order and purposiveness does not exist in a relational vacuum. The Hebrew Bible offers a fundamentally interactive account of the relations between the human self, the social order and natural ecological order, and between all of these and the being of God. This understanding of the interaction between humans, nature and God offers a significant contrast with modern ethical individualism and subjectivism. The Hebrews believed that moral values and purposes were enshrined in the nature of created order. Similarly the Christian doctrine of natural law represents a belief in the moral purposiveness and relationality of the cosmos, and in the relation between the human quest for the common good and the goodness of created order and the other orders of being which inhabit the creation. Thus the moral life may not be reduced to individual human intuitions and emotions, nor may moral judgement be limited to human experience and society. Rather the physical reality of created order, the community of human and non-human species and the ends and purposes which they differently serve, are given in the nature of the creation, and this is why in so many diverse cultures, with no shared religious revelation or truth system, ethical principles such as neighbour love, sexual fidelity and care for the natural environment are widely practised. As Oliver O'Donovan puts it in *Resurrection and Moral Order*, 'the way the universe *is* determines how man *ought* to behave himself in it'.[1]

On this view the natural order is not simply identified with the being of God, as modern pantheists or panentheists such as Fox would have it, but rather is said to reflect the wisdom, goodness and ordering hand of God. The relation of creator to creation is a relation between orders of being which are different in kind and ontologically distinct. Natural created order reflects the being, wisdom and goodness of God in the Hebrew tradition, but this is not to say that the natural order may be monistically identified with the being of God as it is in many non-dualist religions. In the Hebrew concept of created order, and the Christian tradition of natural law, the order and goodness of creation is affirmed as *reflecting* the being of God, and therefore as having a moral significance which is related to the moral purposes and goods of human life. Furthermore human society is to be so ordered as to reflect the justice and goodness of the creator God who has provided the abundance of nature to all living things, and especially for human enjoyment and fulfilment.

I will go on to argue that the primal reverence of the Hebrew traditions for the goodness and wisdom of created order is cognate with the beliefs of contemporary environmental philosophers that natural order and ecological community are essential features of the identity of the human self-in-relation, and that we neglect the relationality of natural and human community at the risk of bringing chaos into the biosphere and anarchy into human social life.

ORDER OUT OF CHAOS

It is difficult for those of us educated in the canons of modern science to imagine how novel and peculiar is the modern denial of *telos* and purpose in the non-human world. Almost all the people who have ever lived, and most people alive in the world today whose religious and cultural traditions have resisted the secularising influence of Western culture, believe that nature is characterised by purposive order and equilibrium which has a deep moral, social and spiritual significance. The anthropologist A. R. Radcliffe-Brown observes that in primitive cultures such as that of the Australian aboriginal, the natural order and the social order are not separate entities but parts of a single order of reality.[2] Disruptions in the predictability and order of the natural world are regarded by primal peoples as evidence of disruption or disharmony in human social order. The maintenance of the order and stability of the natural world and the eschewal of chaos are therefore the central goals of ritual and social and moral systems in primal societies. In the modern world, by contrast, social systems and rituals are constructed without reference to natural systems of order or ecological balance. We build houses on the flood plains of rivers, or on the sides of volcanoes, and blame natural disorder when these houses are inundated with water or buried in larva. We clear cooling forests to rear beef cattle and plant monocrops of groundnuts and maize on fragile savannah and complain of capricious nature when the rivers dry up and the land turns to desert. Modern scientists and ordinary mortals alike are more likely to interpret natural catastrophe or the breakdown of the predictability of natural events such as monsoon rains or temperate seasons as evidence of the chaotic character of the natural world, than as evidence of human foolishness or interference in natural systems. The sometime fertility or predictability of nature is said by many moderns to be merely a human construct rather than evidence of the moral goodness or order of the natural world.

The primal sense for natural order and the primal explanation of natural chaos as evidence of human or cosmic disturbances to this order are not, however, limited to aboriginal peoples. Most of the world's religions share this reverence for nature and the primal awareness of the inter-relationships between human moral life and the order and goodness of the non-human world. Christianity is usually associated with an instrumentalist doctrine of creation which is opposed to this primal world view. This instrumentalist stance is identified with the vocation of humanity, as described in the first creation story of Genesis, to 'have dominion over the fish in the sea, the birds of the air, and every living thing that moves on the earth'.[3] As we have seen, Lynn White and others argue that the concept of dominion is associated with the ruthless exploitation of both living and non-sentient natural resources, particularly since the end of the Middle Ages.

However, in a new anthropologically informed study of the Hebrew Bible, *The Cosmic Covenant*, Robert Murray finds that the Hebrew texts reflect the same awareness of the relationality of human and non-human life systems which characterises all primal cultures, and that the 'dominion' text is misunderstood if it is taken to legitimate an instrumentalist approach to natural systems. Murray argues that there is a profound recognition of a precarious balance between created order and cosmic disorder running through the Hebrew Bible, and he argues that the rituals and laws of the covenant community of Israel are designed to preserve and restore this order, in the face of those cosmic or human forces which threaten to disrupt or overwhelm it.[4]

Murray identifies traces of an earlier creation story than the Genesis myth in different parts of the Hebrew Bible. In this early story the process of creation is conceived as the control of chaos, and the imposition of order and covenant on the raging forces of the cosmos. This tradition is expressed for example in this passage from Jeremiah in the hints of the sea as a power which has to be tamed and controlled:

> Have you no fear of me, says the Lord,
> will you not tremble before me,
> who set the sand as bounds for the sea,
> a limit it never can pass?
> Its waves may heave and toss, but they are powerless;
> roar as they may, they cannot pass.
> But this people has a rebellious and defiant heart;
> they have rebelled and gone their own way.[5]

This primitive idea of the confrontation between the chaotic powers of nature and the ordering power of God forms a central part of the Hebrew concept of covenant, according to Murray. In Jeremiah 33. 20–6 the same word for covenant is used of God's ordering of night and day, and God's blessing of the line of David and the Levites: 'if you could annul my covenant of the day and my covenant of the night, so that daytime and night would not come at their due times, then might my covenant with David my servant be annulled'.[6] The ordering of time and seasons, of oceans and rivers, of deserts and fertile plains, all may be said to belong to the matter of the covenant, and to the divine blessing on king David and the society he ruled. The cosmic covenant involves a fundamental link between the natural order and the social order of Israel and especially the stability and health of her king.

The covenant which was established after the Flood offered the promise that the fruitfulness of the earth would not again be threatened by the bursting forth of the chaotic waters and that Noah and his children would themselves be blessed. It was a covenant made between God and humans 'and living things of every kind',[7] and affirmed that God's ordering of the cosmos would not be again abandoned:

> While the earth lasts
> seedtime and harvest, cold and heat,
> summer and winter, day and night,
> shall never cease.[8]

The terms of the covenant witness to the relation between cosmic order and human order, and the covenantal context in which all life pursues its purposes in the cosmos.[9] The covenant is not simply between humans and God, as anthropocentric exegetes have traditionally held, but is rather a 'cosmic covenant' involving all the orders of creation and linking them with the rituals, ethics and society of humans.

The principle of created order which unites the Genesis 9 account of the covenant and the Genesis 1 account of the original goodness and fruitfulness of the earth takes a liturgical form, according to Murray.[10] The promised succession of day and night in Genesis 9 confirms the centrality in Genesis 1 of the fourth day of the creation in which the great lights are set in the heavens to order the day and the night and to order the times of festivals and seasons and years.[11] This liturgical principle reflects the primal belief that the sacred worship and rituals of human communities interact with the order of nature and the cosmos, and the primal reverence for natural forces as signs of the power and order of God. This relation between human social order and cosmic order is substantiated in the accounts of rituals and in the ritual texts in the Hebrew Bible.[12] Many of these rituals, particularly the liturgies, songs and prayers of the Psalms, refer to the king, and especially king David. The relation between the fertility of the land and the health and wisdom of the king is a dominant theme in Canaanite and Babylonian religions and it finds a strong echo in many of the Psalms:

> O God, endow the king with thy own justice,
> and give thy righteousness to a king's son,
> that he may judge thy people rightly
> and deal out justice to the poor and suffering.
> May hills and mountains afford thy people
> peace and prosperity in righteousness.
> He shall give judgement for the suffering
> and help for those of the people that are needy;
> he shall crush the oppressor.
> He shall live as long as the sun endures,
> long as the moon, age after age.
> He shall be like rain falling on the crops,
> like showers watering the earth.[13]

The orders of the creation, the lights of heaven, are linked with the wisdom and justice of the king, and the fertility of the land with his continuing reign and prosperity. The function of the worship of Yahweh in this cosmology is performative and exemplary. Murray finds evidence of rituals which are designed to subdue hostile forces, and rituals concerned with the bringing about of shalom. The Psalms of Asaph, in particular Psalms 74–79, display elements of rituals designed to preserve the order of heaven and earth and to sustain the blessing which issues from the cosmic covenant,[14] to subdue those human and cosmic elements which still tend to disorder and to invoke the divine name and power as the supreme authority over all earthly powers and forces.[15] At the same time the retelling of the stories of creation and exodus in the temple has an exemplary function, to remind the people of the character of Yahweh,[16] and commend his kindness and compassion for the poor and the alien,[17] as well as his power and might to put down the elements which tend to disorder and chaos.[18]

The true worship of Yahweh is also clearly linked to respect for the natural order in the summary of the law in Exodus, the Ten Commandments. Treating nature as divine gift rather than as an object of worship is inherent in the first commandment to abstain from idolatry of the natural order and instead to worship God alone.[19] From worship of the true God issues both moral order in human life, and harmony in the natural order. Just as cosmic harmony and order are associated with true worship rather than idolatry, and with the divine blessing on the king who worships the God of compassion and justice and rules righteously, so unjust kings, and kings who abandon the true worship of the Lord for the idolatries of graven images or military conquest, are said to be the cause of disharmony and disorder in the land. The divinely originated created order in the cosmos is subverted when the rulers of the people fail to worship the Lord and respect the covenant law of God:

> But this people has a rebellious and defiant heart,
> they have rebelled and gone their own way.
> They did not say to themselves,
> 'Let us fear the Lord our God,
> who gives us the rains of autumn
> and spring showers in their turn,
> who brings us unfailingly
> fixed seasons of harvest.'
> But your wrongdoing has upset nature's order,
> and your sins have kept from you her kindly gifts.[20]

Jeremiah clearly links ecological devastation and the abandonment of the worship and commands of the Lord. Because the people of Israel had turned from the Lord, their land, its mountains and streams, animals and crops, would be laid waste, polluted and destroyed:

Does the snow of Lebanon vanish from the lofty crag?
Do the proud waters run dry, so coolly flowing?

And yet my people have forgotten me; they burn their incense to a
   Nothing.
They have lost their footing in their ways, on the roads of former
   times, to walk in tortuous paths, a way unmarked.
They will make their country desolate, everlastingly derided:
every passer-by will be appalled at it and shake his head.[21]

The prophetic reading of ecological breakdown points to an
apparent conflict between the grand projects of the Hebrew
monarchy, and the unequal society it spawned, and the fertility
of the land, the welfare of the created order. The pride of kings
had denuded valleys of great cedars for their massive building
projects, and the wealthy grew richer while the poor went
hungry. The land suffers and shares in the alienation that
human corruption produces:

> Woe betide those who add house to house
> and join field to field
> until everyone else is displaced,
> and you are left as sole inhabitants of the countryside.
> In my hearing the Lord of Hosts
> made this solemn oath:
> 'Great houses will be brought to ruin,
> fine mansions left uninhabited.
> Five acres of vineyard will yield only a gallon,
> and ten bushel of seed return only a peck'.[22]

The devastation of the land is not only seen as the judgement of
a wrathful God. It is also interpreted as the consequence of the
human rebellion against the created order and wisdom of
nature. Profligacy, waste, greed, injustice and idolatry are all
sins which are contrary to the created order instituted by God,
and so they undermine the goodness and harmony of that
order:

> See how Yahweh lays the earth waste,
> makes it a desert, buckles its surface,
> scatters its inhabitants,
> priest and people alike, master and slave,
> mistress and maid, seller and buyer,
> lender and borrower, creditor and debtor.
> Ravaged, ravaged the earth,

despoiled, despoiled,
as Yahweh has said.
The earth is mourning, withering,
the heavens are pining away with the earth.
The earth is defiled under its inhabitants feet,
for they have transgressed the law, violated the precept,
broken the everlasting covenant.
So a curse consumes the earth
and its inhabitants suffer their penalty,
that is why the inhabitants of the earth are burnt up,
and few men are left.[23]

As we have already seen, environmentalists have often argued that the Hebrew and Christian tradition involves an exploitative disregard of the natural order and that this has given rise to the ecologically damaging attitudes and behaviour which have brought us to our current environmental crisis.[24] Thus Edward Goldsmith, the long-time editor of *The Ecologist*, argues that if Western societies are to regain a sense of respect for the non-human world they need to abandon their roots in the Hebrew and Christian tradition in favour of Taoism or Buddhism, or the new earth religion of ecofeminism.[25] However, Murray's exposition of the cosmic covenant in the Hebrew Bible radically questions this negative prognosis on the ecological orientation of the religions of the Bible. His anthropological reinterpretation provides a rich picture of the cosmic meaning and ecological sensitivities of the Hebrew concept of covenant, for the preservation of order – supernatural, natural, human moral and social order – is the primary function of the covenant and its associated rituals.

But standard Christian exegesis of the Hebrew Bible has interpreted the covenant as being primarily between God and humans, and the creation myth primarily in terms of the dominion of humanity over the creation. Most Christian exegesis of the Hebrew Bible has also played down or positively denied the primal or 'savage' elements in Hebrew traditions. In his study *The Savage in Judaism*, Howard Eilberg-Schwartz argues that this attempt to distance the primal and the Hebrew world-view relates to the colonial and ethnocentric history of

Western anthropological denigration of native or savage cultures.[26] The denial of primal consciousness in the Hebrew Bible is also a feature of attempts to ground Christian theology and practice exclusively in the category of revelation and to deny the relations of Christian revealed truth to natural human creativity and culture, and to the order and beauty of the natural world.[27]

The Hebrew connection between the worship of the God of justice, the justice and wisdom of human society and its leaders and the goodness of the land should not be dismissed merely as a primitive myth, for it expresses a fundamental ecological and theological truth. Human life and society are intricately bound up with the life and community of ecosystems and the biosphere. Corrupt monarchs and dictators who fight wasteful wars and build profligate palaces do indeed ravage the land. As we have seen, recent ecological interpretations of the archaeological evidence of the demise of the great Hebrew cities such as Jericho, Jerusalem and Tyre in eighth century Palestine indicate that their apparently sudden abandonment and subsequent ruin may have been a consequence of an ecological calamity which overtook the region, brought about by overgrazing and over-use which the land suffered under the imperialistic enterprises of the late Israelite monarchy.[28] Kings such as Omri receive hardly a mention in the theological narrative of the Books of Kings because they did not follow the ways of Yahweh, but they were in worldly terms the most successful kings Israel had seen and it is possible that their very political and military prowess contributed to the devastation of lands and cities witnessed to by the prophets. This may also explain why so much attention is given to care for the land, and to limits on the intensity of agricultural production, in the final editing of the law tradition, which took place after most of the damage from deforestation, overcropping and overgrazing had already turned much of the region into semi-desert.

The concept of the cosmic covenant indicates that the ancient Hebrews, like the ancient Greek philosophers, found in the natural order both ethical and ecological significance. In the original goodness of the earth God's goodness and wisdom are clearly displayed. For the Hebrews, the created order represents a transhistorical and transcultural source of moral and aesthetic value, and of ecological balance and harmony, which does not stand in need of human manipulation or perception in order for these values to be realised. Beauty, fecundity, diversity, community are present in the teleological order of the creation. According to the historians, song writers and prophets of the Hebrew Bible it was the denial of the goodness of God, and ingratitude and disrespect for the related goodness of the natural order, that issued in the alienation between humans and nature.

OUT OF EDEN

The vision of nature's original goodness and harmony in the first chapters of Genesis contrasts with other Ancient Near Eastern myths of origin, and it contrasts significantly with modern scientific accounts of human society and the non-human world. The Sumerian myth of origin describes the creation of the world as a consequence of violence between the gods. The warring god Marduk fashions the earth by first killing, trampling and then splitting open the body of the goddess Tiamat, and he fashions humans from the dead body of Tiamat's consort Kingu.[29] The contrast with the Hebrew vision of created order is dramatic. The order of the world is established not by the peaceable word of God but by the chaotic disorder of war between the gods. Reality is fundamentally chaotic, and order only attainable through violence. This myth constructs human societies as endemically warring and aggressive, where the strong must conquer by violence and the weak go to the wall. The implication is that evil and violence are not to be resisted for they are of the essential order of things, the very cause and origin of life itself.[30] Violent and aggressive competition for land and natural resources, between humans and between humans and other species, is of the essence of reality, according to this myth. The violent conquest of nature is legitimated for from violence between the gods was nature born.

Similarly, modern scientific myths of origin have been utilised to characterise the origins and nature of life, both nonhuman and human, as essentially violent, aggressive and competitive, 'red in tooth and claw'. Thus the Darwinist principle of the 'survival of the fittest' is used by biologists such as Richard Dawkins to justify the ethical atomism and individualism of modern commercial behaviour.[31] Many biologists and ecologists argue that natural evolution proceeded by each individual animal, and even gene, pursuing its own interests and competitive advantage with respect to all other animals. Sociobiologists such as Dawkins consequently argue that collective co-operation and care for the weak by the strong are contrary to the laws of nature and may even be dangerous for human societies to pursue.[32] As Mary Midgley argues in *The Ethical Primate*, by such arguments the Victorian sociobiologists sought to justify the depredations of colonialism and industrialism on the happiness and dignity of the landless and the working poor, and the violent industrial assault on the nonhuman world.[33] Humans are the strongest species; their domination and reordering of the non-human world is simply the logical outcome of the evolutionary process.

However, other scientists and philosophers have challenged this representation of animal life and human life as essentially conflictual and competitive. In her remarkable survey of primatial science, *Primate Vision*, Donna Haraway argues that both early sociobiologists and early primatial scientists constructed the primate as essentially an organic machine and that this construct rendered all co-operative or altruistic behaviour problematic, and led primatial observers (and observers of hunter-gatherer human cultures) to focus exclusively on the conflictual, sexual and violent behaviour of individual male primates.[34] However, the emergence of a number of women primatologists, such as Jane Goodall and Diane Fossey, accompanies a new development in ethological studies involving the more careful study of primate communities in the wild, which generated the discovery that the lives of non-human primates are characterised more by co-operation, mutuality and altruism than by competition and conflict.[35] Thus as Stephen Clark argues, the fact that we can find so many aspects of human moral behaviour, at its best more often than its worst, replicated amongst our genetically close relatives can only lead us to the conclusion that human morality has many parallels and correlates in non-human primatial behaviour.[36] We may be justified then in concluding that co-operation, mutuality and altruism are indeed part of the natural order which humans, more than the other animals, have successfully managed to distort and eschew.

Mary Midgley similarly argues that the interaction of plants and non-conscious life forms in ecosystems and food chains can only be described as competitive by an imaginative act which distorts the actual character of their non-conscious existence.[37] Indeed, were hostile competition truly to be the central characteristic of life processes then ecosystems would never be naturally sustained. The order of the universe and of living systems can only be explained with reference to forms of co-operation and mutuality which, while not always conscious, nonetheless may be said to be central to the laws of nature by which life is sustained in all its complexity and diversity. Eugene Odum's theory of ecosystems argued for a directedness within all life communities whose goal is the achievement of a stable biomass in any particular system which can sustain the greatest species diversity.[38] Ecological order is characterised by species diversity, by a stable biomass and by the preservation of nutrients in ecosystems by recycling processes. These processes are reliable and repetitive: they are mostly threatened, not by natural competition or predation, but by humanly originated intervention. Odum, like Leopold, therefore believed that we should try wherever possible to preserve the natural environment in its natural state. Excessive interference by humans would lead to ecological breakdown.

The discoveries of the early scientific ecologists, like the observations of more recent primate ethologists, seem to lend credence to aspects of the Genesis myth of original goodness. Primates and even non-conscious life forms make up communities of being whose collective behaviour in the wild state demonstrates degrees of harmony, mutuality and co-operation.

Primal human societies seem also to be characterised by these same principles to a much more advanced degree, and also far more so than modern Western civilisation. According to Colin Turnbull in his famous study *The Mountain People*, primal peoples are only driven into individualism, stealing and violence of the kind frequently found in modern Western cultures by external forces such as the degradation of natural resources or the shrinking of their terrain consequent on the depredations of modern progress and development.[39] As Turnbull says, in the 'primitive' societies of the world we may still observe degrees of sociality and mutuality long since lost in the violent individualism and atomism which has become the common experience of many urban, and increasingly rural, dwellers, in civilised societies such as those of England or North America.[40] Myer Fortes's studies of the Tallensi in Ghana lend weight to Turnbull's judgement, for Fortes found that the concept of the person, or self-consciousness, in Tallensi culture was fundamentally a *moral* consciousness, not of the self as a locus for the fulfilment of idiosyncratic needs and wants, but as the self located in a natural and social context which orders and constructs the behaviour of the individual.[41] Again, in a major field study of the San peoples whose culture once stretched from East Africa to the Cape, Lorna Marshall found almost no evidence of stealing among the !Kung, one of the San tribes.[42] In her eighteen months with the tribe she witnessed no serious quarrels or fights, and, on the contrary, found a society in which jealousy, envy and ill will were exceptionally rare, and in which human relations were characterised by reciprocity, gift exchange, sociability, security and mutual comfort.[43] My own limited observations of primal culture among the Sengoi peoples in Peninsula Malaysia, and the land Dayaks of Borneo, also tend to bear out these recent anthropological judgements of the inherent moral power, egalitarianism and virtue of many primal cultures as contrasted with the moral deficit associated with modern Western individualism.

The myth of Eden may point then to a time when similar egalitarian cultures predominated in the Ancient Near East, before the disturbances of the wars of conquest and ecological breakdown which occurred in that region during the second millennium BCE, and which are described in the histories of the Hebrew Bible and other historical texts in the region. Archaeological evidence indicates a pattern of civilisation in early Israel where people lived in houses of similar size, in cities or small settlements without walls or defences, where there were few implements capable of being used for warfare, and where peoples and tribes lived in peace and harmony both with themselves and with the non-human world.[44] It is therefore possible that these societies were characterised by the same egalitarianism and lack of domination – of leaders over communities, of men over women, of people over nature – such as we still find in contemporary primal cultures.

The value of the image, particularly as found in Genesis 1, of a non-hierarchical garden in which God, humans and animals lived together in peace and harmony, none fearing the other, is that, like the modern ethological discovery of the non-violence and egalitarianism of many primatial and primal human cultures, it allows us to believe that human beings, and even animal life, are not naturally violent, aggressive and destructive, but that rather these patterns of behaviour are patterns learnt within human cultures which have fallen from the egalitarian ideal of primal paradise, and perhaps also acquired rather than innate in many primatial communities. This myth of origin offers a vision of created order as God intended it to be rather than as it has become distorted by the experience of evil and sin. The power imbalances between male and female, the fear between God and humans and the enmity between humans and nature, are all described in Genesis 2 and 3 as originating not in the nature of things as God intended them to be, but rather in the collusion of Adam, Eve and the serpent, who together deny the goodness and sufficiency of the garden and distrust the good intentions of the creator. Even here there are also hints that the moral fall from original goodness is not exclusively a human fall, but involves other orders of being, both angelic and sub-human, for it is the serpent who is the originator of the evil thought which leads Adam and Eve to transgress the command not to eat of the fruit of the tree of knowledge. The relational community between God, humans and natural species is broken by this first act of distrust: pain in childbirth, alienation between animals and humans and the sweated labour of agricultural tillage are all said to be consequences of this original fall from the paradisiacal harmony and fruitfulness of the garden.

The story of the exile from Eden offers a mythic explanation of evil and disorder in the world which interacts in an intriguing way with the contemporary criticism of humanly originated ecological disorder, and the scientific discovery of the tendencies of ecosystems not dominated by human interference towards stability and harmony. The story affirms that created order contains within it a potentiality for goodness and harmony despite the occurrence of so much natural evil, pain and suffering, and that humans are not fundamentally in conflict with created order, nor with one another or God. The story also offers its hearers or readers grounds for resisting humanly originated evil and domination, both in its oppressive effects on human societies, and its destructive effects on the non-human world. Conflict, competition, distrust and violent destruction are options, tendencies, in human history, which it should be the aim of human communities to resist and reverse. The cosmic covenant, the Jubilee laws, the ethical controls on agriculture and trade may then be read as a demonstration of the efforts of one ancient primal people, guided by their visionaries and prophets with their messages from Yahweh, to construct a society where domination, inequality and competition are challenged and resisted, both in relation to their impacts on human flourishing and on the flourishing of the non-human world.

LIFE, GIFT AND SACRIFICE

In the light of this reading of the heuristic function of the Genesis myth, other features of the story are thrown into a new relief, in particular the dominion over the earth which is conferred on humans in their original blessed and sinless state of paradise, and the charge given to humans to name the animals.[45] Dominion has frequently been misinterpreted as meaning domination and possession. But the Hebrew root of the verb translated subdue or rule means vice-regent or steward and not ruler. God puts humans over nature not as owner or exploiter but as the steward who shares the creative care of the creator. As we have seen, the concept of stewardship of nature is mobilised in the Western tradition from the Fathers to Benedict to refer to the just and gentle care of nature by humans. But it has become associated with instrumentalist attitudes to nature which are linked with environmental exploitation and it may be that the association of stewardship with absolute property rights and land ownership patterns in Western civilisation resulted in its mutation into a metaphor of human control and mastery over nature. Modern human attempts to control the climate, to move the course of great rivers, to excavate mountains, to irrigate deserts or use seas as chemical or sewage sinks have often had disastrous consequences. We still do not understand, and are never likely to be able to manage, the vast and intricate systems which control the climate, or sustain the fragile salinity of the sea or the fecundity of the tropical forest. In this sense then, as I argued above, stewardship has become a misleading and potentially harmful metaphor.

But stewardship is not the only metaphor for moral responsibility within creation which the Hebrew Bible provides. In his innovative analysis of the ecological message of the Bible, *Hope for the Land*, Richard Austin argues that the Hebrew Bible identifies the basic moral responsibility of all life, including human life, with the calling of all life forms to respond to God in praise and worship.[46] This response of gratitude is a fundamental feature of creaturely being which is shared by all the creatures of the earth, humans and animals, landscapes, seas and mountains, earth, wind, fire and rain. The Psalmist charges all things with the first moral duty of the creation, to worship and praise the creator, thereby establishing in as radical a fashion as any deep ecologist the moral agency of animals, and of non-sentient life forms and habitats. The last hymn of the Book of Psalms, Psalm 150, celebrates the common calling of the whole cosmos to worship the Lord in the covenant community, and serves to recall to the assembled worshippers their essential moral and ecological kinship with the whole world of nature: 'Let everything that has breath praise the Lord.'[47] Our own culture has in large part abandoned both the worship of the Lord, and a sense for the sacredness and moral significance of the cosmos, but in the Hebrew perspective humanity and the cosmos have moral significance, and both are required to make a moral response to the creator, a response to God which reflects his glory and offers the return of gratitude, praise and worship:

> Praise him, sun and moon;
> praise him, all you shining stars;
> praise him, heaven of heavens,
> and you waters above the heavens.
> Let them praise the name of the Lord,
> for he spoke and they were created;
> he established them for ever and ever
> by an ordinance which shall never pass away.
> Praise the Lord from the earth,
> you sea monsters and ocean depths;
> fire and hail, snow and ice,
> gales of winds that obey his voice;
> all mountains and hills,
> all fruits trees and cedars;
> wild animals and all cattle,
> creeping creatures and winged birds.[48]

Human praise, the praise of kings and commoners, of young and old,[49] is part of this heavenly chorus, but it is a praise which is also a participation in the whole of creation. This praise is the response of thanksgiving to the creator for the plenitude of creation. It receives creation as gift not as right, as promised land held in trust, not owned or possessed by humans.

This moral responsibility to worship the Lord and reflect his glory may be said to be inherent in the beauty, fecundity and order of the natural world. On the part of humans this response of worship and gratitude involves the active taking of initiatives in relation to the created order, and the creator.[50] Thus Adam and Eve are called upon not merely to be in the garden, but to steward the earth and to replenish it, and not merely to observe the animals but to name them.[51] Naming has a deep personal significance in Hebrew thought. Knowledge of the name of a person gives knowledge of the nature of the person. Naming the animals establishes their otherness, their existence distinctive from humans, their separate purposes and being. For naming, as Jacques Ellul points out, is not an act of exploitation or utilisation, but the expression of 'spiritual superiority, of directing which nevertheless leaves the other *intact*'.[52]

Moral responsibility in relation to nature involves the exercise of creativity which is manifest in the commission to tend the garden and to name the animals.[53] This creativity is to be exercised neither harshly nor cruelly but within the principles and laws of justice, equity and ecology which the Hebrew Torah lays down. The Hebrew Bible thus provides a moral mandate for human intervention in nature, and not just for ceasing from environmental intervention. Modern environmentalism has been rather better at justifying the latter than the former. The Torah therefore may be said to provide a more balanced account of human relations with nature than contemporary environmentalism and environmental philosophy, which often seems to privilege wilderness over any form of human-influenced landscape. The Torah sets our work on and with nature in the moral and religious context of the *telos* of all of life rather than simply commending a withdrawal from engagement with areas of nature that we have previously damaged or over-exploited. The form of the mandate to tend and care for the orders of creation reflects the inherent attitudes of respect and care which are required of humans towards all forms of life. This respect and care is grounded in the Genesis accounts of the goodness which God imputes to the creation: 'and God saw all that he had made, and it was very good'.[54] God cherishes the cosmos, he loves it, and so it is valued, loved, even before we humans encounter it. Respect for life is then a fundamental ethical principle in the Hebrew Bible.

The primary ethical value which arises from this respect is respect for human life because human life most closely reflects the divine image.[55] This issues in a range of moral obligations and responsibilities: to procreate and nurture children, to care for the poor, sick, widows, orphans and aliens, to treat all humans with justice. It also issues in a range of prohibitions: not to kill or maim humans, not to covet their possessions, not to expose or sacrifice children, not to deny the essentials of life – food, clothing, shelter – to the poor or the alien. The duty to bear and nurture children is fundamental to the biblical vision of the moral life but of course it is the very success which contemporary humans have had with this moral duty, at least in terms of bearing, which has partly occasioned the threat to the other species of the biosphere. However, duties to human procreation, and to respect human life and dignity and seek the welfare of the human community are in the Hebrew Torah set alongside duties to other forms of life. Hebrew ethics is not personalist but life-oriented. The primary moral value of life relates to the belief that all life, human and non-human, is in some way related to the life-giving Spirit of God and is therefore worthy of respect. This respect involves a moral claim which animals, both domestic and wild, have upon human society and the land, and which must be balanced with the human quest for nourishment and welfare.[56] Thus animals have a claim to space, nourishment, rest and enjoyment which is not dissimilar to the human claim for such things:

For six years you may sow your land and gather its produce; but in the seventh year you shall let it lie fallow and leave it alone. It shall provide food for the poor of your people, and what they leave the wild animals may eat. You shall do likewise with your vineyard and your olive grove.
For six days you may do your work, but on the seventh day you shall abstain from work, so that your ox and your ass may rest, and your home-born slave and the alien may refresh themselves.[57]

Moral duties are enjoined with respect both for domestic and wild animals. In Genesis 1 and 2 the first humans are represented as vegetarians. They eat plants and fruits but not animals, and animals have no fear of humans. After the flood the Noachian covenant shows God allowing a new and less ideal situation in which animals fear humans as humans may

now kill them for food. Other parts of the Torah reflect a
settled agricultural society in which animals have been domesticated. But moral duties to both wild and domestic animals are
enjoined, even though humans may kill them for food. Domestic animals are to be treated with respect and compassion
and cruelty to them is condemned.[58] They are not to be
overworked, they are to be properly fed, and even the animals
of an enemy should be treated kindly: 'when you come upon
your enemy's ox or ass straying, you shall take it back to him'.[59]
As Lewis Regenstein points out, kindness to animals is also seen
as a sign of virtuous character and the favour of God: Rebecca
is chosen as wife for Isaac by Abraham because she drew water
for Abraham's camels and not just for his servant.[60]

The life and fate of the beast and the life of humanity are
characterised as intricately tied together. Thus Noah and his
family are saved from the flood with all the animals, domestic
and wild, and the cosmic covenant is made between God and
humans and every living creature. Analogously the writer of
Ecclesiastes expresses an ecological sentiment about the
common origin and destiny of human and animal life: 'Men
have no advantage over beasts; for everything is emptiness. All
go to the same place: all came from the dust and to the dust all
return.'[61]

The extension of ethics and law to include animals as well as
humans is often represented as a uniquely modern enterprise.
But the Hebrew Torah went this way many thousands of years
before the modern animal rights movement. Instead of the
language of rights it sets the treatment of animals in the context
of their sharing of the divine-inspired character of all of life,
and in terms of the responsibilities and duties which consequently arise for humans in their treatment of animals. This is
especially demonstrated in the laws concerning the eating of
animals, a practice which is in any case, according to the
authors of Genesis, not part of God's ideal intentions for the
earth. The principle of life which is shared between humans
and animals was believed to reside in the blood and this is why
the Hebrews are enjoined not to eat the blood of animals they
killed, and to slaughter them in such a way as to drain the

blood from the body before preparing it for cooking: 'you must strictly refrain from eating the blood, because the blood is the life; you must not eat the blood with the life. You must not eat it, you must pour it on the ground like water.'[62] The word 'life' here translates the Hebrew *nephesh*, which means breath. The breath of creatures is indicative of divinity because it reflects the breath of the creator Spirit, and the act of breathing and the life-blood are seen as intricately connected, as of course, from medical science, we know that they are. This belief in the sacrality of blood is so strong that it recurs in the New Testament in a command from the Jewish to the Gentile church at the Council of Jerusalem: 'It is the decision of the Holy Spirit, and our decision, to lay no further burden upon you beyond these essentials: you are to abstain from meat that has been offered to idols, from blood, and from fornication. If you keep yourselves free from these things you will be doing right.'[63] Respecting the blood of an animal as the life-force shared with humans is a fundamental feature of the Hebrew attitude to animals and this attitude is manifest in the laws about kindness and respect to living animals. The conditions laid down by the law for animal slaughter also reflect compassion and respect. Thus, for example, mother and young are not to be killed in sight of each other.[64] As Regenstein says, although rudimentary, the regulations governing slaughter are not only kinder than those of surrounding nations, they are also considerably kinder than the practices of modern factory farming and slaughter.[65] Fundamentally these primal beliefs concerning the value of animals, even animals which would be killed and eaten, reflect the idea that the taking of life, including animal life, is always a kind of affront to natural order and must only be done for serious reasons, and in a manner which respects the moral significance of the animal's life. This attitude can still be encountered among certain primal hunters to this day, who say a prayer or perform some kind of ritual when an animal is killed.

This primal belief in the power of blood, and the significance of the sacrifice of a life for food, is of course linked to the practice of animal sacrifice. Because the blood represents the force of life it has moral power which is able to expiate for the sins of the people of Israel in the sacrifices at the altar as well as to provide nourishment: 'the life of a creature is the blood, and I appoint it to make expiation on the altar for yourselves; it is the blood, that is the life, that makes expiation'.[66] The bloody and sometimes wasteful practice of sacrifice is seen by some moderns as disrespectful of animals and the natural order, but the function of sacrificial practice in relation to Hebrew cosmology is complex and, it may be argued, reveals an attitude of deep respect for natural order, including animals as well as the land.[67] The functions of sacrifice in primal cultures and in ancient Israel are complex and multifarious but most scholars would agree they include at least three primary purposes: sacrifice achieves the expiation of pollution, guilt, death and disease; it involves the re-establishment and affirmation of communion, between God and humans, and between persons – especially when particular persons are alienated by some sinful act; and it represents a fundamental attitude of thanksgiving to God or the gods for the gifts of nature or the created order.[68] Thus sacrificial practices involve both the restoration of created order – divine and human – in relation to human actions or natural disasters which threaten that order and its inherent relationality, and the celebration of the fundamental goodness and giftedness of this order.[69] The connection between gift and sacrifice is clearly enunciated in modern scholarship by the anthropologists Henri Hubert and Marcel Mauss, and is a primary, and possibly *the* primary meaning of sacrifice in the Hebrew Bible, as the oldest account, the story of Cain and Abel, makes clear.[70] On this interpretation sacrifice is the offering back to God as gift that which comes from God.[71] This connection between sacrifice and gift clarifies the deep attitude of respect for created order, and for the value of life, which is in fact inherent in the sacrificial tradition.

The practice of sacrifice is gradually eclipsed as the focus of power in Israelite religion moves from a predominantly agrarian culture to a predominantly urban one.[72] Some of the psalmists and most of the prophets regarded sacrificial practices with distaste, arguing that they were a distraction from true religion, and from the quest for true communion, relationality and justice between persons: 'loyalty is my desire not sacrifice, not whole-offerings but the knowledge of God'.[73] According to the New Testament writers, and particularly in the Epistle to the Hebrews, it is the blood of a human who is also the Son of God which ultimately atones for human wickedness, and the need for animal sacrifice is thus for ever abolished. As Hubert and Mauss argue, the sacrifice of a god is the supreme means for the restoration of communion and for expiation in many cultures, and in Christianity the sacrifice of God in Christ on the cross is the supreme instance of restoration and expiation, or redemption.[74] The primal Hebraic understanding of physical sacrifice as restoring created order, and as representing a thank-offering for the goodness and giftedness of this order, presents an ecological perspective on the redemptive implications of the sacrificial death of Christ, for the cosmos as well as for human life.

THE SABBATH OF THE LAND

Alongside the respect for sentient life in all forms the Torah also proposes duties to the ecosystem which sustains life, represented in terms of duties to the land itself. The relationship between Yahweh's ownership and gifting of the land and the calling of the Hebrews is a theme which runs throughout the Torah from the Exodus account of the formation of the people of Israel in the wilderness,[75] to the arrangements for land-use commended in the post-exilic record of the law tradition.[76] In the cosmic covenant, the land is not just the context on which Israel works out her covenant with Yahweh, but a part, a vital part, of the covenant community itself. The land is the object of God's tender care and is gifted to human society, not to be harshly used and manipulated but to be tended and even loved. Richard Austin highlights how the Deuteronomist contrasts Egyptian agricultural practices, which treat the land 'like a vegetable garden', with the moral sensitivity to the soil and its patterns of fertility which is required of the Hebrews, who will farm the Promised Land but recognise that it remains God's and that he will tend and water it.[77] This ethic of love, both divine and human, for the land, together with the admonitions to care for it, runs throughout the traditions of the beauty and fertility of Canaan, 'flowing with milk and honey'.

The most significant indication of the moral status of land is the requirement of the Sabbath of the land. The creator rested on the Sabbath from the work of creation and in this rest the goodness and order of the cosmos are affirmed, blessed and enjoyed by the creator. Humans are given rights to a Sabbath rest, which is established with reference to the Lord's rest. The Sabbath sets boundaries to human work and provides cultic and celebratory space for the people to worship the Lord and enjoy the fruits of their labours and the Lord's land. And the land also is given a Sabbath.[78] Every seventh year it is to lie fallow according to the law, in order that it may recover its strength:

When you enter the land which I am giving you, the land must keep Sabbaths to the Lord. For six years you may sow your fields and prune your vineyards and gather the harvest, but in the seventh year the land is to have a sacred (sabbatical) rest, a Sabbath to the Lord ... in the seventh year the land shall keep a sacred rest.[79]

The Sabbath of the land has ecological value, particularly for the kind of land the Hebrews were farming, which was fragile. Overtilling and overcropping by livestock resulted in soil erosion and eventual desertification, of the kind observed and condemned by the prophets as the consequence of the abuse of land by rich landowners.[80] According to the law codes of Leviticus the abrogation of the Sabbath of the land is linked with the problem of desertification, and the land's neglected need for Sabbaths is represented as a major reason for the exile of the Hebrews:

your land will be desert and your cities heaps of rubble. Then, all the time that it lies desolate, while you are in exile among your enemies, your land will enjoy its Sabbaths to the full. All the time of its desolation it will have the Sabbath rest which it did not have while you were living there.[81]

The people of God are also warned not to forget that the

land does not belong to them. Norman Gottwald argues that the Hebrew conception of divine ownership of the land is similar to the traditional land tenure system in many Asian countries where land was not individually owned but farmed collectively and tenure invested in God.[82] Walter Breuggemann argues that the land is understood primarily in terms of the covenant, which restrained wealth inequality, and that it is consequently considered as the inalienable birthright of the Hebrew.[83] This covenantal concept of Yahweh's ownership of the land has major implications for the patterns of land tenure and economic activity which are legitimised in the Torah. However, as Jeffrey Fager points out, land is evidently bought and sold in Israel, despite the fundamental assumption of Yahweh's ownership. This is why the Jubilee laws establish limits on the private concentration of land by a periodic reform process which returns land to families who have lost it through debt or ineffective farming: land lost in this way 'reverts to the original holder, and he returns to his holding'.[84] By these laws wealth inequality and concentrations of land holdings are restrained. Similarly, lending money at interest is condemned because it tends to drive people into poverty, landlessness and even into slavery. As Douglas Meeks observes, these laws concerning land and usury reflect the original experience of Exodus by which Yahweh called the nation of Israel into being from a state of slavery.[85] Human tenancy of land is provisional on God's promise and his ultimate ownership: 'No land may be sold outright, because the land is mine, and you came to it as aliens and tenants of mine.'[86] As Meeks says, this God is interested in patterns of agriculture, distribution and trade which do not oppress the poor or drive people back into slavery: the Torah is the means by which the Hebrews were called by God to develop an 'economy of life' which reflected their own history of redemption from slavery and the gracious gift from God of the Promised Land.[87] God the redeemer is the God who cares for the defenceless, for the poor and the vulnerable.[88]

The Hebrews are also warned that however successful their farming they must never forget that the fertility of the land arises from God's care for nature rather than simply human manipulation.[89] They should not look for security in the products of the land alone but rather seek the goodness of the whole created order, for in their just and righteous treatment of land, animals and neighbours lies real security, sufficiency and welfare.[90] This is because the God who redeems his people from slavery promises that they shall not again be landless and without food or livelihood, so long as they follow the Torah of life which confers livelihood on all who receive the promise of land. As Meeks argues, in the Torah the sufficiency of the land is related to the justice of God and to the justice of the society of God's people. Where each has access to the means of livelihood, where neighbour does not oppress neighbour with usury or debt slavery, where the poor, the widows and the fatherless are offered hospitality, and where the animals are not cruelly abused, then God's justice is respected, and God will give the land its increase, and the land will meet the needs of God's people and meet them with abundance.[91] But neglect of the worship of the God who is the provider of the land in the covenant which gifted the land to Israel, and neglect of the justice the covenant law requires, brings about real threats to livelihood and security. When the Hebrews turn to idolatry instead of true worship, and deny their dependence on the Lord, they forget that they received the land as a gift not a possession, and they neglect justice. When they take lands from one another by usury or in other unjust ways, then the land turns to desert, their liberation is reversed and their enemies come in to occupy the land of promise and turn them out.

The economic and social practices enjoined in the Torah reflect the relational character of the covenant, and the relational understanding of God, persons and nature in Hebrew cosmology. The Torah and the prophets interpret the threat of exile and the danger of desertification as punishment for the development in Hebrew society of economic practices which denied the relationality of the land to Yahweh, and of Hebrew to Hebrew, as some grew rich at the expense of others.

As we have seen, the commodification of land was one of the first steps in the transformation of relations, both material and cultural, between humans and nature which preceded the modern environmental crisis. The introduction of the concept of absolute land ownership and the commercialisation of the product of the land have been the twin prongs of the assault of historical imperialism and modern capitalism on indigenous peoples and on the tenure systems of pre-modern cultures from the Highlands of Scotland or Ethiopia to the rainforests of Borneo or the Amazon. Western economic relations are predicated on the concept of outright land ownership. But this very concept in relation to land is forbidden by the Hebrew Torah because the Hebrews believed, like most primal peoples, that the land did not belong to them but to God, that they farmed it only as tenants and not as its absolute owners. In many indigenous cultures, including that of ancient Israel, the land is the land of the ancestors and their God (or gods) and in the land reside the memories, hopes (and some believe the spirits) of the people. Land cannot be owned by one generation alone: it represents the common inheritance and posterity of generations past, present and future. Land is also the dwelling place not just of humans but of other species, wild and domesticated: again the idea that the land could belong outright to humans implies a denial of space to the non-human species to whose welfare human welfare is also related.

So fundamental to modern culture and economic relations is the concept of absolute ownership that modernity tends to construct common land as inherently problematic. Colonial administrators and anthropologists used to believe that primitive nomads were not good tenders of the land, and they actively discouraged nomads in preference to settled agriculture. However, more recent social scientific analyses of the life of pastoral nomads have demonstrated that pre-modern land tenure and husbandry systems tend to degrade land less than modern systems reliant on land title and settled commercial agriculture. In a study of nomadism in central Africa, Paul Baxter finds that pastoral nomads who are allowed still to roam are in fact better conservers of fragile soils and ecosytems than many settled farmers.[92] Garrett Hardin, who first coined the phrase the 'tragedy of the commons', argues that the degradation of common land, so ubiquitous in the world today, occurs because of the breakdown of the traditional cultural and social controls on the use of land (and of other natural goods such as air and water) by nomads, herdsmen or fisher folk.[93] The traditional cultural and agricultural systems which relied on common land were better able to respect the integrity of the land and to prevent its desertification and degradation than modern systems of land commodification. This is evident, as we have seen, in the history of the Highland Clearances in Britain. The Highlands of Scotland have been largely turned to peatland desert and denuded of trees and wild animals in the last two hundred years by the agricultural practices of the landowners who acquired the land for large-scale sheep farming, and for sporting estates. A similar fate overtook many colonial lands as the Scottish Clearances in the eighteenth century were replicated all over the colonies in the nineteenth and twentieth centuries.

According to the Hebrew prophets the land turned to desert not when it was farmed equitably by ancestral groups but when it was inequitably acquired for the commercial gain and greed of the rich.[94] Land is part of the covenant community of the ancient Hebrews, and through the covenant character of land moral duties are established in the Torah in relation to the whole biosphere, duties which arise from the cosmic reach of the covenant, from the promised and gifted character of land and from the common origin of all of life in the activity of the creator Spirit. Love and respect for life and ecosystems are not secondary to respect for human life, but relationally intertwined with human identity and purposes in a moral and a natural ecology which is central to the cosmology of created order celebrated in Israel's worship. The welfare and goods of human society are set in the context of the welfare and goods of the covenanted cosmos. Human injustice, the quest for material security by the rich at the expense of the poor, is inextricably related to human and cosmic moral disorder and ecological crisis. The command to love God and neighbour is accompanied by the command to respect the Sabbath, and to keep the Sabbath of the cosmos. When this sacred duty is denied, then the cosmos no longer gives liberally of its fruits and human welfare also declines.

THE SHALOM OF THE EARTH

Just as the post-exilic prophets argued that the peoples of Israel and Judah had been exiled because they failed to worship the Lord, and to respect his justice in relation to the land and their neighbours, so they proclaimed that the return of the exiled Hebrews to the land would require the restoration of integrity and justice in their treatment and distribution of the land. And when the Israelites returned to Jerusalem after the exile in Nehemiah's time, as Austin points out, they renewed the covenant with the land,[95] and they restored the just tenure of those poor farmers who under the last years of the monarchy were evicted from their lands at the hands of ruthless urban landlords.[96] According to Isaiah, the restoration of the land will involve the recovery by every household of the means to livelihood and mutual sufficiency, for God's justice confers on every household the means to meet the basic needs of life, to provide for the flourishing of children and for security in old age:

> No child there will ever again die in infancy,
> no old man fail to live out his span of life.
> My people will build houses and live in them,
> plant vineyards and eat their fruit;
> they will not build for others to live in
> or plant for others to eat.
> They will be as long-lived as a tree,
> and my chosen ones will enjoy the fruit of their labour.[97]

The restoration of the true worship of the Lord, and of the justice of human society, also contributes to the transformation of nature into the peaceable kingdom of shalom and ecological harmony. The *telos* of the cosmos is the restoration of paradise, of the natural relationality between humans and God which the story of Adam and Eve represents as the ideal of divine–human fellowship. Broken covenants, lost blessings, human sin and injustice, and exile from the garden and the land are not the

end of the story. The original peace of the first creation may
have been despoiled by human rebellion but God's sure
purpose is still to restore shalom, harmony, blessing and
fruitfulness to his people, to all living things and to the land:

> Let the wilderness and the dry-lands exult,
> let the wasteland rejoice and bloom,
> let it bring forth flowers like the jonquil,
> let it rejoice and sing for joy.
>
> Then the eyes of the blind shall be opened,
> the ears of the deaf unsealed,
> then the lame shall leap like a deer
> and the tongues of the dumb sing for joy;
>
> for water gushes in the desert,
> streams in the wasteland,
> the scorched earth becomes a lake,
> the parched land springs of water.
>
> The lairs where the jackals used to live,
> become thickets of reed and papyrus.
>
> Therefore the redeemed of the Lord shall return,
> and come with singing unto Zion,
> and everlasting joy shall be upon their heads,
> and sorrow and dying shall flee away.[98]

From the hope of shalom flow the themes of cosmic restoration and redemption, and the ideals of the law tradition,
concerning the treatment of animals domestic and wild, the
tending of the land, the care of the poor and widows and
restraints on economic power and oppression, by which Israel
in exile was to aspire to the goodness and grace of the original
creation, and in response to which Yahweh would restore the
fortunes of Israel and the fertility of the land. First Isaiah
presents an even more radical image, not only of abundance
but of a new ecological harmony where predatorial behaviour
will no longer characterise human and non-human relations:

Then the wolf shall live with the sheep, and the leopard lie down with
   the kid;
the calf and the young lion shall grow up together, and a little child
   shall lead them;

the cow and the bear shall be friends, and their young shall lie down
  together.
The lion shall eat straw like cattle;
the infant shall play over the hole of the cobra, and the young child
  dance over the viper's nest.
They shall not hurt or destroy in all my holy mountain;
for as the waters fill the sea, so shall the land be filled with the
  knowledge of the Lord.[99]

In this passage we see that the effects of the promised
redemption are universalised beyond the tribe of Israel to all
the inhabitants of the globe, Israelite and Gentile, human and
non-human. This same universalising motif is present in Ezekiel's vision of the restored temple giving life to the whole of
nature.[100] Ezekiel creates a particularly powerful and complex
image of the moral and ecological restoration of city, cultus,
people and land. The richness of this ecological vision points to
the possibilities for fulfilment of the created order not only in a
supra-historical realm but within the history of the world and of
human society. The role of apocalyptic and prophecy in the
Bible is not just to predict the future but to encourage and
provoke change and moral fulfilment in the present. The
physical and ecological character of biblical visions of redemption offers hope that the restoration of ecological harmony does
lie within the possibilities of a redeemed human history: this
does not remove the need for social and moral effort in
responding to the ecological crisis, but rather affirms that
human societies which seek to revere God and to mirror his
justice, will also produce the fruits of justice and equity in
human moral order and harmony in the natural world.
According to Ezekiel, even the driest desert can spring to life
again, and the dry bones will rise up again to praise their
creator.

THE DEEP ECOLOGY OF CREATED ORDER

The preceding exposition of the Hebrew Bible may be summarised in the form of a series of propositions which demonstrate the ecological richness of the Hebrew concepts of created

order and covenant, and also the close fit between the covenant and Torah and aspects of the land ethic, of Gaian order and the relationality of self, nature and society which we explored in chapter three above:

1. There is a critical order in the biosphere and humans have a fundamental duty to preserve this critical order, by abstaining from idolatry, and by tending the earth justly and with respect. Where we ignore the worship of God in the greedy pursuit of personal wealth and in grand economic or military projects which radically disrupt the natural order we risk inviting the return of chaos, of unpredictability.

2. 'The king and the land are one': humans are part of the natural created order. The natural and social order are not opposed: they are both aspects of creation, which reflects the order and wisdom of God. When we recognise the rightness of this wisdom we co-operate with God and with nature and we preserve the natural order.

3. Created order involves a relational balance between the strong and the weak, between the various species of the earth, and between persons. Where landowners or princes or merchants appropriate too much of the earth's resources and social relations are characterised by great extremes of poverty and wealth, human community is fractured and the fertility of the land, the predictability of the climate and seasons, will be disrupted even as the poor are removed from their natural inheritance. Social balance and ecological balance are inter-related. Human welfare depends on a recognition of the goodness and relatedness of all the orders of life on earth from the weakest to the strongest.

4. The biblical faith in created order represents a faith in natural wisdom; that the earth will provide her gifts in due season to meet the needs of human flourishing, and that the seas will keep within their sandy boundaries and not inundate the land as they did in the time of Noah (and as they may do again because of global warming). This faith in natural providence also involves trust in nature's abundance; competition for scarce resources is not the natural condition of life. But this faith requires that we ourselves treat the earth

with respect and wisdom, for the abundance of nature is a gift from God. When we cease to worship and respect the giver, we become careless with the gift. When we respect the integrity of created order as reflecting the justice of God, we will seek to preserve the balance and harmony of natural systems, and the earth will give her fruits in due season. If we neglect the wisdom of nature we betray the earth, and we will reap the flood, the drought or the whirlwind.

5. That which is moral in human life is that which tends to preserve the harmony of the natural world and to follow the wisdom of natural systems. The destruction of habitats or the wasting of natural resources are immoral because they disrupt the created order, preventing natural systems from self-regeneration, and bringing about the extinction of their resident species.

6. Respect for natural order, and for the life-blood which moves the human body, also involves respect for all living beings, with which we share the earth. In the future peaceable kingdom which is God's destiny for the earth, all killing will cease, both between humans, and of animals by humans. This new peace recalls and even transcends the original peace of Eden where humans were vegetarians. But in the interim the Bible permits the killing of animals for food, though not for sport or greed. Where animals are domesticated or hunted for food, they must be treated with compassion and respect and their suffering at slaughter minimised. There is also a duty to continue to leave enough land free from human agriculture and settlement for wild animals to thrive.

7. The moral and religious aspects of human life tend to the same end, which is to preserve and restore the stability, harmony and relationality of all things. Ritual and religion are intended for the reordering of relations between persons and Yahweh, for the expression of praise for the giftedness of creation and for the preservation of natural order. The disruptions of natural disasters are signs of disturbances in human and divine relationships, of human mismanagement of nature and society, rather than evidence of natural evil.

The will of God and the good of humans are one – to resist
the power of violence and domination, to uphold the
vulnerable and the weak, to restore the balance between
humans and nature and between rich and poor, to bring
together all things into one harmonious whole, to reconcile
those things which are opposed.[101]

We have found in the Hebrew Bible evidence of an ecological
world-view at least as 'earth friendly' as that which ecologists
such as Edward Goldsmith find in Taoism or in other Eastern
religions. Furthermore we have found in many and perhaps
surprising respects that the Hebrew approach to the natural
order is much closer to the primal world-view than the
instrumentalist view of nature which we find in the subsequent
adaptation of Hebrew creation-thinking in the Western Christian tradition, and more especially in Protestant Reformation
theology and ethics. In the next chapter I will show how this
account of created order in the Hebrew Bible might inform our
understanding of the redemptive activity of God in Christ and a
Christian environmental ethic. I shall especially focus on the
correlations between the concepts of created order, and the
relationality of divine, human and non-human life in the
Hebrew Bible, and the Christian natural law ethic.

CHAPTER SIX

Creation, redemption and natural law ethics

CREATED ORDER AND EASTER FAITH

Christianity emerged from the religion of the Hebrew Bible as a consequence of one single event – the resurrection of Jesus Christ from the dead. If Jesus of Nazareth had lived as an obscure Galilean carpenter's son and a less obscure Jewish prophet and simply been crucified as another political subversive by the Roman state in Palestine we would have heard no more of this man. The resurrection changed his ignominious death from a sad and apparently ill-judged end into a triumphal sacrifice, and his followers from a disillusioned band of peasants into the founders of a missionary religion which ultimately converted the Roman Empire.

The resurrection is not only the historically pivotal event in the birth of Christianity, but, as Oliver O'Donovan argues, the pivotal doctrine of Christianity in relation to the Hebrew understanding of created order.[1] The basic thesis of O'Donovan's powerful theological restatement of Christian ethics, *Resurrection and Moral Order*, is that the resurrection is the starting point of a Christian approach to ethics because 'it tells us of God's vindication of his creation, and so of our created life'.[2] The original *telos* of the created order, its fundamental goodness and harmony, is reaffirmed by the being of God uniquely embodied in the material creation in Christ's life, death and resurrection. The relational alienation – between God and humanity, between persons, between humans and non-humans, and between non-humans – which issues from the Fall is transformed and redeemed by the restoration of created order which is presaged in the resurrection of Jesus Christ who, Christians came to see, was indeed God incarnate, God in a human body, transforming from within the disorder of a fallen creation.

In what is almost certainly the first written witness to the resurrection, St Paul says that it is the response of God to the exile from Eden, the fall from paradise, which is the first judgement of the Hebrew Bible about the human condition: 'as in Adam all die, so in Christ all will be brought to life'.[3] The new life of the Spirit, the spiritual gifts and ethical fruits of the Spirit, above all the gift of love, issue from this fundamental event in which the original goodness and moral significance of the created order, and of humanity's significant place in that order, are reaffirmed and restored. This is why for all Christians Easter Day is the holiest festival in the Christian calendar, more significant than Good Friday or Christmas. Without the resurrection, the child Jesus would not have come to be known as the saviour of the world, and without the resurrection the death of Jesus would not have been seen as the sacrifice by which the sins of the world were atoned. As Paul says 'if Christ was not raised, your faith has nothing to it and you are still in your old state of sin'.[4]

All of Christian belief, worship and ethics springs from this pivotal event. Without it Christ crucified is not good news. Without it death still has dominion. Without it creation remains without hope of restoration. For it is not simply a soul which survives the death of Christ, but Christ is raised as a body, not the same body which died according to Paul, but a body transformed as a seed becomes a plant, though nonetheless a body.[5] This is why the empty tomb is such a vital part of resurrection faith. For in some mysterious way the physical body of Jesus becomes the 'heavenly body' which the disciples witness at various times in small groups and in a group as large as five hundred people.[6]

This orienting belief in the significance of the bodily resurrection of Christ is reflected in Paul's attitude to the body, not, as for so many of his Jewish and Greek contemporaries, as a mode of being to be cast off in death, and whose needs and desires are to be ascetically eschewed in life, but as the 'temple of the Holy Spirit'.[7] The sexual carelessness of the pagans is contrasted by Paul with the sanctification of the physical, sexual and sensual body by the incorporation of every Christian into the transformed and resurrected body of Jesus Christ. The bodies of Christians were not their own to dispose of as they wished, nor were their bodies irrelevant to their spiritual calling and eternal destiny. Rather, as Peter Brown argues in his luminous study *The Body and Society*, the body was a 'visible locus of order, subject to limits that it was sacrilegious to overstep'.[8] Consequently the household ethics of Paul come to form the core of his teaching about created and social order, for it is through the spiritual and moral transformation of Christians in household communities that the social order and sexual mores of Roman society were to be both resisted and changed into the image of the resurrected and spiritual body of Jesus Christ, which is the image of the church.[9] It is in the body of Christ, the visible gathering of households which makes up the true church, that the Spirit who is transforming created order from darkness to light, from Fall to restoration, is working and illuminating. The manifestations of this Spirit are therefore both physical and spiritual, both sensual and moral. The religion of Paul's churches is not an ascetic and disembodied religion but one which embraces bodiliness as the vehicle for the manifestation of the Spirit. This is evident in the centrality of the gifts of the Spirit in the Pauline churches, gifts of healing, prophecy and the sensual ecstatic power of praise.[10]

But these physical and spiritual manifestations of the Spirit are only evidence of transforming and redeeming grace when they are accompanied by the moral fruits of the Spirit's inner work – love, joy, peace, fidelity, goodness, temperance, wisdom, justice.[11] Paul characteristically draws from the Greek virtues tradition in his enunciation of the moral fruits of the Spirit, from Roman political theory in his exposition of the bodily and social character of the church and from the pagan mystery religions with their sensual and ecstatic overtones in his enunciation of the gifts of the Spirit, but all these traditions are transformed as he melds them into a new and powerful statement of the transformation of spiritual, moral, bodily and political order which issues from the resurrection of the body of Jesus Christ and which is effected by the power of the Holy Spirit who raised him from the dead. And this transforming work of the Holy Spirit is not limited to the bodies, households and churches of Christians. The Spirit is said to be already at work in the creation, drawing human history and created order to its destiny of final fulfilment in the eternal plan of God which is revealed in Jesus Christ. Christians worship and order their lives in anticipation of the imminent emergence of this final fulfilment.

The orientation of creation towards its eschatological transformation is brought nearer and anticipated in the events of reconciliation and restoration which are begun in the death and resurrection of Christ. Christ's triumph over death has import for the whole cosmos:

For in him God in all his fullness chose to dwell, and through him to reconcile all things to himself, making peace through the shedding of his blood on the cross – all things, whether in earth or in heaven.[12]

The resurrection of Christ sets in train a series of transforming events which await their final completion in the return of Christ:

Then I heard all created things, in heaven, on earth, under the earth, and in the sea, crying: 'Praise and honour, glory and might, to him who sits on the throne and to the Lamb for ever.'[13]

The ultimate transformation of created order into the Hebrew prophet's vision of the peaceable kingdom of justice where enmity and violence will be no more is at last anticipated in the resurrection, and although, as Stanley Hauerwas puts it, 'we continue to live in a time where there is no peace, when the wolf cannot dwell with the lamb and a child cannot play over the hole of the asp, we believe nonetheless that peace has been made possible by the resurrection'.[14] It is only from the perspective of the resurrection that we can see the creation truly for what it is, which is the product of the holy will of God whose plan is to restore its goodness, wholeness and harmony, and to draw it towards its final end in complete relationality with and reflection of the goodness of God.[15] The resurrection begins in history the work of restoration which is promised and draws the created order towards its goal of harmony and peace.

This embodied, ecclesial and cosmic perspective on the resurrection is underwritten by Paul's cosmic understanding of the effects of the atonement, of the sacrifice of Christ's body on the cross. And here we should recall the primal Hebraic understanding of physical sacrifice as restoring created order, and as representing a thank-offering for the goodness and giftedness of this order. It is clear in the Pauline Epistles, and especially in the Epistle to the Hebrews, that this Hebraic understanding of sacrifice remains paradigmatic for the interpretations which we find in the New Testament of the significance of the death of Christ. In the light of this, and of the supreme example of sacrifice which Christ's death on the cross represents, we can clearly see that God does not abandon his creation to human sin and evil or to ecological injustice and degradation. In the sacrifice of his own being God pays the price which the integrity of nature's order demands, vindicates the being of the cosmos and the justice of the created order and redeems the suffering of the defenceless, the vulnerable and the innocent, human and non-human alike. Though God is the transcendent and supreme originator of the cosmos, and lord of all of life, in the death of Christ God takes into the divine being the suffering and frustration which are the lot of creaturely being after the fall of humanity. But just as the fall of the 'first man Adam' has implications for the whole cosmos, so too does the salvation effected by the 'last man' Christ: as Paul (or a close disciple) indicates in the Epistle to the Colossians the history both of humans and of the cosmos is changed for ever by the death of Christ:

He rescued us from the domain of darkness and brought us into the kingdom of his dear Son, through whom our release is secured and our sins are forgiven. He is the image of the invisible God; his is the primacy over all created things.

For in him God in all his fullness chose to dwell, and through him to reconcile *all things* to himself, making peace through the shedding of his blood on the cross – all things, whether in earth or in heaven.[16]

The continuing experience of suffering, and the continuing agony and groaning of the creation, is made sense of in terms of the experience and hope of salvation and restoration which is begun in this dreadful death which Christians, from the time of Paul of Tarsus, have proclaimed in the sign of the cross as the central act of the world's salvation. Through this great event of redemptive suffering the suffering and frustration of every living thing is drawn into the eternal purposes of God for the restoration of the cosmos:

I think that what we suffer in this life can never be compared to the glory as yet unrevealed, which is waiting for us. The whole creation is eagerly waiting for God to reveal his sons.[17]

According to the Christian idea of atonement then, God does not respond to the predicament of guilt by annulling the moral necessity of judgement on moral evil, including judgement for our destruction of the planet, no more than God unravels the ecological sensitivities and balance of the biosphere. What God does do in the crucifixion is to atone for this judgement, to transform it by drawing it into his own being, thereby restoring the possibilities for life and joy, gratitude and generosity, love and grace in human history, and for fertility and harmony, peaceableness and beauty, reciprocity and stability in the natural world. As Stephen Clark affirms, Christ atones for our debts to the creation, to one another and to God.[18] This paradigmatic act of forgiveness and reconciliation re-establishes the relational structure which is at the heart of the universe and which is first abrogated by human sin and injustice. The possibilities of repentance and renewal in our moral life, of effective resistance to evil and of new and more harmonious relations both in human life and with the order of creation, are all opened up by the crucifixion and the resurrection of Christ from death.

The outworking of the ethical implications of Christ's death and resurrection takes place in the context of the new communities of the New Testament churches, many of them founded by St Paul. These communities, and the ethical schema which Paul developed in correspondence with them, present us with an account of the human self-in-relation which conceives of the embodied self as constituted by its worship of the creator God, and its relations with God, with other selves and with the embodied character of the non-human world. The central significance of persons in the created order for the early Christians, which is productive of a unique ethic of justice and respect for the person, arises from the recognition that, though persons are not of the same substance as God, they are none-theless of supreme value as objects of God's relational care and love. The New Testament concept of the self as constituted by its relations to God as creator emphasises that the central good of human life is relationality to God expressed in worship and spirituality, and relationality to other persons, expressed through an ethic of love and care and mutual responsibility. But this ethic of persons does not lead to personalism. The early Christian emphasis on the embodied character of selfhood, and the redemptive purposes of God for the whole created order, also generates an account of selfhood which, uniquely in the ancient world, locates the order of human life at the heart of all the orders of creation, and in a deep relationality with them.

The understanding of the love of God for persons and creation which we find in the teachings of Jesus translates in later centuries into the love of the desert fathers, and of St Francis and his followers, not only for their fellow monks, and for those penitents who came to them for counsel, but for the wild creatures with whom they shared their wilderness exis-tence. By contrast modern utilitarian individualism represents the individual self as the sole locus of moral purposiveness and meaning in the world. Modern individualism arises, as we have seen, from the distancing of self-consciousness from embodi-ment, and from the disembedding of the self from communities of place as traditionally constituted by the worship of God, and the correlative recognition of divine order in the cosmos and of divine intentionality in human society. The idea that love or justice are central features of God's purposes for human life, and for the life of the non-human world, thus becomes increas-ingly alien to the modern mind, and so moderns pursue their purposes in the world with little reference to their relational impacts upon other groups of poor humans or on the non-human world.

The relationality of all the orders of embodied life is particularly clearly enunciated in the Johannine understanding of incarnation and the Logos doctrine. The cosmic Logos is first encountered in the Christian canon of scripture in the figure of Wisdom in the Hebrew Bible, translated Logos by the Greek Septuagint, and has significant parallels with Hellenistic philosophies of nature. According to the prologue of the Gospel of John, the divine Word, the Logos, who was with the creator in the beginning,[19] and whose life is shared by everything that lives,[20] comes to the creation as embodied presence and in this embodiment he takes into himself the corruption which has entered into creation and heals and restores the whole cosmos, and humanity as the fulcrum of cosmic life and order: 'It was not to judge the world that God sent his Son into the world, but that through him the world might be saved.'[21]

By means of the Logos teaching, the author of the Gospel of John determinatively links the incarnation with the Hebrew story of creation and the Hebrew concept of created order, as the Logos is identified in the Septuagint translation of the Hebrew Bible with the figure of Wisdom, who in the Book of Proverbs and elsewhere is the creative agent of Yahweh. In the Johannine perspective then, the incarnational embodiment of the creator sets forth in human history the face of that energy and power – Logos – which moves and drives the universe from its origin to its destiny. The revelation of Christ as the Son of God reveals within history the creative principle which holds the cosmos together and which draws it to its end and goal: the incarnation confirms and demonstrates the fundamental goodness of created order. Matter itself, as well as humans, plants and animals, is thus revealed as the object of the ordering and creative power of the creator.

THE TRINITARIAN CREATOR

The second-century theologian Irenaeus takes up the Pauline and Johannine interpretation of the cosmic significance of the incarnation, death and resurrection of Jesus Christ, and he develops his theology of nature in opposition to early Christian Gnosticism. Gnosticism was an attempt to answer the philosophical problem of natural evil by positing that the material world is fundamentally evil and opposed to the Gnostic *pleroma* (fullness), the Gnostic God. As Hans Blumenberg argues, the central characteristic of Gnostic theism is that God bears no responsibility for, and cares not, for the material world.[22] Significantly, Blumenberg finds in the influence of Gnostic cosmology on medieval nominalism and scholasticism, and its Greek philosophical counterpart in Epicureanism, the roots of the early modern scientific conception of absolute space and time as realms which are not relationally dependent on the being of God, but which exist independently, absolutely, having their own life and rationality, which are revelatory neither of God nor of a coherent or good order of things.[23] Blumenberg argues that the Gnostic deity is necessarily an immutable as well as a transcendent deity, and that such a deity is also to be found in the writings of medieval theologians such as William of Okham and Anselm of Canterbury. The consequence for Christian theology and its subsequent influence on modern scientific cosmology, particularly after the Reformation, is that creation increasingly becomes secularised and evacuated of theistic order and purposiveness. Blumenberg's thesis represents the antinomy between Irenaeus and the Gnostics as a kind of watershed in the history of Christian, and hence Western thought, and in the origins of modernity. As Colin Gunton argues, this important philosophical tracing of the origins of modernity makes Irenaeus' answer to the Gnostics all the more important.[24]

Against the Gnostic idea that material creation is simply a shadow of the divine light from which the enlightened soul needs liberating, Irenaeus argues that God includes the fullness – *pleroma* – of all things 'in his immensity' and that nothing exists which is unrelated to God who contains all things and commands all things into existence 'by His Word that never wearies'.[25] Against the Gnostic teaching of the primacy of eternal ideas in the mind of God over their material forms,

Irenaeus argues for the primacy of created things in their material embodied substance, and for the origin of created things not in pre-existent matter but in the power and will of God. Against the idea that matter is fundamentally evil and opposed to the purposes of God, Irenaeus teaches that nature and the material world are fundamentally good and blessed by God, and that any tendencies to evil and discord which the material world contains are atoned for and redeemed in the incarnation, crucifixion and resurrection of Jesus Christ, who is God in material, embodied form.

As Gunton argues, the relation between the eternal God and the material, embodied, temporal creation is effected by Irenaeus through the doctrine of the Trinity.[26] The will of God for the creation is established through the partnership of the Father with the divine Logos or Word, and with Sophia or the Spirit of Wisdom: 'there is therefore one God, who by Word (Logos) and Wisdom (Sophia) created and arranged all things'.[27] The eternal God is invisible and incorporeal but as Logos and Sophia this eternal transcendent God becomes visible in the incarnate Son of living flesh who is at one with creation. The creature is related to the invisible God through the Son in the economy of creation/redemption, and through Logos and Sophia God holds all things together and sustains and nurtures them and draws them towards their goal.[28] The salvation and fulfilment of the creation from the natural evil and corruption which originate in the Fall, and *not* in the nature of matter itself, is brought about by the divine Logos being born into the womb of the virgin by the power of Sophia. Corporeal and incorporeal, body and spirit are thereby united and the relation of the creature to the creator, matter and God, finds eternal affirmation and fulfilment. The embodiment of God in the man Jesus Christ confirms the original goodness of created order, and substantial, material embodiment re-establishes the trajectory of this order towards God's good purposes, and redeems that which is unredeemed in the embodied life of the cosmos. But this redemption of the cosmos was already inherent in God's purposes for the creation from the beginning. As Paul Santmire notes, according to Irenaeus God as creator is always near to the creation through the eternal Logos and Spirit who are his 'hands'. And the creation, despite the fall of humanity, largely continues and remains near to God, and subject to His purposes and designs.[29] The whole of creation, as well as humanity, is designed to reflect the beauty, harmony and perfection which is God's, and thus the final eschatological redemption of humanity will be accompanied by the restoration of nature:

The predicted blessing, therefore, belongs unquestionably to the times of the Kingdom, when the righteous shall bear rule upon rising from the dead, when also the creation, having been renovated and set free, shall fructify with an abundance of all kinds of food, from the dew of heaven, and from the fertility of the earth.[30]

Gunton argues that this incarnational and Trinitarian under-standing of creation is central to the recovery of an ecological and relational ethic in which both human and non-human life are conceived as inherently inter-related but also given distinc-tive ontological and physical space in which to *be*.[31] Unlike monistic ontologies of the kind adopted by ecotheologians such as McFague and Fox, Irenaeus' Trinitarian approach to the being of creation establishes a ground for the differentiation of self and other, of the many and the one, for the diversity of human and non-human life and for the embodied and material character of life in the cosmos, including the order of human life. Gunton, after Blumenberg, argues that the modern ten-dency to homogenise nature, to reject its otherness, to deny the relationality of the self to nature and to remake nature entirely for human purposes, has its origins in the gradual dissolution of this early Christian idea of the unity of God's creative and redemptive purposes for the created order and for embodied human life, and the self-in-relation, as part of that order.[32] The early Christian conception of the redemption of embodiment, and its manifestation in a communitarian ethic of self-in-relation, is a vital corrective to the atomism of modern indivi-dualism with its tendency to devalue the distinctiveness of both the human and non-human other, and to locate meaning and moral value exclusively in individual human self-consciousness.

Moral value in the Irenaean synthesis is located in the relations
between persons, in worship and communal life by which
human life together is modelled on the divine life of the Trinity,
and in the relations of God and humans to the embodied
created order.

The Irenaean creation–redemption synthesis, with its roots
in the New Testament, is a unique testament to the theological
and ethical creativity of early Christianity, over against Hellenism, manifest in a new cosmology and ethic which sets
Christ at the heart of reality, both human and non-human,
and which inextricably links God's creative and redemptive
will for human persons and the cosmos. It also demonstrates
the inherent ideological tensions between the Hebraic and
early Christian affirmation of the fundamental goodness of
created order and life in the body, and the Hellenistic tendency
to denigrate finite, embodied life as inherently corrupt and
tending to decay. Christian belief in the resurrection of the
body, of the body of Jesus and of the bodies of believers, and
the related eschatological belief in the 'new creation' which
will be the end of Christ's creative and redemptive work, carry
the Hebrew concept of created order into the Roman world of
Hellenistic philosophy and pagan religion, asserting the fundamental goodness of the world, and of the human body, and the
possibilities for redemption and restoration both of humanity
and nature, the body and the soul. But this resurrection faith is
soon distorted in the subsequent Romanisation and Hellenisation of Christianity and it is here perhaps that we can detect
that first fundamental shift in Christian philosophy which
precedes the gradual displacement of meaning and moral
significance from the created order and embodied human life to
the interior life of the soul and human rationality, and the
subsequent evacuation of teleology and purposiveness from
nature in late medieval and Reformation theology, and early
modern thought. As Blumenberg contends, the early creation–
redemption synthesis is eclipsed by a more exclusive focus on
redemption in subsequent Christian theologies, by a growing
ambiguity about the nature of matter and bodies, and a
growing disjunction between human salvation and the corrup-

tible creation.[33] This shift can already be clearly observed in the writings of the highly influential fourth-century theologian and bishop, Athanasius of Alexandria.

Athanasius treats of the doctrine of creation in his anti-pagan treatise *Contra Gentes*. In this great work of Christian apologetics he argues against polytheism, and in particular the Greek idea of a created demiurge or demi-god who mediates between God and the world, and contends that the one God establishes the whole created order by the power of the divine Logos, the Word who is as much God, of the 'same substance', as God the Father.[34] The divine Word is 'present in all things and extends his power everywhere, illuminating all things visible and invisible'.[35] It is the will of God represented in the invisible Logos which moves the heavenly bodies, and the mountains, seas and living things of the earth: 'by his own will he moves and regulates them, producing a single order'.[36] Consequently the order of creation speaks to the human mind of the wisdom, power and goodness of God.[37] So far Athanasius sounds positively Irenaean. However, when we come to his treatment of redemption in *De Incarnatione* we find no reference to the redemptive purposes of God for the created order as a whole, which, according to *De Incarnatione,* is inherently unstable and corruptible because of its contingency, its finitude, its creation out of nothing.[38] Instead, humanity is the exclusive object of God's redemptive action in the incarnation of his Son: the reason the Word of God came into the corruptible world is to redeem 'the rational race' from the corruption and death which are the inherent nature and end of the rest of the contingent creation, but not the destiny of rational humans who are the image of the invisible God. The incarnate Word effected salvation by taking into the being of God

a body which could die, in order that, since this participated in the Word who is above all, it might suffice for death on behalf of all, and because of the Word who was dwelling in it, it might remain incorruptible, and so corruption might cease from all men by the grace of the resurrection.[39]

It is clear from this passage, and others like it, that for Athanasius, unlike Irenaeus, the redemptive action of God in Christ is not directed to the whole created order, nor even to sensate animals, but only to the rational race of humans. In this radical divorce between creation and redemption, and in the hominisation of redemption, we may detect the clear imprint of Hellenistic, and in particular Neoplatonic assumptions about the corruptibility of matter, bodies and non-rational life which, because they are not eternal but temporal and contingent, are also seen as finite and ever in danger of returning to the non-being from which they originated. Athanasius was the first theologian to establish a new *rapprochement* between the Graeco-Roman world and the Christian, reflecting the changing political realities of his day, as Christianity emerged from its minority sectarian status to become, under the Emperor Constantine, the religion of the Roman Empire. After Constantine's conversion, as John Rist argues, Christian teachers, including the Cappadocian Fathers and Augustine, could now treat paganism not as an adversary but as a defeated foe, but with some pearls of wisdom whose value survived its downfall.[40]

In his 1992 Gifford lectures, *Christianity and Classical Culture*, Jaroslav Pelikan shows with great expository skill the ways in which the triumph of theology over classical culture allowed the further assimilation of elements of Platonic and Neoplatonic thought into the doctrines of God, creation and redemption, and the natural theology of the Cappadocian Fathers.[41] The influence of Platonism is clearly evident in the adoption by Basil of Caesarea of the distinction between matter and form in his *De Spiritu Sancto*, a distinction which is later taken up by the medieval scholastics.[42] This concept of the distinction between forms and matter lies at the heart of Plato's theory of ideas, for by forms he identified the heavenly ideas of living things or objects and by matter, bodies, substance, he indicated their earthy, finite and corruptible realisation in the cosmos. The influence of this theory of ideas is evident again in Gregory of

Nyssa's *De Anima et Resurrectione*, where he argues that the Genesis account of creation describes the development from the heavenly ideas to the particular phenomena in which these ideas were materialised, embodied, in the cosmos.[43] The Cappadocian modification of Platonism allowed that God could be known from the order of creation, without the aid of revelation,[44] but at the same time the Cappadocians taught that only those forms of being closest to the reason and wisdom of God – the invisible angelic powers and the human soul – could reflect the divine nature, for those natures 'of which the senses can take cognisance are utterly alien to deity, and of these the furthest removed are all those that are entirely destitute of soul and of power and of motion'.[45]

This adoption of the Platonic theory of ideas, and the Platonic distinction between the heavenly ideas or forms and their material embodied existence, is closely related to the narrowing of the remit of salvation in the teachings of the Cappadocian Fathers, as in Athanasius, and the deep ambiguity which these Hellenistically influenced theologians felt towards the material world and the human body. In a recent study of Gregory of Nazianzus, Anna-Stiva Ellverson identifies a 'double attitude toward the material world and the creation' in his theology.[46] As we saw in Athanasius, the positive comments about matter occur in passages relating to God's creation of the world, and the negative comments occur in relation to the consideration of humanity's spiritual state, humanity's fall and the Christic work of redemption.[47] This Platonic view leads to a theological anthropology in which man is described as a mingled being, 'temporal and immortal, visible and intellectual, midway between greatness and lowliness, at the same time spirit and flesh, spirit because of the grace, flesh because of the pride'.[48] The purpose of Christ's incarnation as a human is therefore related to this intrinsic weakness of intelligibility and spirit in the first man Adam, and all subsequent humans, as much as it is related to Adam's fall into sin, a fall which was an inevitable consequence of the composite nature of humans as both intelligible spirits and corruptible material bodies.[49] Sin is seen as inherently related to corporeality and matter. Christ's

incarnation as the embodied Son of God is the divine response
to the composite or mingled nature (*mixis*)[50] of humanity as
body and soul, the redeeming of humanity's soul from corporeality: Christ's transformed and resurrected body is the type of
the redeemed human, but of course there can be no such
redemption for creatures who are merely sensible and lack the
intelligibility and spirit which makes of humans the inter-
mediate beings between God and nature in the cosmos.[51]

The Cappadocians distinguished the creative and redemptive
work of God by means of the concept of the *economy* of salvation.
Thus Gregory of Nazianzus used the term economy to distinguish the ineffable transcendence of God from the necessary
immanence of the God who acts as creator and saviour.[52] By
this means the Cappadocians sought to preserve the absolute
transcendence, immutability and *apatheia* of the eternal God,
arguing in relation to Christ that it was his human bodily
nature which suffered and died on the cross, while his divine
nature was preserved in its unchanging form.[53] By contrast, as
Gunton argues, with Hans Urs von Balthasar, Irenaeus uses this
concept of economy to affirm the unity of God's actions
towards the world and humans, from creation to redemption to
the eschaton, a Trinitarian economy which reflects the Trinity
of Father, Son and Holy Spirit. By this Trinitarian economy
'Irenaeus was able to allow history to be itself, by virtue of its
very relation to God. Because all that God does is achieved by
means of his two hands, the Son and the Spirit, it is done both
effectively and in due recognition of the integrity of created
being.'[54] By this means Irenaeus affirms the essential and
dynamic relationality of time and space to God in his roles as
creator, sustainer, redeemer and perfecter of the world.[55]

Thus we see that the radical distinction between creation and
redemption, and the narrowing of the writ of redemption from
its cosmic import in the New Testament and in Irenaeus to its
significance solely for human destiny, commences not with
Augustine, as Gunton argues, but with Athanasius and the
Cappadocian Fathers.[56] However, Gunton is right to indicate
the significant ecological implications of this narrowing of the
import of salvation, for it so clearly contributes to two move-

ments in Christian thought which were to have great consequences in the attitude to created order, the environment, in
later Christian history. Firstly, this new Platonised theology
produces a new asceticism with regard to the human body
which is expounded with great clarity in Peter Brown's *The Body
and Society*,[57] and which eclipses the Pauline emphasis on bodily
resurrection and the transforming effects of the Spirit on the
embodied life of Christians. This in turn contributes to the
rising concentration of Christian spirituality and worship on the
inner life of the individual soul, a concentration which achieves
its first flowering in Augustine's radically new exploration of
interiority in his *Confessions*. As Taylor argues, the subsequent
privileging by Christian theologians of interiority over exter-
iority, of the inner over the outer, of the soul over the body, of
the individual over the community, and of reason over nature
contributes to the modern conception of the self as radically
distinct from the environment of communal relationships, and
physical embodied experiences, in relation to which self-identity
actually emerges. Secondly, as Blumenberg argues, the influence of the Platonic view of matter and life forms as somehow
ontologically weaker than the eternal God and the souls and
minds of humans, mediated to early modern thought through
medieval nominalism, is one of the most significant roots of the
modern secularisation of both human life and the cosmos, and
the modern tendency to reduce the non-human material world
to a homogenised and hominised space which has no independent reality and significance other than its capacity to meet
human needs.[58]

As we have seen, it is the towering figure of Augustine who
mediates the Platonic influence to the Christianity of the
Middle Ages. In many ways his attitude to the body and
sexuality is more positive than that of his Cappadocian forebears. Thus he regards sexuality as part of God's original
intention for the life of Adam and Eve in paradise.[59] The
problem with sexuality and bodies does not reside in physicality
itself but in the corruption of the human will which follows
from the Fall. It is the fallen will which, according to Augustine,
distorted the original goodness of sexuality, friendship and

society, which invented the cruelty of slavery and necessitated the coercion of the state.[60] Tragically emerging from the divine gift of human freedom, it is the fallen will which also so radically disrupts the good order and harmony of the cosmos. But the fallenness of the human will is a function of the contingency of embodied human life. As John Rist shows, it was inconceivable to Augustine that embodied humanness, as part of the material creation which comes from nothingness, could have ever realised the sinlessness of divine perfection.[61] Sin is the inevitable concomitant of contingency and createdness. The soul of Adam, though it was free to choose the good was weak because of its created contingency and so inevitably chose evil.[62] Thus we see how different is Augustine's and Irenaeus' doctrine of creation. For Irenaeus creation is contingent, finite, plural and particular but it is still inherently good, and, as Gunton shows, its goodness is effected by the relationality between the creative and redeeming 'hands' of God, the Son and the Spirit.[63] But Augustine separates the creation of the world from the redemption of the world because, as Gunton argues, his doctrine of creation is finally not Christological and pneumatological but Neoplatonic.[64] Because creation is from nothing it is inherently ontologically, and hence morally, weak, and this moral weakness is supremely focused in humanity. Thus the only place in the cosmos where God may determinatively be known is where the individual human mind and will are being led, by divine revelation and grace, towards knowledge and love of the divine will. Outside of the gracing of human will, the rest of the creation is outside of the divine economy of salvation.

This conception of creation carries with it the concomitant that creation is a product not of Christological care and pneumatological providence so much as of the arbitrariness of divine will. There is an arbitrariness in creation which is a reflection of the absoluteness of God and of the contingent voluntariness of creation. The consequence of Augustine's prioritisation of freedom is a voluntarist doctrine of both humanity and creation, and it is this voluntarism, combined with a divine absolutism, which produces a view of creation which is characterised by what Blumenberg calls the 'disappearance of order'.[65] Augustine answers the Gnostic disregard for matter as naturally evil by means of his focus on human freedom as the origin of evil in the world. But this solution merely transposes the Gnostic problem with matter inward into the human consciousness. The answer to the problems of the world lies not in the cosmos, where the increasingly hidden and absolutely transcendent God of Augustine can hardly be known. Rather the answer lies in human interiority, in matters of the will, and in the direction of human freedom towards love and goodness or away from them. The cosmos, as Blumenberg argues, consequently loses its reliability and its order: the salvation of humans and the creation of the cosmos are counterposed. By this means Augustine 'saved' material existence in the body from Gnostic and Manichaean denunciation.[66] But at the same time Augustine laid the foundation, taken up by the medieval nominalists, for the evacuation of order, purposiveness and moral significance from the external world, beyond the reason and soul of individual humans, which was in turn to legitimate the technical remaking of nature purely in the image of human wants and needs, and the remaking of human society as an order of competing individuals rather than a community of selves-in-relation ordered to the love of God and neighbour.[67] The growing alienation between persons in modern societies, and between modern societies and natural order thus find their theological roots in the nominalist destruction of the reliability and dependability of the cosmos, which, as Blumenberg argues, paved the way for 'the mechanistic philosophy of nature [to] be adopted as the tool of self-assertion'.[68] This destruction of the dependable cosmos is the necessary precondition for the emergence of the technocentrism of modern civilisation as scientifically enabled humans attempt to wrest a 'new humanity' from the deficiency of nature.[69] It is also the precondition for the modern turn to the self as the only sure source of purposiveness and moral significance in a world indifferent to the human fate.

It was the supreme nominalist, William of Ockham, who most clearly enunciated the emergent Augustinian distinctions between the orders of grace and nature, between the absolute will of God and the contingency of matter and between the creative action of God in establishing the world and his redeeming action in saving individual human souls from the world.[70] As Gunton argues, Ockham's famous 'razor' was the philosophical device by which he distinguished between God's causative action in setting the world in motion, and the imputation into nature by human observers of order or rationality.[71] There is no necessity of goodness or providence in creation for the nominalists or else, they argued, the absolute power of the will of God would be compromised by the act of creating. God's creative power is entirely free and hence arbitrary, and so the nature of God may not be read off from nature. Nature is fundamentally indifferent therefore to humanity. All that can be said of it is that God willed it. But God's loving and saving intentions for humans are not tied to this original act of willing of materiality and contingency.

As Blumenberg argues, this new ontological groundlessness of nature, and its newly perceived unfriendliness towards humanity, produces a new urgency in the emergent science of physics, which Ockham himself advanced, for only by the exercise of power over nature through natural science could humanity overcome the hostility of the world.[72] The paradoxical outcome of the nominalist appropriation of Augustine's strong doctrine of the divine will, and his correlative emphasis on human freedom, is that human self-assertion, that very creaturely pride which Augustine regarded as the origin of Adam's sin, becomes the central and definitive mode of humanly being in the cosmos.[73] Thus the new nominalist doubtfulness of the contingent world calls forth humanity's reordering and remaking capacities, and this doubtfulness is taken up with new vigour in the theologies of the Reformation.

Like Ockham, John Calvin dedicates his theological enterprise to the assertion and defence of divine sovereignty over human destiny and the creation, and to the affirmation of God's glory and goodness above all other purposes, human or created. He asserts that the goodness of God for humanity is established in the eternal predestination or choosing of a certain number of elect souls who would be able to realise God's good purposes by overcoming the effects of the Fall within created order. The divine elect, predestined to redemption through the atoning sacrifice of Christ, are eternally distinguished from the rest of created order, and from the eternally damned humans, to which or to whom God has no obligation other than that of judgement. Only in the souls of the elect does there remain an unambiguous reflection of the divine light which at creation irradiated the whole universe.[74] Even in its unfallen state nature has no inherent goodness other than its capacity to witness to the saving power of God for elect souls, and its only legitimacy rests in its potential to be of service to those souls.[75] The influence of the nominalist view of nature as at best indifferent, and after the Fall in some ways hostile, to the good purposes of God for the salvation of elect human souls, also fuels Calvin's emphasis on the human vocation to exercise dominion over the natural world so as to transform it in the service of human industry and human work. The ethical vocation of the individual who experiences inner salvation is to work for the outward transformation of fallen nature so that it may begin to express that same glory of God which is shown forth in the inner work of salvation in the individual who is justified by faith.[76] As Langdon Gilkey puts it, in Calvin's theology the individual is 'strengthened inwardly, given immense creative authority and sent into an "open" world to remold it to God's glory'.[77]

The focus of Reformation theology on the salvation of the soul eclipses the earlier Irenaean and New Testament understanding of the ontological relation between the diversity of created life and the being of God as Father, Son and Spirit, and of the effects of salvation on the whole of created reality. Whereas Calvin still held to the divine intention to restore creation as well as the souls of the elect in the future time of salvation, this view is eclipsed in the strengthening individualism and anthropocentrism of other and subsequent Reformation theologians. Nature gradually ceases to be seen as the object of God's relational and redeeming love manifest in Christ the Lord of nature, who stilled the storm and whose death was announced by an earthquake, and whose resurrection promised the restoration of all created life. In medieval nominalism, and even more explicitly in Reformation theology, nature is essentially available for humans to use and transform at their behest. As Calvin put it, God like a 'provident and industrious head of a family' has 'arranged the motions of the sun and stars for man's use, has replenished the air, earth, and water, with living creatures, and produced all kinds of fruit in abundance for the supply of food'.[78] This anthropocentric and instrumentalist view of nature accompanied a culture which increasingly eschewed the presence and ordering purposes of God in the non-human world and became increasingly instrumentalist and domineering in its attitudes to nature.[79] Although Calvin himself argued against the abuse of nature, nonetheless his emphasis on the depravity of nature, and on the subjection of natural purposes to human purposes, and in particular to the purposes of the elect, preceded, if not legitimated, the abandonment of ethical limits on the human use of nature, and on the commodification of land and its product.

The Reformation theologies of individual salvation and justification also eclipse the early Christian understanding of self-in-relation, for according to Calvin it is not the relations between selves, and between humans and created order, which are salvifically and morally significant but the choosing of particular individual selves by the will of God to be objects of his eternal love and goodness. This Protestant intensification of Augustine's emphasis on the individual self as the locus of divine activity in the world gives rise to a new form of religious individualism which is deeply corrosive of the relationality of human and ecclesial community, and of the relations of human community to the non-human world. The natural law ethic of the Middle Ages reflected a theology of cosmic and social order and relationality in which persons were set in a divine hierarchy of being, and a divine purposiveness for all life from angels to animals. The social order of land and humans was also conceived as a divine order. Through the worship of the church, and the ordering of agricultural and town life around the interaction of the natural seasons and the divine liturgy, the life of medieval society was purportedly directed and ordered by and towards the love of God and God's redemptive purposes for the cosmos. The advent of Protestant individualism not only removes the sacred significance of the divinely ordered cosmos. It also corrodes the theological and ethical underpinnings of human social relations, exposing the mass of humanity after the Reformation to the naked assertion of social power by political actors, landowners and merchants freed from the restraint of traditional natural law ethics and the conserving influence of monasticism. The liberation of self-assertion and social power from these traditional communitarian and ethical constraints occasions the most profound shake-up in human relations to the land, and to nature, and leads to the rise of the ordering and dissolving power of money in human society as the supreme symbol and vehicle of this newly liberated social power.

We can then see that there is a theological ground within the Christian doctrines of God, creation and redemption, and particularly in the Christ events, for the recognition of the moral value of the non-human world, and of the deep relationality of human life and self-consciousness to the created order. However, the early Christian schema of creation/redemption is gradually eclipsed under the influence of Hellenistic philosophy, and in particular of Platonism, and the good and salvific purposes of God for any part of the created order other than human souls are further eclipsed in Protestant theologies of election. The consequent metaphysical and moral dubiety of nature, and the rise of individualism, are both significantly linked to the modern technical domination of nature, and to the hominisation of the non-human world. The turn to the self eventually issues in a threat not only to the particularities, and distinctive moral goods, of the non-human world, but also in a threat to humanness itself, or as C. S. Lewis puts it, to 'the end of man', for as moderns have sought to ground human goods entirely in an account of human interiority, the very subjectivity of such accounts, and their lack of correlates in the material world of bodies and the cosmos, renders modern human societies peculiarly vulnerable to forms of totalitarianism and genocide such as Nazism and the Holocaust or more recently the Pol Pot and Rwandan massacres.[80] Similarly the modern conception of the uncreated, randomly evolved, character of the human being leaves modern humans peculiarly vulnerable to technocentric subversion, a subversion brought potentially much closer by recent advances in genetic science and planned medical therapies involving the genetic modification of the human germline. The nominalist and modernist evacuation of any signs of God as creator from the cosmos eventually leads to the substitution of chance and the laws of physics for the divine providence of the creator. In the end, as Dietrich Bonhoeffer notes, we 'cease to know the world as God's creation', and so 'the earth is no longer our earth, and then we become strangers on earth', and from strangers we finally become earth's subjects: through the power of technology 'the earth grips man and subdues him'.[81]

It becomes clear then that the recovery of an ecological ethic in the modern world requires the recovery of a doctrine of creation redeemed, and the worship of a creator who is also redeemer of the creation. It will also involve the reaffirmation of the relationality of God as creator to all that is created, to the materiality and embodiedness of all life, and of all human selves-in-relation, and not simply to the life of certain elected souls. As Gunton argues, a Trinitarian doctrine of creation re-establishes the ontological ground for the materiality, substantiality and relationality of the particular individuals and plural orders which constitute life on earth.[82] It also re-establishes the theological framework in which the human relation to creation may be truthfully constructed. The non-human world on this account does not simply consist of matter and sub-human life forms which have either been constructed by chance, or by a divine being who brings them into being and then places them entirely at the service of humans. Creation is rather the gifted and blessed state of embodied being for which God intends goodness and blessing from the beginning of the cosmos, an intention which is reaffirmed in the coming of Christ and the gift of the Spirit. The divine origin and purposiveness of embodied, created order is affirmed by the incarnation. In the crucifixion of Christ God shows that the suffering of the embodied creation consequent upon sin, sickness and death, are both of fundamental concern to God, and at the same time occasions for his overwhelming love and grace. In the resurrection God vindicates the created order from the frustration and evil which the Fall has occasioned, showing that it is the divine intention not only to restore the created order but to make it new, a 'new creation' in which the deep relationality of all *things* as well as all persons is, in the eschaton or the last days, finally affirmed.

Through this account of divine purposiveness in created order, and of the embodied relationality which characterises that order, we can critique the modern scientific evacuation of meaning and purposiveness, and hence of moral significance in the natural order; we can critique the focus of modern utilitarian individualism on individual self-consciousness and interiority as the exclusive locus of moral value and the touchstone of moral order; and we can critique the modern idolatry of consumerism which substitutes worship of the gift for the worship of the giver and so subverts the goodness of the gift. The reality of the natural order is both purposive and relational, and embodied human persons are central to this natural purposiveness and relationality, but they are also subjectively constructed *through* this reality, both as bodies and by their relations to other persons, and to particular places and features of the natural order. Any conception of reason or soul or self which eschews this subjective construction of the person through the order of nature and bodies, as well as through the order of persons and consciousness, is a denial of the incarnational understanding of creation/redemption, of the suffering of God in the excruciating physical reality of the cross and of the promised new creation which begins in the bodily resurrection of Jesus Christ from the dead.

This new creation, remains though, an interim reality, a way of being in the world which begins to restore relationality between persons and God, and between persons and created order in terms of their own bodies, of human society and of the embodied life of the biosphere, but which also recognises the not yet of creation/redemption, the ultimate incompleteness of Christian life and of created order, as we await the final work of grace and judgement which leads to fulfilment and the final victory of good over evil, of life over death and of joy over suffering. But even in the context of this eschatological interim, as we have seen, Christians began to develop an account of the moral significance of the self-in-relation and of created order and nature, which was productive of a deep respect for both human persons and non-human life, a respect moreover which was in sharp contrast to the pagan barbarity of contemporary Roman ethics and social practice. The centrality of the moral valuation of persons in the New Testament is evident in the life of Christ, in his relations with particular women and men, and it is particularly evident in the new communities of the early church and their elaboration of a pattern of worship and a household ethics in which the Jewish respect for personal, social and created order as gifted and sustained by God is affirmed and renewed.

The moral implications for non-human life of this new vision of creation redeemed find their clearest expression in the New Testament in the Synoptic Gospels, where the Lordship of Christ in relation to the creation is consistently affirmed. The baptism of John, the temptations of Jesus in the wilderness, the nature miracles, the turning of water into wine, the agrarian parables, the healing of ailments and disease; all these events and stories portray a relationship between Jesus as the Son of Man and the natural order which is reminiscent of the deep respect for created order, and God's salvific purposes for that order which we encounter in the Hebrew Bible. Jesus is portrayed as one who lives in supreme harmony with the natural order. He encounters the presence of God on the mountains, he calms the noise of nature on the Sea of Galilee and as Lord of nature his death causes ruptures in the natural order – the eclipse of the sun and the earthquake described in the passion narrative. Like the Hebrew prophets, the teachings of Jesus in the Gospels portray a harmonious relationship between God, humanity and nature, a relationship of blessing and abundance, and a relationship which human avarice and materialism are most likely to mar: 'consider how the lilies grow in the fields; they do not work, they do not spin; yet I tell you even Solomon in all his splendour was not attired like one of them'.[83] Or again God is one who takes care of the sparrows and birds of the air, and also numbers the hairs on the head of the human person. The natural provision of the creation for animals, their dependence on seasons and natural foods, is contrasted with human greed and materialism. Humanity is enjoined to learn the same dependence on God as the animal world already shows.

This portrayal of Christ as Lord of nature in the Synoptic Gospels, and the deep respect for created order which is manifest in the teachings of Jesus, as in the Jewish scriptures, is taken up in the letters and ethics of Paul in a more personalist form. The priority of Paul's ethics is the new relations between persons which the new creation in Christ constitutes for Christian households and communities, relationships which are fundamentally characterised by love, *agape*, which is the supreme gift or fruit of the Holy Spirit who transforms the moral inclinations, habits and life-styles of Christians from within. It is through the indwelling of the Spirit that Christians are enabled to begin to experience in their bodies and minds, in their households and in Christian churches, that transformation which is the promise of the resurrection for the whole created order. But at the same time Paul does not wish to deny the morality and potential goodness and flourishing of the created order and of human society beyond the lives of those spirit-filled individuals who are enabled to experience the fruits of faith which are the work of the Holy Spirit in the believer and in the community of faith. It is equally the work of the believer to discern within the created order of human society, and of nature, that which is conducive to the more general flourishing of the human condition, and not simply the flourishing of Christians.

The moral significance of natural created order for Paul is particularly evident in the first two chapters of the Epistle to the Romans, where he affirms two fundamental aspects of the moral teaching of both Jewish and Gentile (especially Stoic) philosophers of his day. The first of these is that there is clear evidence in the natural order of divine attributes and power, evidence which is available to all people as a source of moral guidance and reasoning – what the Stoics variously call logos or natural law.[84] The second is Paul's affirmation of conscience: 'When Gentiles who do not possess the law carry out its precepts by the light of nature, then, although they have no law, they are their own law; they show that what the law requires is inscribed on their hearts, and to this their conscience gives supporting witness.'[85] Like the Stoics, Paul argues that the light of nature is a moral source and guide for all people of good conscience, even for those who lack the wisdom of the Jewish legal tradition or great powers of reasoning or the indwelling divine grace and virtue of the Holy Spirit. Both these passages have of course been the subject of great controversy in Christian theology precisely because they do argue for a natural relationality between the 'new creation' of Christian living, Christian love and Christian community and the already existing order of nature and human society. These passages above all others in the New Testament affirm that the Christian ethic is not simply an ethic *for* Christians, but is rather what Oliver O'Donovan calls a 'natural ethic' because it involves an understanding of the moral order of the world, and of the restoration of that order in Christ, which is an order which addresses all people and not just Christians.[86] It is in the tradition of natural law, particularly as elaborated by Thomas Aquinas, that this 'natural ethic' reaches its fullest expression in the Christian moral tradition. I will argue that natural law as elaborated by Aquinas gives expression to the Hebraic ideas of created order, natural justice, natural wisdom and the relationality of human and non-human life, and at the same time to the Christian belief in the restoration of natural created order from the ambiguity of fallenness and sin, of human evil and natural evil in the Christ events.

NATURAL LAW ETHICS

Like Paul and the Hebrew prophets, but unlike Augustine, Aquinas argues that much of what can be known about God, and about the way we are to live, can be known from our natural experience of reason, and our reasoned observation of the natural order. Natural knowledge of truth is available to us because the cosmos is a realm in which the being of God manifests itself as being-in-action.[87] Like the New Testament writers, Aquinas does not believe that matter, embodied life, is inherently ontologically weak or problematic. He regards being itself as of the essence of divinity, and therefore inasmuch as everything which *is* has being, in *being* it manifests the divine being. Therefore, he says, all acts-of-being manifest the being of God for without God's being nothing can be: 'As long as one thing is, God must be present in it in that it is.' And so God 'must therefore be in all things'.[88] As Brian Davies shows, Aquinas uses the traditional idea of the ubiquity of God, which we encounter in Psalm 139, to argue for an intimate relation between God and every existent thing and place: 'he [God] is in every place giving it existence and the power to be a place, just as he is in all things giving them existence, power and activity'.[89] But this understanding of the ubiquity of God is clearly distinguished from pantheism, for the sense in which God is in every place is fundamentally a teleological sense: that is God is in everything in the sense that 'things are ordered to the ultimate end which God intends'.[90] Aquinas therefore eschews not only pantheism, but also the nominalist idea of arbitrariness in physical material being, and by extension its modern scientific equivalent in the idea of chance or random-ness in atomic or biological events.[91] The universe may be said to manifest in its beauty and order and is-ness various, though not all, of the attributes of God, and these attributes may therefore be truly if partially known from observing the uni-verse. Aquinas, unlike Augustine, believed that nature was a true mirror of the divine, and that the divine image is manifest in nature even after the Fall: 'Not only are individual creatures images of God but so too is the whole cosmos.'[92] Therefore Aquinas argues that every being pursues a goal which is a movement towards the creator: 'Each and every creature tends toward this – that it may participate in the Creator and be assimilated to the Creator insofar as it is able.'[93] Each individual being is, however, unable to reflect the perfection of God's nature and goodness. But when all beings in their relations with one another are observed as part of the whole which is the universe, we are drawn by this very multiplicity and relationality to reflect on God whose goodness and essence is much greater than any one human thought, word or concept can convey. It is the whole, and the inter-connections between the diverse beings which make up the whole, which together manifest the wise ordering of the universe by the active being of God: 'God deliberately brings about multitude and distinction in order that the divine goodness may be brought forth and shared in many measures. There is beauty in the very diversity.'[94]

This positive doctrine of creation, and of being in creation, means that there are for Aquinas not one, but two sources of our knowledge of God, and of truth: one is reasoned reflection on the order of things, or natural theology; the other is reflection on the revelation of God in the Bible which is the knowledge of faith. In a similar way there are two sources to guide us in how we are to live: nature and faith. The Bible indicates the character of the moral life to the faithful through the commandments and the life of Christ. In faithful worship we receive the indwelling Holy Spirit who brings forth in us the fruits of virtuous living, and especially the 'theological virtues' of faith, hope and, above all, love. These virtues are also acquired in the spiritual community of persons-in-relation. But nature may also guide us as to what is moral and virtuous. For Aquinas, as for Paul, conscience is the natural voice of the moral law which is part of the law of nature, guiding us to our proper end and purpose, which is established for every being in creation by natural law.

Aquinas states the central precept of natural law as follows: 'the first principle of practical reason is one founded on the notion of good, viz., that good is that which all things seek after. Hence this is the first precept of law, that good is to be done and pursued, and evil is to be avoided.'[95] Through his doctrine of natural law, Aquinas encapsulates Aristotle's belief in the rationality and purposiveness of the natural created order. God not only causes the universe to come into being but he is the origin of the purpose which every kind of being pursues in the course of its life, which is why each purpose which is pursued according to nature can be described as inherently good and right: 'Everything in nature moves and acts for an end that is a good since the end of something acting in nature is a natural appetite. Therefore everything that acts acts for a good.'[96]

Aquinas distinguishes between the goods of different orders of being, and in particular between the goods pursued by humans and those pursued by non-humans. In some aspects their goods are related. Thus the goods of appetite such as the gathering and eating of food, sexual procreation and the education and nurture of offspring are shared by both animals and humans.[97] But humans by virtue of their reason have a higher set of goods which are unavailable to animals and in pursuing these they will pursue those goods or virtues which through their reason humans are ordered to realise: 'there is in man a natural inclination to the good of the rational nature which is his alone. Thus man has a natural inclination to know the truth about God and to live in society.'[98] Humans are ordered by God both to a relationality with God, and with one another, which is, according to Aquinas, distinctive and determinative for human moral well-being. These respective goods of the different orders of being are set by Aquinas in an all-embracing teleology which represents the whole and its many parts as tending towards return to God, and as reflecting by its very nature and being the essence of God's goodness, which is compassion and justice: 'So the order of the universe, embracing natural and voluntary things alike, manifests the judgement of God.'[99]

There are a number of parallels between Aquinas' account of natural law and the account of created order and natural justice which we encounter in the Hebrew Bible:

1. Aquinas regards created order as a sphere of blessing and goodness which reflects deeply the imprint of its maker. Nature is ordered by God for its own purposes and these purposes are fundamentally good.
2. We are guided by nature and reason to do what is right.

There is a common inheritance of morality shared by all humans which is part of our nature. This natural morality is also shared in part with the other orders of creation which, in seeking their own goods, reflect to some degree the same teleological orientation which humans express when they pursue the good life and virtue: the goods of both humans and of non-humans are goals to which created order as a whole, and in all its diversity, is directed by the providence of the creator.

3. There is harmony and beauty in the diversity of things in the natural order and these are both reflections of God's own being.[100] All things are directed towards God in the goods which they pursue. But all things also tend towards a natural harmony of interdependence. This interdependence reflects the justice of God in the order of the cosmos. Created order is therefore also a moral order.[101]

4. The transforming work of divine grace in humans, and in the non-human world, is directed towards the restoration of this harmony and interdependence. The principle of restoration is the principle of justice: 'Justice preserves all existing things to the extent that the nature of each thing receives and upholds it according to its own particular kind.'[102]

5. The end of human government is the promotion of the common good which is characterised by a state of justice in which all are rendered their due according to the natural equity of proportion manifest in natural justice.[103] The human self is constituted not by its individual self-consciousness and individual fulfilment but by the richness of its relations with God and created beings. The order of society should therefore be directed towards the maximisation of opportunities for goodness and virtue in human relationships, including love as well as justice.

6. Human production or exchange which is designed to meet natural needs or necessities, and to provide security for a person's household, is 'praiseworthy because it serves natural needs', but forms of trade and money exchange which promote private gain and greed – and particularly usury – are contrary to natural justice.[104]

Despite the positive view of creation and of the moral significance of natural order which we find in Aquinas' philosophy, and which is reflected in his doctrine of natural law and natural justice, there are limitations in his elaboration of a natural law ethic with regard to the non-human world. In his earliest work *Summa Contra Gentiles* Aquinas argues that animals and plants are fundamentally ordered for human ends, and that humans may therefore do what they will to animals in their quest for food and other life necessities: 'animals are ordered to man's use in the natural course of things, according to divine providence'.[105] The domestication and killing of animals for meat is therefore clearly permitted. But even cruelty against animals may not be ruled out on moral grounds if it serves human purposes.[106] This ordering of all things for human purposes reflects the natural law presumption of the superiority of human reason over all non-rational beings, for by reason humans are closer to God and to divine incorruptibility.[107] In his adherence to reason as the essence of the human soul, and as that which marks humans off from the rest of corruptible nature, Aquinas clearly reflects the common inheritance of both Plato and Aristotle, and of Greek philosophy generally. This adherence to reason as the uniquely divine aspect of human life is also manifest in Aquinas' qualitative distinction between natural law as available to animals only in terms of base instincts, but to humans as rationally motivated virtue.[108]

The other problem is with Aquinas' tendency to discount the significance of natural evil, and to underestimate the effects of the Fall in the non-human world and for human life. Thus he argues that natural evil is part of God's providential order of things and that particular instances of corruption or suffering express God's overall providence. Lions prey on other animals because they need to live, but this is simply an instance of an overall purposive good in the order of things; 'the defect in one thing yields to the good of another, or even to the universal good: for the corruption of one is the generation of another, and through this it is that a species is kept in existence'.[109] Thus much evil that is suffered both by humans and non-humans can be explained 'as part of the good of the whole natural order' as

Bryan Davies puts it.[110] We may not wish to dissent from this, as it is a sensible account of the actual biological reality of predation and even perhaps of parasitism. But the Irenaean view of creation/redemption which I outlined above points to the idea that these apparently necessary evils may not be part of God's eternal intention for the cosmos, either before creation, or at its final restoration. In other words to take the interpenetration of creation by redemption seriously we must concur with Isaiah that natural evil will at some point be addressed by God in his final redemption of created order. We may also want to say, as Jürgen Moltmann among others does, that in taking the form of a human body, and undergoing death, God has indicated in the clearest way possible that the suffering of creation is of deep and fundamental concern to the creator, and, even if this suffering is in part inherent in the physical and embodied interaction of diverse parts in the ordering of the whole, nonetheless this suffering is in some way redeemed through the cross or the 'holy tree'. There is of course another kind of evil, which is caused directly by human agency, but in relation to this kind of evil Aquinas argues that it is primarily evidence of a lack of good, and again it would seem that at this point he underestimates the deep reality of sin, and the effects of the Fall, however we may understand these effects as being transmitted, whether biologically or socially.[111] Here too it would appear that his doctrine of humanness is insufficiently Christological and redemptionist, and rather too reliant on his account of original causation and derivative being.

However, despite these problems, natural law ethics as we encounter it in Aquinas, and embryonically in the first two chapters of Romans, provides the strongest conceptual base within the Christian tradition for an ecological ethic. It affirms that the natural order is a moral order, even though subject to elements of moral ambiguity arising at least partly from the Fall, that this order is determinative for human society and morality, that human goods are interdependent with the goods of the non-human world, that this order is represented in each human person by the powers of conscience and reason and that this naturally located morality is found in every human culture.

Natural law is not just a religious ethics in the sense of being tied to one religious tradition – Christianity. The belief in natural law is found in most of the world's religious traditions including both primal religions and the world faiths of Buddhism, Islam, Hinduism and Judaism. This cultural ubiquity reflects the claim of Aquinas and others that natural law is an ethic which is located not just in human philosophy but in the inherent order and relationality of the cosmos, and of human persons.

As we have seen, the combination of nominalism and the Reformed emphasis on the ubiquitous consequences of the Fall involved the rejection of Aquinas' argument that goodness and moral law remain in the natural order of human and non-human life. The Reformers sought to construct an ethic which was exclusively based on revelation in scripture instead of the duality of nature and revelation obtaining in the natural law perspective. However, there were Reformed theologians who pursued the natural law tradition. Calvin adopted the traditional language of natural law in his consideration of the Ten Commandments, of human conscience and of justice,[112] though it plays no role in his view of the non-human world, and was largely ignored by his followers and interpreters. But the influence of natural law remained particularly strong in England and may be traced in the plays of William Shakespeare, in the theology and philosophy of the seventeenth-century Anglican divine Richard Hooker, in the poetry of Gerard Manley Hopkins and in the novels and essays of the twentieth-century Christian apologist C. S. Lewis. As Robert Murray points out, the plays of Shakespeare affirm the relationality between nature and human society expressed in the Hebrew Bible, and which also finds its correlate in the natural law tradition.[113] Thus in *A Midsummer Night's Dream* changes in the weather and in the fertility of the fields are attributed to the argument between Oberon and Titania, while in a number of plays the decline of kingship is linked with the decline of political and natural order for, as Hamlet declares, 'the king and the land are one'. Similarly in many of Shakespeare's plays a felicitous marriage creates a new harmony both in human society and in cosmic order, as for example in the wonderful conclusion of *Twelfth Night.*

In a more systematic way Richard Hooker adopts the pre-Reformation natural law tradition and makes it an essential part of his ethics and political theory. Hooker, like Aquinas, believes that the world is ordered to a divine plan, and that everything natural, especially human, tends toward the good, even though humans frequently frustrate this tendency by misconstruing what is the good, and what they truly desire.[114] But sin does not succeed in frustrating the law of nature, as argued the Puritans, against whom Hooker wrote. The Bible confirms and redirects us to the law of nature rather than opposing or superseding it.

Like Aquinas, Hooker believes that all levels of reality are relationally inter-connected from the highest which is God to the lowest which is inanimate nature, and all reflect the same law: 'God therefore is a law both to himself and to all other things besides.'[115] The inter-connectedness of things means that there is nothing in nature which is not in some function needed by the whole, and nothing lives entirely for itself: 'God hath created nothing simply for itself: but each thing in all things, and of every thing each part in other hath such interest, that in the whole world nothing is found whereunto any thing created can say "I need thee not." '[116] For Hooker, as for Aquinas, God is the ultimate source of motion and purpose in nature, and so God is also the source of nature's dependability such as the regularity of its seasons or the motions of the stars: 'those things which nature is said to do, are by divine art performed, using nature as an instrument'.[117] Because the order of the world reflects the divine essence and divine law, human reason, which observes nature, will be led to the knowledge that there is a God.[118] Similarly knowledge of the good after which humans are to strive if they are to find fulfilment and happiness arises from nature as well as from reason and revelation: 'For that which all men have at all times learned, Nature herself must needs have taught and God being the author of Nature, her voice is but his instrument.'[119] Like Aquinas, Hooker finds the highest good in the human knowledge and love of God and so from true religion flow all the other virtues, including justice, by which human life is directed to its own good. But justice is not arbitrary, it is not confined in its judgements to what is contained in the Bible: we learn of justice from both nature and scripture.[120] This vision of the pervasiveness of justice reflects Hooker's cosmological assumptions concerning the relationality of the world. Hooker views the human person, and relations between selves in political and ecclesial communities, in a deeply relational way. Thus individuals and communities are held in tension and balance and as with Aquinas the moral value of individuals is closely connected to the contribution of each individual to the richness and diversity of the whole.

Hooker is of course the classic exponent of the Anglican *via media* and in his philosophy of God, human society and nature he steers a middle path between the supernaturalism of Catholicism and Puritanism and the new humanism of the continental Renaissance. He is critical of the supernatural biblicism of Puritanism, which repudiated nature in its insistence on the principle of *sola scriptura*.[121] But he also criticises the supernaturalism of Roman Catholicism in its excessive reliance on ritual and in the superstition surrounding the ceremonies of the church.[122] Instead, Hooker presents a political philosophy, and a philosophy of nature, which are both oriented around the incarnation, which by divine infusion is said to draw human society towards its true end in the relational expression of the virtues, and towards a harmonious balance and conformity with the created order which is also charged with the natural grace of divinity. As John Marshall says: 'Hooker accepts the supernatural, but he recognises the natural, and it is the recognition of the proper balance between them which is the source of his particular merit in theology.'[123] Both nature and supernature reflect the same eternal law and goodness whose purpose is to restore the richness and wholeness of life. In this way, Hooker comes closer to the account offered above of a creation/redemption schema for he views the whole of created order not only in terms of the Aristotelean-influenced Thomistic account of original and providential causation, but also in terms of the incarnation which, for Hooker much more than for Aquinas, involves a significant change in the nature of created order, albeit a change which is anticipated in the original plan of creation:

for with power he [Christ] created the world, but restored it by obedience. In which obedience as according to his manhood he had glorified God on earth, so God hath glorified in heaven that nature which yielded him obedience, and hath given unto Christ even in that he is man such fullness of power over the whole world (Luke 21. 27), that he which before fulfilled in the state of humility and patience whatsoever God did require, doth now reign in glory till the time that all things be restored (Acts 3. 21). He which came down from heaven and descended into the lowest parts of the earth is ascended far above all heavens (Ephesians 4. 9), that sitting at the right hand of God he might from thence fill all things with the gracious and happy fruits of his saving presence.[124]

In many ways, and not least because of his profoundly incarnational approach, Hooker's theology, and his version of natural law ethics, are even more suggestive of an ecological ethic than Aquinas'. Hooker develops a political vision which encapsulates the Hebrew and early Christian conceptualisation of the relational self or the self-in-relation while at the same time suggesting that this new order of relations between persons also has implications for human relations with the natural order, and more especially with the landscape to which the ecclesiastical polity is ordered for both its care and sanctification. Hooker's ideals were of course encapsulated in social form in the restoration of the parish system in the Carolingian era, and in the partial transfer of monastic care for land and human social order to the new secular clergy. But this parish system itself became deeply corrupt in the seventeenth and eighteenth centuries and ultimately failed to provide an effective bulwark against the combination of growing mercantile individualism and the rise of state power over local communities or parishes, as manifested in the Enclosures, and the ultimate transformation of human relations with nature which the Enclosures presaged in every parish in the land.

NATURAL LAW IN ECOLOGICAL PERSPECTIVE

Thomist natural law has been generative of political ideals and theory throughout the transition from the pre-modern hierarchy of church and royalty to the democratic states of modern Europe.[125] Thomism has also been a consistent source of criticism of the excesses and human indignities perpetrated under various modern political and economic practices and ideologies, including industrial capitalism, *laissez-faire* economics, communism and fascism. The influence of natural law theory continues to pervade contemporary European political thought and practice, as instanced in the concept of subsidiarity enshrined in recent treaties of the European Union and first promulgated in the natural law ethics of Pope Pius IX. This concept argues for the legitimacy of local and natural associations: the powers of the state must always be held in check by the associations of workers, peasants and local communities through which the natural right of the person to livelihood and the necessities of life may be asserted and maintained against corporatism or statism.[126] It reflects the deeply relational view of the human self which is enshrined in natural law thinking.

In moral theory also, natural law retains a prominent role and especially in contemporary Catholic moral theory. However, it is in the moral field that natural law theory is most criticised, partly because it has become associated with the strange Papal dictum against artificial contraception. This dictum is however based on an entirely false premise, which is that the natural function of human sexuality is purely concerned with the procreation of children. In nearly all human cultures, and even in parts of the animal world, sexuality is associated as much with companionship and pleasure between sexual partners as it is with procreation. This is why older people who are past child-bearing age, continue to enjoy sexual intimacy, as of course do many mammals. Perhaps only a celibate order of priests could imagine that pleasure and companionship are not a natural part of the sexual experience. It is unfortunate that natural law morality should have been brought into disrepute by the Papal denial of the natural richness of human sexuality.

However, this problem about the natural character of human sexuality points to two fundamental issues regarding moral theory in relation to natural law. The first of these concerns the idea that nature itself can or should exercise moral authority over the moral goods and purposes of human life. David Hume, and most philosophers since Hume, reject this idea for reasons we reviewed at the beginning of this chapter. This rejection, as we have seen, is expressed in terms of the putative undesirability of deriving an 'ought' from an 'is', or Moore's 'naturalistic fallacy'. The second and related problem concerns empirical observation. If nature is to function as an authority or source in human moral reasoning and intuition, this gives moral significance to the observation and interpretation of human nature and even of non-human nature. Thus the debate over the morality of artificial contraception relies on different judgements about the empirical character of human sexuality.

Natural law ethics has achieved a new prominence in recent legal and moral theory, partly because of the rise of the modern concept of human rights. The creation of the United Nations after the Second World War involved the construction of a new doctrine of human rights designed to enshrine in international agreement respect for the person such that the dreadful genocide of the Nazi regime would not be repeated. The 1948 UN Universal Declaration speaks of duties to the community and of rights and freedoms which no polity may deny except in the defence of the rights of others, though it offers no conceptual or philosophical ground for the assertion of these human rights.[127] With the demise of natural law reasoning most philosophers assert that the recognition of human rights relies on intuitions or feelings about what is right and wrong.[128] However, Alasdair MacIntyre argues that the assertion of rights purely on the basis of intuition or emotion means that in practice they are moral fictions: they have no basis in either reasoned argument or in empirical reality. This reliance of the modern world on a doctrine of respect for persons which is primarily emotivist results, MacIntyre argues, in those peculiar forms of modern moral expression – moral indignation and protest – which so characterise the environmental movement, and which make modern societies so prone to radical and even violent disagreement about moral ends and purposes.[129] Thus arguments about rights are reduced to *what I feel strongly about.* Strength of feeling therefore becomes a central moral validator in modern societies. And yet at the same time we want to continue to assert that human rights are universal, that they do not depend on cultural perceptions or personal feelings. They are somehow of the order of persons, somehow given in the very nature of our humanness and therefore cannot be said to rest simply on human intuition. If human rights are simply sentiments about persons, then torture and genocide have no universally valid moral counter: they are only wrong for those persons who don't like these ways of behaving because they run counter to their moral intuitions. Some would argue that the modern erosion of the universal and natural basis of morality is the key reason why modern societies, despite their putative moral progress, so frequently torture, kill, maim or starve their citizens, or the citizens of neighbouring or distant territories.

In response to the problems of intuitionism or emotivism, moral philosophers such as Germain Grisez and Jean Porter in the United States, John Finnis in England and Pierre d'Entrève in France have sought to repristinate Thomist natural law theory. The central moral argument of the modern revival of the natural law tradition concerns the rational and objective basis of the recognition of natural or human rights. Grisez identifies natural law with 'objective principles originating in human nature' which indicate a given standard of conduct between persons which is universally knowable, and which as we have seen St Paul refers to in Romans 2. 14–16.[130] Thus in every culture and civilisation there are certain, though very limited, goods or purposes which are universally recognised as being of the essence of a good human life. Moral goodness, and those particular goods through which goodness is realised, may in other words be located in the universal character of humanness, and displayed to each person in the inner voice of conscience which prompts knowledge of and conformity to the good of self and others. When human relationships and society are ordered so as to realise these goods, then persons experience human flourishing and find fulfilment.

Finnis argues that there are certain basic values or goods which anthropologists have found in every culture and civilisation.[131] These include: concern and respect for human life, the value of procreation and a preference for stability in sexual relations; a concern for truth manifest in the education of the young about safety and religion; friendship, justice and co-operation between individuals and groups; a quest for the common good; the recognition of property; the importance of reciprocity; the value of play; and respect for the dead. From these anthropological observations Finnis arrives at a more precise list of seven basic goods or values which all societies may be said to recognise and from which, through practical reasoning, we may conclude why we morally ought to do some things and to avoid others. These values are briefly: life itself, which includes all the biological necessities without which life cannot be sustained such as food, shelter and physical security; curiosity or knowledge; play; aesthetic experience; sociability; practical reasonableness; and religion.[132]

According to Finnis, these basic goods become moral values and actions by the application of practical reasonableness and conscience. We learn to respect these values in others and in our own life plans by recalling that our time on earth is limited, that all the values need to be held in harmony and respected in every action, that we have a duty to impartially promote these values in others as well as in ourselves and that the requirements of cost-benefit efficiency can never justify the overriding of these values in others or in ourselves. In pursuing these basic values for ourselves and others we are aided by conscience and by relations in community: it is unreasonable to act in a way which is contrary to conscience, and it is reasonable to act in such a way as to promote the common good, the good of community and not just our own private good or gain.[133]

Through this analysis of the nature and requirements of the good, Finnis is able to construct a conceptual foundation for justice, duties, obligations and rights in human morality, law and society which demonstrates the many advantages of natural law theory over consequentialism and utilitarianism. It gives a much richer and more relational account of the good than is offered by consequentialism: this richness reflects the diversity and also the harmony of the goods which humans are ordered to pursue. It generates a relational account of justice at the heart of morality because the recognition of the goods of every person requires that societies should be so ordered as to give each person the same possibility of experiencing these goods. Wealth and property must be distributed so as not to give a small number of persons excess while the basic values are denied to many others through poverty. Limits on human inequality in relation to these basic values are therefore morally essential.

Natural law also provides an account of motive as well as of the good. We achieve fulfilment and happiness when we pursue the good. But only a rational person, and a person who begins to experience such virtues as prudence, justice, temperance and love, can know fully that this fulfilment is the result of pursuing the good. Doing good is therefore in some senses the consequence of both nurture and habit. As to the latter, the more often we do it, the more accustomed we become to doing it and the more we want to do it.[134] As to the former, we become good, we acquire our knowledge of the good from our interaction with significant others, especially as children.[135] Goodness is not simply an innate category. We are nurtured in good conscience as in bad in our experience of being as self-in-relation, especially in our relations to parents and siblings. The role of both habit and nurture in the expression of the good indicates both the teleological and the relational character of the goods by which we become more human, more fully ourselves and more fully able to live in harmony with, and to promote the goods of, those around us. We cannot come to know the goods of sociability and security, and to promote these in our relations with others, without experiencing them ourselves as children who are securely loved and befriended, as well as biologically nourished, by parents. Equally when we direct our lives towards the good, we experience the happiness, the Johannine 'fullness of joy' which, when we seek purely for pleasure, eludes us.

The nature of the good is also intrinsically concerned with harmony and balance. If we pursue one particular good – knowledge – to the exclusion of another good – such as sociability – we may cease to be able to promote the goods in others, and in turn to experience their promotion of our goods. The accumulation of great knowledge may give an individual a marketable skill – especially in the 'information age' – but when he falls ill or becomes lonely he may be bereft of those relationships of mutuality through which the other aspects of his being, his other goods, might have been addressed and restored. The goods which we pursue must then, as Finnis argues, be pursued in a harmonious balance if we are to experience true flourishing and fulfilment.[136]

Finnis's account of the nature of the human good provides a much richer discourse for the description of the human moral life than that of utilitarian individualism. It overcomes the subjectivism of the standard modern account of morality, and presents a powerful challenge to societies where human goods are ordered purely on the basis of cost-benefit equations, and of prior property relations. This is highly significant for the construction of an ecological ethics, for it involves a rejection of essential features of modern capitalist or free market dogma, including the materialist goals of modern societies, the equation of material wealth and economic growth with the human good and the denial of the common good in preference for individual wealth maximisation. The highest human good in the natural law ethics as enunciated by Finnis and Grisez, as also by Aquinas and Hooker, is located in the orientation of the human self towards the love of God and of other persons in human communities of nurture, place, work and religion. This approach represents a morally principled rejection of the values inherent in the material rapaciousness of modern consumerism with its assault on the beauty and order of the natural world, and its systematic denial of the natural rights and inheritance of the poor – including tribal peoples, landless migrants and the descendants of landless migrants in the blighted unemployment blackspots of the developed world – not only in relation to biological necessities but also to those other goods including culture, sociality and religion without which the good life is unattainable.

However, there remains a fundamental problem in relation to environmental ethics with the position which Finnis, and also Grisez, advance. Their anthropologically and sociologically informed adaptation of Aquinas' natural law ethics is radically different in one respect from Aquinas, and this is that nature has ceased to be a source of natural law and moral guidance and significance, except inasmuch as human reason can be said to be part of our human nature.

Ever since the Enlightenment it has been a central part of the Western project to define and orient ourselves towards the good in such a way as to remove divine authority and guidance (especially in the form of the Bible) and nature from the moral project. Immanuel Kant argued that the good is good because of its conformity to the character of the good, not because God says it is good. If God's actions or commands can be said to be good, this is because God, like humans, is subject to the same ethical imperative. Thus to say that God says an action is good adds nothing to the statement that an action is good. The good is logically prior to God. This eschewal of God in describing the nature of morality reflects the rise of rationalism in Enlightenment philosophy and in modern culture. But it also reflects the demise of nature as a moral source in modern Western philosophy. Modern scientists, like Enlightenment philosophers, argue that nature is not inherently good, that it is not constructed on any divine plan and that it manifests no teleological or purposive behaviour other than that imputed to it by sensate beings, and in particular by the most rational of these beings – humans. Neither God nor nature can therefore be involved in the human definition of what is the good, and of how we are to live good and morally rich and fulfilling lives. This is why David Hume, and G. E. Moore, argue that we can never derive an 'ought' from an 'is'. Empirical facts about the natural world, or even about human behaviour, cannot tell us how we are to live. The ethical imperative, the good, is autonomous: it has a logical order of its own which cannot be derived from state-ments of fact about, or observations of, the nature of the universe. As Peter Singer so concisely puts it, according to the modern account 'ethics is no part of the structure of the universe'.[137] Enlightenment thinkers, such as Hume, argued that the workings of the cosmos must be entirely independent of God's volition, for a good God would not allow the evil and suffering that there is in the world. Therefore God must either not exist, or be incapable of interfering. Thus Hume argued that the natural order is fundamentally evil. It cannot be said to represent moral good because it frequently visits natural dis-aster and death on humans. Similarly the suffering inflicted by one species on another, or sometimes even by individuals of a species on their own offspring, is evidence of the inherently amoral or immoral character of natural order.[138]

However, by eschewing the moral significance of natural order the modern Western style of ethics requires that morality be located exclusively within human moral intuitions. Part of the grounds for modern intuitionism, in addition to the eschewal of divine agency in the cosmos, is that humans are said to demonstrate a morality which is vastly superior to that which is to be found amongst animals. But in reality the comparison between human and animal morality is by no means an unambiguous one. Humans are rare amongst animal species in waging war on their own kind, and in inflicting methods of torture on members of their own species which in ingenuity and technical skill far exceed animal-originated evil, both in manifest intent and in the degree of suffering inflicted. The behaviour of those animals which kill some of their own young in order that others may survive is not without human parallels, as the ancient and modern history of child abuse and of the intentional killing of human progeny both before and after birth, sadly attests. Furthermore, the idea that animals are inherently competitive, that the weakest always go to the wall, must be balanced against the evidence of the strong caring for the weak within many species, and of the often co-operative mutuality between different orders of species which is observed in every ecosystem and habitat.

Even if we can admit that nature is not entirely evil, it may be argued it is still nonsensical to seek to link human moral order and natural order as directly as primal peoples, such as the ancient Hebrews, do. Causative links between human moral behaviour and natural order such as those adhered to by the Hebrew prophets are surely only possible in a primal world-view which substitutes magic for the scientific understanding of natural cause and effect.

Finnis accepts the validity of Hume's is–ought distinction, described by G. E. Moore as the 'naturalistic fallacy', and the consequent division of fact and value. To justify his position, Finnis makes the surprising claim that Aquinas himself did not regard nature as a moral source, and therefore did not make any moral inferences from factual observations: 'from end to end of his ethical discourses, the primary categories for Aquinas are the "good" and the "reasonable"; the "natural" is, from the point of view of his ethics, a speculative appendage added by way of a metaphysical reflection'.[139]

A significant consequence of this exclusion of nature as moral source is that Finnis nowhere in his work acknowledges that any thing or any being other than rational human beings has any goods which humans may legitimately acknowledge as making a claim on their own rational moral consideration: 'Where a choice must be made it is reasonable to prefer human good to the good of animals.'[140] This is one of very few references to animals in Finnis's work, and I can find no mention of natural ecosystems or of the biosphere in his work. This approach also explains the remarkable lack of concern for non-human life and the biosphere which we encounter in recent Papal teaching, which is much influenced by the Grisez–Finnis school of natural law interpretation, and which has been much criticised by the environmental theologian Sean McDonagh for this lack.[141]

Nature is discounted as a moral or normative source by Finnis because he rejects any relationship between factual statements and judgements about the good. He explicitly opposes a fundamental feature of Thomist, and Aristotelean, teleology, and this is that the good obliges us to conform to it because not to conform to it is contrary to our nature and is therefore contrary to the order of the universe. But, Finnis argues, to deny the good is often good for us: 'to act contrary to justice is frequently advantageous to oneself and one's friends'.[142] We often avoid the good because we lack the motive to achieve it, and here he cites Hume in support: 'It is one thing to know virtue, and another to conform the will to it.'[143] The only reason according to Hume that we conform our actions to virtue is that virtue gives us pleasure, or avoids pain.[144] But, as we have seen, the New Testament itself, as well as Aquinas, has an answer to this line of argument for Paul says that the Gentiles know by the nature of the world and their own consciences what is the good. They sometimes do not do it because they are, like all people, sinful: 'The good which I want to do, I fail to do; but what I do is the wrong which is against my will and if what I do is against my will, clearly it is no longer I who am the agent, but sin that has its dwelling in me.'[145] But this law of sin is contrary to the law of nature, and the law of God, which are according to Paul and Aquinas one and the same. To do the good is to conform to our nature, but through the inheritance of sin we often do what is contrary to our nature. In other words even when we do not conform to the good, the good still exercises a hold over us, we still experience the obligation of the good. This is why according to Paul and Aquinas we need grace and the Holy Spirit as well as nature, for without the grace of God we cannot by our own efforts alone restore our lost virtue, recover our true nature and set our lives on the goal which is the good for us and which will bring us true fulfilment.

Despite his professed adherence to Hume and Moore, Finnis himself finds it almost impossible to avoid making judgements about the good from factual statements. Thus his rich account of basic human values and of the good is informed by a number of anthropological studies which he cites in support of his argument.[146] His use of such empirical studies of the character of the good in different societies demonstrates that in practice it is almost impossible to avoid making statements about what is good, what we ought to do, without also making statements about what human societies normally and naturally do. It is only possible to avoid the fact–value relationship if morality is located entirely in human intuition and feeling. If, as Hume argued, the good is simply what we like, what gives us pleasure or what we feel like doing, then it is possible to agree with Hume that statements about what is good, and factual statements, are of two different logical orders. However, if, as Finnis wishes to do, we claim that there is an objective order of goodness which we encounter in certain universal features of our humanness, and this can be demonstrated in anthropological accounts of different cultures, then intuitionism is clearly rejected and it then becomes impossible in practice to avoid fact–value inferences.

Finnis's rejection of nature as moral source, and his attempt to locate natural law purely within the structure of human reason, is at fundamental variance with the account of the good offered by Aquinas. As Jean Porter argues, 'for Aquinas, every creature necessarily seeks its own good'.[147] Thus the human quest for the good is also a quest for fulfilment and happiness. When we conform our lives to the good we will find happiness, according to Aquinas, because the good is that form of life which we are best fitted to live. The human quest for happiness is then, as Porter says, 'only one instance of a universal and necessary dynamism of all creatures'.[148] Factual beliefs or empirical arguments about what makes us happy will therefore be of motivational significance, for we will tend to conform our actions to what we perceive makes us happy. The paradox, though, is that humans frequently misconstrue their own happiness. We saw this in chapter two above in the discussion of materialism and consumerism. The evidence shows that most people most of the time find more happiness in sociability, marriage and the nurture of children than they do in buying and possessing material objects, but our culture has a range of hidden and overt persuaders which try to convince us otherwise. The uniqueness of our humanness then is that we do not automatically, like animals, live according to what natural law determines is the good for us. We need to exercise our reason and our intuition – there need be no dualism here such as the rationalists and intuitionists sought to construct – in ordering our lives and societies to the good for us. However, if the good for us is to live in conformity with our nature, with the objective moral order of nature in us and in the non-human world, then the moral ends both of our individual actions and of human communities, must include within them reference beyond human life to the whole of the natural order whence we not only derive normative values about human life and the good, but also those biophysical attributes of nourishment and aesthetic beauty which are, as Finnis argues, essential elements of the human good.

But in what senses can the non-human world be said to be moral and to be ordered towards the good? We have already seen how in the Hebrew Bible, in the New Testament, in Irenaeus and in Aquinas, there are a range of ways in which the non-human world may be said to be ordered to the good, and furthermore, a range of ways in which this good not only acts as a normative good for humans but as a physical constraint upon human purposes when these purposes come too much into conflict with the natural order. But modern science, like modern moral philosophy, tends to deny this objective and naturally located moral order in which the ancients believed. As Oliver O'Donovan puts it: 'on the one hand scientific thought is anxious to free nature from immanent purposiveness; on the other, moral philosophy wishes to free the will from any purposiveness in nature'.[149] O'Donovan, like Hans Blumenberg, traces this eschewal of purposiveness in the world to a correlative over-emphasis on the human will. And, again in a way reminiscent of Blumenberg, O'Donovan argues that the modern denial of the moral significance of nature is closely related to the nominalist and scientific denial of the divine creative ordering of nature, and the correlative eschewal of teleology or purposiveness in the non-human world.[150]

In an examination of the nature of scientific claims and of scientific language, Edward Goldsmith finds that scientists who mostly dislike the idea that nature is teleological develop a range of subterfuges for avoiding talking about purpose, goals or *telos*.[151] Darwin spoke of competition and survival as if these were adequate to explain the origins and evolution of life. But why do beings want to survive? Survival implies a *telos*, a purpose or goal. Similarly the principle of natural selection is teleological because it describes intention, purpose: 'ecology has to be teleological, for purposiveness is possibly the most essential feature of the behaviour of living things'.[152] The biologist E. O. Wilson, who consistently denies the existence of purposive or teleological order in nature, nonetheless in his *The Diversity of Life* implies a teleological orientation in the biosphere when he says, 'the most wonderful mystery of life may well be the means by which it created so much diversity from so little physical matter'.[153] In place of teleological order, with its origin in created order, modern biologists put 'genetic programming'. Living things are said to be *programmed* to seek out and maximise their opportunities according to the innate laws of natural selection and evolution, which are basically generalisations about the interaction of species and environments in the unravelling of the original genetic order of DNA. The 'selfish gene' carries within it the will to live, and to make the best of the opportunities its environment avails.[154] Thus human moral purposiveness, just as much as purposive behaviour in non-human life, can be explained as simply the outworking of that original genetic programme.[155]

However, against this denial of teleology by biologists and geneticists, we find, as we have seen, that in the writings and observations of ecologists such as Eugene Odum and organic chemists such as James Lovelock, ecosystems are said to be purposive and also deeply relational. Similarly as we have seen we find in the work of modern ethologists accounts of the purposive, relational and moral activity of animals. We may in other words say that there are certain goods which are analogous to human goods, after which each aspect of reality is ordered, including both the biosphere as a whole, particular eco-regions within it and particular species within these regions. If we re-examine Finnis's list of basic values, we find that many of these values are experienced at least in part by the higher primates. Thus most primates respect the life of their own species most of the time;[156] they seek to provide nourishment and nurture for their young, often manifesting co-operative behaviour in their efforts; they enjoy play and sociability; and they employ practical reason in tackling tasks such as extracting termites from a termite mound or in identifying a shelter. In their experience of these basic values, animals may even be said to share some of the features of human moral experience, particularly in their social instincts and the quest which animals share with most humans for the good of the whole community rather than purely individual interest.

James Rachels cites a story of Charles Darwin which illustrates powerfully Darwin's judgement that the moral instincts of animals and humans are not so far apart as people traditionally believed. A group of baboons was walking across a valley in Abyssinia when they were surrounded by a large pack of dogs. The adult males initially scared the dogs away so the other baboons could make their escape, but one young baboon was stranded and surrounded: 'now one of the largest males, a true hero, came down again from the mountain, slowly went to the young one, coaxed him, and triumphantly led him away – the dogs being too much astonished to make an attack'.[157] After recounting this story from Darwin's *The Descent of Man*, Rachels tells how more recent primate research has confirmed and extended Darwin's belief in the moral instincts, and altruism, of animals. In a rather cruel experiment on rhesus monkeys two monkeys were put in two cages side by side and one was given food in such a way that if it ate the food the monkey in the other cage received an electric shock. The experiment was run over a number of days and repeated many times and the researchers found that the great majority of monkeys would forgo food rather than cause pain to the other monkey. One monkey went hungry for five days and another for twelve rather than cause pain to the monkey in the wired cage.[158]

Inter-species altruism is also not unknown. I observed on a television film whose subject was African elephants an incident in which a goatherd in Zimbabwe had taken his goats to feed from the shoots of a copse of young trees. A group of elephants then approached the copse and began to feed on the same trees, and most of the goats, and the goatherd, left the copse. However, one small goat stayed behind feeding on the trees, and was in danger of being trampled by a growing group of elephants. The camera then recorded one of the adult elephants going over to the small goat, picking it up gently with its trunk and removing it from the copse to a place of safety. Other accounts of inter-species altruism occur in animal ethology literature.

Darwin explained the existence of con-species and inter-species altruism primarily in terms of kinship. Kin altruism is the most common form amongst most animals, and indeed amongst humans. Even humans are less often altruistic to strangers than friends or family.[159] However, a recent experiment in human game theory offers an even more significant explanation for the altruistic instinct which is evident in both animal and human behaviour. The experiment is described by Peter Singer and concerns a logical puzzle about co-operation called the Prisoner's Dilemma.[160] Two prisoners are in separate cells in a Ruritanian gaol. Each prisoner is told that the authorities are seeking to get both prisoners convicted of plotting together against the state. Each prisoner is invited to confess to the crime and each is told he will then be released while the other prisoner will get ten years in gaol. If both refuse to confess they are told they will get eight years. The prisoners are held in separate cells and cannot communicate. As Singer says, from a purely self-interested point of view it is rational to confess in this situation.[161] But if both prisoners confess they both spend a lot of time in gaol. Thus to act in a self-interested way results in both parties being worse off. This is true of many moral dilemmas, especially of an environmental kind.[162] But we often fail to see that co-operation will bring greater good to us as well as others. And we have been particularly encouraged *not* to think this will be the case by those economists and moral philosophers who argue that justice and wealth creation are best served by each individual pursuing her own particular good, and perhaps that of her immediate family, without regard to some more general concept of justice or common good.

An American games theorist, Robert Axelrod, demonstrated this point particularly powerfully by inviting a number of games theory researchers to take part in a tournament in which the Prisoner's Dilemma was repeated two hundred times and where the aim of the game was to spend the minimum time in gaol. The twist was that after the first time each 'prisoner' got to hear what the other prisoner did. The strategy which won the tournament was a 'tit-for-tat and random niceness' strategy operated by prisoner A in which prisoner A started off being nice and not confessing. If prisoner B confessed then the next time prisoner A would also confess. But if prisoner B did not confess, then prisoner A did not confess either. The 'tit-for-tat and random niceness' strategy reduced the amount of time both parties spent in gaol and worked better for both parties singly or together than any other strategies, including selfish ones and extremely altruistic ones in which prisoner A continued to refuse to confess even when prisoner B confessed every time.[163]

As Singer argues, Axelrod's game is of great moral significance, for it demonstrates that even without a prior moral sense of right and wrong, and without full knowledge of the long-term consequences of an action, co-operative behaviour, 'randomly nice' strategies which also resist selfishness, will always do better. Applied in an evolutionary perspective, Axelrod's game demonstrates that groups of animals or species which consistently pursue co-operative rather than selfish strategies, are more likely to thrive and survive than those which are mean. This is especially so, as Singer argues, if all 'nice' animals withdraw their co-operation from animals which consistently behave badly.

The Axelrod game is particularly significant in a natural law context for it seems to demonstrate that co-operation, friendship and justice are not simply human constructs or sentiments, nor simply projections on to reality arising from the rational structure of the human brain, but fundamental features of nature which are potentially operative in every form of social interaction amongst both animals and humans. The game also undermines another of Finnis's reasons for adhering to the naturalistic fallacy, which is his claim that 'to act contrary to justice is frequently advantageous to oneself and to one's friends'.[164] The game disconfirms this judgement, and the naturalistic fallacy, by indicating that the fundamental moral principle of relational reciprocity, which pervades human societies, must also be pervasive in the non-human world because even non-human species tend to flourish and thrive in contexts where they are 'nice' to one another.[165] The main context in which the principle does not seem to work so well, as Singer notes, is in those modern cultures and social forms which are increasingly characterised by anonymity.[166] Axelrod's game works because of repetition between parties who become known to one another. In modern urban cultures a growing number of interactions take place between people who may never meet again. Similarly, because of the mobility of modern life, the deleterious effects of human activities on the environment are often at a distance from the places of residence, the places which are *known* and valued by those who generate these activities. Anonymity is a crucial ethical problem both in human relations and in relations between humans and nature, and one to which we must return in the final chapter.

The pervasiveness of relational reciprocity as an ethical principle in primatial and human societies is matched, according to the primal world-view of the Hebrew Bible and other primal religions, by the reciprocal relationships between human society and the inanimate natural order. Again, modern scientists mostly tend to dismiss the kind of open system reciprocity which the primal world-view holds to, preferring to envisage biophysical reality as a large machine whose various functions and activities are controlled by the original programming of DNA or even of atoms. But as we have seen, ecologists such as Odum and Aldo Leopold, and climatological and atmospheric observations associated with the Gaia hypothesis, indicate that in wholes as well as in parts, the principle of relational reciprocity does indeed hold true. In an ecologically revised Thomist perspective, we may say then that natural law is operative at every level of reality, and ecosystems like animals pursue certain goods after which they are teleologically ordered by the creator. Christians, like Taoists, can affirm in an ecologically informed account of natural law, that the order and stability of the world, and the reciprocal relationship between this order and the moral order of human society, is built into the very nature of reality.

C. S. Lewis in *The Abolition of Man* argues that most people until modern times believed in the existence of natural law, and that this belief is reflected in the respect present in most pre-modern cultures not only for life itself but for non-conscious objects such as mountains, trees and rivers.[167] But he identifies a selfist tendency in the modern world to treat all value as merely representations or projections of the self and the sentiments of the self on to relationships with others and with nature. Nature consequently ceases to operate as an objective external sphere of value and moral order for modern societies. The human conquest of nature brings about the rejection of the idea that goodness and virtue are part of the structure of the universe as has been commonly believed by Platonists and Confucianists, Christians and Hindus alike.[168] Consequently moderns identify as their moral lights instinct and sentiment rather than the traditional ordering of reason and desire through education in the virtues and in the nature of what Lewis calls the Tao. The denial of the self-evident harmony and beauty of the natural world coincides with the denial of the self-evident naturalness of virtue, of respect for life and of care for posterity. The rational recognition of the fundamental order, goodness and wisdom of the Tao is, according to Lewis, essential to the moral life of virtue and the quest for goodness. When nature is recast as material stuff without intelligible order or moral value, human reason and morality loose their moorings in the external world. Consequently that which makes us distinctively human – our reason – is undermined and we fail any longer to live in accordance with natural law, or the Tao, for we fail to perceive the objective reality of truth and goodness. The rejection of the Tao results not so much in the end of nature but in the 'end of man', for when we abandon the idea that the world has an intelligible order to which it is our duty as humans to conform, we give ourselves up to impulse and instinct: 'at the moment then of Man's victory over nature, we find the whole human race subjected to some individual men, and those individuals subjected to that in themselves which is purely "natural" – to their irrational impulses ... Man's conquest of nature turns out, in the moment of its consummation, to be Nature's conquest of Man.'[169] Lewis suggests that the modern conquest of nature results in the dissolution of the moral project of the self, as well as the end of nature. We no longer know how we are to live, or what it is to be good: 'for the wise men of old the cardinal problem had been how to conform the soul to reality, and the solution had been knowledge, self-discipline, and virtue. For magic and applied science the problem is how to subdue reality to the wishes of men: the solution is a technique.'[170]

But, as Lewis acknowledges in *Mere Christianity*, even when we do recognise natural law as the clue to the meaning of the universe, we still frequently fail to choose the good in our own relations with other persons and with the non-human world.[171] Though we are ordered to the good, we frequently persuade ourselves that something other than the good is best for us. In other words humans have a capacity, unique in the natural order, to act in a way which is contrary to their natural ordering. It is this moral freedom which gives humanity its unique place in the universe. But nonetheless, as O'Donovan argues, the natural order still establishes the conditions in which our freedom as moral agents is exercised.[172] The sinful exercise of this freedom in ways which harm both ourselves and the biosphere, and the modern eschewal of the natural limits on this freedom in the moral order of creation, combine to produce a form of civilisation which is uniquely destructive of the non-human world and subversive even of the conditions of human flourishing, both for indigenous peoples whose survival is increasingly threatened, and for the moral and social ecology of human life in modern urban industrial societies in both North and South.

In sum, we can see that the ecological repristination of the natural law tradition which I have begun to flesh out in this chapter presents from within the Christian ethical tradition significant resources for an environmental ethic. While I have sought to show the close connections between an ecologically revised natural law ethic and the creation/redemption schema of the New Testament and Irenaeus, belief in natural law or the Tao of nature is not limited to Christians and is widely shared in the different religious cultures of the world.

Most secular environmental philosophies of the 'shallow' variety have to argue for the preservation of the environment from the perspective of human interest and human welfare. But, as O'Donovan says, such an approach 'offers no stable protection against the exploitation of nature by man, since he can discern nothing in the relations of things to command his respect'.[173] The ecological revision of natural law presents from within the Christian tradition a moral valuation of natural order, and an account of relationality and the human self-in-relation, which arises from the objective reality of the biophysical world as well as from Hebrew and Christian revelation, and one that does not rely on human sentiment or on human reason alone. The shift of modern moral consciousness from the natural order to human sentiment is, as I argued in chapter two, a principal cause of the environmental crisis. The recovery of a more objective and naturally located basis for human moral life would seem to be a prerequisite for reordering human life towards a more relational social order in which the richness of human goods is more fully pursued, and in which the goods of the non-human world are also affirmed and conserved.

CHAPTER SEVEN

Natural law and ecological society

THE TECHNOLOGICAL SOCIETY

The modern social form may be most accurately characterised, as Jacques Ellul proposes, as a technological society.[1] The domination of *techne,* according to Ellul, occurs not just in relation to the domination of machines, but in relation to the powers of technical, statist and corporatist processes by which central human ends – work, play, religion, family – are converted into means to ends, the principal ends being economic efficiency and the technological servitude of the state and the corporation.[2] The social transformations involved in the technological society are essentially to do with the transformation of social power, and its relocation from families, tribes and local communities, where nature's wealth and human productivity were located in the pre-modern world, to the landowner, the corporate manager and the rulers or servants of the state. Technology, and the economy of money which is its supreme manifestation, achieves an autonomy from divine command, from human community and from natural order, eliminating moral value and spiritual significance along with natural necessity.

The technological domination of modern life therefore involves a threefold subversion of human flourishing as religion, human community and nature are all transformed and corroded by the social power which is mobilised in the pursuit of technological progress and prowess. The technological society involves the death of God as technical progress is substituted for divine creation/redemption as the origin and end of human life and the cosmos, and the idolatry of consumer artefacts is substituted for the worship of God; the technological society involves the subversion of human community as the traditional moral order and government of human life by communities of kinship, place, religion and *ethne* are dissolved by the social and technical power of nation states and corporations; and the technological society involves the 'end of nature' as the natural world is increasingly subject to human technical reordering, and we rarely experience nature in its unhominised state as a prior order of reality to human claims and interests.[3]

The elimination of religion would seem to be an inevitable concomitant of the technological society. Technique and technology offer us both in daily life, and in social hope, the promise of material salvation from meaninglessness and suffering, and transmute the discernment of good and evil into a calculus of human risks. In daily life the new car, the foreign holiday, the latest multimedia computer are socially constructed as objects which will meet our own and our children's desires for happiness and fulfilment. These artefacts are invested with sacred, idolatrous power which both legitimates the technological remaking of the world, and desacralises that world and its order by supplanting the creator God for the creator technologist.[4] Technique and technology also present the social hope of a transformed society where more people will have better health, greater economic security, more comfort, greater leisure. The new global organisation of production spreads jobs and consumerism to every corner of the planet, and, it is argued, in its wake will spread improved longevity, reduced child mortality and higher incomes. Salvation from the natural vicissitudes and threats to life on the subsistence farm or in the rainforest is offered by the globalised iconography of progress – symbolised by *Dallas* or McDonalds – while the jobs and factories which may bring the icons within reach are purveyed by the new global employers of international capitalism. As the spiritual quest for salvation is transformed into material advancement, so the threats to life in the pre-modern world, and the traditional fear of divine judgement, are transformed into the horizons of the risk society.

The modern horizon of risk correlates in an intriguing way with the lost horizon of divine purposiveness for human life and the cosmos, for whereas in pre-modern eras the principal opportunities in, and threats to, life were in some senses regarded as related to the providential agency of God in creation, in the modern era the horizon of humanly originated opportunities and risks replaces the horizon of divinely originated opportunities and dangers in the natural order.

The technological society not only eliminates God from the human horizon, but also threatens to undermine human security. In North America, in much of Northern Europe and in the modernised metropolitan areas of much of the rest of the world, the technological domination of human life and natural order is far advanced. And yet cities, and even some rural areas, are plagued by crime and violence and rates of depression and suicide are rising, while people increasingly seek the escape of drug and alcohol abuse, or the addiction of the flickering screen. The most technologically advanced societies are also those which are experiencing rising divorce rates, growing numbers of children who have never lived in stable families and who grow up in poverty, the collapse of local community networks and support structures, endemic unemployment and the casualisation of much of the employment that remains. Technique and technology do not consistently or even frequently deliver those real goods towards which, according to the natural law tradition, human life is directed. Children cannot play safely in car-dominated streets. Sociable communities are corroded by the degrees of personal mobility demanded by corporations, states and technological work patterns, and enabled by automobiles and aeroplanes. Family stability and security are threatened by unemployment and job mobility and the individualistic quest for sexual fulfilment where other kinds of fulfilment have begun to fail. The security of life itself is threatened for many in modern Western cities who live in fear of street robbery or violence, domestic burglary, rape and even murder. The grave moral and social problems of that most technologised society, North America, are perhaps the clearest illustration of the failure of the modern myth of technique. As Douglas John Hall says, 'only in North America has the experience of technological existence been full enough and long enough for people to know that technology does not solve all human problems and bring the good life'.[5] Hall, like C. S. Lewis, remarks on the irony that in pursuing the technical conquest of nature, human nature is ultimately threatened, for in preferring technological solutions to every human problem, we have ultimately surrendered ourselves to technology and thus 'the mastery of nature has to mean the mastery of human nature'.[6] Thus technological domination presages not only the death of God and the end of nature but also the end of humanity. The nadir of this tendency is surely the idea that future societies will be more and more dominated by intelligent machines which will order and control ever-increasing aspects of technological processes, from global currency flows and urban traffic to food procurement and animal husbandry. In this technological future the human 'factor' as characterised by playfulness or compassion looks increasingly out of place. Machines will serve productive efficiency so much better than humans, who are prone because of their fondness for other humans to errors of judgement.

Technology has of course brought real progress in aspects of human well-being. Modern hygiene, sewerage systems and medical technology have eradicated much disease, we no longer fear that our children will not survive childhood and more of us live three score years and ten than in previous eras. Similarly it may be argued that modern civilisation shows great progress in comparison to the moral standards of our pre-scientific forebears. People are no longer subjected to slavery or serfdom, and human rights are enshrined in the laws of most countries of the world. However, the empirical evidence for both these assertions is less unambiguous than it might be.

On the first count of progress in hygiene and the treatment of disease, and hence reductions in child mortality and increases in longevity, there are a number of points which might balance an excessive optimism about modern achievements. While we have indeed made considerable progress in human hygiene, diet and health in this century, this progress is much less obvious in the Third World, especially if we contrast the health, hygiene and diet of people before colonialism with their current conditions in sub-Saharan Africa and parts of South Asia and Latin America. I have witnessed at first hand the profound contrast between the health and happiness of those nomads who have managed to retain their traditional life-styles in the shrinking jungles of West Malaysia and Borneo and indigenous peoples who have been forcibly resettled in concrete and tin houses, their children sent to alien schools and their adults set to work in workshops and other forms of unskilled wage labour. Indigenous peoples all over the world are fighting a last desperate struggle against the forces of modernity for the survival of their ancient and more natural ways of life. They have seen what has happened to their kin who have been subjected to modern life-styles. Those who have not died from Western diseases or from the technological violence of military force, become addicted to alcohol or drugs, or become a prey for rape and theft by their Westernised neighbours. Even if they retain their physical integrity they lose their culture, their values, their religion, their happiness and very often their sanity. If modern technology genuinely offers a better way to the primitive life of these ancient cultures, why is it that so many indigenous peoples have organised for hundreds of years to try to resist the advances of modernity? It is also worth recalling that many of the medicines utilised by Western doctors in the modern struggle with disease originated in forest plants in the Third World and have been utilised for thousands of years by primal people to treat disease, to guard against infection and to promote longevity.

Even if we confine the argument over human health to people living in the modern West, there are signs of regress alongside progress, as children's health in cities is increasingly threatened by pollution, asthma, injury from cars and new drug-resistant strains of viral infection which have arisen partly as a consequence of the over-use of modern drugs such as antibiotics, and especially as a consequence of their wasteful use as growth enhancers in commercial animal husbandry. In addition the increasingly artificial and :nhealthy diet of children and many adults, and their lack of natural exercise, is giving rise to a host of new diseases.

Our bodies may on the whole be healthier as a consequence of modern technology but there are increasing signs that the remaking of human life by technology is having very deleterious effects on the human psyche, and on human happiness and fulfilment. These are surely not unrelated to the technological subversion of spirituality and religious belief. In Christian tradition, a human life is only rightly ordered when directed towards the creative and redeeming love of God. Only in relation to this love are the other goods of human life – long life, companionship, material comfort and security – likely to be ordered for human flourishing and fulfilment. We are certainly justified in speaking of progress in human health and comfort as the fruits of the technological society, but this progress may have been bought at the price of faith in God and the orientation of human life and society towards divine purposiveness. Such a price is, in terms of Christian ethics, surely too high to pay.

On the issue of moral progress, the evidence concerning modernity is even more questionable. Animal rights philosophers and activists claim that the ascription of rights to animals is part of the moral progress of modern humans who first ascribed rights to slaves, then women and now animals.[7] But the appalling indignities inflicted by modern agricultural techniques on millions of contemporary farm animals are by no means evidence of moral progress, but quite the opposite. The religious texts of all the world's religions, including as we have seen the Hebrew Bible, enjoin kindness and compassion for animals. Compared to the sheer quantity of suffering involved in the wholesale incarceration of animals in the cruel cages of factory farms, and their lamentable live transport systems, even the cruelty of animal experimentation begins to look less significant. The primal hunter may be carnivorous, but he does not subject the animal to a lifetime of cruelty and deprivation before it serves him for a meal. Most primal peoples regard wild animals as their fellow creatures which are worthy of respect, even in the act of hunting, rather than as inferior forms of life with no feeling or sensibility to pain worthy of human moral consideration.

But it is in the treatment of humans rather than animals that the most telling evidence against the argument for the moral superiority or progress of modern technologically ordered societies lies. Tribal and territorial conflict stretches back into the annals of our fallen history, but the modern twentieth century has seen genocide and tyranny on a more technically advanced level, and a greater scale, than any previous era, including the holocaust of six million Jews in the Second World War, the slaughter of one million Cambodians, half a million Rwandans, and the violent assaults on indigenous peoples in every part of the globe where they remain.

According to the Hebrew Bible history has a shape and an order to it but it is not an order of progress from evil to goodness. On the contrary the Hebrew Bible teaches that we began on this earth in paradise and our life since represents a lack as compared to this original blessing and grace. The moral order of history is therefore not progress but movement between right and wrong, good and evil. These alternatives are eternally available to us as humans. The freedom to choose good or bad is part of the essence of our humanness, of the 'image of God' as the Hebrew Bible calls it. But this voluntary order of right and wrong in human life interacts with a natural order of right and wrong which reflects the involuntary character of goodness in the created order, and this in turn reflects the unoriginated nature of God who is good. But our voluntary choosing of right and wrong is not without consequence in our relations with one another, with the non-human world and with God. When we do right, when we conform our actions to what is the good according to nature and conscience, then we experience well-being and happiness in our relations with God, with others and with the cosmos. When we consistently choose evil, flouting conscience and natural law, then disaster follows, in alienation from God and self, in broken relationships and in ecological breakdown.[8] The moral perspective of the Hebrew Bible on history is, as Robert Gordis puts it, a 'law of consequence embedded in the universe'.[9] Historicism, the belief in the inevitability of progress in human history, is therefore profoundly at variance with the biblical view of history.

C. S. Lewis suggests that we may begin to eschew a false historicist idea of progress when we find it possible to live in the world without destroying nature, or technologically transforming nature into the mere servant of our wants, for in changing our way of living we may also recover a more traditional kind of wisdom. According to the tradition of natural law humans learn what is good for them, and how they are to live, in stable human communities and relationships where moral virtues and values are instilled.[10] The shape of the moral life is also informed, at least partly, by the forms, orders and regularities of nature, and the attempt to construct human communities which live in harmony with the order of the creation. But how are such values and such communities of virtue to be sustained in the technological society, and how might they impact upon the decision-making processes of states and corporations as these affect the environment? There may be societies which successfully eschew subservience to *techne*. Where a nation state gives recognition to the independent cultures and mores of an indigenous *ethne* and its land claims this is all the more possible, if a rare eventuality. But most of us already inhabit the technological society. How can we bring to bear a set of values in relation to daily life and social hope which both preserve human goods against technological subversion and recognise and conserve the distinctive but related goods of the non-human world?

In preceding chapters I have explored the idea that the goods of the human and non-human world are intricately related in the Hebrew and Christian traditions, and that human ecology and natural ecology are therefore inextricably bound together. The recognition and valuing of certain key human goods is therefore central both to the well-being of human life and to the flourishing of the non-human world. This reciprocity between human and non-human goods is focused in the prophetic tradition on the ideas of justice and equity. Excessive inequalities between humans are not only opposed to divine justice, which is enshrined in the law of the covenant community, but also to the natural law of the land and of created order. Excessive inequalities generate ecological imbalances on the land as surely as they generate unhappiness and discontent in human society. They do so precisely because of the abrogation of the limits on human wealth and luxury which arise from the created order and from a moral vision of human society, because, as Aquinas believed, like the Hebrew prophets before him, when individuals pursue their own goods without regard for the common good, then ultimately both the common good and the good of those individuals who neglect their duties to the community of persons and the community of the non-human world are threatened and subverted. The non-human world primarily enters human calculations about resource use, and distribution, as land. The ecological reform of technological processes, including those of economics and industrialism, must then begin with an ethical account of the land, and its centrality to both human and non-human goods, and with a form of economics which treats of the land as the central resource in relation to human and non-human welfare.

NATURAL JUSTICE AND THE GIFT OF LAND

As I argued in chapter five, land is central to Hebrew religion, as to all primal religions, and it is as land that nature is primarily located in the moral world of the primal Hebrews. Land is the source of blessing, the locus of creativity and the provider of all that makes human life possible and fulfilling – gardens for herbs, flowers and relaxation; fields for fruits, food and work; forests for fuel, shelter and imagination; rivers and lakes for travel, fishing and awe; mountains and hills for water catchment, walking and contemplation. But in the Hebrew religion, as in all primal religions, land is conceived as the gift of Yahweh and not as the possession of humans. It is in relation to the divine ownership of land that *radah*, vice-regency, over the land is given to humans, according to the Genesis story. Humans are not given dominion in the sense of absolute rule over the land for it does not belong to them. They are, though,

God's representatives, charged by God to tend the land, to care for it on behalf of its rightful owner. Each aspect of the created order has its own good which it is designed to realise, but the highest good is relationality between God and the creation, a good which is above all a possibility for humans, who are closest to the 'image' of God in creation. The Ten Commandments are first and foremost designed to promote this relationality through true worship and right living, and to proscribe idolatry of created things or of work which would obscure or prevent the fundamental relationality of God and humans. The breaking of the original openness of the relationship between God and humans is what causes Adam and Eve to hide from the Lord who walked in the garden. But this relationality between God and the creation is not confined to humans. Every aspect of the creation, mammals and fish, land and sea, is described in Job and Proverbs as reflecting the wisdom and ordering power of God, and every part of the creation has the potential to respond in praise to God, according to the Psalms. The calling of humans to be the vice-regents of the creation does not abrogate the relationality of all creation to God, but rather establishes an order of goods in which human goods are more closely connected with relationality to God than the goods of the rest of the creation.

This same hierarchy of goods is reflected in the natural law ethics of Aquinas and Hooker, who both affirmed that the common good of the cosmos is ordered by a rational God ultimately to serve rational creatures. Aquinas proposes a hierarchy whereby all other goods in the cosmos are ordered to serve human goods, hence the charge of anthropocentrism which is laid against Christianity, including the natural law tradition. Versions of deep ecology, such as those rehearsed in chapter three, argue that any conflict between human goods and the goods of the non-human world should be resolved in favour of the integrity of whole ecosystems rather than of humans. This leads some environmentalists, for example, to advocate abandoning aid to famine victims. They have exhausted the ability of the land, their ecosystem, to feed them. The logic of the law of nature is that human numbers should be diminished to such a point that the ecosystem can recover. Against the moral problems of such an ecocentric position, we may concur with Aquinas that the human good must take priority where human goods and natural goods come into conflict. But this prioritisation is only exercised in the context of the recognition of the independent and interdependent moral value and goods of the non-human world, a recognition that Aquinas' excessive devotion to rationality as the central characteristic of divine order in the cosmos tends to deny, hence his statements about the moral insignificance of cruelty to animals.

This is why I argued previously that the natural law tradition needs ecological revision, and cannot be applied in a fundamentalist way from medieval philosophy to modern ethical problems. Many of the features of human life which Aquinas identifies with practical rationality and even aspects of the quest for virtue are, as I argued in the last chapter, also present in the non-human world. For this reason the hierarchy of goods which human life should be ordered to promote must include not only human goods, but those of the non-human world as well. Such an ecological revision of natural law may also bring it into closer harmony with the primal world-view of the Hebrews, for the Hebrews believed that the gift of nature, the gift of good, fertile land, carried with it moral obligations. The gift of the land was to the whole community of Israel and was to be distributed justly, and the principle of justice applied both between human neighbours, and between the needs of humans and the needs of wild animals for land. Each human had a claim on the land, for food and shelter and space, but so did wild animals. The denial of these claims was contrary to the righteousness, the justice of God which was enshrined in the divine law, and contrary to the common good of the land on which both peoples and animals resided.

This ecological revision of natural law also finds confirmation in Aquinas' reflections on the virtues, and especially on the nature of justice, which is the supreme form of virtue, that virtue which is closest to the 'divine mind'. According to Aquinas 'the proper act of justice is nothing else than to render to each one what is their own', their own being 'that which is due to them according to equality of proportion'.[11] Justice entails the idea of equality, that each person is a reflection of the divine image and should receive according to their due. Injustice is that state in which 'one attributes to oneself too many of the benefits and too few of the burdens'.[12] Excessive inequality is proscribed by natural law ethics because it denies to persons that which is their due. According to Jean Porter, Aquinas is quite clear about what is due to persons. Each person 'has a claim not to be deprived of his life, or of the material goods necessary to support life and to maintain a family'.[13] So much we can also adduce from the Ten Commandments, which are the revealed form of the natural law – 'do not murder', 'do not steal', 'do not covet your neighbour's goods'.[14] The denial of the essential goods which are necessary for someone to maintain a family is theft, according to Aquinas: 'each according to their due' means that a society is unjust and contravenes natural law when it forces people off their lands, and denies them their inherited claim to land and shelter and livelihood. Equality is the *sine qua non* of natural law ethics because each person who is truly a person is capable of reason and virtue, and therefore each person is due those basic goods of land, food, shelter, livelihood, without which the higher goods can never be attained.

But does the same principle of justice apply to beings which are not persons? In the *Commentary on Dionysius* Aquinas argues that this rendering of what is due is characteristic not only of the just state and just rulers, but also of the justice of God in the cosmos as a whole: 'just as through the ordering of distributive justice in a city governed by a first citizen, the entire political order is preserved, so through this ordering of justice the entire universe is preserved by God'.[15] And again '[divine] justice truly consists in this: that it gives to all things according to their proper worth and that it preserves the nature of each thing in its proper order and power'.[16] In these passages we can see that the ecological revision of Aquinas I am proposing is prefigured in Aquinas' writing on the cosmic and universal nature of justice. Aquinas argues, like the

Hebrew prophets, that the order of the universe itself manifests the justice of God: 'whatever is done by God in created things is done according to proper order and proportion wherein consists the idea of justice'.[17]

But if the goods of humans and non-humans are both morally considerable, then how are we to live in the world? We cannot live without uprooting plants for food, without cutting trees for wood and fuel and, in most human cultures, without supplementing our diet with fish and meat. According to Aquinas all these lower orders of life are ordered to the maintenance of the higher order, which is persons. But this does not mean that the principle of justice has no relevance to these lower orders. The ordering of the goods of both humans and non-humans is described in terms of the central concept of the common good. If human affairs are to be ordered according to the principle of justice then, Aquinas argues, the common good must be the primary concern of the polity and its leaders.[18] Individual goods will have the best chance of being realised in a polity which aims to preserve the common good of the whole, where no class of individuals has a privileged claim on those goods which make for life and fulfilment. By pursuing the common good each individual being will also realise its own good, the good for which it is designed and ordered. Individual fulfilment is in other words reciprocally related to the harmony and balance of the whole. Aquinas' cosmic understanding of the common good means that when human societies are ordered to the common good this will also tend to preserve the good of the non-human and material creation also. The good of each individual being, both mortal and immortal, human and non-human, is most likely to be realised when the common good of the whole is respected and this respect for the whole, and each element of the whole in due proportion, is the content of justice. The presumption of a Thomistic natural law ethic will then, as Porter argues, be against the waste or destruction of natural resources, against cruelty with regard to animals and for the conservation wherever possible of the stability and order of both ecosystems and non-human species.[19]

In the Hebrew Bible the idea of the common good of both

Israel and the land is implicit in the concept of created order. When the created order is treated with respect, and when human claims on this order are just and equitable, then both human society and the land flourish. Nature will be fruitful with its gifts, which God in his providence confers freely, when humans respect the covenant between God, people and land, and practise the good life as God ordains in the law and the covenant.[20] Abundance of gift, of provision is the covenant intention of the Lord provided the people follow in his ways. Such provision requires human co-operation and creativity; it requires the work of tending and caring for nature, and above all the moral and spiritual work of worship and gratitude towards the creator, and the quest for righteousness. Scarcity is not the normal condition of human experience in the natural world, according to the Hebrew Bible.

Isaiah's vision of human well-being argues for the legitimate aspiration of every human household to the ability to earn its own living and to provide shelter and the necessities of life without debilitating or demeaning dependence upon other economic actors.[21] His vision of natural sufficiency contrasts with the scarcity of land, food and livelihood experienced by the growing numbers of the poor in the increasingly marketised society described in Isaiah 10. The poor had no food, the destitute no house or land because the avariciousness of others had taken it from them. Where scarcity arises, it is explained by the prophets primarily in terms of the abandonment of the covenant, and the distortion of the order of creation which God has set in nature and affirmed in his promise of blessing. Instead of the hidden hand of the market, as Donald Meek argues, the Hebrew Bible proposes God as the hidden hand who correlates abundance and gift with moral righteousness, and scarcity and famine with moral failure.[22]

Jesus and many of the Fathers taught similarly that the abundance of nature's gifts are the provision of God and are the accompaniment of the life of goodness, justice and piety:

Do not ask anxiously "what are we to eat, what are we to drink, what shall we wear?" All these are things for the heathen to run after, not for you, because your heavenly Father knows that you need them all.

Set your mind first on God's kingdom and his justice before everything else, and all the rest will come to you as well.[23]

Trust in God, and the quest for justice will mean that God,
working through the natural order, will supply material needs,
for God is the 'source of all good gifts'. Barry Gordon argues
that Jesus, no more than Paul, did not mean that his followers
should therefore abandon work or property, for Jesus was
preaching to Jews who worked on the land in accordance with
their calling as the chosen people, and who practised land
inheritance, as far as the harsh tax regimens of Roman imperial
rule allowed.[24] Rather Jesus meant that work, livelihood and
the use of a person's gifts and inheritance should be set in the
perspective of the new reality of the Kingdom, in which all are
called to celebrate at the banquet table of the Messiah, rich and
poor, tax-collector and sinner, and to know God as the one who
heals their infirmities and forgives their sins. The contrasting
harsh economic realities of Roman occupation are strongly
denounced by Jesus in the light of the Kingdom ethic. In his
preaching he frequently recalled the Jubilee tradition of debt
forgiveness, thereby questioning the authority of Roman
economy over the people of God and the land, and he often
provided bread for the hungry and fish for empty nets when his
followers did not experience the abundance of God's provision.

We may call the biblical understanding of land and natural
abundance an economy of gift. According to the anthropologist
Marcel Mauss this economy of gift is to be found in most primal
cultures where reciprocity in gift exchange is the primary mode
of exchange relations.[25] Similarly Karl Polanyi argues that
most exchange and distribution of surplus in primal cultures
takes place in the form of the exchange of gifts, a process of
exchange which enhances the reciprocal character of social life,
and also redistributes surplus so that all are satisfied.[26] When
someone kills a piece of game he holds a feast for the community. Regular feasting is a form of economic exchange as well as
an enhancement of social life for, by giving his surplus to the
feasters, the hunter in turn will be able to eat at others' feasts
when he has no meat, and children and old people who do not

hunt will also be provided for. The vernacular economy is embedded, as Edward Goldsmith argues, in social relations which satisfy people's basic requirements and at the same time maintain exchange activity in balance with the self-renewing capacities of the biosphere.[27] Modern economics by contrast works to generate natural scarcity in land, food and shelter, and artificial scarcities in clothes or manufactured goods, for without scarcity people will not enter the cash economy as wage labourers and buy market products. But, as Goldsmith, along with many anthropologists, notes, scarcity was not a feature of vernacular societies. Colonialists found this lack of scarcity particularly frustrating. They frequently wanted to persuade native peoples to enter the wage economy as miners or plantation workers, but as long as traditional agricultural and economic systems survived, indigenous peoples had no desire to become wage labourers.[28] Indeed traditional agriculture was so successful at meeting the needs of people for food and artefacts without destroying the soil or disrupting the biosphere that some agronomists argue that the traditional agricultural systems of India, Ethiopia and China compare very favourably in terms of both efficiency and ecological sensitivity with the systems utilised in North America and in parts of Europe which are so rapidly eroding the soil and draining subterranean aquifers.[29] A World Bank report noted with regard to Kenya: 'over much of the country nature's bounty produces enough to eat with relatively little expenditure of effort. Until enough subsistence farmers have their traditional lifestyles changed by the growth of new consumption wants, this labour constraint may make it difficult to introduce new crops.'[30] Today in Kenya millions are facing food shortages as the harvests of the new commercial crops have either failed because the soil has been exhausted by more intensive farming methods, or because the rains have failed as so much of the natural vegetation has been removed for commercial mono-crops and because the crops are exported by commercial farmers for cash or to meet government debt repayments. As we have seen, the introduction of modern agricultural systems in these regions has often resulted in the destruction of soils and of traditional social structures so that famine, rural migrancy and poverty have become the common experience of millions in societies which formerly fed themselves more than adequately. The economy of scarcity is substituted for the economy of gift. Land and its product become commodities. Production moves out of scale with the natural limits of the land, and economic exchange moves out of local community control into the control of large enterprises and bureaucracies.

In most primal societies both exchange systems and land tenure patterns reflect social custom and tradition; they are embedded in social and natural relationships. The land is vested in the care of tribal chiefs for the good of the whole people, who all legitimately have a claim to land for their needs and those of their household. Traditional pre-modern land tenure patterns can still be observed operating in surviving vernacular cultures. The rights of each family and pastoralist to particular trees, patches of forest, grazing areas, watering holes or grasslands are controlled in a highly complex local economy of social controls which makes the human use of common land ecologically harmonious. Each family or household has access to what is seen as its natural due. Homelessness, that growing scourge of Britain and North America, is virtually unknown in vernacular cultures past and present. When land tenure is informed by the principles of natural justice, not only are human goods met in an equable manner, but the harmony and goods of the non-human order are conserved as well. It is when these principles of natural justice, and the social controls which encapsulate them, are abrogated by modern forms of land tenure and commercial pressures on land, that the 'tragedy of the commons' is brought about.

An essential part of moral formation in traditional societies is for children to learn the obligations or duties owed to others, in relation to such diverse foci of moral claims as fruit trees, sexual fidelity, respect for other children and animals and the moral authority of tradition and of the elders. In traditional cultures these moral claims and duties, inasmuch as they impinge on land use, are highly complex and balanced in their exercise and in the respect due to them, for land is held in common, and not

possessed by any one individual or household. Access to
common land is then *the* fundamental natural right of traditional communities, access which moral arrangements in these
societies are designed to uphold and respect.

The Hebrew Bible reflects this location of fundamental
moral claims in its covenant and salvation theology of land and
in the laws regulating land use. Divine liberation comes for the
enslaved people of Israel in the form of the gift of land. This gift
of land makes of the disparate Hebrew tribes a common people
with interests in common, interests which their land laws, and
other economic mechanisms, upheld and respected. Because
the land is given to Israel as a gift, and a sign of her salvation,
the people of God are not to abuse the land, nor are they to
appropriate to themselves more of the land than they may justly
require for their own needs and those of their household. This
community between humans and the land means that the
human good, when pursued with justice and equality, involves
the promotion of non-human goods as well. This is why the
good king is also a king who presides over fertile lands, rich
forests and a beneficent climate, and why unjust rulers who
allow the wealthy to live in great luxury at the expense of the
poor experience failing harvests, famines, climate change and
ecological disaster. The advent of a new commercial ethos
under the Israelite monarchy undermines this fundamental
ethic, and is the occasion for one of the most powerful stories in
the Hebrew Bible, the story of Naboth's vineyard.[31] King Ahab
took a liking to an ancient vineyard near the royal gardens
belonging to a neighbour, Naboth. Ahab offered to buy the
vineyard from Naboth and compensate him, but he refused
because it had been in his family for generations. Ahab's wife,
Jezebel, finding the king disconsolate because he could not get
what he wanted, conspired to have Naboth stoned on a false
charge of blasphemy, and then forged documents transferring
his ancestral vineyard to King Ahab. The prophet Elijah then
went to the king and charged him with murder and unlawful
seizure of land, and because of this one act of land plunder,
Elijah prophesied the downfall of the lineage of Ahab. The
cataclysm of the downfall of the Northern Kingdom of Israel,

and the eventual exile from the land of many of its people, is presaged, according to the writers of the Books of Kings, by an act of land plunder, which carried with it the implicit denial of the law of God, and of the promise of the land through which Yahweh had liberated the Hebrews from slavery.

The gift of the land carried with it duties and privileges, claims and responsibilities, which included the recognition of the inviolability of land tenure for every household in Israel,[32] and even the recognition of the rights of strangers or aliens to glean and find food when they were on Israelite land. Respect for the equality of these rights on the part of every member of the community is a fundamental tenet of the ethic of land enshrined in the legal codes of the Hebrew Bible, hence the Jubilee laws which required the return of ancestral lands where these had been lost through indebtedness. Similarly the natural law ethic which emerged within the Christian tradition affirmed the fundamental equality of all persons, and their equal rights to certain fundamental human goods, including a private place of shelter and domicile, common land to grow vegetables and for animals to graze and access to common forests and rivers for fuel, fish and hunted meat. As we have seen, for Aquinas these natural rights to sustenance and domicile represented a permanent check on the property rights of the rich. Where the poor were denied their natural needs, it was legitimate for them to steal from the rich:

in case of necessity everything is common property and thus it is not a sin for someone to take the property of another that has become common property through necessity ... Human law cannot violate natural or divine law. The natural order established by Divine Providence is such that lower ranking things are meant to supply the necessities of men.[33]

In England, as we have seen, such rights were enshrined in land usage until the Norman Conquest, when a less equitable form of feudal land tenure was imposed, although such rights survived in modified form until the Enclosures of the seventeenth century. In Scotland such rights were preserved until the eighteenth century, when the clan chiefs initiated the Highland Clearances, with the encouragement of the English barons who wanted to put down peasant power in Scotland after the Act of Union in 1707. In seventeenth-century London, George Winstanley argued for the natural law basis for land rights when he protested the rights of squatters who had been removed from enclosed lands: 'Therefore I say, the Common Land is my own land and equal with my fellow Commoners, and our true property by the law of creation.'[34] In Scotland the Highland Land League adopted as its motto a text from Ecclesiastes, 'The profit of the earth is for all.'[35] The Highland land-reformer John Murdoch argued that the Highland Clearances for commercial greed and gain were contrary to the law of Moses. Like the Hebrews and many other indigenous and primal peoples, Murdoch argued that land was the gift of God to the people, and he cited the prophetic word of Nehemiah against the sin of land theft: 'Restore O pray you, to them, even this day, their lands, their vineyards, their oliveyards, and their houses.'[36]

This approach to a natural law ethics has clear implications for land use and development policies in both the Third World and the First World. In the Third World this approach will involve the clear rejection of the trends towards concentration of land holdings by commercial interests in modern development policies and programmes. The first principle of land use in a natural law ethic relates to the natural claims of indigenous people to the land. These claims originate in divine providence and in the order of nature, and are a fundamental feature of the naturally located moral order which is still recognised in those last surviving primal cultures of the non-Western world. No government action, no development project which involves the enforced removal of indigenous peoples from tribal lands, whether for logging, for hydroelectric schemes, for national parks or any other 'progressive' purpose is compatible with a natural law ethic. These removals find their justification in every conceivable branch of Western scientific, political and economic study, but they lie at the root of the dissolution of the harmonious relation between modern humanity and the lands of the earth. Development economists and Western 'experts' have colluded with the misrepresentation of native peoples as ignorant or even positively destructive of the ecological balance of their traditional lands. Development banks and aid agencies, especially the World Bank and the International Monetary Fund, have similarly colluded with Third World governments who want to mobilise the natural resources of indigenous peoples for their own and their urban supporters' commercial gain.

Even in conservation measures the connection between ecological balance and traditional customs and economies is frequently if not invariably ignored. World Wild Fund for Nature campaigns to preserve the elephant and the rhino across Africa have encouraged governments to establish centralised game reserves for species conservation and for tourist camera 'hunters'. These reserves are established by removing the people from the land, which is given over entirely to the animals, sometimes surrounded by electric fences. In this way the animals themselves end up more like the occupants of a zoo than species genuinely conserved in their natural habitats while the grazing rights of local people are destroyed. In turn, local people come to perceive the wild animals, which their pastoral life-styles have preserved for thousands of years, as competitors with them for land, rather than as fellow members of an ecological community. Thus native groups such as the Masai are at once alienated from conservation campaigns and their cultures driven to the edge of extinction by the use of nomadic lands for animal conservation.[37]

Contemporary African governments of course dislike pastoral nomads, just as historically European governments disliked the peasant economy of common land. They would prefer to round up nomads and put them in 'settled villages' which are often no better than concentration camps, while trying to draw these displaced peoples into the cash economy. This process of displacement of people who have lived in harmony with nature by those who see nature merely as a commercial resource – whether for the tourist gaze, the logging camp or the cattle ranch – is replicated all over the world by the forces of modernisation. Frequently governments justify their eviction of native peoples from land for conservationist reasons. However, if the rights of native peoples are put at the heart of the conservation agenda, rather than marginalised, there is evidence that conservation programmes are more successful. As the biologist and wildlife conservation manager Richard Bell argues, it is when elephants and other animal populations are taken out of the control of local people and conserved by governments, from paternalistic, racist and profit motives, that their numbers have begun to decline: 'in effect a wall has been erected between rural communities and the resources among which they live'.[38] Consequently impoverished local people who are denied legitimate benefits from wildlife cease to have an interest in its conservation, and hence the rise in poaching. In Zambia and Zimbabwe efforts are now being made to give back to local rural people control over their own natural resources. Historically they were the best guardians of these resources and, Bell's projects have shown, they remain a better guard against poaching and other threats to animal life than centralised government or WWF conservation schemes.[39] Paradoxically, when the needs of indigenous people and human ecology are prioritised the diversity and stability of the host ecosystem is also maintained and preserved. Thus the ethical priority of the natural law tradition on human goods turns out in practice to have an explicit conservationist and ecological payoff. When the goods of indigenous peoples, not animals or trees, are first recognised and advanced, then they will tend in turn to care for the forests and plains which they inhabit. Many Western conservationist agencies, such as the WWF, are regarded in a very ambivalent way by native peoples because they seem to give priority to natural resources over humans. Ultimately this perverse prioritisation is a new form of imperialism, which, though it may find justification in some versions of ecocentric environmentalism, does a grave disservice both to human welfare and to the environment. The welfare of humans and the land is intricately, reciprocally related. No conservation programme which neglects, or worse undermines, human justice can ultimately hope to be successful, short of turning patches of savannah or rainforest into heavily guarded zoos.

The juggernaut of modernity is, though, difficult to stop, and the history of the transition of societies throughout the world from pre-modernity to modernity is a history of the under-mining of the natural claims of indigenous peoples to land and traditional forms of livelihood. Modern states, banks, aid agencies and companies justify their impacts on indigenous peoples by claiming that the take-over of their land will contribute to the increase in aggregate general welfare, even though the welfare of particular communities or households whose moral interests stand in the way of 'progress' will be undermined. The compulsory purchase powers, or mercenary gun rule, through which governments and commercial land-lords eradicate local community land tenure are justified on this utilitarian basis, and find their ideological warrant in the language of agronomy and modern economics. Thus agrono-mists argue that the commercialisation of agriculture remains the essential precursor to the banishment of famine in the modern world. But food scarcity is a daily reality in many parts of the non-Western world precisely because of the movement of so much land from traditional, low-impact, sustainable methods of farming for local human needs, to the exploitation of land for cash crops which do not feed local people and on land which is frequently unsuitable in the long-term for this kind of development. Many of the most publicised famines in recent years have arisen not as a result of the failure of vernacular hunter-gathering, nomadism and peasant farming but from the mismanagement of centralised agricultural systems by urban-based governments, and from ecologically and humanly disas-trous wars between these governments and disadvantaged ethnic groups in regions such as Eritrea and Southern Sudan.

Even in the most highly developed of Western monocrop chemically-driven agricultural systems, the North American wheat prairies, soil erosion, drought and the expense of modern chemicals threaten the prosperity of North American farmers, and the long-term fertility of their fields. The last forty years of chemically-driven agriculture has seen a constant acceleration in rates of soil loss, and a shift from dependence of farmers on the micro-organisms and insects which maintain and replace healthy soil to bags of fertilisers and pesticide sprays supplied by chemical companies and subsidised by government agencies.

The increases in arable production per acre have been fourfold but at enormous cost to the soil, to biodiversity and to the taxpayer, who has funded the drainage of marginal lands as well as ever more intensive production on prime arable land. But the net result has been very expensive agricultural surpluses which, when dumped on foreign markets or given as food aid, have been deeply damaging to less heavily subsidised and intensivised agricultural markets, and especially to the peasant farmers of Africa. However, the losses of soil, the silting of rivers and fisheries and the poisoning of the land with chemicals which eventually seep into drinking water, are also heavy costs which this new form of intensive agriculture has generated. As Richard Body argues, modern farmers are encouraged by subsidies and tax incentives to work against the natural cycle of soil reproduction, while natural elements which used to aid the reproduction of soil – leaves from trees and hedgerows, animal manure, worms and beetles – are systematically replaced with chemicals.[40]

There is evidence, particularly in South East Asia, that equitable land distribution is the natural precursor of economic development in the non-agricultural sector, as Jean Dreze and Amartya Sen demonstrate in the case of post-war South Korea.[41] It may be argued on the basis of the South East Asian experience that significant changes in the access of people to natural resources through land reform programmes is not only the precursor to a more ecologically sustainable pattern of farming than the monocrop commercial style so favoured by Western-style agronomy, but also the precursor to other kinds of improvement in life quality and aggregate welfare.

Land reform in most parts of the Third World only comes about as a result of considerable pressure from displaced peoples and communities. Many are the wars which have begun in former colonies as a consequence of pressures for reform of colonially imposed land tenure systems and the concentration of land in the hands of commercial farmers and estate owners. The Mau Mau rebellion in Kenya, the guerrilla war in the Philippines, the Tamil rebellion in Sri Lanka, the civil war in Ethiopia and unrest in many parts of Central

America are all linked to landlessness, rural poverty and the desire to overthrow colonially imposed land laws and commercial farm and plantation systems.[42] However, as D. Christodoulou argues, even where governments have legislated to reverse land concentration originating in colonial times, landowners and commercial interests, often backed by the military, have effectively resisted the enactment of land reform legislation. He cites examples throughout Latin America, the Philippines and sub-Saharan Africa. Similar struggles continue all over the world as forest peoples, pastoralists and agrarian villagers seek to defend their traditional communities and ways of life from the extractive quest of modern commercial loggers and farmers for a quick profit from nature. The struggles of Amazonian Indians and of rubber tappers in Brazil for recognition of native land tenure have become particularly well known in environmental circles, and more widely through television documentaries, especially since the assassination of Chiko Mendes, the informal leader of the rubber tappers, by mercenaries employed by landowners.[43]

The denial of native land tenure was the first act of colonialism during European expansionism. The recognition of inherited land tenure is a fundamental feature of an ecologically revised natural law ethic. The quest of native peoples for the return of their stolen lands is the first step in the reversal of the racism and genocide to which they have been subjected on every continent at the hands of Europeans. In New Zealand, Australia and North America, tribal groups have been challenging the legality of government land theft with little success. In these countries, as well as in most Third World countries, indigenous peoples find that their land rights are not recognised in the law courts. Indeed frequently indigenous peoples are reduced to the status of secondary citizens, controlled by a government department for native affairs, which not only refuses to recognise their historic rights but denies them equal legal standing with other citizens. This denial of basic legal and political status makes all the more urgent the quest of native peoples for self-determination as well as the return of their lands. It is ironic, and tragic, that in the century which has seen the proclamation of the Universal Declaration of Human Rights so many indigenous peoples should have been brought to the verge of extinction, either by brutal attacks on their villages, lands or persons, or by the subversion of their health, culture and food-gathering systems by the incursions of loggers and farmers. Because of the failure of many national governments to even recognise the justice of the cause of indigenous peoples, these groups are increasingly seeking legal redress in international courts and forums, such as the United Nations, whose charter commits its members to the principle of self-determination and respect for human rights of all peoples on the earth.

While some may agree that in the Third World land reform and a reorientation of development priorities towards small farmers, or fisherfolk, might be of immense value, it is of course more problematic to apply this kind of approach to the ecological problems of modernised societies such as those of Europe or North America. The enclosure of the land may be the first step in the creation of modern industrialised societies but how might a natural law ethic of natural justice inform the ecological reformation of societies where this enclosure is already complete and the product of nature and the land are completely tied to a modern system of cash exchanges, commercial trade and industrial production?

THE ECONOMY OF THE LAND

In the ancient world, as in the primal world, livelihood, not trading and exchange, was the fundamental form of economic life. Aristotle expressed the difference between exchange and livelihood in his *Politics* by means of a significant distinction between what he called 'chrematistics' and 'oikonomia'. Chrematistics was the activity of making money and of accumulating wealth. Aristotle was critical of wealth acquisition for its own sake, for it 'led to the opinion that there is no limit to wealth and property'.[44] Oikonomia on the other hand was the activity of household management, the acquisition of objects to satisfy the needs of the household. This form of acquisition was limited by the physical needs of the household. As John O'Neill comments, 'the amount of household property which suffices for a good life is not unlimited'.[45] In household management things are acquired in order to meet actual needs, whereas in chrematistics acquisition is pursued for its own sake. Aristotle's contrast between exchange and household management relies upon his teleological account of ethics, an account which is clearly reflected in Aquinas' natural law and virtue ethics. Humans are created to realise certain goods and virtues. The uninhibited pursuit of wealth will not enable these goods to be realised. Social and political practices and institutions should then be designed in such a way as to discourage reliance on the activity of exchange, on market activity, as it obscures the quest for the good life. It also creates scarcity as those who seek personal aggrandisement through unlimited acquisition necessarily achieve this at the expense of others who consequently find it more difficult to meet the needs of their own households. Chrematistics, market activity, creates scarcity.

According to modern economists, scarcity is the central reality of economic life.[46] The existence of scarcity is resolved by the mobilisation of exchange activity in the market. Economic historians generally assume that people living in market-oriented societies are therefore assured of a greater abundance of the necessities of life than those living in non-market societies. Thus ancient economies are said to be characterised by conditions of famine and economic insecurity which are only lifted when formal trade relations become established. Where there is no trade, or trade and exchange is over-restricted by taxation or redistributive regulation, prosperity is said to be lacking or is undermined.[47] However, as we have seen, there is considerable evidence to the contrary.

In our own society economic activity is almost exclusively identified with chrematistics. As I argued in chapter two, in a marketised society people come to confuse the goods which make for happiness with market goods which are presented, by advertisers and in cultural signals, with the claim that they will make people happy. This means that many of those engaged in exchange activity confuse material acquisition with the good

life, and at the same time make it harder for others who aspire
to live the good life to achieve their aspirations as scarcity is
exacerbated by the excessive consumption of some groups at
the expense of others. This confusion of exchange activity with
genuine human goods is also a principal occasion of environmental exploitation.

The impact of the shift to chrematistics is first felt in relation
to land and rents in developing societies. As we have seen, in
eighth- and seventh-century Israel the rising urban middle class
achieved greatly increased wealth at the expense of the rural
poor whose lands were taken from them, and who could not
afford the inflated prices of basic commodities such as grain
and corn.[48] As Morris Silver notes, 'the central image is one
that is familiar to modern Americans, namely the blight of
poverty amid affluence'.[49] Along with affluence grow corruption and injustice, and not only the poor but nature itself begins
to suffer.[50] The Clearances in the Highlands of Scotland, whose
depopulated but glorious hills are my frequent weekend retreat,
similarly resulted in the deportation and immiseration of
hundreds of thousands of families, while their former lands
suffered a process of environmental degradation under intensive sheep and game farming which reduced much of the
Highlands to near-desert. Scotland now has one of the most
inequitable land ownership patterns in the world, while hundreds of thousands of urban poor continue to languish in
overcrowded high-rise and low-rise housing schemes on the
edge of Scottish cities, many with no access to the means of
livelihood except for social security payments. As we have seen,
the process continues throughout the developing world as
ancestral lands are taken over for commercial exploitation and
millions every year move to vast insanitary squatter settlements
on the fringes of the growing environmental disaster areas of
the world's megacities.

Modern economists and historians argue that this process of
mass immiseration is the necessary price of progress. Without
the enclosures and the clearances we would not have had
commercial farming, and 'free' labour to fuel industrial development in the cities. But if the participants in this vast

experiment had been invited in advance to decide for themselves whether or not they were prepared to face the privations
of enforced migration, slum living, child labour, foul factory
air and polluted cities for the eventual realisation of higher
rates of population growth and material acquisition, is it
conceivable that they would have agreed? Even as the promise
of mass economic prosperity is now held out to the successors
of these immiserated masses as the final proof of the industrial
development experiment, the spectre of mass unemployment
and poverty again rears its head in advanced Western economies. In the United States and Britain in the past fifteen years
the number of children born into poverty has increased
fivefold, and the diseases of poverty have returned to the cities,
including tuberculosis and respiratory problems associated
with damp housing, and other conditions related to inadequate
diet.[51] Long-term unemployment is the growing experience of
millions living on the urban periphery of advanced capitalism
in prosperous countries in the Northern hemisphere, as well as
in poor developing economies in the South.

Alfred North Whitehead argues that the reason why modern
economists confuse immiseration with progress is because
modern economic theory does not measure real indices of
human welfare or life quality such as stable families, secure and
fulfilling work and healthy food, and nor does it measure
indices of natural wealth such as mature forests, diverse flora
and fauna, clean air, clear waters. Instead modern economists
rely exclusively on idealised measures of wealth and welfare –
profit, prices, rent and wages. Whitehead identifies this idealist
character of modern economics as the 'fallacy of misplaced
concreteness'.[52] Modern economists idealise that which is concrete – land, human work – while they make concrete that
which is merely the product of the mind – price. Land only
enters into economic equations in the form of land price and
rents. Herman Daly argues that this idealism is a major
contributory factor in the degradation of nature, for by making
concrete that which is merely a human construct – price and
profit – it ignores the real biophysical factors which underlie
wealth creation, and the real limits to exchange activity pre-

sented by the needs of human communities for stability, order and access to the biophysical necessities of land, water, air and species communities.[53] This also explains why societies which are experiencing economic growth, the supreme indicator for the modern economist of an increase in human welfare, may not necessarily be societies in which human welfare and utility are increasing. Economic growth can take place in ways which, far from advancing human goods, may actually detract from them. This is particularly evident where growth means more 'efficient' labour-saving technologies and hence higher unemployment. Consumer choices may increase with economic growth but if the quality of life in human communities and the natural environment is radically reduced in the process, the consumer has no way of expressing a preference for a state of affairs in which stable jobs and communities take precedence over labour-shedding technologies, or clean air and quiet towns over out-of-town supermarkets.[54]

Instead of growth Edward Mishan argues that modern states should be seeking stability of human communities and stability of natural ecosystems, for in seeking stability rather than growth human welfare is more likely to be genuinely advanced by productive and exchange activities.[55] Similarly Herman Daly proposes that the only ecologically sustainable economy is a 'steady-state' economy which is characterised by a constant human population, utilising a constant stock of artefacts sufficient for a good life, where the production of new artefacts is held in equilibrium with the depreciation of old ones, and where artefacts are long-lasting and made in such a way as to minimise waste and pollution, and to maximise the re-use of materials.[56] Daly argues that the mania for the maximisation of economic growth involves the minimisation of morality: it defers justice and it rations love.[57] It is a way of putting off until tomorrow the need to redistribute resources to those who have too little for the good life today. The promise of growth makes those who already have too much feel comfortable while it acts as an opiate for the poor, who are told that, although they have nothing today, they will one day have something, provided enough money is made by the rich tomorrow and therefore not diverted to the poor today. Daly contrasts this approach with the Sermon on the Mount, which requires that restitution of evil should be made today and not put off until tomorrow: 'So do not be anxious about tomorrow, for tomorrow will look after itself. Each day has troubles enough of its own.'[58] Instead of allowing the distribution and quantity of money to determine and order human goods and human welfare, we should first seek an account of human and non-human goods from the objective source of our Western Hebrew and Christian moral inheritance, informed by an appreciation of the biophysical limits of created order, and then seek to order our economic and productive systems so as to promote the just distribution of these life goods while respecting biophysical limits. This approach calls into question both the supremacy of the consumer, and the quest for perfect competition in deregulated markets, advocated by many free market economists, particularly in Britain and the United States. But, as I argued in chapter two, there is mounting evidence that the quest for human fulfilment through market supremacy is in any case a chimera. As Robert Lane and Paul Ormerod argue, markets in goods and services only serve human welfare, and analogously environmental welfare, where they are carefully regulated by political and civil institutions through which human communities express democratic collective control over markets and their impacts on human life and the environment.[59]

Many environmental economists believe radical reform of market economics is unnecessary, and indeed that the only way of overcoming ecologically damaging poverty, as well as other environmental problems, is through further economic development and growth. Reformist environmental economists such as David Pearce, Anil Markandya and Edward Barbier argue that it is possible to adapt the economic preference for growth and for market transactions as the vehicle to distribute economic rewards, by introducing environmental and human 'disutilities' or costs into market transactions, so that market decisions and consumer choices would begin to reflect the real environmental costs of particular products or technologies.[60] Similarly they argue that it is possible to attach market values to particular environmental goods such as an undisturbed mountain or an unpolluted coastline and then let the market decide when human development – such as quarries or sewage treatment – should take precedence over these values. But Daly argues that cost-benefit analysis is the problem not the cure, and that progress towards a steady-state economy, which serves human moral goods, values environmental goods and recognises biophysical limits, lies in linking economic activity much more closely to the economy of nature – and in particular to land. For land and not money is the real key to the economic and productive process. If land and not money or price is placed at the centre of distribution and taxation systems, then, Daly argues, the goods of the land, and the ecosystems and species which make up the land, will inevitably be drawn back into economic analysis. Daly proposes a variety of instruments for achieving this end.

The key instrument is a device to remove land from processes of speculation and accumulation by taxing the product of the land at a rate close to its rental value.[61] This proposal, which was first enunciated by Ricardo, and restated with new vigour by Henry George in his Land Tax campaign,[62] would tend over time to reverse the commodification and the absolute ownership of land, returning land to the status of public trust, and thus allowing local communities, regional and national governments, to decide on optimal land use and land conservation in terms of the agreed priorities of local communities for food production, settlement, forestry and wilderness. Such an approach would enable a dramatic extension of current wilderness areas, allowing species threatened with extinction in Europe and North America by intensive agriculture and urban land speculation, to recover. By decommodifying land, and removing the attraction of unearned income from land ownership and speculation, the land tax would allow for greater regulation of land use to discourage topsoil erosion, pollution or waste dumping, so that the health of the land is prioritised over harmful development activities.[63] This approach would also allow for more ecologically benign zoning of human activities so that cities or towns could be designed in such a way as to minimise travel, and hence energy consumption, for example by integrating housing, recreation and food-growing areas and workplaces in new 'green settlements' – many of them located in currently derelict areas within cities – while leaving more of the land free of the transport corridors, industrial parks and monocrop wastelands which are so rapidly eroding the tranquillity and biodiversity of the countryside.

Another approach to land reform in industrialised societies is the idea of community land ownership, a concept which is growing in popularity in both inner urban and rural areas in Britain and North America. In some inner cities in America local community groups, often mobilised around a local church, have used local savings, public grants and tax allowances to acquire land from inner city landlords, and then begun to use this land for the welfare of the local community and its environment. Land has been given over to low cost rented housing, to small workshops and to inner city farms and gardens which provide employment and help to green the inner city, and bring inner urban peoples back into touch with the natural order.[64] At the same time this approach ensures that rents from land and housing are reinvested in the local community, helping to generate a virtuous circle of local economic and environmental uplift. The same project to bring land back into community ownership has begun to attract advocates in Scotland in the last decade as groups of crofters and local residents have sought to free themselves from the tyranny of absentee landlords and from the ecological degradation and very limited employment opportunities which are engendered in Highland sporting estates. A number of attempts have been made by local people to form trusts to buy back land from landowners at market price, with the help of both public funds, voluntary giving and private savings and so far two or three groups of crofters have already been successful, most notably the crofters of Loch Assynt, who have bought back their land from its former absentee owners and have begun to initiate a number of employment, forestry and hydroelectric schemes which are designed to enhance both the local environment and wealth and job creation in the local community. The long-term vision in returning the land to the people interacts with a number of other visions for the greening of Scotland and the return of employment and ecological diversity to the Highlands. These include: the replanting of indigenous Scots pines and the recovery of the Caledonian forest; the subsequent development of traditional forest and timber-related employment opportunities, including woodcraft, joinery, furniture-making, as well as the sale of sawn timber; the reintroduction of mixed farming to lands eroded by hundreds of years of sheep and deer ranging; the reintroduction of undomesticated wildlife, including wolves and other small mammals; the return of a proportion of the land to 'unproductive' wilderness areas where sheep and deer are excluded, including not only forest but wetland, ox-bow lakes and diverse heather patches, so that species diversity and natural fertility may begin to return amongst over-eroded and overgrazed hills and monocropped plains.[65]

Community ownership of land creates far more opportunities for balancing human welfare and the goods of the natural order than the large landed estates which currently dominate the Scottish landscape, and which still reflect the original act of theft by which land was stolen from indigenous farmers and crofters in the eighteenth century. It also offers a much lower cost and longer-term model of economic development in the Highlands, and indeed in much of lowland Scotland, than the development model favoured for many years, which has involved large public subsidies to big capital-intensive projects such as aluminium smelting, steel mills, paper mills and nuclear power. These projects, whose set-up costs involve massive public borrowing, have often not provided the long-term jobs and prosperity for which their proponents hoped, while they have done nothing to address fundamental imbalances in the Scottish economy between land use, biodiversity and human welfare.

The land tax and community land ownership have vital implications for planning and decision-making regarding the human use of natural resources, for they bring the ethical and philosophical concept of self-in-relation, which I argued above is central to the Christian understanding of human and created order and natural law, into the heart of economic and political processes as these affect both land use and human welfare. Because of the dominance of utilitarianism in modern ethical thinking, modern states, bureaucracies and corporations tend to treat of the welfare of individual persons in terms of an aggregate of human welfare. They frequently in practice abrogate the welfare of particular individuals, and their local environmental goods, in the name of some larger aggregate utility, expressed either in market measurements of cost and benefit or in terms of a public planning procedure, or both. But when local communities are reinvested with economic and hence political control of their local environment through community land ownership, local environmental goods are much less likely to be abrogated by aggregate measurements of human welfare. The local welfare of local people interacts much more transparently with local environmental goods than the welfare of the nation state or the profits of the corporation, which, under traditional cost-benefit measurement procedures, require very considerable erosion of environmental goods before these show up in balance sheets or market transactions. Treating the land as central to human welfare, and to the political as well as economic empowerment of local communities, will also therefore have the effect of enhancing the conservation of natural resources and environmental quality in the context of local decisions designed to maximise opportunities for land use for local employment, for food and resource production, for recreational and spiritual use and for the conservation of land for the independent flourishing of wildlife in all its natural diversity.

A popular manifestation of this project to recover a relationship with the land may be identified in the quest of 'New Age' nomads in England for a new style of self-sufficient communal life on agricultural land. This contemporary nomadism illustrates the deep desire of many dispossessed city dwellers to recover self-sufficiency and the capacity to earn a living on the land independently of the large technical and industrial processes which have generated so much poverty, unemployment and human misery in inner city areas. This new nomadism finds a coherent voice in a new advocacy group led by George Monbiot of Green College, Oxford, which calls itself 'This Land is Ours' and which models itself on the eighteenth-century Diggers in calling for a redistribution of land to the people of Britain. Some groups of nomads have settled on former agricultural land by buying the title, erecting informal housing, and developing community woodlands, farming and crafts. But current British planning laws outlaw this kind of resettlement of agricultural land, while urban land which is zoned as development land is too expensive for poor people to build their own houses, or grow their own food. The British government has responded to the new nomads, who have emerged partly as a consequence of the growth of long-term urban unemployment and home/landlessness, and partly reflect the growth of ecological consciousness, by attempting to outlaw informal camping in the 1994 Criminal Justice Act. A more appropriate response, in the light of the foregoing analysis, would be to reform taxation and planning laws to foster a more creative and ecologically benign use of land in both rural areas and cities, for example to provide more opportunities for food-growing by unemployed people in cities, and to reverse the loss of rural employment consequent on the industrialisation of agriculture by changes in agricultural subsidies and incentives towards less intensive, and less ecologically destructive, farming methods. Governments have heavily subsidised the advance of chemical and industrial farming, and the consequent depopulation of the countryside. In rural areas, the consequences have included the poisoning of the land, the erosion of the soil, the destruction of rural communities and services and rising rates of depression and suicide amongst increasingly isolated farmers and farm-workers. At the same time the cities have failed to provide enough jobs for their burgeoning populations, while people living in cities become increasingly alienated from the land, and unconscious of the vital connections between human health and life quality and the health and biodiversity of the land. In the end the economic rationale of efficient industrial food production subverts both the sum of human good and environmental quality.

The principal contemporary alternative to industrial agriculture is organic or biodynamic agriculture in which preference is given to the careful management of natural cycles and mechanisms in both animal husbandry and food-growing in place of the drug and chemical dependency of modern animal husbandry and monocrop techniques. The organic approach to agriculture reflects the natural law philosophy which puts moral as well as economic value on the natural systems of soil fertility and climate regulation. As E. F. Schumacher says:

Although ignorance and greed have again and again destroyed the fertility of the soil to such an extent that whole civilisations foundered, there have been no traditional teachings which failed to recognise the meta-economic value and significance of 'the generous earth'. And where these teachings were heeded not only agriculture but also all other factors of civilisation achieved health and wholeness. Conversely, where people imagined that they could not 'afford' to care for the soil and work with nature, instead of against it, the resultant sickness of the soil has invariably imparted sickness to all the other factors of civilisation.[66]

In Britain and in North America there is a strong case for shifting agricultural subsidies from chemically dependent and machine-intensive agriculture towards organic agriculture, not only for its ecological advantages, but for the spin-off of jobs and improvements in rural life, and in food quality, that such a shift would involve. Chemical farming involves fewer jobs but many risks, risks to human health, risks to the farm worker and risks to the welfare of rural communities. To give just one example of the risks to human health, the widespread use of organophosphate pesticides in Britain is linked by some scientists with uniquely high incidences of breast and stomach cancers, with the growing incidence of immunological problems in some agricultural workers, rural dwellers and consumers of foods with high pesticide residues and with certain diseases in treated livestock.[67] Chemically dependent monocropping, and intensive animal husbandry methods, use much more energy and generate much more pollution, as oil-derived chemical fertilisers are substituted for animal waste on fields. Unwanted and concentrated animal waste from factory farms is now a major cause of ground-water and river pollution, while the feeding of animal by-products arising from factory farms to other intensively reared animals, which are naturally herbivores, has resulted in one of the greatest modern farming disasters, the decimation of the British cow population by bovine spongiform encephalopathy or mad cow disease. This style of agriculture generates far fewer jobs than more traditional methods of plant and animal husbandry, thus undermining the quality of life and welfare of many rural communities, which often become little more than dormitories for industrial centres. And all these problems are in addition to the problems of soil erosion, reductions in biodiversity and appalling levels of cruelty to animals involved in intensive farming. The new valuation of land, and of work on the land, that I am proposing issues from the Hebrew land ethic, will involve a shifting of our economic and productive priorities back to agriculture and food production, a much greater concern with food quality and animal welfare and a greater attempt to conserve the biodiversity of the countryside instead of treating it simply as a spare resource for industrial farming. But this ecological reform of land use and agriculture in rural areas will of course depend on the ecological reform of industrialism itself, and the monetary system which sustains the developmental priorities, and ecological abuses, of advanced industrial civilisation.

REFORMING INDUSTRIALISM

As I argued in chapter two, the motive force behind the modern dissolution of vernacular economies of gift and barter is the unfettered power of money. Money is the spirit, the abstracting force which draws the modern self towards material satiety and the world towards ecological catastrophe, and money dissolves the natural relations of beneficence between the goods of natural systems and human welfare. As we have seen, the sociologist Georg Simmel argues that the motive power behind the modern dissolution of vernacular economies of gift and barter is the unfettered power of money.[68] Analogously, Herman Daly argues that it is the free movement of capital and finance which is the key instrument of environmental degradation, and the shift from ecologically harmonious life-styles and stable communities to ecological and social breakdown.[69] In this perspective, the key obstacle to reorienting industrial economies towards the preservation of the goods of human and ecological communities is not only the abstract or idealised character of economic theory and the money economy, but also the increasingly international character of capitalism. The globalisation of capitalism and markets in the twentieth century, which has its origins in the colonial experience, has produced a situation of capital mobility which is unprecedented and which is eroding the ability of national and local communities to control their own affairs.[70] The effects of this globalisation are already being felt in Europe and North America as these regions struggle to compete with the lower wages and infrastructural costs of manufacturing in the Pacific Rim countries: mass unemployment and lower wages are eroding the affluence of the Western worker as, without national controls, capital owners seek the most advantageous – low cost, low taxation – environment in which to invest. Just as globalisation threatens national prosperity it also threatens national environments. One of the key factors in the relocation of industrial plants is the weaker environmental and health and safety regulations of many Third World countries.

None of this would have surprised Adam Smith or Ricardo, who both believed that for free trade to be advantageous to particular nations it was necessary to assume a significant degree of capital immobility and of nationalist interest and sentiment on the part of the owners of capital, whose Britishness, or Frenchness would lead them to invest in their own community, and to put its interests above those of the interests of other nations:

By preferring the support of domestic to that of foreign industry, he intends only his own security; and by directing that industry in such a manner as its produce may be of the greatest value, he intends only his own gain, and he is in this, as in many other cases, led by an invisible hand to promote an end which was no part of his intention.[71]

Welfare is promoted by the invisible hand of capitalism, according to Smith, because the self-identity, and therefore the welfare, of the capitalist, is linked inextricably to his own national community. As Daly comments, 'of course he [the capitalist] acts in his own interest, but when the self is constituted by internal relations of community it is not surprising that private interest should promote community welfare'.[72] In a globalised economy where the market transcends national interests, boundaries and regulations, self-interested individualism is truly liberated from concerns for welfare of any particular national, regional or local communities. Capitalists are free in a global market to pursue profit without any regard for the welfare of their fellow humans. This is why John Maynard Keynes argued against free trade in the 1930s: the 'divorce between ownership and real responsibility' made possible by the phenomenon of capital flight and the internationalisation of capitalism had undermined the comparative advantage which free trade was traditionally said to confer on nations who participated in it in the early modern economic order.[73]

The extreme problems that deregulated free trade have produced both for the wealth of nations and for the environment can be seen with special clarity when we observe the effects of enforced trade liberalisation on Third World nations. As we have seen, under structural adjustment debtor nations are forced by the World Bank and the International Monetary Fund to concentrate their labour and natural capital on the production of primary commodities for external trade in order to earn foreign exchange to repay their debts. The land is literally raided as timber, minerals and cash crops are mobilised to pay foreign debts, with few compensating infrastructural or taxation benefits for the surrounding communities whose land is polluted and degraded by such activity. The comparative advantages of free trade have not been realised in these circumstances, as the prices of commodities have fallen dramatically with increased production, while Third World environments are ravaged and tens of thousands of self-sufficient rural communities are destroyed and national governments find themselves unable to buy enough food to substitute for lost indigenous production. Frequently, as Daly points out, the only winners in this situation are transnational corporations who are able to exploit falling commodity prices, falling wages and rising food prices to their own considerable advantage.[74]

The debt crisis itself is of course a consequence of a free trade regime. Great quantities of surplus capital, mostly generated by the oil price rises of the early seventies, were sold to Third World governments to finance large development projects, and were often utilised for other purposes, such as the purchase by Third World politicians and bureaucrats of property and bank credits in New York, Geneva or London. Such capital flight is enabled by a globalised financial and trade system which has divorced trade and capital from community responsibility and moral order.[75] The consequent debt burdens have resulted in huge flows of commodities and finances from Africa, Latin America and parts of Asia to Western banks and economies, and the systematic impoverishment of millions of humans and of environments in many parts of the Third World. The early advocates of free trade never envisaged the degree of capital mobility which the modern world now experiences, nor the degrees of global impoverishment which such mobility generates.

In traditional pre-modern economies the order of exchange is closely related to the natural order of available biological resources, and to the moral order and relationships of human communities. On some Pacific islands the medium of exchange was a limited biological commodity, conch shells, while in other economies it might have been pearls, snakeskins or goats. Such limited systems of exchange were the servants of the welfare and needs of particular human communities. The exchange system was embedded in social relations in particular communities, and held in check by relational and communal ties which discouraged excessive exchange accumulation, and by biophysical limits on the unit of exchange, whether conch shells, pearls or goats. The purpose of exchange activity was the mutual benefit of those involved. This is what Marcel Mauss means when he talks of the 'economy of gift'. However, as people are forced into the cash nexus of the modern money economy by the processes of modernisation and development they themselves, as well as their lands, are effectively commodified. The medium of exchange ceases to be a medium in which needs are mutually met and welfare is collectively enhanced. Instead people are subject to coercion and poverty which force them into economic migrancy to sell themselves and often their children into some form of wage slavery. The growing impoverishment of the urban periphery of the modern West and the modern Third World testifies to the massive scale of immiseration which these coercive tendencies of the abstract money economy generate when disembedded from biological limits and community responsibility.

The heart of the ecological and human enigma of modern industrial civilisation is that the money economy and industrialism have become autonomous to particular human and biotic communities. The international economic system is too global, too vast and anonymous, to allow for feedback between imbalances between costs and benefits arising from particular kinds of production or consumption, to be reflected in the market price of these activities. The solution is not only to bring economic and productive activity back into scale with biophysical limits, but also to bring economic and industrial activity back into relation with human needs and human welfare, and into the control of local polities and local communities. The need to bring economic processes back into democratic control goes to the heart of the theological and ethical arguments which I have explored in previous chapters. The autonomy of money in the modern world is the social form of the denial of the creative and ordering activity of God in the world, and the shift from forms of human sociality oriented around the self-in-relation – to God, human communities and nature – towards atomised forms of human behaviour, and the related tendency of modern states and markets to aggregate total human welfare in ways which frequently harm the welfare of particular human communities and individuals, and of the non-human world. The economy of God the creator/redeemer is by contrast an economy oriented in Aristotelean and New Testament terms to the welfare of each *oikos* or household, where real economy, real wealth, is measured in terms of the realisation by each household of those goods which make for human flourishing, including sociability, play and religion.[76] Economic relations on this account should reflect the relational character of created order, and the relational character of the self, which, as we have seen, are both grounded in the Hebrew and Christian traditions on a relational account of the being of God. But how in a globalised economy can we begin to rebuild the moral economy which must underlie the economy of wealth creation if industrialism is not to undermine both human goods and communities and ecological integrity? How can we begin to draw anonymous and dehumanising economic and industrial processes back into scale with the face-to-face character of human communities and the self-in-relation, and the localised and particular character of ecological goods and biodiversity?

Some economists argue that ecological reorientation can take place through the sovereignty of the consumer.[77] Thus through environmental education and information, ecologically sensitised consumers can be encouraged to make decisions in the market which will favour clean technologies over dirty ones, recycled and biodegradable packaging and low-energy consumer durables or machines. But in reality consumers are not sovereign. There are many kinds of environmental decision-making which are not amenable to this kind of approach. Consumers may prefer subsidised trains to subsidised roads and heavy traffic jams, but in Britain and North America state or national governments discourage the building of new railways while they freely subsidise the building of new roads from public taxes. Consumers may prefer deposit and return bottles to the messy and expensive business of trashing or recycling non-returnable bottles, but where manufacturers collectively decide to abolish the returnable bottle, consumers can do nothing about it. The idea of consumer sovereignty as a mode of environmental decision-making represents an abdication of political responsibility to the autonomy of the market. What is needed is a more radical approach to political economy where local communities are empowered both to resist the human and ecological depredations of globalising industrialism, and to foster more humanly and ecologically beneficent forms of technology and artefact production.

Herman Daly and John Cobb advocate the practice of bioregionalism as a way of bringing economic and industrial activities and processes back into scale with human communities and ecological balance.[78] In a bioregional approach, economic practices and markets are primarily organised in relation to local or 'bioregional' communities, which are mostly smaller than nation states. Through the devolution of political and economic sovereignty to smaller communities, it is possible for local communities to begin to regain control over those universal technical processes which tend to degrade local environments. In a bioregional approach jobs are created locally, and goods are mostly traded locally, minimising the transport and trading of goods across vast distances and in an anonymous market.[79] Bioregionalism involves a new relationship between the factors of production and the local conditions of the environment and of human welfare so that feedback from the degradation of either occurs quickly and locally. In the global economy feedback between investors and the environment where capital is mobilised may never occur because of the global scale and hence anonymity of the economic process. Bioregionalism ensures that producers and consumers and the environment are maintained in a relationship of proximity which discourages the devil-may-care waste and pollution of so much globally organised production.

Daly and Cobb illustrate the bioregional approach with reference to population control. They note that the biggest environmental impacts are made not by more African children but by more North Americans and Europeans. They point to the rising incidence of teenage pregnancy in Britain and North America, the millions consequently born into poverty and without two parents, as symptomatic of the breakdown of community under the influence of the economic orthodoxy of the market, and the failure of community to express any kind of moral control over the procreative activities of the population. They propose that the aim of community control over population growth should be to match the number of people, and their resource use, to the welfare of the community, 'where community includes concern for the future and for non-human species as well as presently living humans'.[80] Population stabilisation, or zero population growth, is, they argue, the desired option for both developed and developing countries. A variety of measures are proposed whereby communities might express greater control over the individual's procreative abilities. One proposal is the idea of a licence to have a child. Every adult receives a licence which he or she may either use or sell to someone else who may want more than the two children such a policy would prescribe for two parents.[81]

The same approach of community decision-making can be applied to resource use as to population control. In modern market-oriented democracies, markets in houses and consumer durables are already regulated to a surprising degree. New washing-machines may only be sold if they are electrically safe, and if they conform to the specifications and claims of their manufacturers. However, there are in most countries no legal requirements relating to how much water a washing-machine may consume, or how long a washing-machine should last. Similarly there are few restrictions on the kind of detergents which may be used, despite the higher environmental costs of some detergents over others. New cars in most developed countries must conform to certain emission standards, even though these standards are still low enough to contribute to city smog, rural ozone pollution and human ill-health. Regulations also require the fitting of safety equipment, for the passengers, though the regulations concerning the impact of cars in collisions with pedestrians are tragically inadequate. Car use is also regulated to the extent that licences and taxes must be paid, and in some countries tolls on certain bridges and roads, and speed is kept within enforced limits. However, there are no regulations on the number of cars a household may own, or the frequency with which they may be driven. Housing is similarly controlled by a range of regulation concerning drainage, electrical safety, protection against climate offered to occupants and window-size. Planning permits govern the building of new houses. Again, though, there are no regulations on the number of houses an individual may possess, or on the maximum energy consumption of a house of a given size. But given the extent of existing legal regulation of washing-machines, automobiles and houses, it is clearly inaccurate to describe their production, marketing and consumption as 'free'. Nations as political communities already express considerable degrees of control over markets for food, consumer durables, cars and houses. The political and communal recognition of the true environmental costs of washing-machine or car use would suggest not an abolition of markets in these goods but a much tighter regulation of their production, purchase and use than obtains under present arrangements. But there is considerable reluctance on the part of national governments to force producers to make low-energy and long-life consumer durables and automobiles. The source of this reluctance is largely the influence not of consumers, who are often ignorant of the energy consumption of different washing-machines or the emission standards of different car engines, but of producers. Producers and corporations are consistently reluctant to accept that their products damage particular local environments and need tighter regulation, and they exercise their reluctance in powerful lobbying of national governments to ensure that they are allowed to continue producing with the minimum of restraint. Producer power is the other side of the supposed freedom of the individual consumer in the market. The production of cars and washing-machines is in the hands of a small number of corporations in any one country. These corporations exercise power over consumers and over the political process which is largely beyond the control of individual consumers, or even of communities of consumers and voters. Increasingly as these corporations are international, they are also beyond the control of national governments.

One of the most ingenious proposals for reorienting the production and consumption processes of industrialism towards both human flourishing and environmental goods relates to taxation reform. Charles Pigou was the first economist to propose a shift in taxation to reflect the environmental costs of production and consumption, and such taxes are sometimes known as Pigovian taxes.[82] The clearest case for an ecological tax reform, aside from the land tax already proposed above, relates to energy consumption. Present taxation arrangements are primarily focused on human work through taxes on income and employment (National Insurance). This means that labour-saving technologies receive a tax advantage, and that income taxes thus contribute to increased unemployment and social dislocation, while the increased energy and natural resource consumption involved in more mechanised technologies on farms or in factories is actually favoured by current taxation policies, thus contributing to global warming. Shifting the taxation burden from productive work which gives people a stake in society towards the consumption and use of energy will therefore have profound social as well as ecological benefits. And yet such a radical shift in taxation policies does not involve any enhancement of political control over people's lives, nor any increase in public spending, but simply a rebalancing of existing government controls over economic processes or market forces in a more ecological direction. Indeed this approach is likely to reduce dependence of individuals on the state because by favouring human work over energy consumption it will produce less unemployment. It will also enable market activities to more fairly reflect their environmental impacts, for the sale price of a consumer durable or an item of food will reflect the true environmental costs of its production and transport. This approach will produce market circumstances in which less polluting and less energy-intensive technologies are automatically favoured by market conditions. It is a good example of the way in which the political and democratic management of market forces can be used constructively to enhance both human and ecological goods, while not undermining the obvious advantages of market economies over centrally planned economies as systems of information which bring together purchasers and producers in relationships of mutual benefit. What this taxation reform will do is to enhance dramatically the capacity of the information communicated by the prices of goods and services to reflect environmental as well as human and technological considerations. The energy tax, like the land tax, enables the abstract money system to more accurately reflect the impacts which money exchange behaviour is having on both human and non-human flourishing. Again, though, this approach will also necessitate reforms to the global system of production and exchange, such as those involved in the bioregional proposal considered above, for without such reforms, international corporations will simply shift their production and pollution to regions where they do not have to pay Pigovian taxes of this kind.

Another approach to the communal and ecological reform of industrial production arises from a consideration of car use and transport policy. Private cars are a luxury enjoyed by roughly 15 per cent of the world's population. The rest, the vast majority of contemporary humans, still rely on legs, bicycles, animals, buses and trains for transport. Cars are the archetypal product of the free market, affluent consumer society: they symbolise individual freedom. But, as André Gorz notes, the enjoyment of the motor car is not infinitely expandable to the whole population of any one country, or of the globe.[83] In countries which have achieved mass car ownership, there is a correlative reduction in the freedom and enjoyment which car ownership confers as more and more cars are added to the roads. Vacation traffic jams, and ride-to-work traffic jams are the common experience of Western car-owning democracies. Because of the number of cars on the road, the average speed of traffic in Western cities is now slower than it was in the days of horse-drawn transport. Cities in turn have become increasingly noisy, polluted and unhealthy places. People move to the suburbs or the country hinterland to escape the polluted city that their cars have created, and they drive back to the city every day, so compounding the problem. The car generates crime, danger and ill-health. Car crime is the largest form of crime in the Western world. Because of the dangers of traffic, children cannot safely play outside their houses in most residen-

tial areas in car-dominated societies. The freedom of the child
in a pre-industrial village to wander and roam is a distant
dream for a child in a car-owning democracy. Parents are
afraid for their children to walk to school, and children living
on main roads, in city centres or near motorways are at great
risk of acquiring respiratory problems which may affect their
health for life. More people die in car accidents every year than
from HIV/AIDS. The life chances of trees and wild animals as
well as humans are dramatically reduced by car pollution and
impacts with cars. The car destroys communities as roads are
driven through villages and town centres, and flyovers divide
city space. Just as the car promises individual freedom it
threatens community security, and it destroys the environment.

More than any other single commodity, the control of the
production, consumption and use of cars is an environmental
priority. Cars and their production are the single largest source
of waste metal, air and noise pollution and oil consumption,
and the second largest contributor to global warming after
space heating. The roads cars use are the largest utiliser of
quarried materials, and the largest cause of environmental
degradation as rare heathlands, tropical forests, mountainsides
and lowland farmland are covered with tarmacadam for the
car. But the car is the archetype of consumerism and affluence.
Cities, suburbs, shops, the whole of human life, especially in
North America, are designed around the car. Producers and
voters will not happily oversee its demise, despite the fact that
hundreds of thousands of people world-wide are slaughtered
and maimed by this mode of transport every year.

Communal resistance to the encroachments of the car on
human living-space and wilderness is growing. A large road
expansion scheme in England was dramatically curtailed by the
government in 1994 at least partly as a consequence of the
informal alliance of New Age travellers, home-owners and
conservationists which fought road schemes in East London
and Essex, at Twyford Down, Winchester and in other parts of
Southern England by means of direct action, civil disobedience
and obstruction as well as lobbying at local, national and
international level. Similar resistance to road schemes is

growing in other parts of the developed and developing world. Local communities are also beginning to demand safer space in which to live. Traffic calming, pedestrianisation and lower speed limits are all being utilised in parts of Europe to stem the assault of the car on the quality of life in towns and cities.

But Gorz suggests a more radical vision of cities and life without cars and mass transportation. Suburbanised cities serve a system of transportation which is an adjunct of the social division of labour. The division of social life into work place, house place, leisure place, shopping place makes for the disintegration of human life and of community so that we never imagine 'that work, culture, communication, pleasure, satisfaction of needs, and personal life can and should be one and the same thing: a unified life, sustained by the social fabric of the community'.[84] Instead of the mass division of social life into sectors connected up by cars, we need to recover neighbourhoods and communities 'where people can work, live, relax, learn, communicate, and knock about, and which they manage together as their place of life in common'.[85] People will rely less on the car as a means of escape when they come to love the place where they live, where they nurture it and thrive in it, without noise, pollution and the desert wastes of car-scaped cities and suburbs. In Gorz's ideal of medium-sized towns and small cities, bicycles, taxis, trams and buses could replace the car completely, while for those who wish to journey out of town the car could remain an option, though he prefers communally owned or rental vehicles to private cars.[86]

In the short-term we will not do away with the need for mass transportation altogether, although trends such as home-working and community planning for integrated work and living-space could dramatically reduce the need for transportation. Where mass transportation is needed, the resources which are currently utilised in private transport could be much more effectively utilised in public transport, and with much lower environmental impacts. In Britain, as in North America, there has been a big decline in public transport provision in the last forty years. Only air transport is encouraged to expand, while many rural and suburban trains and railway lines have been decommissioned, and the remaining trains and buses deregulated and privatised. A few British cities, notably Manchester and Sheffield, have experimented successfully with new tramways which have shown the possibilities for a clean, quiet transport revolution in cities. But public spending on such schemes is severely restricted by central government while private toll roads and bridges are encouraged instead.

The efforts of local communities in resisting the encroachments of the car on their quality of life are too often unsuccessful in the face of the conspiratorial partnership of commercial car and road makers and liberal governments. This is indicative of a wider problem with Western political and democratic societies. The encroachments of the market have in many cases severely weakened community structures and associations. Human as well as natural ecology has been gradually but systematically undermined. This process has in turn undermined the legitimacy of political power. Thus the remobilisation of community control over local space, technical processes and environmental quality is not only a key feature of ecological renewal. It is also essential to the recovery of genuine political control of those economic, productive and bureaucratic processes by which the state and the corporation have ceded social power from local human communities. The redressing of environmental problems through the reactivation of local community structures and institutions will also help in the development of a response to many of the human problems which modern 'developed' societies now experience. Rising rates of property crime and violence against the person, rising levels of suicide and depression, the growth of family breakdown and of one-person households, and other features of advanced industrial societies – these concomitants of individualism, social atomism, of private wealth and public squalor, also indicate the need for the rebuilding of human associational and community structures as Amitai Etzioni and Paul Hirst, amongst others, argue.[87]

As we have seen, this reactivation of community and associationalism is a common feature of local environmental protest. People in villages, towns or cities band together and rediscover

the values of neighbourliness and common action when faced
with the external threat of a new motorway, a toxic waste
incinerator or another unwelcome development project.
Similar local resistance to global industrialism and capitalism is
also increasingly evident in the developing world. The land tax
concept, community land ownership and land reform, bioregionalism and the devolution of economic and political power
from corporations and nation states to local communities are all
suggestive of a new localised vision of human self-government
and the common weal which can effectively challenge the
subversion of both human and environmental goods by the
faceless power of technological processes. However, relocating
environmental decision-making and political economy in local
communities will not alone achieve the radical reorientation of
industrialism which is required by the environmental crisis.
What is also required is a radical change of heart, of orientation, from the wasteful and intemperate surfeit of consumerism,
and the technologies which drive the throw-away society, to a
simpler style of life involving fulfilment through patterns of
artefact production and consumption, work and play which
consume less energy and fewer natural resources. But it is
unlikely that this kind of radical reorientation of personal life-
style can take place without a moral and spiritual reorientation
to more traditional sources of human fulfilment than the
shopping mall and the motorway.

PAROCHIAL ECOLOGY

The world-wide spread of the environmental movement has
produced a growing political and bureaucratic awareness of
environmental problems both at national and international
levels in recent years. Governments in Europe and North
America have dramatically extended the range of legislative
and regulatory control of the industrial remaking of the environment, even though, and at the same time, they continue to
sponsor the further spread of industrial development and
intensive industrial agriculture across the land. Western industrial development is gradually moving from dirtier to cleaner

technologies and some corporations are trying to find ways to close the 'product cycle', for example by building chemical plants which reuse and recycle materials which were traditionally discharged as effluent to atmosphere or estuaries. Some research continues to be sponsored by governments into renewable energy production, although inertia and market forces continue to allow fossil fuel-based energy production and high energy consumption behaviour to dominate, despite the employment opportunities which would be created by energy conservation measures such as enhancing building insulation, and despite the greatly improved possibilities for solar and wind power production which have become apparent in recent years. Official environmentalism in Britain and the United States is much attenuated by the commitment of governments in these countries to market approaches to social decisions, including decisions about natural resource use. The privatisation of public utilities in these countries has reduced public control over energy production, water use, river pollution, sewerage, transportation and waste handling, and weakened democratic control of the environmental impacts of these key social and economic activities. The language of 'sustainable development' fills government reports on environmental issues but the preference for market solutions to environmental problems dramatically reduces the willingness to generate public plans for reductions in energy consumption in transport or electricity systems, or reductions in sewage and chemical pollution of rivers and oceans. Governments with a stronger sense of the need for social control of market forces have made much further advances in environmental reform. For example in Sweden and Germany there is much closer regulation of industrial and domestic waste production, and incentives and laws which encourage the sorting and recycling of waste at both household and factory level. In Holland an integrated transport policy has substantially reduced the use of private cars both within cities and for journeys between cities.

The ecological repristination of natural law ethics which I outlined above provides a strong ethical argument for the legitimacy of democratic regulation and control over markets, technologies and environmental resource use. The quest for the common good, and the orientation of social processes towards those goods which make for the flourishing of both human communities and non-human species and communities, are the central goals of the polity in the natural law tradition. But the pursuit of the common good in this tradition also involves a presumption in favour of the exercise and sharing of social power by local human communities, rather than the concentration of sovereign power in centralised states or transnational corporations. The rise of the modern nation state and of the transnational corporation have limited the powers of groups of citizens to conserve and mobilise their own natural resources for the welfare of their own communities and habitats. In addition to more international and government regulation of economic and market processes, the ecological reform of political economy requires that local communities are empowered to find new ways of expressing democratic control over economic and technological processes, and of controlling their impacts on human and non-human goods in particular regions and habitats.

The Rio Earth Summit represented the global flowering of a new international response to the environmental crisis. It produced a very substantial report, *Agenda 21*, which includes a range of proposals for bringing human expansion of economic and productive activities more into line with the biophysical limits of the planet, and attempts to set targets for reductions in energy and natural resource use, for preserving biodiversity and for changing consumption behaviour. However, the rhetoric of Rio has rarely matched up to the more short-term and economistic inclinations of most national political leaders. The proceedings of the conference gave little ground in any case for optimism about the preparedness of international actors and the richest nation states to radically shift the terms under which development is pursued in the global market. The Climate Change Convention set no target dates for reducing or even stabilising emissions of greenhouse gases because of pressure from the richest and most energy-consumptive economy, the United States.[88] The United States also opposed a biodiversity treaty on the grounds that it involved a potential threat to its own global prominence in biotechnology. Malaysia and India opposed any treaty on forest preservation, arguing that the attempt to impose logging restrictions on developing nations was a form of imperialism on the part of rich nations, most of whom had already cut down their forests.

Wolfgang Sachs observes that the emergence of an international ecocracy is not without ambiguity for like sovereign national governments, global environmentalism can also subvert the environmental responsibilities and potential of local communities.[89] The new ecocracy conjures up the chimera of global resource management which is in reality the continuation of the Western myth of limitless economic growth facilitated by new levels of human technological control over nature. But of course the character and extent of this control, and of the possibilities for global resource management, are illusory. Industrialised societies release thousands of toxins and pollutants into the sinks of air and water every year, but we monitor perhaps fifty of them. The remainder we leave to chance and dispersal. Resource management is too exalted a term for the neglectful pollution and destruction of precious resources which Western development entails. Climate, oxygen production, carbon recycling: these key processes on which all known life depends are too vast and complex for even the most sophisticated computers and dedicated scientists to 'manage'. Perhaps the greatest danger of international environmentalism is not so much the mirage of environmental control it sets before those who have economic and political power, but the illusion such meetings as the Rio Summit create that something is being done, that ordinary people and local communities have no need to worry, that transnational agri-business, ecocrats or the United Nations have already got the problem in hand.

Most environmental problems are not global in origin or in character but local. Christine von Weizsäcker notes that the new concern for biodiversity on the part of many Western governments and companies treats biodiversity as a form of global economic capital which can be charted, captured, managed and improved by global biotechnology.[90] But species diversity is not a global phenomenon to be managed by transnational biotechnology companies. Diversity is maintained in particular local habitats with boundaries of mountains, rivers or oceans, and human cultural boundaries which have evolved in correlation with the various ecologies of different regions. However, monocrop agriculture recognises no boundaries, ecological or cultural, and where those habitats are destroyed no amount of biotechnology can replace the lost diversity, or remake the ecological systems which ensured the continuing mutation of species necessary for future diversity. The continuing impact of monocrop zoning in commercial agriculture in both the developed and developing worlds is the principal cause of the loss of species diversity. The proposed biotechnological guardianship of diversity may then not be the opponent but the handmaid of modern agriculture's intensive assault on wild nature.

It may be that the very capacity of modern technologically enabled humans to conceive of the earth as one global space, and for a small but growing elite to travel and range widely in that space in their lifetime, contributes to the illusion of global resource management, and of the environment as a global problem which is only resolvable on a global scale. Global environmentalism is a dangerous distraction from the urgent need to recover local and communal mechanisms of environmental control, of ecological resource management, of trade and food production, of livelihood procurement and wealth creation. It raises the spectre of a kind of global resource policing, and of world government, which have often been part of the ecotopian vision of a world after environmental breakdown, and are simply the continuation of Western scientific imperialism and control projected into a post-crisis future.

Green consumerism, ecocracy, even environmental protest movements, ultimately cannot succeed in radically changing the direction of modern civilisation so long as they avoid the moral and spiritual vacuum which lies at its heart. The ecological repristination of the natural law tradition argues for a fundamental connection between the reorientation of society towards the common good of humanity and the cosmos and the situation of persons in moral and worshipping communities where the quest for the common good is enriched and legitimated by the spiritual quest. The dissolution of these communities by the disembedding forces of money, modern individualism and global mobility is clearly linked with modern civilisation's spiritual vacuum. The natural sustaining reciprocities between particular human cultures and communities and particular kinds of species diversity and ecological community are dissolved by the global mobility of the products of nature as these are drawn into the cash nexus. Mobility is deeply destructive of morality and human communities and relationships. This is as true of the mobility of persons engendered by the modern motor car and air transport as it is of the mobility of the product of nature engendered by the modern cash economy. But the dissolution of human communities and cultures is not regarded by most modern scholars as problematic, for in modern philosophy and social theory moral significance is located exclusively in the mind, and more especially in the sensations, of each individual person. Thus provided we advance the pleasurable sensations of the majority of individual persons, the destruction of cultures and communities, and of their moorings both to particular places or lands and to particular religious traditions, represents no threat to human welfare. However, as we have seen, this process of cultural and communal dissolution ultimately also subverts the moral capital on which every form of civilisation must rely. Paradoxically it also undermines the true sources of pleasure as the chimera of consumption is substituted for the true happiness which originates in the richness of human interaction in human communities. In the ecological repristination of natural law ethics essayed in this book, the true flourishing of persons and of the creation lies in the realisation of those moral goods or excellences which, according to the Hebrew and Christian traditions, persons, societies and the non-human world are teleologically ordered to realise in different but related ways. The fundamental good is the orientation of life towards God as the giver of life, an orientation which is expressed in the first commandment of the Decalogue, which is the revealed form of the natural law, the commandment to worship God and God alone, and not to idolise – and hence abuse – any other feature of created reality. The centrality of worship in this vision of ethics points to the moral significance of worshipping communities in which the dependence of all life on God, and the gifted and relational character of all forms of life on earth, are celebrated and affirmed, and in which those values or virtues which make for the good life, and the common good, of both human society and the land, are pursued and legitimated. In this approach, the moral quest is fundamentally concerned with the recovery of relationality, to God, to other persons and to the land and all created things. This relationality finds expression in the pursuit of those moral practices which are known as the virtues: love and justice, temperance and prudence, fidelity and courage, hope and peaceableness. These virtues enable us to become more fulfilled as persons, to live in solidarity with one another and to live in harmony with the created order. They represent a set of principles which point to the embedded character of the moral life in the structure of human consciousness and human relationships, and in the structure of created order.

The virtues have profound ecological as well as human significance and resonance. Love is the first of all the virtues, for in ordering our loves, for God, for persons and for created things aright, we are enabled to recover a sense of emotional security with God and with other persons which balances our cravings for material security, and for satiety and excess, the emotional drivers of so much of our disordered consumerism. The love of God and the love of life, life in all its diversity, are also intricately connected, for in loving the giver we are enabled to love and respect the gifts of the creation. Secondly justice is crucial to an ecological perspective on human society, for as we have seen, the oppression of the poor is intricately connected with the destruction of environments and habitats throughout human history as well as in the contemporary developing world. The just distribution of those biophysical goods which make for human flourishing – housing, food, clothing, fuel – is essential to a civil society in which crime and social disorder are minimised, and in which the poor do not have to steal, or to destroy their environment, in order to provide for their children. And justice will also involve a recognition of the legitimacy of the claims on natural resources of non-human species, of the moral requirement to leave space beyond human settlement and agriculture for wildlife and wild habitats to flourish. Finally justice requires that those abstract economic and technological forces which reconstruct human life and society in the modern world must be subjected to democratic control, and must be made to reflect the balance of both human goods and of ecological goods, which they either promote or hinder. Temperance is an essential ecological virtue, for it involves the right ordering of human appetites so that these do not lead either to abuse of one's own person, or other persons, or to abuse and excess consumption in relation to the non-human world. Without temperance we cannot distinguish between a genuine need for food or material security and comfort, and an ecologically harmful quest for luxury or excess. Prudence is also of profound ecological significance, for the waste and pollution of non-renewable or pristine natural resources is clearly imprudent, if not in terms of our own welfare, then in terms of the welfare of our children and grandchildren. Equally prudence would encourage us to be cautious about mobilising technologies whose hazards are not fully understood and accounted for. Fidelity is also a key virtue from an ecological perspective for fidelity requires that we respect and conserve our relations with those persons and places which together have brought us to life and given us our sense of self: as the fifth commandment has it, 'Honour your father and your mother, so that you may enjoy long life in the land which the Lord your God is giving you.'[91] Courage or fortitude is again of profound value for it is precisely this virtue which is needed in the ecological reform of modern civilisation, and of its moral and spiritual traditions. Only a courageous politician would propose the radical reform of a taxation system towards taxes on land and energy on the basis of the long-term projections of coming environmental catastrophe which extend far beyond the life of any elected government and in the face of opposition from corporations and landlords. Hope is essential if we are to believe that we can change direction before it is too late, that voters and consumers, corporations and governments, are amenable to moral arguments about ecological destruction, and the justice of the cause of radical reform of our global trading system. And finally peaceableness is profoundly important, for without it we will continue to imagine that our life on this planet is one of inevitable conflict, with our neighbours for scarce resources, and with natural systems for human control of the planet.

As we have seen, this approach to ethics challenges the moral individualism which drives the supremacy of the market in modern economic theory and the modern global order, and it demonstrates the limitations of the narrow account of human and animal welfare offered by different versions of utilitarianism. It has profound ecological significance because it situates the quest for the good in the context of particular relationships, responsibilities, communities, places and habitats, and especially those which have formed us and made us as persons, and because it reaffirms the connections between persons, cultures, traditions and ecosystems which are so rapidly being eroded by the globalisation of North American and European consumerist icons and aspirations. The realisation of the virtues is, though, only possible in the context of stable relationships of nurture and care, and of stable communities which are oriented towards both moral and spiritual fulfilment. It is a truism, confirmed by the growing modern experience of divorce, that the child who lacks a stable parenting environment is a child who as an adult may lack certain of those psychic and moral qualities without which the possibilities for adult fulfilment will be diminished. It is difficult to acquire or to sustain the moral virtues which enable us to live as good persons, and to pursue our own goods in ways which are in harmony with the goods of other persons and the environment, in the absence of stable moral communities in which these virtues may be formed. This is why the ecological crisis of contemporary industrial capitalism is also a moral crisis, for the same processes which are dissolving natural ecological harmony, diversity and goodness are dissolving the natural moral goods of traditional human communities. But this recognition brings us back to the fundamental moral and ecological conundrum with which this book has been concerned. If the crisis of the environment is also a moral crisis, and if the processes of modernity which are destroying nature are also destroying human moral virtue, where are we to find the moral resources to radically change the direction of modern civilisation?

The ancient Hebrews, like most primal peoples, oriented their social customs, exchange relations, their work on the land and their tending of nature around the worship of Yahweh. The liturgical calendar established the times and seasons of their daily life and work, religious rituals affirmed the fertility of the land and their delight in the beneficence and beauty of the natural order was also a delight in the goodness and beauty of Yahweh. Europe under Christendom experienced a similar coming together of the liturgical and the agricultural and productive cycles and still in the last surviving primal cultures this same reciprocity between worship, spirituality and life-style can be observed. The forces of technological modernity which undermine human and ecological communities have also undermined the religious and spiritual orientation by which they were characterised. The orientation of the pre-modern village around the parish church, and the medieval city around the cathedral, and of the working week and year around holy days and liturgical seasons, is a fading folk memory for much of Northern Europe. The worship of the Lord has moved to the margins of social life, and religious feasts, ceremonies and ritual entertainments such as passion plays and sacred music are secularised and repackaged as the orgy of Christmas consumerism, or the compact disc of Gregorian chant.

But in the current phase of 'high modernity', as Anthony Giddens dubs it (more accurately I believe than those who speak of the advent of post-modernity), we can observe the mutual emergence of movements of ecological resistance and protest, and of a new quest for spiritual meaning and the transcendent.[92] The range of single issue protest groups, and

the plurality of modern new religious movements and spiritualities, may not represent a coherent challenge to the trajectory
of modern Western civilisation. But the emergence of these not
unrelated quests for ecological harmony and spiritual fulfilment
in modern societies is a sign of hope, for it is in the articulation
of these two quests that a vision of an alternative society may be
generated. But the problem with the modern supermarket of
religions is that it purveys transcendence as one more commodity rather than offering a genuinely alternative way of
living. As Robert Wuthnow notes, the new religions – charismatic Christianity, Western-style Terevada Buddhism, resur-
gent New Age paganism – offer transcendental experience as
one more life-style choice, but their adherents often tend to
eschew those works of community building, charity and engagement with the social and relational structure of life which were
the characteristic moral outcomes of more traditional forms of
religious community.[93] Apart from the embedded social structures associated with traditional religious communities, many
modern spiritualities do not seem to generate caring behaviour,
either in relation to other humans or to the natural order, but
only a privatised quest for inner emotional states of peace,
harmony or ecstasy. Religion itself in the latest manifestations
of charismatic ecstasy would seem to have more to do with
adapting mind states to the alienation and moral disorder of
technologically dominated societies than with challenging the
autonomy and power of technology to undermine human
community and the self-in-relation. The very adherence of
these new styles of Christian religion to technologically enabled
worship – worship as entertainment – would seem to be one
more confirmation of the power of technological modernity to
undermine and reshape human selfhood and community.

But what distinguishes the traditional natural law-influenced
vision of religious community from these modern ersatz religious styles is precisely the association of religion with particular
places and communities and with those virtues which make for
individual flourishing and the common good of all. Hooker's
vision of the worship and polity of the church as the focal point
of the productive, ritual, family and moral life of English society

is an essential feature of his enunciation of a natural law tradition which is genuinely incarnational, which locates the experience of transcendence, the nurture of children and of society in the expression of the virtues, and in the context of worshipping communities. This reflects the pre-modern function of the parish church as the focus for the human experience of place, land, settlement, community government and transcendence. But with the differentiation of social life into the distinct spheres of work and consumerism, leisure and education, domesticity and religion, the maintenance of the territorial character of religious community seems to be no more than a quixotic historical reminder of a former undifferentiated, local and less mobile style of life, and a reminder which becomes increasingly attenuated by financial pressures and by the privatisation and congregationalism of modern religious inclinations. The decline of religion and the technological altering of the natural and the human environment seem to be two sides of the same coin. How then might religious communities and parish churches, which affirm face-to-face and neighbourly contact as a vital feature of church and community life, influence and change the technological society in a more ecological direction?

Firstly it seems clear that churches and worshipping communities have to try to recapture to some extent the links between the world of work – of industry and agriculture, of economy and consumerism, of science and technology – and the worship and common life of the parish. The enormous gulf between the liturgy and life of the parish and the working world of many of its members is one which must be bridged within the church's own worship and community, through rituals, sermons, teaching and discussion materials and media which encourage church members to reflect on the ethical implications of their incorporation into technological processes and global markets from the perspective of the creator/redeemer whose actions are for all the cosmos and not just for a diminishing group of Christians. Since the Second World War the churches have attempted to bridge this gulf through sending clergy into the workplace as chaplains. Increasingly churches are seeing that this approach has not bridged the gap.[94] It is clearly far more useful for local churches to provide contexts in which people can bring Christian ethical insights to bear on their experiences at work or in the shopping mall, and to develop a liturgical and educational and spiritual environment in which these experiences can be critiqued and correlated with an understanding of the wholeness of the human good, and the goods of the non-human world, as indicated in the Christian ethical tradition as presented here. The central vehicle for remaking these lost connections is the work of ritualisation in worship.

Tom Driver argues that ritual is one of the features of human behaviour which is shared with animals.[95] Rituals are inherited and learned behaviour patterns which represent the interaction of biophysical and cultural factors in the environmental and social construction of life both for primates and for humans. Rituals connect us to the social world and to our environment, and enable us to develop many motor and linguistic functions without which we could not live as adults, nor engage with other adults. Driver also suggests that the biophysical connections between nature and culture which are constructed and learnt in ritual are an essential part of ecological consciousness. Correlatively Driver suggests that the evacuation of ritual is a central feature of the impact of technology and the machine on human life and culture as instanced in the subversion of traditional ritualised, and less destructive, conflict resolution by the mechanised battlefield.[96] Similarly the modern factory shift subverts the rhythm of work, play, rest and worship of the pre-industrial age, while the TV dinner destroys the rite of the family meal, the shared grace for the gifts of creation, and the shared communication of the common meal. The loss of ritual is also a central feature of the modern subversion of community, and the shift of moral consciousness from its interactive locus in the natural and social order to the intuitions and sensations of individual minds. Driver argues that liberating and holistic ritualising is a vital force in the reconstruction of moral communities in society, and in the empowerment of these communities in the quest for transformation, and for ecological justice.[97]

As we saw in chapter five above, the ritual recognition of

ecological justice in the Bible is most powerfully represented in the Book of Psalms. The reading of the Psalms forms the basis for the worship of the monastery, and until recently played a central role in Christian worship. The revival of Psalm reading and singing will be vital to the ecological renewal of Christian worship. In Hebrew society ritual played a vital role in sustaining nature's order and the order of human society, and in healing divisions and fractures in the natural and social order. In Christian tradition the linkages of space, time and seasons to the liturgical year played a similarly important role in integrating worship with the patterns of life on earth. Artificial lighting, office and factory time, frozen and air-flown food, air-conditioning and central-heating isolate modern humans from this sense of the natural ordering of times, seasons and places. In attending to the cycles of the earth, and the cycles of the liturgical year, Christian worship can do much to overcome the consequent alienation between human consciousness and the natural order, through rituals which explicitly remake these lost connections. The most powerful ecological prayers in Christian history were written by the patron saint of the modern ecological movement, St Francis of Assisi. He identified the spiritual significance of nature as the sphere of divine blessing and the first locus of praise and worship in the *Canticle of the Brother Sun*:

> Praised be you my Lord through our Sister Mother Earth.
> Who sustains and governs us
> And who produces varied fruits with coloured flowers and herbs.[98]

Christian worship since the Reformation has mostly rejected the Franciscan way, and has tended in a very cerebral direction, and, perhaps especially since the Industrial Revolution, has begun to lose its traditional connections to place and land, time and seasons, focusing ritual action primarily on the minds and intuitions of individual participants. Contemporary liturgists, such as the Episcopalian priest Scott McCarthy, have created eucharistic and seasonal prayers and rites, ceremonies of light and darkness, rituals in the open air and forms of thanksgiving for water, minerals, animals and food designed to remake these lost connections.[99] Such rituals are not only recollections of our kinship with creation but they also enact the Christian vision of the incarnate God who becomes one with creation to restore its original *telos* and order. They not only recall the Christ event, but are also performative, bringing salvation into present reality: challenging the oppression of the poor and the theft of their lands and livelihood, inspiring compassion for vulnerable persons and vulnerable animals or habitats, and transforming social relations between ritual participants as an anticipation of the quest for justice and love in society as a whole. The ecological reform of local and parish worship will involve the recovery of holistic rituals which reconnect worshippers to their kinship as embodied beings with the whole creation and with animals, to the dependence of human society on the ecosystems which give life to humans and animals alike and to the natural goods and goals by which all created life is marked by the purposive hand of the beneficent creator and is directed towards its final restoration.

Secondly parish churches can be a place in which a true care for the earth is recovered and mobilised. I have already rehearsed some examples of this kind of mobilisation in the recent involvement of inner urban churches in Britain and America in Community Land Trusts, where the neighbourhood church acts as the focus for people of the neighbourhood to begin to reclaim patterns of housing, employment, production, exchange and natural environment which are conducive to human flourishing, and to a more ecologically balanced environment, in the heart of the city. Similarly we might conceive of rural churches becoming more involved in attempts to restore a balance in rural areas between the commercial pressures of industrial farming and the urgent need to restore biodiversity to chemically altered fields, forests and rivers. Churches might also encourage reflection on the land ethic in the biblical traditions and its implications in terms of a return to a less invasive style of agriculture, relying more on natural fertility, and on labour-intensive methods of fertilising and pest control, which might also help to achieve a better balance between human and mechanical activity on the land and so overcome the appalling loneliness which is driving a small but sadly growing number of farmers to suicide in isolated rural areas, as well as undermining the ecology of rural communities. The rural parish might also become a focus for efforts by small farmers (crofters in Scotland), and rural residents, to reclaim and buy back land from large landowners and commercial farms, for a better mix of rural activity and land use, and for a new relationship between people and land in rural areas.

Another vital way in which the local parish church can become involved in a new kind of care for the earth might be in terms of land audit, whereby each parish or local church undertakes an audit of land use, pollution, and ecological degradation in its own area. Such an audit would provide a remarkable knowledge base which could be utilised in efforts to restore ecological integrity to degraded areas, to challenge polluting and destructive industrial and agricultural practices and to promote better environmental practice amongst local firms or local farmers. The parish is a uniquely local institution. The parish church is defined by its proximity to land and is in an ideal position to capitalise on this proximity for an ecological audit of the land. Resistance to pollution and environmental neglect is an essentially local phenomenon. It was when fishermen on the Hudson River upriver from New York City began to lobby local power utility and chemical companies about their polluting outfalls into the river, and took this lobbying into local law courts, that the river began to improve and the fish returned. It was when local people protested about the health effects of a heavy oil-burning power station in the East End of London that the power company closed the polluting plant. Local people care for their local parish. If the creation–redemption schema which we have found in the Christian tradition is a truthful interpretation of this tradition, then part of the church's mission is to explore the implications of this schema with local landowners and users, farmers and companies, and to mobilise communities to reclaim their own land, to restore its beauty and balance and to recover its potential both as a source of wealth for local people, and as a locus for the realisation of the distinctive goods of non-human species.

Finally churches are places where the divine story of salvation and hope for human life and the cosmos is declared and experienced and anticipated in worship: hope in the redeeming creator, the God who takes created embodied life into divine being, the man who dies on the tree of life in sacrifice for the life of the cosmos, and the Spirit of life who not only brooded on the face of primeval waters but continues to urge the creation at every level to realise those goods of harmony and reciprocity, of co-operation and creativity, of community and diversity, which we find reflected both in biotic and in human communities. The greatest danger of environmental apocalypticism is that it encourages an attitude of helplessness. We are all bound to a web of relationships through which *we* are cutting the rainforests and trawling the oceans and eroding the soil and polluting the air and poisoning the soil. This web creates wealth and brings poverty, it promises life and brings death, it is modelled on interactivity and spreads individualism. The story of the dying and rising creator presents us with the possibility that we can remake this web from within as God also chose to do. In the local parish we need to develop worship, liturgies and educational media which enable people both to live and thrive in the midst of ecological ambiguity and at the same time to develop a spirituality and mentality of fruitful resistance. Above all in these communities we need to learn to foster those central and determinative practices of living by which the goods of human flourishing, and the goods of the non-human world, will be sustained and encouraged against their threatened subversion by technological processes. These practices include: the lively and embodied worship of an embodied God; the nurture of children in stable families; the recovery of good work as craft and art, as service of others and of nature and not simply as service of the machine and of the accountant's measure; the recovery of hospitality as a central Christian practice where in the ritual of the hand-prepared meal we reclaim time and food and the products of the land as gifts to human relationality; the making of ritual in which the relationality of human and non-human life is affirmed and enacted – the Christian sacramental elements of bread, wine and water testify deeply to this relationality but so equally do celebrations of winter's dark night in the Christmas Mass, or of spring's life reborn in the celebration of the resurrection of Christ on Easter Sunday; the exchange and sharing of gifts which reflect personal creativity and not just the designed ephemeralism of the shopping mall, and an exchange which reflects also a desire to share those artefacts which we may have bought as consumers rather than succumbing to the false security of outright possession; the making of music and dance, stories and drama which reconnect and remake human communities through collective cultural production and which challenge the disembodied and denatured togetherness of the TV game show and the electronic community. Perhaps the most determinative practice of all for Christians in relation to the modern environmental crisis is the inculcation of those habits of mind and morality which emanate from the traditional orientation of Christian living towards heaven. The ultimate teleological directedness of human life towards salvation and heaven, rather than towards pleasure or material possessions for their own sake, is an orientation which subverts the modern location of fulfilment entirely within the materialist quest for satiety, and which encourages instead the development of the practices of prayer and meditation, and of those virtues, such as justice and prudence, which not only make for whole persons and the wiser use of natural resources but are also said to prepare the person for the life of heaven.

In these practices Christian communities may seek to sustain those goods and virtues which characterise the flourishing of persons-in-relation, and which enable them to resist the currents of materialism and individualism which threaten to undermine both human community and the relationality of human life to the non-human world. The central ecological virtue remains that of justice, for without a witness to justice it is doubtful that parish churches or any other kind of Christian community can be said to be places of good news to those people who are excluded from the riches of the North, and for those animals and plants, fish and rivers, mountains and lakes, oceans and wildernesses, whose beauty, order and fecundity is every day threatened by the advancing juggernaut of modern consumerism. The source of the Hebrew and Christian view of justice is the worship of the just God. Christian communities, local churches, are places where this God of justice is worshipped and adored, and where God's reign of justice is looked for and evoked. The Hebrew prophets proclaimed that this justice would one day rain down not only on communities of humans but on the land, and on the life forms which teem over the face of the earth. St Paul, and the writer of the Book of Revelation, speak of a time when the whole cosmos will be brought into relationship with the supreme justice of the Lord who is God in Christ. Christians have often proclaimed this justice to people of their own race and gender and class. They have more rarely proclaimed it amongst people different from themselves. Far more rarely has it been proclaimed to those orders of life which are not human flesh and blood. But the connections between human justice, and the good of the land and its non-human inhabitants, remain as clear today in environmental disasters which destroy the land of greedy landowners who have exiled the poor and extinguished the wild animal and burnt the tree and leaf, as they did in the time of Isaiah and Amos. Parish communities cannot be so parochial that they neglect these wider, global connections. In remaking connections between worship and land, community and environment, ritual and seasons, hospitality and nature's wealth, Christian communities are also called to remember the universality of the church and of Christ's work, and the globality of our modern way of life. We cannot wish this globality away. But we can challenge its deleterious effects on the poor of the world, and on their degraded environments, as we in Northern Europe and North America continue to consume an unreasonable proportion of nature's limited resources and produce an unconscionable amount of global pollution and waste. Some of the ways in which we challenge these global processes will be precisely to remake and recover local methods of work and wealth creation which do not unduly exploit the land, which do not consume resources tilled or mined thousands of miles away and which remake connections between human community and natural created order in our own back yards. But in other ways we must continue to recognise that the world is also a parish and that justice and the integrity of creation can only be advanced when we act and lobby and think in such a way as to influence and challenge global actors and decision-makers about the ecological and human effects of their companies and agencies in distant lands and among alien peoples. The ecological slogan 'think globally, act locally' remains in the end a profoundly important message for the ecology of the parish.

Notes

I FROGS, FLOODS AND FAMINES

1 See especially Julian Simon and Herman Kahn (eds.), *The Resourceful Earth* (Oxford: Blackwell, 1984) and Richard North, *Life on a Modern Planet: A Manifesto for Progress* (Manchester: Manchester University Press, 1995). See also David E. Cooper, 'The Idea of Environment' in David E. Cooper and Joy A. Palmer (eds.), *The Environment in Question: Ethics and Global Issues* (London: Routledge, 1992), pp. 165–80.

2 Intergovernmental Panel on Climate Change, *Climate Change: The IPCC Scientific Assessment* (Cambridge: Cambridge University Press, 1990).

3 Alexander Pekham, *Global Warming* (London: Franklin Watts, 1991).

4 E. G. Nisbet, *Leaving Eden: To Protect and Manage the Earth* (Cambridge: Cambridge University Press, 1991), pp. 62 ff.

5 Marcia D. Lowe, 'Cycling into the Future' in Lester R. Brown, Alan Durning et al. (eds.), *State of the World 1990: A Worldwatch Institute Report on Progress Toward a Sustainable Society* (London: Unwin, 1990), pp. 119–34.

6 Debora MacKenzie, 'Polar Meltdown Fulfils Worst Predictions,' *New Scientist*, 1990 (1995), p. 4.

7 See the discussion of the term pollution by Mary Douglas, *Risk and Blame: Essays in Cultural Theory* (London: Routledge, 1992), pp. 4–5.

8 Nisbet, *Leaving Eden*, p. 78.

9 Donella Meadows, Dennis L. Meadows and Jorgen Randers, *Beyond the Limits: Global Collapse or a Sustainable Future?* (London: Earthscan, 1992), pp. 155–7.

10 Hilary F. French, 'Clearing the Air' in Brown and Durning, *State of the World 1990*, p. 106.

11 Chris Rose, *The Dirty Man of Europe: The Great British Pollution Scandal* (London: Simon and Schuster, 1990), p. 147.

12 *Ibid.*, p. 145.

13 Nisbet, *Leaving Eden*, pp. 81, 82.
14 Rose, *Dirty Man*, p. 32.
15 *Ibid.*, pp. 59, 60.
16 *Ibid.*, p. 69.
17 Rachel Carson, *Silent Spring* (Harmondsworth: Penguin, 1965).
18 Meadows and Randers, *Beyond the Limits*, p. 89.
19 Rose, *Dirty Man*, p. 2.
20 *Ibid.*, p. 197.
21 Department of the Environment, verbal evidence to House of Commons Environment Committee, Second Report: Toxic Waste, vol. 2, p. 35 cited in Rose, *Dirty Man*, p. 202.
22 Brian W. W. Welsh and Paul Butoria (eds.), *Dictionary of Development: Third World Economy, Environment and Society*, 2 vols. (London: St James Press, 1990), vol. 1, p. 305.
23 *Ibid.*, vol. 1, p. 306.
24 Lester R. Brown and John E. Young, 'Feeding the World in the Nineties' in Brown and Durning, *State of the World 1990*, pp. 59–78.
25 Statement of John F. Timmons, Professor of Economics, Iowa State University, to the Joint Hearing before the Subcommittee on Natural Resources and the Environment of the United States of America House of Congress, 25, 26 July 1979 (Washington: House of Congress, 1979), pp. 230, 231.
26 Welsh and Butoria, *Dictionary of Development*, vol. II, p. 910.
27 Organisation for Economic Cooperation and Development, *The State of the Environment* (Paris: OECD, 1991). See also Jeffrey R. Rae, 'An OECD Perspective on Agriculture and the Environment' in F. A. Miller (ed.), *Environment and Agriculture* (Reading: Centre for Agricultural Studies, University of Reading, 1991).
28 Nisbet, *Leaving Eden*, p. 137.
29 Piers Blaikie, *The Political Economy of Soil Erosion in Developing Countries* (London: Longman, 1985), pp. 58, 59.
30 Walter Rodney, *How Europe Underdeveloped Africa*, cited in Teresa Hayter, *The Creation of World Poverty: An Alternative View to the Brandt Report* (London: Pluto Press, 1982) pp. 31–2.
31 *Ibid.*
32 World Commission on Environment and Development, *Our Common Future* (Oxford: Oxford University Press, 1987), p. 123.
33 See further Paul Harrison, *The Third World Tomorrow: A Report from the Battlefront in the War Against Poverty* (London: Penguin, 1981).
34 *Ibid.*, p. 45.
35 *Ibid.*, pp. 45–6.
36 North, *Life on a Modern Planet*, pp. 48 ff.

37 J. V. Thirgood, *Man and the Mediterranean Forest: A History of Resource Depletion* (London and New York: Academic Press, 1981), p. 257.

38 Donald Hughes, *Ecology in Ancient Civilizations* (Albuquerque: University of New Mexico Press, 1975).

39 *Ibid.*

40 See further Clive Ponting, *The Green History of the World* (London: Penguin, 1988).

41 Norman Myers, *The Primary Source: Tropical Forests and Our Future* (New York: W. W. Norton, 1984).

42 *Life After Logging. The Role of Tropical Timber Extraction in Species Extinction* (London: Friends of the Earth, 1991), p. 14.

43 Robert Hunt of Trinity Theological College, Singapore, personal testimony.

44 The teak forests of Burma, now Myanmar, may be an exception: the nineteenth-century Belgian forester Derek Brandis selected a very few large trees per acre, he only moved logs in the rainy season when the ground was slippery, he did not build large logging roads as he used rivers and elephants rather than the machines now used and he used the local tribal peoples to help him not only to extract the wood but to preserve the forests: see Derek Brandis, 'The Burma Teak Forests', *Garden and Forest*, 9 (1896). I am indebted to Michael Lyons, consultant to the International Tropical Timber Organisation, for this reference. For a range of arguments for and against 'sustainable' timber harvesting in rainforests, and a consideration of the potentially greater and more long-term economic benefits to be derived from the harvesting of non-timber rainforest products see *The Rainforest Harvest: Sustainable Strategies for Saving the Tropical Forests? Including the Proceedings of the International Conference Held at the Royal Geographical Society, London 17th–18th May 1990* (London: Friends of the Earth, 1992).

45 Myers, *Primary Source*, p. 146.

46 Evelyn Hong, *Natives of Sarawak: Survival in Borneo's Vanishing Forests* (Pulau Pinang, Malaysia: Institut Masyarakat, 1989). See especially ch. 3, 'Swidden as a Rational Agricultural System'.

47 Myers reproduces a series of satellite images showing the destructive effects on the forest of roads cut through the Brazilian Amazon in order that shifted cultivators can settle and clear patches of forest: *Primary Source*, pp. 182–3. The extraordinarily extensive fires from this kind of government-encouraged migration and informal forest clearance are also a major environmental hazard, and a cause of air pollution problems in certain tropical cities: again see the satellite pictures of these fires in *Primary Source*, pp. 180–1.

48 See further Bruce Rich, *Mortgaging the Earth: The World Bank, Environmental Impoverishment and the Crisis of Development* (London: Earthscan, 1994), pp. 34–8.

49 Nisbet, *Leaving Eden*, p. 101.

50 Thirgood, *Man and the Mediterranean Forest*, p. 163.

51 *Life After Logging.*

52 Myers, *Primary Source*, p. xviii.

53 R. M. May, 'How Many Species?', *Philosophical Proceedings of the Royal Society* (1990) no. 330, pp. 293–304.

54 *Our Common Future*, p. 150.

55 Myers, *Primary Source*, p. 106.

56 *Our Common Future*, p. 149.

57 Paul R. Ehrlich, *Extinction: The Implications of the Loss of Our Biological Heritage* (Murdoch, WA: Murdoch University Press, 1985).

58 Eugene P. Odum in his classic textbook *The Fundamentals of Ecology* (Philadelphia: W. B. Saunders, 1953) argued that ecosystems were directed towards the achievement of maximal biodiversity. He therefore believed that the landscape should be left in as natural a state as possible to allow this internal directedness of nature to thrive. Some contemporary ecologists have challenged this view. See further Donald Worster's insightful discussion of this controversy in 'The Ecology of Order and Chaos' in *The Wealth of Nature: Environmental History and the Ecological Imagination* (New York: Oxford University Press, 1993), pp. 156–70.

59 Ehrlich, *Extinction*, ch. 5.

60 Stephen Jay Gould, *Wonderful Life: The Burgess Shale and the Nature of History* (London: Penguin Books, 1991), pp. 301 ff.

61 For these and many other examples of the potential benefit of unexploited and threatened species to humans see Ehrlich, *Extinction*, ch. 4.

62 Meadows and Randers, *Beyond the Limits*, p. 23.

63 The word 'commons' is often used in environmental literature to refer to such things as oceans, air, forests, land.

64 Meadows and Randers, *Beyond the Limits*, fig. 2/4, p. 25.

65 *Ibid.*, p. 29.

66 *Population, Resources and the Environment: The Critical Challenges* (London: United Nations Population Fund, 1991), p. 12.

67 *Ibid.*, p. 24.

68 *Ibid.*

69 Anne H. Ehrlich and Paul R. Ehrlich, *Earth* (London: Methuen, 1987), pp. 82, 83.

70 *Population, Resources and the Environment*, pp. 11 and 22. See also Rich, *Mortgaging the Earth*, pp. 186, 187.

71 As Roy A. Rappaport, among others, points out, the use of terms such as carrying capacity and environmental degradation are not without conceptual difficulties. However, he argues that these difficulties can be overcome for the purposes of assessing the relative ecological impacts of, for example, different agricultural systems: Roy A. Rappaport, *Pigs for the Ancestors: Ritual in the Ecology of New Guinea People*, enlarged edition (New Haven: Yale University Press, 1984), pp. 88 ff. For a strong advocacy of the value of the term in relation to human and animal populations see Garrett Hardin, *Living Within Limits: Ecology, Economics and Population Taboos* (New York: Oxford University Press, 1993), ch. 20.

72 *Population, Resources and the Environment*, p. 72.

73 *Ibid.*

74 Alan Durning, *How Much Is Enough? The Consumer Society and the Future of the Earth* (London: Earthscan, 1992), and M. K. Hubert, 'Energy Resources' in W. W. Murdock (ed.), *Environment: Resources, Pollution and Society*, cited in Paul H. Connett, 'The Disposable Society' in F. Herbert Bormann and Stephen R. Kellert, *Ecology, Economics, Ethics: The Broken Circle* (New Haven: Yale University Press, 1991), p. 99.

75 Avijit Gupta, *Ecology and Development in the Third World* (London: Routledge, 1988), p. 24.

76 Paul Harrison, *The Greening of Africa* (London: Paladin, 1987).

77 North, *Life on a Modern Planet*, p. 48.

78 *Population, Resources and the Environment*, pp. 61–2.

79 J. Hardoy and D. Satterthwaite, *Environmental Problems in Third World Cities: A Global Problem Ignored?* (London: International Institute of Environment and Development, 1990).

80 See further William M. Adams, *Green Development: Environment and Sustainability in the Third World* (London: Routledge, 1990), pp. 114–15.

81 *Our Common Future*, p. 29.

82 For an analysis of the effects of political corruption and external debt repayment on the environment in Africa see Lloyd Timberlake, *Africa in Crisis: The Causes, the Cures of Environmental Bankruptcy* (London: Earthscan, 1987).

83 Susan George, *A Fate Worse Than Debt* (London: Penguin 1989), and also Rich, *Mortgaging the Earth*.

84 Frances Stewart, 'Are Adjustment Policies in Africa Consistent with Long-Run Development Needs', *Development Policy Review*, 9 (1991), pp. 412–36.

85 See again Rich, *Mortgaging the Earth*, ch. 2.

86 See for example *Our Common Future*, and also the report of the Rio

Earth Summit *Agenda 21* reproduced in Stanley P. Johnson, *The Earth Summit: The United Nations Conference on Environment and Development (UNCED)* (London: Graham and Trotman, 1993). On the problems with the language of sustainability see for example Wolfgang Sachs, 'Global Ecology and the Shadow of Development' in Wolfgang Sachs (ed.), *Global Ecology: A New Arena of Conflict* (London: Zed Books, 1993).

87 Adams, *Green Development,* p. 200.

88 See for example Martin W. Lewis, *Green Delusions: An Environmentalist Critique of Radical Environmentalism* (Durham, NC: Duke University Press, 1992).

89 Evidence of this shift in attitudes in countries all over the world is provided in a recent Gallup survey of environmental attitudes: Riley E. Dunlap, George H. Gallup Jr, Alec M. Gallup, *Health of the Planet: Results of a 1992 Environmental Opinion Survey of Citizens of 24 Nations* (Princeton, NJ: George Gallup International Institute, 1993).

90 David Bellamy, public lecture, Edinburgh Regional Chambers, 2 June 1995.

91 C. S. Lewis, *The Abolition of Man* (London: Oxford University Press, 1943), p. 43.

92 Seyyed Hossein Nasr, *Man and Nature: The Spiritual Crisis in Modern Man* (London: George Allen and Unwin, 1968).

93 *Peace with God the Creator, Peace with All of Creation: Message of his Holiness Pope John Paul II for the Celebration of the World Day of Peace, 1 January 1990,* reprinted in Margaret Atkins, *Must Catholics Be Green* (London: Incorporated Catholic Truth Society, 1995), p. 29.

94 Robin Grove-White, 'Environmentalism: A New Moral Discourse?' in Kay Milton (ed.), *Environmentalism: The View from Anthropology* (London: Routledge, 1993), pp. 18–30.

95 Jonathan Sacks, *Faith in the Future* (London: Darton, Longman and Todd, 1995).

96 *Ibid.,* p. 14.

2 THE ORIGINS OF THE ENVIRONMENTAL CRISIS

1 Paul R. Ehrlich, *The Population Explosion,* British edition (London: Arrow Books, 1991).

2 Donella H. Meadows et al., *The Limits to Growth* (New York: Universe Books, 1972).

3 Robin Attfield, *The Ethics of Environmental Concern,* second edition (London: University of Georgia Press, 1991).

4 Theodore Roszak, *Where the Wasteland Ends: Politics and Transcen-*

dence in a Postindustrial Society (London: Faber and Faber, 1972), Rupert Sheldrake, *The Rebirth of Nature: The Greening of Science and God* (London: Rider, 1990), Edward Goldsmith, *The Way: An Ecological World View* (London: Rider, 1992).

5 Lynn White, 'The Historical Roots of our Ecologic Crisis', *Science*, 155 (1967) pp. 1203–7.

6 Rosemary Radford Ruether, *Gaia and God: An Ecofeminist Theology of Earth Healing* (London: SCM Press, 1993) and Mary Daly, *Gyn-Ecology: The Metaethics of Radical Feminism* (London: Women's Press, 1984).

7 See for example Anne Primavesi, *From Apocalypse to Genesis: Ecology, Feminism and Christianity* (London: Burnes and Oates, 1991).

8 Anthony Giddens, *The Consequences of Modernity* (Cambridge: Polity Press, 1991).

9 Ian G. Simmons, *Changing the Face of the Earth: Culture, Environment and History* (Oxford: Blackwell, 1989), pp. 82 ff.

10 John H. Bodley, *Cultural Anthropology: Tribes, States and the Global System* (Mountain View, CA: Mayfield Pub., 1994), p. 56.

11 There are many detailed studies of the culture and ecological impacts of present-day hunter-gatherer societies. See for example Roy A. Rappaport's fascinating ethnographic study of the Tsembaga people in New Guinea in the 1960s, *Pigs for the Ancestors: Rituals in the Ecology of New Guinea People*, enlarged edition (New Haven: Yale University Press, 1984). He finds that, except in a few localised areas, Tsembaga hunter-gathering and cultivation did not give rise to ecological degradation. This is in marked contrast to the ecological effects of the current assault on the forests of New Guinea by Japanese and Korean logging companies.

12 Bodley, *Cultural Anthropology*, p. 50.

13 Marshall Sahlins, *Stone Age Economics* (Chicago: Aldine, 1972), pp. 42 ff.

14 In Sarawak, East Malaysia I met a doctor who regularly visited isolated groups of tribal Ibans by helicopter, and saw them at clinics in small settlements, who identified malnutrition as their principal health problem: see also Evelyn Hong, *Natives of Sarawak: Survival in Borneo's Vanishing Forests* (Pulau Pinang, Malaysia: Institut Masyarakat, 1989), p. 87.

15 Sahlins, *Stone Age Economics*, ch. 1. See also Bodley's description of 'rainforest affluence' based on his own field research in the Amazon in his *Cultural Anthropology*, p. 57.

16 Allen Johnson, 'In Search of the Affluent Society' in David Hunter and Philip Whitten (eds.), *Anthropology in Contemporary Perspective*, cited Bodley, *Cultural Anthropology*, p. 57.

17 See for example the harrowing account of the degraded moral life of a tribe moved out of its original territory in Uganda in Colin Turnbull, *The Mountain People* (London: Cape, 1973). See also the discussion of cultural genocide and the moral issues involved in Barbara Rose Johnston (ed.), *Who Pays the Price? The Sociocultural Context of Environmental Crisis* (Washington, DC: Society for Applied Anthropology and Island Press, 1994), esp. Barbara Rose Johnston, 'Introduction' and Jason W. Clay, 'The Yanomami Holocaust Continues'.

18 The prevalence of our knowledge of environmental disaster in settled agrarian cultures over our knowledge of such disasters in hunter-gatherer and nomadic cultures might be explained as simply a function of the development of literacy and literary records in more developed agrarian cultures. However, as we have seen, ethnographic and ecological studies reveal a clear contrast between the ecological impacts of intensive forms of agriculture and the impacts of contemporary hunter-gatherer and nomadic cultures.

19 Clive Ponting, *The Green History of the World* (London: Penguin, 1988), ch. 4.

20 *Ibid.*

21 E. L. Jones, *The European Miracle: Environment, Economics and Geopolitics in the History of Europe and Asia* (Cambridge: Cambridge University Press, 1987).

22 Alfred W. Crosby, *Ecological Imperialism: The Biological Expansion of Europe* (Cambridge: Cambridge University Press, 1986).

23 Donald Worster, 'The Vulnerable Earth: Toward a Planetary History' in Donald Worster (ed.), *The Ends of the Earth: Perspectives on Modern Environmental History* (Cambridge: Cambridge University Press, 1988), pp. 3–22.

24 Crosby, *Ecological Imperialism.*

25 A Maori cited by Alfred W. Crosby, 'Ecological Imperialism: The Overseas Migration of Western Europeans as a Biological Phenomenon' in Worster (ed.), *The Ends of the Earth*, pp. 103–17.

26 Chris C. Park, *Sacred Worlds: An Introduction to Geography and Religion* (London: Routledge, 1994), pp. 229 ff.

27 L. T. C. Rolt, *High Horse Riderless* (Bideford: Green Books, 1988), ch. 1.

28 Sean McDonagh, *To Care for the Earth: A Call to a New Theology* (London: Geoffrey Chapman, 1986), p. 130.

29 Immanuel Wallerstein, *Capitalist Agriculture and the Origins of the European World-Economy in the Sixteenth Century: The Modern World-System*, 2 vols. (London: Academic Press, 1974), vol. 1.

30 Robert S. Lopez, *The Commercial Revolution of the Middle Ages, 950–1350* (Cambridge: Cambridge University Press, 1976), p. 50.

31 Karl Polanyi, *Origins of Our Time: The Great Transformation* (London: Victor Gollancz, 1945), p. 181. Polanyi's judgements are controversial but they continue to find support in that tradition of radical English historiography represented by such figures as Eric Hobsbawm and Edward Thompson.

32 Lopez, *Commercial Revolution*, pp. 48–55.

33 Alvaro Soto, 'The Global Environment: A Southern Perspective', *International Journal*, 47 (1992), pp. 679–705.

34 Nicholas Georgescu-Roegen, 'Economic Theory and Agrarian Economics', *Oxford Economic Papers*, 12 (1950), cited in Herman Daly and John B. Cobb, *For the Common Good. Redirecting the Economy towards Community, the Environment and a Sustainable Future* (London: Green Print, 1990), p. 460. See also George Dalton (ed.), *Tribal and Peasant Economics* (Austin: University of Texas Press, 1967).

35 According to Chesterton, 'the key to the mystery of the Merry Peasant is that the peasant often is merry. Those who do not believe it are simply those who do not know anything about him.' G. K. Chesterton, *The Everlasting Man* (London: Hodder and Stoughton, 1925), p. 185. Chesterton's judgement is not without support amongst modern medieval historians. See for example the account of the quality of life enjoyed by peasants in a feudal English manor in H. S. Bennett, *Life on the English Manor* (Cambridge: Cambridge University Press, 1937), esp. pp. 3–25.

36 Wallerstein, *Capitalist Agriculture*, ch. 3.

37 *Ibid.*, pp. 21–2.

38 See the powerful analysis of the origins and effects of the Enclosures in Edward P. Thompson, *Customs in Common* (London: Merlin Press, 1991).

39 *Ibid.*, esp. ch. 2.

40 See further Wendel Berry, *The Gift of Good Land: Further Essays Cultural and Agricultural* (San Francisco: North Point Press, 1981).

41 Wallerstein, *Capitalist Agriculture*, pp. 128–9.

42 Immanuel Wallerstein, 'The West, Capitalism and the Modern World-System', *Review*, 15 (1992), pp. 561–620.

43 John A. Hall, 'States and Economic Development: Reflections on Adam Smith' in John A. Hall (ed.), *States in History* (Oxford: Blackwell, 1986).

44 *Ibid.* See also Paul Kennedy, *The Rise and Fall of the Great Powers* (London: Unwin Hyman, 1988), pp. 16 ff.

45 J. L. Bolton, *The Medieval English Economy 1150–1500* (London: Dent, 1980), p. 334.

46 O. Langholm, *Economics in the Medieval Schools* (Leiden: Brill, 1992).

47 See the fictionalised account of a disputation on this very point between Franciscan monks and the cardinals in Umberto Eco, *The Name of the Rose*, Eng. trans., British edition (London: Secker and Warburg, 1983).

48 R. H. Tawney, *Religion and the Rise of Capitalism* (Harmondsworth: Penguin, 1938), p. 183.

49 *Ibid.*

50 *Ibid.*

51 Alasdair MacIntyre, *After Virtue* (London: Duckworth, 1981), p. 234.

52 Some landless groups, such as the tribal peoples of the Cordillera mountains in North Luzon, Philippines, and Aboriginal Australians, have attempted to use North American and Australian courts to challenge the violent expropriation of land in colonial times.

53 See further Michael S. Northcott, 'A Place of Our Own?' in Peter Sedgwick (ed.), *God in the City* (London: Mowbrays, 1995).

54 George Hendry, *Theology of Nature* (Philadelphia: Westminster Press, 1980), p. 17.

55 Richard Bentley, *The Folly of Atheism*, cited in Keith Thomas, *Man and the Natural World* (London: Penguin, 1986), p. 18.

56 Thomas, *Man and the Natural World*, p. 25.

57 *Ibid.*, p. 23.

58 Max Weber, *The Protestant Ethic and the Spirit of Capitalism*, Eng. trans. (London: George Allen and Unwin, 1930). The evidence for and against Weber's thesis is widely disputed. For a relatively recent historically detailed account of its explanatory utility in Scotland see Gordon Marshall, *Presbyteries and Profits: Calvinism and the Development of Capitalism in Scotland* (Oxford: Clarendon Press, 1980).

59 Thomas Aquinas, *Summa Theologiae* ii–ii, 67, 7.

60 Weber, *The Protestant Ethic*.

61 Thomas, *Man and the Natural World*, pp. 143 ff.

62 Thompson, *Customs in Common*, ch. 2.

63 Again see Bennett, *Life on the English Manor* for evidence of this contention.

64 Soto, 'The Global Environment'.

65 Weber, *The Protestant Ethic*, pp. 48–50.

66 Adam Smith, *Theory of the Moral Sentiments*, vol. iv, cited in Peter Singer, *How Are We To Live? Ethics in an Age of Self-Interest* (London: Mandarin, 1994), pp. 40–1.

67 Tawney, *Rise of Capitalism*, pp. 227 ff.

68 See for example Christopher Kaiser, *Creation and the History of Science* (London: Marshall Pickering, 1991).

69 Hans Blumenberg, *The Legitimacy of the Modern Age*, Eng. trans. (Cambridge, MA: MIT Press, 1983), p. 149.

70 *Ibid.*, p. 150.

71 John Hedley Brooke, *Science and Religion: Some Historical Perspectives* (Cambridge: Cambridge University Press, 1991), pp. 137–41.

72 *Ibid.*

73 Blumenberg, *Legitimacy of the Modern*, p. 187.

74 Kant's views are expounded with great clarity by Brooke, *Science and Religion*, pp. 203–9.

75 See Bryan Appleyard's useful discussion of this point in his *Understanding the Present: Science and the Soul of Modern Man* (London: Pan Books, 1992), p. 68.

76 Blumenberg, *Legitimacy of the Modern*, p. 214.

77 Brooke, *Science and Religion*, pp. 204–6.

78 Stephen W. Hawking, *A Brief History of Time* (London: Bantam Press, 1988), p. 175.

79 Alexander Abian, 'Hate Winter? Here's One Man's Solution: Blow up the Moon', *Wall Street Journal* (1991), cited in Goldsmith, *The Way*, p. 317.

80 René Descartes, *Discourse on Method*, Discourse v. Keith Thomas identifies Pereira as the originator of the Cartesian beast-machine doctrine which came to be identified with Descartes: Thomas, *Man and the Natural World*, p. 33.

81 Descartes, *Discourse on Method*, Discourse v.

82 The judgement that the human brain is 'nothing but a pack of neurons' is described by Francis Crick, the discoverer with Watson of DNA, as the 'astonishing hypothesis' of modern science about human consciousness, astonishing because it flies in the face of cultural assumptions about human identity, but nonetheless a hypothesis which is, he argues, well proven: Francis Crick, *The Astonishing Hypothesis: The Scientific Search for a Soul* (London: Simon and Schuster, 1994).

83 Appleyard, *Understanding the Present*, pp. 149, 150.

84 For an account of the scientific and ecological implications of chaos theory see Ilya Prigogine and Isabelle Stengers, *Order Out of Chaos: Man's New Dialogue With Nature* (London: Flamingo, 1985).

85 Appleyard, *Understanding the Present*, p. 159.

86 See Thomas S. Kuhn's classic study *The Structure of Scientific Revolutions*, 2nd enlarged edition (Chicago: Chicago University Press, 1975), and also Bruno Latour, *Science in Action: How to Follow Scientists and Engineers Through Society* (Milton Keynes: Open University Press, 1987).

87 Mary Midgley, *Science as Salvation: A Modern Myth and its Meaning* (London: Routledge, 1992), p. 77.

88 Carolyn Merchant, *The Death of Nature: Women, Ecology and the Scientific Revolution* (New York: Harper and Row, 1979).

89 Evelyn Fox Keller, *Reflections on Gender and Science* (New Haven: Yale University Press, 1985).

90 Donna Haraway, *Primate Vision: Gender, Race and Nature in the World of Modern Science* (New York: Routledge, 1989), p. 11.

91 Brooke, *Science and Religion*, p. 292.

92 Donald Worster, *The Wealth of Nature: Environmental History and the Ecological Imagination* (New York: Oxford University Press, 1993), p. 166.

93 Descartes, *Discourse on Method*, and Francis Bacon, 'Novum Organum', as cited in Langdon Winner, *The Whale and the Reactor: A Search for Limits in an Age of High Technology* (Chicago: Chicago University Press, 1986), p. 123.

94 Blumenberg, *Legitimacy of the Modern*, pp. 384 and 388.

95 Charles Taylor, *Sources of the Self: The Making of the Modern Identity* (Cambridge: Cambridge University Press, 1989), p. 232, and Blumenberg, *Legitimacy of the Modern*, p. 389.

96 Blumenberg, *Legitimacy of the Modern*, pp. 391 and 403 ff.

97 Midgley, *Science as Salvation*, pp. 152 ff. See also the discussion of clones and cybernetics in Haraway, *Primate Vision*, pp. 216–7 and 368–9.

98 Midgley, *Science as Salvation*, pp. 147 ff.

99 Robert Wallace summarises Lowith's views in his 'Translator's Introduction' to Blumenberg's *Legitimacy of the Modern*, pp. xi–xxxi. Wallace explains that Blumenberg's assertion of the legitimacy of the modern age is conceived in opposition to Lowith's critique of progress and modernity expressed in Karl Lowith, *Meaning in History*, Eng. trans. (Chicago: Chicago University Press, 1949).

100 Richard Stivers, *Evil in Modern Myth and Ritual* (Athens, GA: The University of Georgia Press, 1982), p. 89.

101 MacIntyre, *After Virtue*, p. 53.

102 Attfield, *The Ethics of Environmental Concern*, ch. 5.

103 Krishan Kumar, *Prophecy and Progress: The Sociology of Industrial and Post-Industrial Society* (London: Penguin, 1978), p. 303.

104 Winner, *The Whale and the Reactor*, p. 174.

105 For a preliminary discussion of the ethics of the genetic modification of non-human life see further Paul B. Thompson, *The Spirit of the Soil: Agriculture and Environmental Ethics* (London: Routledge, 1995), pp. 32–41.

106 Ulrich Beck, *Ecological Enlightenment: Essays on the Politics of the Risk Society*, Eng. trans. (Atlantic Highlands, NJ: Humanities Press, 1995).

107 *Ibid.*, p. 17.

108 *Ibid.*, p. 79.

109 Taylor, *Sources of the Self*, p. 340.

110 See further Lincoln Allison, *Ecology and Utility: The Philosophical Dilemmas of Planetary Management* (Leicester: Leicester University Press, 1991).

111 Taylor, *Sources of the Self*, p. 13.

112 *Ibid.*, p. 56.

113 *Ibid.*, pp. 211 ff.

114 David Braine, *The Human Person: Animal and Spirit* (London: Duckworth, 1993), esp. ch. 1.

115 Neil McKendrick, 'The Consumer Revolution of Eighteenth-Century England' in Neil McKendrick, John Brewer and J. H. Plumb, *The Birth of a Consumer Society: The Commercialization of Eighteenth Century England* (London: Hutchinson, 1983).

116 *Ibid.*, p. 19.

117 Jonathan Swift, *Prose Works*, VII, cited in McKendrick, 'The Consumer Revolution', p. 19.

118 Daniel Horowitz, *The Morality of Spending: Attitudes Towards the Consumer in America 1875–1940* (Baltimore: Johns Hopkins University Press, 1985), p. 167.

119 Angus Campbell, *The Quality of American Life*, cited in F. E. Trainer, *Abandon Affluence!* (London: Zed Books, 1985), p. 194.

120 *Ibid.*

121 Louis Harris, *The Anguish of Change*, cited in Trainer, *Abandon Affluence!*, p. 195.

122 Michael Argyle, *The Psychology of Happiness* (London: Methuen, 1987).

123 *Ibid.*, p. 173.

124 Robert E. Lane, *The Market Experience* (Cambridge: Cambridge University Press, 1991).

125 Fred Hirsch, *The Social Limits to Growth* (London: Routledge & Kegan Paul, 1977).

126 John K. Galbraith, *The Affluent Society*, fourth British edition (London: Penguin, 1987).

127 Alexis de Tocqueville, *Democracy in America*, 2 vols., cited in Wilfred McClay, 'Where Have We Come Since the 1950s?' in Robert Wuthnow (ed.), *Rethinking Materialism: Perspectives on the Spiritual Dimension of Economic Behaviour* (Grand Rapids, MI: Eerdmans, 1995), pp. 25–71.

128 Francis Fukuyama, *The End of History and the Last Man* (London: Hamish Hamilton, 1992), p. 331.

129 *Ibid.*

130 A. Hirschmann, *Shifting Involvements. Private Interests and Public Action*, cited in Liisa Uusitalo, *Environmental Impacts of Consumption Patterns* (Aldershot: Gower, 1986), p. 34.

131 MacIntyre, *After Virtue*, pp. 60 ff.

132 Taylor, *Sources of the Self*, p. 339.

133 Giddens, *Consequences of Modernity*, p. 24.

134 *Ibid.*, p. 25.

135 Douglas Meeks, *God the Economist: The Doctrine of God and Political Economy* (Minneapolis: Fortress Press, 1989). See also Timothy Gorringe, *Capital and the Kingdom: Theological Ethics and Economic Order* (Maryknoll, NY: Orbis, 1994).

136 See further Paul Ekins (ed.), *The Living Economy: A New Economics in the Making* (London: Routledge & Kegan Paul, 1986), and Goldsmith, *The Way*, pp. 297 ff.

137 Anthony Giddens, *The Nation State and Violence: Volume Two of A Contemporary Critique of Historical Materialism* (Berkeley: University of California Press, 1985), p. 340.

138 Thomas Malthus, *An Essay on the Principle of Population* (London: J. Johnston, 1798).

139 See Johnston, *Who Pays the Price?* for a number of contemporary studies of the continuing assault of loggers, traders, industrialists and development agencies on the cultures, life-styles, lands and human rights of indigenous peoples in many parts of the world from Alaska and the Amazon to the Russian Far East and Papua New Guinea.

140 See further Mahathir Muhammad, *The Malay Dilemma* (Singapore: Times Books International, 1970).

141 The demise of leisure in societies with lots of labour-saving machines and higher levels of consumption is noted by E. F. Schumacher in his *Small is Beautiful: Economics as if People Mattered* (London: Abacus, 1974), p. 48.

142 White, 'The Historical Roots of our Ecologic Crisis'.

3 THE TURN TO NATURE

1 From William Wordsworth, *Lines Composed a Few Miles Above Tintern Abbey*.

2 Alan Bewell, *Wordsworth and the Enlightenment: Nature, Man, and Society in the Experimental Poetry* (Yale: Yale University Press, 1989), p. 141.

3 Charles Taylor, *Sources of the Self: The Making of the Modern Identity* (Cambridge: Cambridge University Press, 1989), p. 355.

4 *Ibid.*, p. 357.

5 Wordsworth, *Tintern Abbey*.

6 Taylor, *Sources of the Self*, pp. 374 ff.

7 *Ibid.*, p. 379.

8 Eugene C. Hargrove, *Foundations of Environmental Ethics* (Englewood Cliffs, NJ: Prentice Hall, 1989), ch. 3.

9 *Ibid.*, p. 83.

10 *Ibid.*, p. 87.

11 Keith Thomas, *Man and the Natural World* (London: Penguin, 1986), p. 192.

12 Marjorie Hope Nicholson, *Mountain Gloom and Mountain Glory: The Development of the Aesthetic of the Infinite*, cited in Hargrove, *Environmental Ethics*, p. 87.

13 Hargrove, *Environmental Ethics*, pp. 92–3.

14 *Ibid.*, p. 78.

15 Thomas, *Man and the Natural World*, ch. 1. As we have seen, Thomas also finds a growing and cruel streak in attitudes to animals, and their treatment in laboratories, in the wild and on farms, in early modern Europe. The parallel development of these two trends is still reflected in modern Europe to this day in the conflict between modern intensive animal husbandry, with its cruel effects on the dignity and life enjoyment of farm animals, and campaigners for animal welfare and animal rights.

16 John Bulwer, *Anthropometamorphis* (1653), cited in Thomas, *Man and the Natural World*, p. 278.

17 Mark Sagoff, *The Economy of the Earth* (Cambridge: Cambridge University Press, 1988), p. 154.

18 Alasdair MacIntyre, *After Virtue* (London: Duckworth, 1981), p. 62.

19 *Ibid.*, ch. 2.

20 Peter Singer, *Animal Liberation*, second edition (London: Cape, 1990).

21 *Ibid.*, p. 21.

22 *Ibid.*, p. 224.

23 *Ibid.*, p. 20.

24 Robin Attfield, *The Ethics of Environmental Concern*, second edition (London: University of Georgia Press, 1991), p. 153.

25 Attfield's extensive consideration of utilitarian styles of consequentialism in *Environmental Concern*, and his reliance on them at times, has led Andrew Brennan among others to characterise him as a utilitarian: Andrew Brennan, *Thinking About Nature: An Investigation of Nature, Value and Ecology* (London: Routledge, 1988), p. 168.

Attfield in a recent essay challenges this characterisation of his work though he does not deny his reliance on utilitarian arguments, albeit nuanced and combined with arguments from other traditions including the Judeo-Christian tradition: Robin Attfield, *Environmental Philosophy: Principles and Prospects* (Aldershot: Avebury, 1994), p. 137.

26 Attfield, *Environmental Concern*, p. 62.

27 Attfield does, however, propose a series of adaptations of cost-benefit analysis which go some way to mitigating the traditional environmental problems with cost-benefit analysis. See further his *Environmental Concern*, pp. 141–3, and ch. 3 in Robin Attfield and Katherine Dell (eds.), *Values, Conflict and the Environment* (Oxford: Ian Ramsey Centre and St Cross College, 1989). But see also ch. 5 of this report, 'An Alternative Approach', by Oliver O'Donovan and Robin Grove-White, who argue that the adaptations of cost-benefit theory proposed by Attfield and others still fail to provide sufficient opportunities for valuing, preferring and protecting environmental goods when these are threatened by human projects such as motorways or intensive agricultural practices.

28 Immanuel Kant, *Lectures on Ethics*.

29 Hargrove, *Environmental Ethics*.

30 *Ibid.*, p. 192.

31 *Ibid.*, p. 198.

32 Kieran Cronin, *Rights and Christian Ethics* (Cambridge: Cambridge University Press, 1992), pp. 85–6.

33 Tom Regan, *The Case for Animal Rights* (London: Routledge, 1988), p. 243.

34 *Ibid.*

35 *Ibid.*, p. 153.

36 *Ibid.*, p. 334.

37 Holmes Rolston, *Environmental Ethics: Duties to and Values in the Natural Environment* (Philadelphia: Temple University Press, 1988), p. 81.

38 Christopher Stone, *Should Trees Have Standing? Towards Legal Rights for Natural Objects* (Los Altos, CA: William Kaufman, 1974).

39 See further Mary Ann Glendon, *Rights Talk: The Impoverishment of Political Discourse* (New York: Free Press, 1991).

40 MacIntyre, *After Virtue*, pp. 64–7.

41 Carol Gilligan, *In a Different Voice: Psychological Theory and Women's Development* (Cambridge, MA: Harvard University Press, 1981).

42 Rolston, *Environmental Ethics*, pp. 109 ff.

43 *Ibid.*, pp. 138 ff.

44 *Ibid.*, p. 176.

45 *Ibid.*, pp. 254 ff.

46 Rolston's position contrasts sharply with that of biocentrist Paul Taylor, who enunciates the first principle of a biocentric ethics as the belief that 'humans are members of the Earth's Community of Life in the same sense and on the same terms in which other living things are members of that Community': Paul W. Taylor, *Respect for Nature* (Princeton, NJ: Princeton University Press, 1986).

47 Aldo Leopold, *A Sand Country Almanac and Sketches Here and There*, first published 1949, paperback edition, (New York: Oxford University Press, 1968), pp. 214–15.

48 *Ibid.*

49 *Ibid.*, p. 225.

50 *Ibid.*, p. 220.

51 Ecological critics of modern agriculture have echoed Leopold's arguments. See for example Paul B. Thompson, *The Spirit of the Soil: Agriculture and Environmental Ethics* (London: Routledge, 1995), and Vandana Siva, *Monocultures of the Mind: Biodiversity, Biotechnology and the Third World* (Penang, Malaysia: Third World Network, 1993).

52 J. Baird Callicott, *In Defence of the Land Ethic: Essays in Environmental Philosophy* (Albany, NY: State University of New York Press, 1989), p. 25.

53 Garrett Hardin, 'The Economics of Wilderness', *Natural History*, 78 (1969), cited in Callicott, *In Defence of the Land Ethic*, p. 27.

54 See further Harold Turner, *From Temple to Meeting House: The Phenomenology and Theology of Places of Worship* (The Hague: Mouton, 1979).

55 For a consideration of the ethical significance of the Christian desert tradition see Susan Power Bratton, *Christianity, Wilderness and Wildlife: The Original Desert Solitaire* (Scranton, PA: University of Scranton Press, 1993).

56 See further Leslie Sponsel, 'The Yanomami Holocaust Continues' in Barbara Rose Johnston (ed.), *Who Pays the Price? The Sociocultural Context of Environmental Crisis* (Washington, DC: Society for Applied Anthropology and Island Press, 1994), pp. 37–46.

57 See further a number of the essays in Robert Wuthnow (ed.), *Rethinking Materialism: Perspectives on the Spiritual Dimension of Economic Behaviour* (Grand Rapids, MI: Eerdmans, 1995).

58 James Lovelock, *Gaia: A New Look at Life on Earth* (Oxford: Oxford University Press, 1979).

59 James Lovelock, *The Ages of Gaia: A Biography of Our Living Earth* (Oxford: Oxford University Press, 1989), p. 212.

60 *Ibid.*, p. 218.

61 *Ibid.*, p. 131.

62 See below, chapter 5.

63 Lovelock, *Ages of Gaia*, p. 212. Lovelock uses the analogy of a cancer in *Gaia: A New Look*, p. 139.

64 According to Matthews 'if selves exist, then, the scope of selfhood must extend all the way up to the cosmic level': Freya Matthews, *The Ecological Self* (London: Routledge, 1991) pp. 146–7. Devall and Sessions speak of the self as representing organic wholeness, and the unfolding of the self as including even the tiniest microbes in the soil in Bill Devall and George Sessions, *Deep Ecology* (Salt Lake City, UT: Gibbs Smith, 1985), p. 67.

65 Val Plumwood, *Feminism and the Mastery of Nature* (London: Routledge, 1993), pp. 126 ff.

66 Matthew Fox, *Original Blessing: A Primer in Creation Spirituality* (Santa Fe, NM: Bear and Company, 1983).

67 Plumwood, *Mastery of Nature*, p. 128.

68 Colin Gunton, *The One, the Three and the Many: God, Creation and the Culture of Modernity* (Cambridge: Cambridge University Press, 1993), p. 153 and ch. 2.

69 Arne Naess, *Ecology, Community and Lifestyle*, Eng. trans. (Cambridge: Cambridge University Press, 1989).

70 *Ibid.*, p. 81.

71 *Ibid.*, p. 85.

72 Plumwood, *Mastery of Nature*, p. 174.

73 Gunton, *The One, the Three and the Many*.

74 Plumwood, *Mastery of Nature*, pp. 182 ff.

75 I am indebted to Edward Goldsmith for his extensive references to this alternative tradition in Western anthropology in *The Way: An Ecological World View* (London: Rider, 1992). See for example A. R. Radcliffe-Brown, *Structure and Function in Primitive Society* (London: Cohen and West, 1965), and Marcel Mauss, *The Gift: Forms and Functions of Exchange in Primitive Societies* (London: Cohen and West, 1954). For a more contemporary approach see John H. Bodley, *Tribal Peoples and Development Issues* (Mountain View, CA: Mayfield Pub., 1988).

76 Goldsmith, *The Way*, pp. 287 ff. See also E. F. Schumacher, *Small is Beautiful: Economics as if People Mattered* (London: Abacus, 1974).

77 Rene Dubos, 'Will Man Adapt to Megalopolis?' in *The Ecologist*, cited in Goldsmith, *The Way*, p. 289.

78 See especially Mauss, *The Gift* for an account of the relational character of primitive economic systems.

79 See especially Gilligan, *In a Different Voice*.

80 Val Plumwood, 'Plato and the Bush', *Meanjin*, 49 (1990), pp. 524–36. See also John H. Bodley, *Cultural Anthropology: Tribes,*

States and the Global System (Mountain View, CA: Mayfield Pub., 1994), p. 76, on the ethnocentrism of anthropological judgements of indigenous peoples.

81 Gilligan, *In a Different Voice.*

82 *Ibid.*

83 Zygmunt Bauman, *Postmodern Ethics* (Oxford: Blackwell, 1993), pp. 50–69. See also Virginia Held, *Feminist Morality: Transforming Culture, Society and Politics* (Chicago: University of Chicago Press, 1993), esp. pp. 64 ff.

84 See for example Held's account of the significance of mothering and her contrast of the particular moral identification of mothers with their children and the universalising and distancing moral implications of the free market: *ibid.*, pp. 70–3.

85 Plumwood, *Mastery of Nature*, p. 183.

86 One of the worst examples of this kind of environmental terrorisation is the story of the burning and destruction of villages in the oil-rich area of Ogoniland in the Niger Delta, the imprisonment without trial of community leaders, including the internationally renowned writer Ken Saro Wiwa, and the murder of others. The appalling legacy of injury to human health and ecological destruction resulting from environmentally neglectful drilling and refining activities in the area led local people to begin a community protest for compensation from the oil companies concerned, a protest which was ruthlessly put down by the Nigerian military in order that drilling and refining activities in Ogoniland could recommence: Ken Saro Wiwa, *Genocide in Nigeria* (Lagos, Nigeria: Saros, 1992). Just before this book went to press Ken Saro Wiwa was tragically and secretly executed by the Nigerian military regime after a summary military trial.

87 Warwick Fox, *Towards a Transpersonal Ecology: Developing New Foundations for Environmentalism* (Boston: Shambala, 1990), pp. 250 and 263.

88 *Ibid.*, p. 105.

89 Val Plumwood, 'Nature, Self and Gender: Feminism, Environmental Philosophy, and the Critique of Rationalism' in Robert Elliot (ed.), *Environmental Ethics*, Oxford Readings in Philosophy, (Oxford: Oxford University Press, 1995), p. 163.

90 Bodley points out that Australian aboriginals need an immense amount of knowledge about their environment, its plants, animals, birds, fish, water sources and climate in order to live as hunter-gatherers. By comparison, as he says, a group of modern urbanites dropped into a wilderness would hardly survive without loss; Bodley, *Cultural Anthropology*, p. 22.

91 Gunton, *The One, the Three and the Many*.
92 1 John 3.
93 MacIntyre, *After Virtue*, esp. pp. 169 ff.
94 William Cobbett, *Political Register*, cited in MacIntyre, *After Virtue*, p. 222.
95 MacIntyre, *After Virtue*, p. 222.
96 Plumwood, *Mastery of Nature*, p. 185.
97 *Ibid.*, and Rolston, *Environmental Ethics*, ch. 5.

4 THE FLOWERING OF ECOTHEOLOGY

1 For example Clare Palmer, 'A Bibliographical Essay on Environmental Ethics', *Studies in Christian Ethics*, 7 (1994), pp. 68–97.
2 For a comprehensive bibliographical survey of the field of ecotheology and of Christian responses to environmental crisis see Joseph K. Sheldon, *Rediscovery of Creation: A Bibliographical Study of the Church's Response to the Environmental Crisis* (Metuchen, NJ: The American Theological Library Association and the Scarecrow Press, 1992).
3 Teilhard de Chardin, *The Phenomenon of Man*, Eng. trans. (London: Collins, 1959).
4 *Ibid.*, p. 283. See also Teilhard de Chardin, *Man's Place in Nature: The Human Zoological Group*, Eng. trans. (London: Collins, 1966), pp. 79 ff.
5 Teilhard de Chardin, *The Future of Man*, Eng. trans. (London: Collins, 1964), p. 231.
6 *Ibid.*, p. 237.
7 Thomas Berry takes the Teilhardian approach in a much more ecocentric direction. Space precludes a detailed consideration of his work but see particularly his *The Dream of the Earth* (San Francisco: Sierra Club Books, 1988), and Brian Swimme and Thomas Berry, *The Universe Story: From the Primordial Flaring Forth to the Ecozoic Era – A Celebration of the Unfolding of the Cosmos* (San Francisco: Harper, 1992). In *The Universe Story* Berry and Swimme argue that the present 'technozoic' era is marked, as Teilhard also argued, by the comprehensive influence of humans on the life systems of the planet, but, unlike Teilhard, they see the technocentric orientation of this domination as deeply opposed to the evolutionary progress of life on earth, and call for the development of an 'ecozoic' civilisation which involves a new 'biocartic' form of human governance of the earth.
8 Sean McDonagh, *To Care for the Earth: A Call to a New Theology* (London: Geoffrey Chapman, 1986), pp. 77 ff.

9 *Ibid.*, p. 87.
10 Francis Schaeffer with Udo Middleman, *Pollution and the Death of Man*, new expanded edition, (Wheaton, IL: Crossway Books, 1992). Lynn White's article is reprinted as appendix A in this book.
11 *Ibid.*, pp. 49–55.
12 *Ibid.*, p. 57.
13 *Ibid.*, pp. 93, 94.
14 *Ibid.*, p. 90.
15 See for example George Hendry, *Theology of Nature* (Philadelphia: Westminster Press, 1980), pp. 189 ff.
16 See for example Robin Grove-White and Oliver O'Donovan, 'An Alternative Approach' in Robin Attfield and Katherine Dell (eds.), *Values, Conflict and the Environment* (Oxford: Ian Ramsey Centre and St Cross College, 1989), p. 74.
17 See for example, McDonagh, *To Care for the Earth*, pp. 121–5, and William Dryness, 'Stewardship of the Earth in the Old Testament' in Wesley Granberg-Michaelsen (ed.), *Tending the Garden: Essays on the Gospel and the Earth* (Grand Rapids, MI: Eerdmans, 1987).
18 Robin Attfield, *The Ethics of Environmental Concern*, second edition (London: University of Georgia Press, 1991), p. 25.
19 Laurence Osborn, *Guardians of Creation: Nature in Theology and the Christian Life* (Leicester: Apollos, 1993).
20 'Final Document: Entering into Covenant Solidarity for Justice, Peace and the Integrity of Creation' in D. Preman Niles (ed.), *Between the Flood and the Rainbow: Interpreting the Conciliar Process of Mutual Commitment (Covenant) to Justice, Peace and the Integrity of Creation* (Geneva: World Council of Churches, 1992).
21 *Ibid.*, p. 174.
22 Philip Sherrard, *The Rape of Man and Nature: An Enquiry Into the Origins and Consequences of Modern Science* (Ipswich: Golgonooza Press, 1987), p. 40.
23 *Ibid.*, pp. 70 ff.
24 *Ibid.*, p. 90.
25 *Ibid.*, p. 93.
26 *Ibid.*, p. 94
27 Philip Sherrard, *Human Image: World Image: The Death and Resurrection of Sacred Cosmology* (Ipswich: Golgonooza Press, 1992).
28 Paulos Gregorios, *The Human Presence: An Orthodox View of Nature* (Geneva: World Council of Churches, 1978), pp. 82 ff.
29 *Ibid.*, p. 85.
30 *Ibid.*, p. 89.

31 *Ibid.*, p. 99.

32 John Paul II, *Sollicitudo Rei Socialis: Encyclical Letter of the Supreme Pontiff John Paul II to the Bishops, Priests, Religious Families, Sons and Daughters of the Church and All People of Good Will for the Twentieth Anniversary of Populorum Progressio*, reprinted in Daniel J. O'Brien and Thomas A. Shannon (eds.), *Catholic Social Thought: The Documentary Heritage* (Maryknoll, NY: Orbis Books, 1992), p. 411.

33 *Ibid.*, pp. 412–14.

34 *Ibid.*

35 *Peace with God the Creator, Peace with All of Creation: Message of his Holiness Pope John Paul II for the Celebration of the World Day of Peace, 1 January 1990*, reprinted in Margaret Atkins, *Must Catholics Be Green* (London: Incorporated Catholic Truth Society, 1995).

36 *Ibid.*, p. 22.

37 *Ibid.*, p. 30.

38 John Paul II, *Veritatis Splendor: Encyclical Letter Addressed by the Supreme Pontiff John Paul II to all the Bishops of the Catholic Church Regarding Certain Questions of the Church's Moral Teaching* (London: Catholic Truth Society, 1993), p. 123. See further my review of the encyclical in *Theology*, 97 (1993), pp. 141–3.

39 John Paul II, *Evangelium Vitae: Encyclical Letter Addressed by the Supreme Pontiff Pope John Paul II to all the Bishops, Priests and Deacons, Men and Women Religious, Lay Faithful and All People of Good Will on the Value and Inviolability of Human Life* (Dublin: Veritas Pub., 1995), pp. 74 and 94.

40 The new catechism hardly advances the issue either, with only a very brief reference to the 'integrity of creation' with no explication of the significance of the phrase, and a slight consideration of the human stewardship of animals, in which it is argued that it is contrary to human dignity if animals are made to suffer or die needlessly: *The Catechism of the Catholic Church*, Eng. trans. (London: Geoffrey Chapman, 1994), pp. 516, 517.

41 See further chapter six below.

42 Rosemary Radford Ruether, *Gaia and God*, British edition (London: SCM Press, 1993), p. 2.

43 *Ibid.*, p. 185.

44 *Ibid.*, pp. 185 ff.

45 *Ibid.*, p. 211.

46 *Ibid.*, p. 250. Process theology is discussed under the heading of ecocentric approaches below.

47 *Ibid.*, p. 249.

48 *Ibid.*, p. 250.

49 *Ibid.*, p. 254.

50 *Ibid.*, p. 258.

51 *Ibid.*, pp. 268 ff.

52 For a much more radical version of Christian ecofeminism, which rejects the 'fall/redemption' tradition altogether, see for example Anne Primavesi, *From Apocalypse to Genesis: Ecology, Feminism and Christianity.* (London: Burnes and Oates, 1991). See also Andrew Linzey's review of the same in *Scottish Journal of Theology*, 45 (1992) pp. 265–8.

53 Jürgen Moltmann, *God in Creation: An Ecological Doctrine of Creation*, Eng. trans. (London: SCM Press, 1985) and, *The Spirit of Life: A Universal Affirmation*, Eng. trans. (London: SCM Press, 1992). The inclusion of Moltmann under the category theocentric may perhaps be challenged in the light of my consideration of Cobb, McDaniel and others under the heading ecocentric. However, it is arguable that Moltmann's doctrine of creation is derived primarily from a new reading of the doctrine of God as Trinity whereas process theologians such as Cobb and McDaniel derive their starting point from a scientific reading of evolutionary process, and construct a new doctrine of nature from this, and then proceed to construct a new doctrine of God. Moltmann himself claims a more theocentric character to his own approach when he says 'the aim of our investigation is not what nature can contribute to our knowledge of God, but what the concept of God can contribute to our knowledge of nature'; *God in Creation*, p. 53, cited in Sally McFague, *The Body of God: An Ecological Theology*, British edition (London: SCM Press, 1993), p. 83.

54 Moltmann, *God in Creation*, p. 98.

55 *Ibid.*, p. 100.

56 *Ibid.*, p. 280.

57 *Ibid.*, pp. 278–95.

58 See especially the reflections on the image of God and the soul in chs. 9 and 10 of Moltmann, *God in Creation*.

59 James Nash, *Loving Nature: Ecological Integrity and Christian Responsibility* (Nashville, TN: Abingdon, 1992), p. 99.

60 On the concept of biophilia see further Edward O. Wilson, *Biophilia* (Cambridge, MA: Harvard University Press, 1984).

61 *Ibid.*, p. 137.

62 See especially Alexander Schmemann, *The World as Sacrament* (London: Darton, Longman and Todd, 1966).

63 Arthur R. Peacocke, *Creation and the World of Science: The Bampton Lectures 1978* (Oxford: Clarendon Press, 1979), pp. 289–91, and John Habgood, 'A Sacramental Approach to Environmental

Issues' in Charles Birch, William Ekin and Jay B. McDaniel (eds.), *Liberating Life: Contemporary Approaches to Ecological Theology* (Maryknoll, NY: Orbis Books, 1990).

64 Peacocke, *Creation and the World of Science*, p. 291.
65 Habgood, 'A Sacramental Approach', p. 51.
66 Stephen R. L. Clark, *How to Think About the Earth: Philosophical and Theological Models for Ecology* (London: Mowbrays, 1993), p. 142.
67 *Ibid.*, p. 143.
68 *Ibid.*, pp. 142–4.
69 Andrew Linzey, *Animal Rights: A Christian Assessment of Man's Treatment of Animals* (London: SCM, 1976).
70 Andrew Linzey, *Christianity and the Rights of Animals* (London: SCM Press, 1987), p. 16.
71 *Ibid.*, pp. 19, 20.
72 *Ibid.*, pp. 31–8.
73 *Ibid.*, p. 45.
74 *Ibid.*, p. 82.
75 *Ibid.*, p. 84.
76 Andrew Linzey, *Animal Theology* (London: SCM Press, 1994). The most distinctive new element in this work is the focus in chapter two on the vulnerability of God in Christ, and particularly in Christ crucified, which in turn is seen as indicative of God's particular identification with the vulnerable – both vulnerable humans, the poor and the downtrodden, and vulnerable animals: this is then used as an exemplar of a revised human attitude to the defencelessness of animals, particularly their defencelessness against modern methods of factory farming, hunting and slaughter.
77 John B. Cobb, *Is it Too Late? A Theology of Ecology* (Beverly Hills, CA: Bruce, 1972).
78 *Ibid.*, pp. 76 ff.
79 *Ibid.*, p. 107, his italics.
80 *Ibid.*, p. 112.
81 *Ibid.*, p. 134.
82 *Ibid.*
83 Charles Birch and John B. Cobb, *Liberating Life: From the Cell to the Community* (Cambridge: Cambridge University Press, 1981), pp. 195–7.
84 *Ibid.*, pp. 152, 153.
85 John B. Cobb and Herman Daly, *For the Common Good: Redirecting the Economy towards Community, the Environment and a Sustainable Future* (London: Green Print, 1990).
86 Clark, *How to Think About the Earth*, p. 82.

87 Jay B. McDaniel, *Of God and Pelicans: A Theology of Reverence for Life* (Louisville, KY: Westminster/John Knox Press, 1989), pp. 19 and 35 ff. Cobb also hints at this approach when he speaks of God coercing and compelling Life in certain directions in *Is it Too Late?*, p. 134, and McDaniel draws on a later, more explicit account of the origin of evil by Cobb in John B. Cobb and David Griffin, *Process Theology: An Introductory Exposition* (Philadelphia: Westminster Press, 1976).

88 McDaniel, *Of God and Pelicans*, p. 35.

89 *Ibid.*, pp. 37, 38.

90 *Ibid.*, p. 41.

91 *Ibid.*, p. 45.

92 *Ibid.*, p. 67.

93 *Ibid.*, p. 77.

94 On the emotional life of elephants see further Jeffrey M. Masson and Susan McCarthy, *When Elephants Weep: The Emotional Lives of Animals* (Rockland, WV: Wheeler, 1995).

95 In terms of avowals of pantheism McDaniel sounds at times just as radical as Fox. See for example his comments on the importance of erotic love for the Earth which is God's body in *Of God and Pelicans*, p. 91. But at other points he seems to want to stay closer to traditional Christian language about God's relation to the cosmos.

96 Matthew Fox, *Original Blessing: A Primer in Creation Spirituality* (Santa Fe, NM: Bear and Company, 1983).

97 *Ibid.*, p. 48.

98 *Ibid.*, pp. 53 ff.

99 *Ibid.*, p. 73.

100 *Ibid.*, p. 210.

101 *Ibid.*, pp. 129 ff.

102 Matthew Fox, *Creation Spirituality: Liberating Gifts for the Peoples of the Earth* (San Francisco: Harper Collins, 1991), p. 20.

103 *Ibid.*, pp. 73 and 143.

104 *Ibid.*, p. 167.

105 *Ibid.*, p. 187.

106 *Ibid.*

107 *Ibid.*, p. 290.

108 Grace Jantzen, *God's World, God's Body* (London: Darton, Longman and Todd, 1984).

109 *Ibid.*, p. 150.

110 McFague, *The Body of God*, p. 252, note 18.

111 *Ibid.*, p. 19.

112 *Ibid.*, p. 20.

113 *Ibid.*, pp. 84 ff.
114 *Ibid.*, p. 113.
115 *Ibid.*, p. 126.
116 *Ibid.*, p. 133.
117 *Ibid.*, p. 204.
118 *Ibid.*, p. 211.
119 Her discussion of natural evil does not include a discussion of predation: *ibid.*, pp. 174–8.
120 *Ibid.*, p. 179.
121 *Ibid.*, p. 19 and also p. 252, note 18.
122 *Ibid.*, pp. 73 ff.
123 Peter Singer, *How Are We to Live? Ethics in an Age of Self-Interest* (London: Mandarin, 1994), ch. 6.
124 Ruether, *Gaia and God*, pp. 115 ff. See also Walter Wink, *Engaging the Powers: Discernment and Resistance in a World of Domination* (Minneapolis: Fortress Press, 1992).
125 Singer suggests that it is the weak sense of individual selfhood in contemporary Japan which explains the inability of individuals and local communities to resist the ecological depredations of the society as a whole: Singer, *How Are We To Live?* p. 128. I would also propose that this weak sense of selfhood is closely related to the lack of differentiation between God and the embodied self in pantheistic thought.

5 THE ORDER OF CREATION

1 Oliver O'Donovan, *Resurrection and Moral Order* (Leicester: Inter-Varsity Press, 1986), p. 17.
2 A. R. Radcliffe-Brown, *Structure and Function in Primitive Society*, cited in Edward Goldsmith, *The Way: An Ecological World View* (London: Rider, 1992), p. 182.
3 Genesis 1. 28.
4 Robert Murray, *The Cosmic Covenant: Biblical Themes of Justice, Peace and the Integrity of Creation* (London: Sheed and Ward, 1992).
5 Jeremiah 5. 21–3.
6 Murray's translation in *The Cosmic Covenant*, p. 4.
7 Genesis 9. 12.
8 *Ibid.* 8. 22.
9 Murray, *The Cosmic Covenant*, ch. 3.
10 *Ibid.*, p. 47.
11 Genesis 1. 14–18.
12 Murray, *The Cosmic Covenant*, ch. 5.
13 Psalm 72. 1–6.

14 Psalm 74. 12 ff.
15 Psalm 76. 7–8.
16 Psalm 77. 11–15.
17 Psalm 74. 21.
18 Psalm 75. 4 ff.
19 Exodus 20. 4–5.
20 Jeremiah 5. 23–5.
21 *Ibid.* 18.14–16.
22 Isaiah 5. 8–10.
23 *Ibid.* 24. 1–6 (from the Jerusalem Bible).
24 Thus according to Peter Marshall 'many of the ecological ills of Western civilisation may be traced to the Judeo-Christian tradition'; Peter Marshall, *Nature's Web: An Exploration of Ecological Thinking* (London: Simon and Schuster, 1992), p. 108.
25 Goldsmith, *The Way*, esp. pp. 26 ff.
26 Howard Eilberg-Schwartz, *The Savage in Judaism: An Anthropology of Israelite Religion and Ancient Judaism* (Bloomington and Indianapolis: Indiana University Press, 1990), ch. 3.
27 *Ibid.*
28 The ecological devastation which overtook the whole Ancient Near Eastern region in the second century BCE is described by Clive Ponting in *The Green History of the World* (London: Penguin, 1988), pp. 69 ff.
29 Rosemary Radford Ruether, *Gaia and God*, British edition (London: SCM Press, 1993), p. 17.
30 Walter Wink, *Engaging the Powers: Discernment and Resistance in a World of Domination* (Minneapolis: Fortress Press, 1992), p. 15.
31 Richard Dawkins, *The Selfish Gene* (London: Penguin, 1977). See also the critical essay on this style of sociobiology by Mary Midgley, 'Gene-Juggling' in Ashley Montagu (ed.), *Sociobiology Examined* (New York: Oxford University Press, 1980).
32 In addition to Dawkins, *Selfish Gene*, see also J. L. Mackie's welcome for this biological support for philosophical egoism in his essay 'The Law of the Jungle', *Philosophy*, 53 (1978), cited in Midgley, 'Gene-Juggling', p. 108.
33 Mary Midgley, *The Ethical Primate: Humans, Freedom and Morality* (London: Routledge, 1994), p. 125.
34 Donna Haraway, *Primate Vision: Gender, Race and Nature in the World of Modern Science* (New York: Routledge, 1989), pp. 226–8 and 311.
35 *Ibid.*, esp. ch. 7. Ethological observations are not unambiguous with regard to primatial morality as Haraway recognises. Jane Goodall's field studies of chimpanzees uncovered a pattern of behaviour amongst a small group of males which included both

infanticide and cannibalism, though this discovery was notable precisely because it conflicted with most other field observations; Haraway, *Primate Vision*, p. 184. See also Helmut Kummer, 'Analogs of Morality among Nonhuman Primates' in Gunther S. Stent (ed.), *Morality as a Biological Phenomenon: The Presuppositions of Sociobiological Research*, revised edition, (Berkeley, CA: University of California Press, 1980).

36 Stephen R. L. Clark, *The Nature of the Beast: Are Animals Moral?* (Oxford: Oxford University Press, 1982), ch. 10.

37 Midgley, *The Ethical Primate*, p. 126.

38 Odum's ideas are clearly summarised in Donald Worster's essay 'The Ecology of Order and Chaos' in Worster, *The Wealth of Nature: Environmental History and the Ecological Imagination* (New York: Oxford University Press, 1993).

39 Colin Turnbull, *The Mountain People* (London: Cape, 1973), p. 288. Turnbull found a desperately morally degraded culture of violent individualism among the Ik mountain people on the border of Uganda. The reasons for their moral degradation were not, however, innate to their culture, which showed evidence of real goodness and virtue prior to their recent 'fall' but rather to the destruction of their way of life by outside forces.

40 *Ibid.*, pp. 288 ff.

41 Myer Fortes, *Religion, Morality and the Person: Essays in Tallensi Religion* (Cambridge: Cambridge University Press, 1987), p. 285.

42 Lorna Marshall, 'Sharing, Talking and Giving: Relief of Social Tensions among the !Kung' in Ricard B. Lee and Irven DeVore, *Kalahari Hunter-Gatherers: Studies of the !Kung San and their Neighbours* (Cambridge, MA: Harvard University Press, 1976).

43 *Ibid.*, pp. 370, 371.

44 Roland de Vaux, *Ancient Israel*, vol. 1, pp. 72–3, cited in Jeffrey A. Fager, *Land Tenure and the Biblical Jubilee: Uncovering Hebrew Ethics through the Sociology of Knowledge* (Sheffield: JSOT Press, 1993). See also Wink, *Engaging the Powers*, p. 36.

45 Genesis 1. 28 and 2. 20.

46 Richard Cartwright Austin, *Hope for the Land: Nature in the Bible* (Atlanta: John Knox Press, 1988), p. 49.

47 Psalm 150. 6.

48 Psalm 148. 3–10.

49 Psalm 148. 11–12.

50 Austin, *Hope for the Land*, p. 49.

51 Genesis 1. 28.

52 Jacques Ellul, 'Technology and the Opening Chapters of Genesis', Eng. trans. in Carl Mitcham and Jim Grote, *Theology and*

Technology: Essays in Christian Analysis and Exegesis (Lanham, NY: University Press of America, 1984).

53 Austin, *Hope for the Land*, pp. 43 ff.

54 Genesis 1. 31.

55 *Ibid.* 1. 27.

56 Austin, *Hope for the Land*, p. 98.

57 Exodus 23. 10–12.

58 Genesis 49. 6–7.

59 Exodus 23. 4.

60 Lewis G. Regenstein, *Replenish the Earth: A History of Organized Religion's Treatment of Animals and Nature – Including the Bible's Message of Conservation and Kindness to Animals* (London: SCM Press, 1991), p. 23.

61 Ecclesiastes 3. 19.

62 Deuteronomy 12. 23–4. This association of blood with life is characteristic of Hebrew attitudes to blood at death, but other forms of the shedding of blood such as menstruation or the male circumcision wound have a different significance: Eilberg-Schwartz, *Savage in Judaism*, p. 179.

63 Acts 15. 28–9.

64 Leviticus 22. 28.

65 Regenstein, *Replenish the Earth*, p. 50.

66 Leviticus 17. 14.

67 See Linzey's discussion of animal sacrifice in *Animal Theology* (London: SCM Press, 1994), pp. 104–5, in which he argues that the view that sacrifice meant disrespect to the victim is giving way to a fuller understanding of sacrifice as a supreme act of valuing.

68 This understanding of sacrifice is informed by the following essays: Douglas R. Jones, 'Sacrifice and Holiness' and Robert Hayward, 'Sacrifice and World Order' both in Stephen W. Sykes (ed.), *Sacrifice and Redemption: Durham Essays in Theology* (Cambridge: Cambridge University Press, 1991).

69 Myer Fortes argues that a primary function of sacrifice is both to ward off natural dangers, and to propitiate natural forces in relation to disasters such as storms or droughts, which may be seen as an indication of the anger of the gods; see his 'Endpiece: Sacrifice among Theologians and Anthropologists' in Fortes, *Religion, Morality and the Person*, esp. p. 297.

70 Henri Hubert and Marcel Mauss, *Sacrifice: Its Nature and Function*, Eng. trans. (London: Cohen and West, 1964).

71 This view is enunciated by Eric Mascall in *Corpus Christi*, cited in Linzey, *Animal Theology*, p. 104.

72 Nancy Jay, among others, observes that a primary function of

sacrifice in agrarian society is to affirm the kinship and communion of the large extended families, and the large number of males, required to sustain extensive herds of domesticated animals. This explains why sacrifice is rarely found in societies with smaller family units, including both hunter-gatherer and urban societies and hence the eclipse of sacrifice in the more urban-based religion of post-exilic Israel; Nancy Jay, *Throughout Your Generations Forever: Sacrifice, Religion and Paternity* (Chicago: Chicago University Press, 1992). Jay's highly creative overall thesis is that the form of communion which most sacrificial systems are primarily oriented to establishing and affirming is that between males, and the male lineage, hence the exclusive role of males in the performance of the acts of sacrifice, and hence also the common taboo against blood from menstruation and child-birth which is regarded as polluting and dangerous, whereas the blood from animal sacrifices is regarded as purifying.

73 Hosea 6. 6.
74 Hubert and Mauss, *Sacrifice*, pp. 93 ff.
75 Exodus 19. 5–6.
76 Leviticus 25. 2 ff.
77 Deuteronomy 11. 1–2, 10–15 cited in Austin, *Hope for the Land*, p. 90.
78 Jürgen Moltmann in his *God in Creation: An Ecological Doctrine of Creation*, Eng. trans. (London: SCM Press, 1985) draws attention to the Jewish significance of the Sabbath as the completion of creation, and of human work: see esp. ch. 11.
79 Leviticus 25. 2–3.
80 Isaiah 5. 8–10.
81 Leviticus 26. 32–5.
82 Norman K. Gottwald, 'Early Israel and the "Asiatic Mode of Production" in Canaan' in *SBL Seminar Papers*, cited in Fager, *Land Tenure*, p. 93. Similar land tenure systems operated in most premodern agrarian and hunter-gatherer societies, as argued above in ch. 2.
83 Walter Breuggemann, 'Reflections on Biblical Understandings of Property', *International Review of Mission*, 64 (1974) cited in Fager, *Land Tenure*, p. 86.
84 Leviticus 25. 28, and see Fager, *Land Tenure*, pp. 93–7. Some scholars argue that these ideals with respect to land ownership and debt forgiveness were rarely if ever practised by the Hebrews, most notably Maurice Silver, whose free market reading of the Hebrew Bible, *Prophets and Markets: The Political Economy of Ancient Israel* (Boston: Kluwer-Nijhof Pub., 1983) not only contrasts

dramatically with the view being presented here, but also with much of the archaeological and historical evidence, as Fager shows; Fager, *Land Tenure*, pp. 86–7.

85 Douglas Meeks, *God the Economist: The Doctrine of God and Political Economy* (Minneapolis: Fortress Press, 1989), ch. 4.

86 Leviticus 25. 23.

87 Meeks, *God the Economist*, p. 83.

88 The requirements of the Torah to care for animals can also be read in this same perspective, as Linzey argues in ch. 2 of Linzey, *Animal Theology*, entitled 'The Moral Priority of the Weak'.

89 Deuteronomy 8. 11–18.

90 Austin, *Hope for the Land*, p. 92.

91 Meeks, *God the Economist*, pp. 174 ff.

92 See for example Paul T. W. Baxter, 'The New East African Pastoralist' in John Markakis (ed.), *Conflict and the Decline of Pastoralism in the Horn of Africa* (London: Macmillan, 1993), and Peter Rigby, *Persistent Pastoralists: Nomadic Societies in Transition* (London: Zed Books, 1985).

93 Garrett Hardin, 'The Tragedy of the Commons', *Science*, 162 (1968), pp. 1243–8.

94 Isaiah 5. 8–10.

95 Nehemiah 10. 31.

96 *Ibid.* 5. 1–13, cited in Austin, *Hope for the Land*, pp. 104, 110.

97 Isaiah 65. 20–2.

98 *Ibid.* 35. 1–2, 5–7, 10.

99 *Ibid.* 11. 6–9.

100 Ezekiel 47. 1–12.

101 In the preparation of these seven principles I am much indebted to Goldsmith's *The Way*. However, Goldsmith argues that this kind of ecological world-view finds little support in the Jewish and Christian tradition.

6 CREATION, REDEMPTION AND NATURAL LAW ETHICS

1 Oliver O'Donovan, *Resurrection and Moral Order* (Leicester: Inter-Varsity Press, 1986), to which I am much indebted.

2 *Ibid.*, p. 13.

3 1 Corinthians 15. 22.

4 *Ibid.* 15. 17.

5 *Ibid.* 15. 35 ff.

6 *Ibid.* 15. 6.

7 Romans 1. 24–7.

8 Peter Brown, *The Body and Society: Men, Women and Sexual Renuncia-*

tion in Early Christianity (New York: Columbia University Press, 1988), p. 51.

9 *Ibid.*, pp. 50–3.
10 1 Corinthians 12–14.
11 *Ibid.* 13 and Galatians 3.
12 Colossians 1. 19–20.
13 Revelation 5. 13.
14 Stanley Hauerwas, *The Peaceable Kingdom: A Primer in Christian Ethics* (London: SCM Press, 1984), pp. 88–9.
15 *Ibid.*, p. 20.
16 Colossians 1. 13–15, 20, my italics.
17 Romans 8. 18–19.
18 Stephen R. L. Clark, *How to Think About the Earth: Philosophical and Theological Models for Ecology* (London: Mowbrays, 1993), p. 82, and esp. the citation of Romans 3. 21–5.
19 John 1. 1.
20 *Ibid.* 1. 4.
21 *Ibid.* 3. 17.
22 Hans Blumenberg, *The Legitimacy of the Modern Age*, Eng. trans. (Cambridge, MA: MIT Press, 1983), p. 148.
23 *Ibid.*, p. 149.
24 Colin Gunton, *The One, the Three and the Many: God, Creation and the Culture of Modernity* (Cambridge: Cambridge University Press, 1993), p. 53.
25 Irenaeus, *Against Heresies*, II, 1. 2 and II, 2. 5.
26 Gunton, *The One, the Three and the Many*, pp. 158 ff.
27 Irenaeus, *Against Heresies*, IV, 20. 1.
28 Irenaeus, *Proof of the Apostolic Preaching*, ch. 47.
29 Paul Santmire, *The Travail of Nature: The Ecological Promise of Christian Theology* (Augsberg, MN: Fortress Press, 1972), pp. 39–40.
30 Irenaeus, *Against Heresies*, V, 33. 3, cited in Santmire, *Travail of Nature*, p. 43.
31 Gunton, *The One, the Three and the Many*, and Blumenberg, *Legitimacy of the Modern*, pp. 148–51.
32 *Ibid.*
33 *Ibid.*
34 R. M. Thomas, 'Introduction' in his translation of Athanasius, *Contra Gentes and De Incarnatione* (Oxford: Clarendon Press, 1971), p. xix.
35 Athanasius, *Contra Gentes*, 42.
36 *Ibid.*, 44.
37 *Ibid.*, 45.
38 Athanasius, *De Incarnatione*, 4.

39 *Ibid.*, 10.
40 According to Rist, Middle Platonism was taught to pagans and Christians alike in the late third century in Alexandria. Rist detects the influence of Platonism in both *Contra Gentes* and *De Incarnatione* and argues that this influence is indicative of the adoption of Christianity by the emperor, allowing Christian teachers to 'pick and choose' those remnants of pagan philosophy which were regarded as worthy of Christian repristination after paganism's defeat by Christianity: John M. Rist, 'Basil's "Neoplatonism": Its Background and Nature' in Paul J. Fedwick (ed.), *Basil of Caesarea: Christian, Humanist and Ascetic: A Sixteen Hundredth Anniversary Symposium* (Toronto: Pontifical Institute of Medieval Studies, 1981), esp. pp. 173–9.
41 Jaroslav Pelikan, *Christianity and Classical Culture: The Metamorphosis of Natural Theology in the Christian Encounter with Hellenism* (New Haven: Yale University Press, 1993).
42 Basil, *De Spiritu Sancto*, 26. 61, cited in Pelikan, *Christianity and Classical Culture*, p. 95.
43 Gregory of Nyssa, *De Anima et Resurrectione* (On the Soul and the Resurrection), 46. 57, cited in Pelikan, *Christianity and Classical Culture*, pp. 96–7.
44 Pelikan, *Christianity and Classical Culture*, p. 252.
45 Gregory of Nazianzus, *Orationes*, 38. 10, cited in Pelikan, *Christianity and Classical Culture*, p. 261.
46 Anna-Stiva Ellverson, *The Dual Nature of Man: A Study in the Theological Anthropology of Gregory of Nazianzus* (Uppsala: University of Uppsala, 1981), p. 34.
47 *Ibid.*, p. 35 and references to Gregory of Nazianzus, *Orationes*, on p. 103, notes 135 and 136.
48 Gregory of Nazianzus, *Orationes*, 38. 11, cited in Ellverson, *The Dual Nature of Man*, p. 47.
49 *Ibid.*, 40. 7, cited in *ibid.*, p. 60.
50 *Ibid.*, 14. 7, cited in *ibid.*, p. 37 and p. 104, note 144.
51 *Ibid.*, 45. 22, cited in Pelikan, *Christianity and Classical Culture*, p. 272.
52 Pelikan, *Christianity and Classical Culture*, p. 265.
53 *Ibid.*, pp. 270–4.
54 Gunton, *The One, the Three and the Many*, p. 159.
55 Gunton goes on to argue that the divorce between creation and redemption commences with Augustine. I believe it begins earlier, with Athanasius, and as the inevitable consequence of the hellenisation of Christian philosophy consequent on the 'conversion' of the pagan Constantine. For a discussion of the dubiety of Con-

stantine's conversion to Christianity see Alasdair Kee, *From Christ to Constantine: The Triumph of Ideology* (London: SCM, 1977), in which Kee also argues that it has taken the Christian religion more than fifteen hundred years to awaken to the effects of the Constantinian era.

56 The same Platonic influences are also of course evident in Origen and many other third-century Christian theologians: see further Brown, *The Body and Society*, esp. chs. 8–10.

57 As Brown shows, Gregory of Nyssa believed that the original physical body of Adam was radically different from our own. Sexuality and even the 'garments of skin' of the human body were a result of the fall, and evidence of the 'merciful afterthought' of God who provided them in order that Adam and Eve could survive outside paradise, and so that through sexual reproduction humanity might achieve a continuity through time which her new fallen mortality would otherwise deny: *ibid.*, pp. 294–6.

58 Blumenberg, *Legitimacy of the Modern*, pp. 152 ff.

59 Brown, *The Body and Society*, p. 404.

60 *Ibid.*

61 John Rist, *Augustine: Ancient Thought Baptized* (Cambridge: Cambridge University Press, 1994), p. 106.

62 As Rist comments, Augustine could have argued that human freedom always held open the possibility of equality of option, for good or evil, but Augustine did not choose this path: *ibid.*, pp. 107–8.

63 Gunton, *The One, the Three and the Many*, p. 55.

64 *Ibid.*, p. 54. See also the citation of Augustine, *Confessions* 12. 9 on p. 56, note 21, in *The One, the Three and the Many*, in which Gunton shows that Augustine distinguishes in Platonic fashion between the creation of an intellectual creature and the material creation, the intellectual having ontological and chronological priority.

65 Blumenberg, *Legitimacy of the Modern*, p. 137.

66 I do not wish to give credence to the dismissal of the Fathers by some ecofeminists, and the charge that they actually hated their bodies and the natural order because of their doctrine of sin/fall/redemption. Gregory of Nyssa's account of the great beauties of his family's estate cited by Brown in *The Body and Society*, p. 292, and his brother Basil of Caesarea's deep respect for animals and non-sensate life, manifest in his wonderful exposition of creation in his *Hexaemeron*, are testimony enough to the love for nature which the Fathers clearly felt. The point is not that the Fathers either despised nature, or encouraged the abuse of animals or their own bodies. Indeed the ethic of asceticism, and

the spiritual quest for meaning in the life of the soul rather than in material things, contributed to a style of life which involved considerable restraint on materialism and personal wealth, and which was conducive to the 'wise use' of natural resources, as Margaret Atkins argues in 'Flawed Beauty and Wise Use: Conservation and the Christian Tradition', *Studies in Christian Ethics* 7 (1994) pp. 1–16. The point is rather that by examining the ideological prefiguring of the modern secularisation of the cosmos and the modern abuse of nature in the Platonising of early Christian thought we may also be able to recover and repristinate a Christian theology of creation and of embodied material life which can help to resolve those inherent tensions in modern Western philosophy and culture between reason and nature, self and society, civilisation and ecology, economy and biological limits, which are so implicated in the environmental crisis.

67 Blumenberg, *Legitimacy of the Modern*, pp. 136–43.
68 *Ibid.*, p. 151.
69 *Ibid.*, p. 139.
70 *Ibid.*, pp. 152–3.
71 Gunton, *The One, the Three and the Many*, p. 57.
72 *Ibid.*, p. 155. See also André Goddu, *The Physics of William Ockham* (Leiden: E. J. Brill, 1984).
73 Blumenberg, *Legitimacy of the Modern*, pp. 137–9.
74 John Calvin, *Institutes*, II, 2. 19.
75 *Ibid.*, I, 14. 2.
76 Santmire, *Travail of Nature*, p. 126.
77 Langdon Gilkey, *Reaping the Whirlwind*, p. 176, cited in Santmire, *Travail of Nature*, p. 127.
78 Calvin, *Institutes*, I, 14. 2.
79 Keith Thomas, *Man and the Natural World* (London: Penguin, 1986), p. 25.
80 C. S. Lewis, *The Abolition of Man* (London: Oxford University Press, 1943), pp. 34ff.
81 Dietrich Bonhoeffer, *Creation and Fall: A Theological Interpretation of Genesis 1–3*, Eng. trans. (London: SCM Press, 1959), p. 38.
82 Gunton, *The One, the Three and the Many*, esp. pp. 204 ff.
83 Matthew 5. 28–9.
84 Romans 1. 19–20.
85 *Ibid.* 2. 14–15.
86 O'Donovan, *Resurrection and Moral Order*, pp. 16–17.
87 Etienne Gilson, *The Christian Philosophy of Thomas Aquinas* (London: Victor Gollancz, 1957), p. 101.

88 Aquinas, *Summa Theologiae*, 1, 8. 1 cited in Gilson, *Philosophy of Thomas*, p. 102.

89 Aquinas, *Summa Theologiae*, 1a, 6. 2, cited in Bryan Davies, *The Thought of Thomas Aquinas* (Oxford: Clarendon Press, 1992), p. 100.

90 Aquinas, *Summa Contra Gentiles*, III. 65. 2, cited in Davies, *Aquinas*, p. 159.

91 Davies, *Aquinas*, pp. 159–61.

92 Aquinas, *Compendium Theologiae*, II, 5, cited in Matthew Fox, *Sheer Joy: Conversations with Thomas Aquinas on Creation Spirituality* (San Francisco: Harper, 1992), p. 66.

93 Aquinas, *Summa Theologiae*, 1, 103. 2, cited in Fox, *Sheer Joy*, p. 88.

94 Aquinas, *Compendium Theologiae*, 1, 102, cited in Fox, *Sheer Joy*, p. 97.

95 Aquinas, *Summa Theologiae*, I–II, 94. 2.

96 Aquinas, *Summa Contra Gentiles*, III, 3.

97 Aquinas, *Summa Theologiae*, I–II, 94. 2.

98 *Ibid.*, I–II, 94. 3.

99 *Ibid.*, 1, 21. 1. In his *Commentary on the Psalms* Aquinas says that compassion is part of the divine ordering of all things in the cosmos: 'Psalm 32', cited in Fox, *Sheer Joy*, p. 390.

100 Aquinas, *Commentary on Dionysius' De Divinis Nominibus*, p. 340, cited in Fox, *Sheer Joy*, p. 104.

101 Aquinas, *Summa Theologiae*, 1, 21. 1.

102 Aquinas, *Commentary on Dionysius' De Divinis Nominibus*, p. 771, cited in Fox, *Sheer Joy*, p. 411.

103 Aquinas *Summa Theologiae*, II–II, 58. 11.

104 *Ibid.*, II–II, 77. 4 and 78. 1.

105 Aquinas, *Summa Contra Gentiles*, III–II, 112. 12.

106 *Ibid.*, III–II, 112. 13.

107 *Ibid.*, III–II, 112. 7.

108 Aquinas, *Summa Theologiae*, I–II, 94. 2.

109 *Ibid.*, 1a, 22. 2, cited in Davies, *Aquinas*, p. 162.

110 Davies, *Aquinas*, p. 93.

111 *Ibid.*, pp. 94–6.

112 Susan Schreiter, *Theater of His Glory: Nature and Natural Order in the Thought of John Calvin* (Durham, NC: The Labyrinth Press, 1991), p. 78.

113 Robert Murray, *The Cosmic Covenant: Biblical Themes of Justice, Peace and the Integrity of Creation* (London: Sheed and Ward, 1992), pp. 157–60.

114 Richard Hooker, *Of the Laws of Ecclesiastical Polity*, 1, 2. 3.

115 *Ibid.*

116 Hooker, Sermons, III, 2, cited in John Marshall, *Richard Hooker*

and the Anglican Tradition (London: Adam and Charles Black, 1963), p. 86.

117 Hooker, *Ecclesiastical Polity*, I, 3. 4, cited in Marshall, *Hooker*, p. 89.

118 Marshall, *Hooker*, p. 87.

119 Hooker, *Ecclesiastical Polity*, I, 8. 3 cited in Marshall, *Hooker*, p. 97.

120 Marshall, *Hooker*, p. 118.

121 *Ibid.*, p. 120.

122 Hooker, *Ecclesiastical Polity*, v, 3. 1–4. 3.

123 Marshall, *Hooker*, p. 121.

124 Hooker, *Ecclesiastical Polity*, v, 55. 8.

125 Paul E. Sigmund, 'Thomistic Natural Law and Social Theory' in Paul E. Sigmund (ed.), *St Thomas Aquinas on Politics and Ethics* (New York: W. W. Norton, 1988).

126 *Ibid.*, p. 184.

127 Article 29 of the Universal Declaration of the United Nations, cited in John Finnis, *Natural Law and Natural Rights* (Oxford: Clarendon Press, 1980), p. 212.

128 Alasdair MacIntyre, *After Virtue* (London: Duckworth, 1981), p. 67.

129 *Ibid.*, p. 68.

130 Germain Grisez, *Christian Moral Principles*, vol. 1 of *The Way of the Lord Jesus*, 2 vols. (Chicago: Franciscan Herald Press, 1983), p. 173.

131 Finnis, *Natural Law*, pp. 83, 84.

132 *Ibid.*, pp. 85 ff.

133 *Ibid.*, ch. 5.

134 See further Peter Singer, *How Are We To Live? Ethics in an Age of Self-Interest* (London: Mandarin, 1994), p. 169.

135 See further Carol Gilligan, *In a Different Voice: Psychological Theory and Women's Development* (Cambridge, MA: Harvard University Press, 1981), esp. chs. 2 and 5.

136 Finnis, *Natural Law*, p. 126.

137 Singer, *How Are We To Live?*, p. 188.

138 Jay McDaniel highlights a particularly harsh instance of parental treatment of offspring in the behaviour of pelicans: only one of a pelican's two chicks can survive each year so the weakest has eventually to be pushed out of the nest to die on the ground: McDaniel, *Of God and Pelicans: A Theology of Reverence for Life* (Louisville, KY: Westminster/John Knox Press, 1989), pp. 19–20.

139 Finnis, *Natural Law*, p. 36.

140 *Ibid.*, p. 111.

141 Sean McDonagh, *The Greening of the Church* (London: Geoffrey Chapman, 1990), ch. 9.

142 Finnis, *Natural Law*, p. 40.
143 David Hume, *Treatise on Human Nature*, III, i, 1, cited in Finnis, *Natural Law*, p. 41.
144 Alasdair MacIntyre, 'Editor's Introduction' in Alasdair MacIntyre (ed.), *Hume's Ethical Writings*, cited in Jean Porter, *The Recovery of Virtue: The Relevance of Aquinas for Ethics* (Louisville, KY: Westminster/John Knox Press, 1990), p. 47.
145 Romans 7. 19–20.
146 Finnis, *Natural Law*, pp. 83 ff.
147 Porter, *Recovery of Virtue*, p. 47.
148 *Ibid.*
149 O'Donovan, *Resurrection and Moral Order*, p. 46.
150 *Ibid.*, p. 49.
151 Edward Goldsmith, *The Way: An Ecological World View* (London: Rider, 1992), p. 24.
152 *Ibid.*, p. 27.
153 Edward O. Wilson, *The Diversity of Life* (London: Penguin, 1994), p. 33.
154 Richard Dawkins, *The Selfish Gene* (London: Penguin, 1977).
155 Edward O. Wilson, *On Human Nature*, p. 32, cited in John Bowker, *Is God a Virus? Genes, Culture and Religion* (London: SCM Press, 1995), p. 36.
156 But see the discussion above; ch. 5, note 35.
157 Charles Darwin, *The Descent of Man*, cited in James Rachels, *Created from Animals: The Moral Implications of Darwinism* (Oxford: Oxford University Press, 1990), p. 148.
158 Rachels, *Created from Animals*, p. 150.
159 *Ibid.*, p. 157.
160 Singer, *How Are We To Live?*, pp. 132–4.
161 *Ibid.*, p. 134.
162 *Ibid.*
163 It may be argued that this conclusion is closer to Jesus' perfect law of love than it might appear at first sight. Many of Jesus' moral injunctions involved the same kind of double moral orientation: firstly random 'niceness' or goodness such as in turning the other cheek or going the extra mile, and, secondly active resistance to evil, as in his commendation 'if any one wants to sue you and takes your shirt, let him have your cloak as well' (Matthew 5. 40): in the act of giving the cloak as well as the shirt, the person becomes naked and shames the one who demands the shirt. See further in this vein John Howard Yoder, *The Politics of Jesus: Vicit Agnus Noster* (Grand Rapids, MI: Eerdmans, 1972), pp. 90 ff. and also Walter Wink, *Engaging the Powers:*

Discernment and Resistance in a World of Domination (Minneapolis: Fortress Press, 1992), pp. 175 ff.

164 Finnis, *Natural Law*, p. 40.

165 Alvin Gouldner, 'The Norm of Reciprocity', *American Sociological Review*, 25 (1960), cited in Singer, *How Are We To Live?*, p. 150.

166 Singer, *How Are We To Live?*, p. 143.

167 C. S. Lewis, *The Abolition of Man* (Oxford: Oxford University Press, 1943).

168 *Ibid.*, pp. 14–16.

169 *Ibid.*, p. 41.

170 *Ibid.*, p. 46.

171 C. S. Lewis, *Mere Christianity* (London: Collins, 1955), pp. 15 ff.

172 O'Donovan, *Resurrection and Moral Order*, p. 37.

173 *Ibid.*, p. 52.

7 NATURAL LAW AND ECOLOGICAL SOCIETY

1 Jacques Ellul, *The Technological Society*, Eng. trans. (London: Cape, 1965).

2 *Ibid.*, p. 141.

3 Bill McKibben, *The End of Nature* (London: Penguin, 1989).

4 Ellul, *Technological Society*, pp. 143–5.

5 Douglas John Hall, 'Toward an Indigenous Theology of the Cross' in Carl Mitcham and Jim Grote (eds.), *Theology and Technology: Essays in Christian Analysis and Exegesis* (Lanham, NY: University Press of America, 1984), p. 252.

6 *Ibid.*, p. 253.

7 See for example Andrew Linzey, *Animal Theology* (London: SCM Press, 1994).

8 Robert Gordis, 'A Basis for Morals: Ethics in a Technological Age' in *Judaism*, 25 (1970) pp. 22–43.

9 *Ibid*, p. 42..

10 See for example Giddens's observations on the effects of modern reproductive technology on the character of human sexuality: Anthony Giddens, *Modernity and Self-Identity: Self and Society in the Late Modern Age* (Stanford, CA: Stanford University Press, 1991), p. 206.

11 Aquinas, *Summa Theologiae* II–II, 58. 11 cited in Matthew Fox, *Sheer Joy: Conversations with Thomas Aquinas on Creation Spirituality* (San Francisco: Harper, 1992), p. 416.

12 Aquinas, *Ethics*, v, 50. 11, cited in Fox, *Sheer Joy*, p. 409.

13 Jean Porter, *The Recovery of Virtue: The Relevance of Aquinas for Ethics* (Louisville, KY: Westminster/John Knox Press, 1990), p. 136.

14 Exodus 20. 13, 15, 17.

15 Aquinas, *Commentary on Dionysius' De Divinis Nominibus*, 22, cited in Fox, *Sheer Joy*, p. 411.

16 *Ibid.*, 781, cited in *ibid.*, p. 413.

17 Aquinas, *Summa Theologiae*, 1, 21. 4, cited in *ibid.*, p. 405.

18 See Porter, *Recovery of Virtue*, pp. 125 ff. for a fuller account of the common good in Aquinas.

19 *Ibid.*, p. 178.

20 In addition to chapter 5 above, see also Barry Gordon, *The Economic Problem in Biblical and Patristic Thought* (Leiden: E. J. Brill, 1989), ch. 2.

21 Isaiah 65. 20–3.

22 Douglas Meeks, *God the Economist: The Doctrine of God and Political Economy* (Mineapolis: Fortress Press, 1989), pp. 75 ff.

23 Matthew 6. 31–3.

24 Gordon, *The Economic Problem*, p. 46.

25 Marcel Mauss, *The Gift: Forms and Functions of Exchange in Primitive Societies* (London: Cohen and West, 1954), esp. pp. 8–18.

26 Karl Polanyi, 'Societies and Economic Systems' in George Dalton (ed.), *Primitive, Archaic and Modern Economics: Essays of Karl Polanyi*, cited in Edward Goldsmith, *The Way: An Ecological World View* (London: Rider, 1992), p. 304.

27 Goldsmith, *The Way*, p. 307.

28 John Bodley, *Cultural Anthropology: Tribes, States and the Global System* (Mountain View, CA: Mayfield Pub., 1994), p. 56.

29 Goldsmith, *The Way*, pp. 309 ff.

30 World Bank, *Accelerated Development in Sub-Saharan Africa*, cited in Goldsmith, *The Way*, p. 313.

31 1 Kings 21.

32 Leviticus 25. 23–4.

33 Extract from Thomas Aquinas, *Summa Theologiae*, II–II, 66. 7 in Paul E. Sigmund (ed.), *St Thomas Aquinas on Politics and Ethics* (New York: W. W. Norton, 1988).

34 George Winstanley, 'New Year's Gift for Parliament and Army', cited in Francis Reed, *On Common Ground: De Prima Materia* (London: Working Press, 1991), p. 12.

35 Donald E. Meek, 'The Land Question Answered from the Bible: The Land Issue and the Development of a Highland Theology of Liberation', *Scottish Geographical Magazine*, 103. (1987). The text cited is Ecclesiastes 5. 9.

36 John Murdoch, 'The Highlanders' Jubilee: The Solution of the Land Question According to the Bible', Land League pamphlet cited in Meek, 'The Land Question'. The text cited is Nehemiah 5. 1–13.

37 The history of these kinds of conservation projects in Africa is told in Edward Pearce, *Green Warriors: The People and the Politics Behind the Environmental Revolution* (London: Bodley Head, 1991), ch. 4.

38 Richard Bell as quoted in Pearce, *Green Warriors*, p. 89. The quote from Bell originates in Sue Armstrong and Fred Bridgland, 'Elephants in the Ivory Tower', *New Scientist*, 1679 (1993) p. 39.

39 *Ibid.*

40 Richard Body, *Our Food, Our Land: Why Contemporary Farming Practices Must Change* (London: Rider, 1991), ch. 2.

41 Jean Dreze and Amartya Sen, *Hunger and Public Action* (Oxford: Clarendon Press, 1989), p. 195.

42 D. Christodoulou, *The Unpromised Land: Agrarian Reform and Conflict Worldwide* (London: Zed Press, 1990), ch. 10.

43 For an account of the struggle of the rubber tappers in Brazil see Susanna Hecht and Alexander Coburn, *The Fate of the Forest: Developers, Destroyers and Defenders of the Amazon* (London: Penguin, 1990), pp. 214 ff.

44 Aristotle, *Politics*, 1256b, cited in John F. O'Neill, *Ecology, Policy and Politics: Human Well-Being and the Natural World* (London: Routledge, 1993), p. 169.

45 O'Neill, *Ecology, Policy and Politics*, p. 169.

46 *Ibid.*, p. 170.

47 This approach is well illustrated in Maurice Silver, *Prophets and Markets: The Political Economy of Ancient Israel* (Boston: Kluwer-Nijhof Pub., 1983): Silver contends that the reason for the break-up of the kingdoms of Israel and Judah and the exile of their peoples was the attempt by the prophets to impose an ideal of economic equality through a system of social regulation which reversed the production and trading advances of eighth- and seventh-century Israel, and destroyed the economic base which generated the prosperity the prophets railed against.

48 Amos 5.

49 Silver, *Prophets and Markets*, p. 125.

50 Hosea 4. 1–4.

51 See further Michael S. Northcott, 'Children' in Peter Sedgwick (ed.), *God in the City* (London: Mowbrays, 1995).

52 Alfred North Whitehead, *Science and the Modern World*, cited in Herman Daly and John B. Cobb, *For the Common Good: Redirecting the Economy towards Community, the Environment and a Sustainable Future* (London: Green Print, 1990), p. 36.

53 Daly and Cobb, *For the Common Good*, esp. pp. 97ff.

54 *Ibid.*, p. 119.

55 Edward J. Mishan, *The Costs of Economic Growth* (London: Penguin, 1967).

56 Herman E. Daly 'The Steady-State Economy: Toward a Political Economy of Biophysical Equilibrium and Moral Growth' in Herman E. Daly and Kenneth E. Townsend (eds.), *Valuing the Earth: Economy, Ecology, Ethics* (Cambridge, MA: MIT Press, 1993).

57 *Ibid.*

58 Matthew 6. 34.

59 On the increasing costs and diminishing returns consequent on attempts to model human societies on the 'laws' of free market economics, see further Paul Ormerod, *The Death of Economics* (London: Faber, 1994); on the inability of market activity to deliver human fulfilment and quality of life see further Robert Lane, *The Market Experience* (Cambridge: Cambridge University Press, 1991).

60 See for example David W. Pearce, Anil Markandya, Edward B. Barbier, *Blueprint for a Green Economy* (London: Earthscan, 1989).

61 *Ibid.*, pp. 256 ff.

62 See Henry George, *Progress and Poverty* (London: J. M. Dent, 1911) for a full exposition of the land tax philosophy.

63 Daly and Cobb, *For the Common Good*, p. 259.

64 See further Northcott, 'A Place of Our Own' in Sedgwick (ed.), *God in the City*.

65 See further the collection of short papers and addresses in Denis Mollison (ed.), *Wilderness With People: The Management of Wild Land* (Edinburgh: John Muir Trust, 1992).

66 E. F. Schumacher, *Small is Beautiful: Economics as if People Mattered* (London: Abacus, 1974), p. 90.

67 Body, *Our Food, Our Land*, pp. 46–7.

68 Georg Simmel, *The Philosophy of Money* (London: Routledge, 1978).

69 Daly and Cobb, *For the Common Good*, ch. 11 and see further Simmel, *The Philosophy of Money*.

70 Paul Kennedy, *Preparing for the Twenty-First Century* (London: Harper Collins, 1993), p. 53.

71 Adam Smith, *The Wealth of Nations*, p. 423, cited in Daly and Cobb, *For the Common Good*, p. 215.

72 Daly and Cobb, *For the Common Good*, p. 235.

73 John Maynard Keynes, 'National Self-Sufficiency' in *The Collected Writings of John Maynard Keynes*, vol. XXI, cited in Daly and Cobb, *For the Common Good*, p. 216.

74 Daly and Cobb, *For the Common Good*, p. 229. See also Susan George, *Costing the Earth* (London: Penguin, 1991).

75 *Ibid.*, p. 234.

76 Meeks, *God the Economist*, pp. 33ff.

77 On the concept of consumer sovereignty see further Russel Keat, in Abercrombie and Keat (eds.), *The Enterprise Culture* (London: Routledge, 1993). For a critical discussion of the concept of consumer sovereignty see Peter G. Perry, *Consumer Sovereignty and Human Interests* (Cambridge: Cambridge University Press, 1986).

78 Daly and Cobb, *For the Common Good*, pp. 241 ff.

79 Andrew McLaughlin, *Regarding Nature: Industrialism and Deep Ecology* (Albany, NY: State University of New York Press, 1993), pp. 206 ff.

80 Daly and Cobb, *For the Common Good*, p. 242.

81 *Ibid.*, pp. 244–6.

82 Charles N. Pigou, *The Economics of Welfare* (London: Macmillan, 1920).

83 André Gorz, *Ecology as Politics*, Eng. trans. (London: Pluto Press, 1987), pp. 69 ff.

84 *Ibid.*, p. 77.

85 *Ibid.*, p. 76.

86 *Ibid.*

87 See further Amitai Etzioni, *The Spirit of Community: The Reinvention of American Society* (New York: Simon and Schuster, 1993) and Paul Hirst, *Associative Politics: New Forms of Economic and Social Governance* (Cambridge: Polity Press, 1994).

88 Wolfgang Sachs, 'Global Ecology and the Shadow of Development' in Wolfgang Sachs (ed.), *Global Ecology: A New Arena of Conflict* (London: Zed Books, 1993).

89 Wolfgang Sachs (ed.), *Global Ecology*.

90 Christine von Weizsäcker, 'Competing Notions of Biodiversity' in Sachs, *Global Ecology*.

91 Exodus 20. 12.

92 Anthony Giddens, *The Consequences of Modernity* (Cambridge: Polity Press, 1991), esp. pp. 151 ff.

93 Robert Wuthnow, *Acts of Compassion: Caring for Others and Helping Ourselves*, pp. 153–6, cited in Larry L. Rasmussen, *Moral Fragments and Moral Communities: A Proposal for Church and Society* (Minneapolis: Fortress Press, 1993).

94 See further Michael S. Northcott, *The Church and Secularisation: Urban Industrial Mission in Northeast England* (Frankfurt: Peter Lang, 1989).

95 Tom Driver, *The Magic of Ritual: Our Need for Liberating Rites that Transform Our Lives and Our Communities* (San Francisco: Harper Collins, 1991), pp. 19 ff.

96 *Ibid.*, pp. 32 ff.

97 *Ibid.*, pp. 152 ff.
98 From Regis J. Armstrong and Ignatius C. Brady (eds.), *Francis and Clare: The Complete Works* (London: SPCK, 1982), pp. 38–9.
99 Scott McCarthy, *Celebrating the Earth: An Earth-Centred Theology of Worship with Blessings, Prayers and Rituals* (San Jose, CA: Resource Publ. Inc., 1991).

Index

acid rain, 10
aestheticism, 87–9, 98, 106, 156, 158, 174, 240, 248
Africa, 1, 4, 14–17, 20–1, 25, 28, 31, 33, 45, 49, 80, 81, 101, 177, 191, 261, 277, 280–1, 297, 329n, 332n, 358n, 367n, 368n
agriculture: intensive, 280, 288, 293; monocrop, 34, 63, 279–80, 289, 293, 312; organic, 293
alienation, 53, 74, 103, 105–6, 118, 128, 131, 171, 179, 199, 217, 263, 318, 321
altruism, 175, 250, 251–2
Amazon, 35, 43, 191
animal husbandry, 14, 28, 63, 100–1, 191, 260–1, 293, 342n
anonymity, 253, 300
anthropocentrism, 23, 146, 168, 219, 266
anthropology, 116, 120, 172–3, 177, 213, 240, 246, 345–6n
Antony, St, 147
apocalypticism, 7, 195, 324
Aquinas, Thomas, 54, 226–48, 265–9, 275, 283, 337n, 362–7n
Aristotle, 54, 228, 231, 235, 245, 282, 299, 368n
asceticism, 138, 201, 215, 362n
Athanasius, 211–14, 359–60n
atmosphere, 1, 3, 6–10, 19, 81, 112, 309
atonement, 145, 203, 204
Attfield, Robin, 40, 95, 103, 129, 333n, 339n, 342–3n, 348n
Augustine, St, 138, 212, 214–16, 218, 220, 227, 361n
Austin, Richard, 180, 187, 193, 336n, 355–6n
Australia, 4, 84, 166, 281, 337n, 346n
autonomy, 55, 103, 243, 257, 298, 300, 318

Axelrod, Robert, 251–2

Bacon, Francis, 63, 65–6, 339n
Basil of Caesarea, 212, 360n, 361n
Bauman, Zygmunt, 117, 346n
Beck, Ulrich, 69, 340n
Benedict of Nursia, 180
Berry, Thomas, 126, 347n
biocentrism, 104, 141–2, 344n
biodiversity, 22, 27–8, 280, 289–94, 299, 310–11, 322, 331n, 370n
biophilia, 140, 144, 350n
bioregionalism, 300, 304, 308
blood, 184–5, 187, 197, 202–3, 326, 356–7n
Blumenberg, Hans, 57–8, 65, 207, 209–10, 215, 217–18, 248, 338–9n, 359n, 361–2n
Borneo, 18, 67, 90, 177, 191, 261, 330n
Braine, David, 71, 340n
Brazil, 19, 281, 368n
Breuggemann, Walter, 189, 351n
Brown, Peter, 166, 201, 215, 327–9n, 345n, 353n, 358n, 361n
Buddhism, 37, 119, 172, 233, 318

Callicott, J. Baird, 107–8, 111, 344n
Calvin, John, 54, 218–20, 233, 362–3n
Canada, 19
cancer, 1, 23, 345n
capitalism, 50–1, 64–5, 76, 80, 105, 157, 191, 237, 242, 258, 285, 295–6, 308, 316
carrying capacity, 26, 332n
cars, 4, 6, 21, 36, 74, 118, 140, 258–9, 261, 301, 304–9, 313
Carson, Rachel, 12, 327, 329n
chaos, 33, 61–2, 151, 165–7, 170, 196, 331n, 338n

New Studies in Christian Ethics